The Internet
FOR
DUMMIES®
12TH EDITION

Middlesbrough College

00083873

The Internet
FOR
DUMMIES®
12TH EDITION

by John R. Levine
Margaret Levine Young

WILEY

Wiley Publishing, Inc.

The Internet For Dummies®, 12th Edition

Published by
Wiley Publishing, Inc.
111 River Street
Hoboken, NJ 07030-5774

www.wiley.com

Copyright © 2010 by Wiley Publishing, Inc., Indianapolis, Indiana

Published by Wiley Publishing, Inc., Indianapolis, Indiana

Published simultaneously in Canada

For general information on our other products and services, please contact our Customer Care Department within the U.S. at 877-762-2974, outside the U.S. at 317-572-3993, or fax 317-572-4002.

For technical support, please visit www.wiley.com/techsupport.

Wiley also publishes its books in a variety of electronic formats. Some content that appears in print may not be available in electronic books.

Library of Congress Control Number: 2009942329

ISBN: 978-0-470-56095-2

Manufactured in the United States of America

10 9 8 7 6 5 4 3 2 1

WILEY

About the Authors

John R. Levine was a member of a computer club in high school — before high school students, or even high schools, had computers — where he met Theodor H. Nelson, the author of *Computer Lib/Dream Machines* and the inventor of hypertext, who reminded us that computers should not be taken seriously and that everyone can and should understand and use computers.

John wrote his first program in 1967 on an IBM 1130 (a computer somewhat less powerful than your typical modern digital wristwatch, only more difficult to use). He became an official system administrator of a networked computer at Yale in 1975. He began working part-time — for a computer company, of course — in 1977 and has been in and out of the computer and network biz ever since. He got his company on Usenet (the Internet's worldwide bulletin-board system) early enough that it appears in a 1982 *Byte* magazine article on a map of Usenet, which then was so small that the map fit on half a page.

Although John used to spend most of his time writing software, now he mostly writes books (including *UNIX For Dummies* and *Internet Secrets,* both published by Wiley, and *Windows Vista: the Complete Reference,* published by Osborne / McGraw-Hill) because it's more fun and he can do so at home in the tiny village of Trumansburg, New York, where in his spare time he was the mayor for several years (yes, really, see www.Trumansburg.ny.us) and can play with his daughter when he's supposed to be writing. John also does a fair amount of public speaking. (Go to www.johnlevine.com to see where he'll be.) He holds a B.A. and a Ph.D. in computer science from Yale University, but please don't hold that against him.

In high school, **Margaret Levine Young** was in the same computer club as her big brother, John. She stayed in the field throughout college against her better judgment and despite John's presence as a graduate student in the computer science department. Margy graduated from Yale and went on to become one of the first PC managers in the early 1980s at Columbia Pictures, where she rode the elevator with big stars whose names she wouldn't dream of dropping here.

Since then, Margy has co-authored more than 25 computer books about topics that include the Internet, UNIX, WordPerfect, Microsoft Access, and (stab from the past) PC-File and Javelin, including *The Internet For Dummies Quick Reference* and *UNIX For Dummies* (both published by Wiley), *Windows Vista: The Complete Reference,* and *Internet: The Complete Reference* (both published by Osborne/McGraw-Hill). She met her future husband, Jordan, in the R.E.S.I.S.T.O.R.S. (that computer club we mentioned). Her other passion is her children, along with music, Unitarian Universalism, reading, knitting, gardening (you can never grow too much garlic), and anything to do with eating. She lives in Vermont (see www.gurus.org/margy for some scenery) and works as a software engineer for the Unitarian Universalist Association (www.uua.org).

Please visit both authors online at net.gurus.org.

Dedication

John dedicates his part of the book (the particularly lame jokes) to Sarah Willow, who surprises and delights him every day, and to Tonia, now and always.

Margy dedicates this book to her niece Alana Margaret Schumb. And, of course, to Jordan, Meg, and Zac.

Authors' Acknowledgments

We thank Kenneth Sutton for information about *Second Life,* Zac Young and James Curran for information about online games, and Kasey Melski for help with *World of Warcraft.*

Mark Enochs hustled us through the editorial process despite our attempts to drag it out while (no doubt at great personal cost) making us look like better writers than we are. Rebecca Whitney is the editor for whom we get down on our knees and beg when we begin each update to this book. Steve Hayes gets us organized, which is no easy task. Thanks also to the rest of the gang at Wiley Publishing, especially those listed on the Publisher's Acknowledgments page.

Margy thanks Jordan for holding everything together. We all thank Bill Gladstone at Waterside Productions for encouragement. The entire contents of this book were edited and submitted to the publisher using the Web — practicing what we preach. We thank our Internet providers: Finger Lakes Technologies Group (Trumansburg, N.Y. Hi, Paul!), Lightlink (Ithaca, N.Y. Hi, Homer!), and Shoreham.net (Shoreham, Vermont. Hi, Don and Jim!).

Finally, thanks to all the smarties (we wouldn't say wiseacres) who sent us comments on the previous editions and helped make this one better. If you have ideas, comments, or complaints, about the book, whisk them to us at `internet12@gurus.org`.

Visit our Web site at `net.gurus.org` for updates and more information about the topics in this book.

Publisher's Acknowledgments

We're proud of this book; please send us your comments through our online registration form located at `http://dummies.custhelp.com`. For other comments, please contact our Customer Care Department within the U.S. at 877-762-2974, outside the U.S. at 317-572-3993, or fax 317-572-4002.

Some of the people who helped bring this book to market include the following:

Acquisitions and Editorial

Senior Project Editor: Mark Enochs

Executive Editor: Steve Hayes

Copy Editor: Rebecca Whitney

Technical Editor: Lee Musick

Editorial Manager: Leah Cameron

Editorial Assistant: Amanda Graham

Senior Editorial Assistant: Cherie Case

Cartoons: Rich Tennant
(`www.the5thwave.com`)

Composition Services

Project Coordinator: Sheree Montgomery

Layout and Graphics: Carrie A. Cesavice, Samantha K. Cherolis, Joyce Haughey, Ronald G. Terry

Proofreaders: Leeann Harney, Lauren Mandelbaum

Indexer: Potomac Indexing, LLC

Publishing and Editorial for Technology Dummies

Richard Swadley, Vice President and Executive Group Publisher

Andy Cummings, Vice President and Publisher

Mary Bednarek, Executive Acquisitions Director

Mary C. Corder, Editorial Director

Publishing for Consumer Dummies

Diane Graves Steele, Vice President and Publisher

Composition Services

Debbie Stailey, Director of Composition Services

Contents at a Glance

Table of Contents

Part III: Web Mania 87

Introduction

Welcome to *The Internet For Dummies,* 12th Edition. The Internet has become so interwoven in today's life — work, school, politics, and play — that ignoring it is no longer an option. This book describes what you do to become an *Internaut* (someone who navigates the Internet with skill) — how to get started, what you need to know, and where to go for help. And, we describe it in plain old English.

When we first wrote *The Internet For Dummies* 16 years ago (yikes!), a typical Internet user was a student who connected from college or a technical worker who had access through work. The World Wide Web was so new that it had only a few hundred pages. The Net has grown like crazy to include a billion (dare we say it?) normal people, connecting from computers at home or work, along with students ranging from elementary school to adult education. This 12th edition focuses on the parts of the Net that are of the most interest to typical users — how to find things on the World Wide Web, download interesting things from the Net, send and receive electronic mail (e-mail), and shop, invest, chat, and play games online.

About This Book

We don't flatter ourselves to think you're interested enough in the Internet to sit down and read the entire book (although it should be a fine book for the bathroom). When you run into a problem using the Internet ("Hmm, I *thought* that I knew how to find somebody on the Net, but I don't seem to remember"), just dip into the book long enough to solve your problem.

Pertinent sections include

- ✔ Understanding what the Internet is
- ✔ Staying safe online
- ✔ The types of Internet connections
- ✔ Climbing around the World Wide Web
- ✔ Finding people, places, and things
- ✔ Communicating by e-mail
- ✔ Hanging out with friends using instant messaging and chat

✔ Getting stuff from the Net

✔ Putting your own stuff online with Web sites and social networks

How to Use This Book

To begin, please read the first two chapters. They give you an overview of the Internet and some important safety tips. If you have children or grandchildren, read Chapter 3, too. When you're ready to get yourself on the Internet, turn to Part II and read Chapter 4. Parts III through VI egg you on and provide support — they describe the Web and e-mail and other stuff you can do on the Internet.

Although we try hard not to introduce a technical term without defining it, sometimes we slip. Sometimes, too, you may read a section out of order and find a term that we define a few chapters earlier. To fill in the gaps, we include a glossary at the end of this book.

Because the Internet is ever-changing, we put additional information online, which we can update more often than this book can be republished. The *Internet For Dummies* authors have a Web site with updates, history, and other interesting articles, at net.gurus.org.

When you have to follow a complicated procedure, we spell it out step by step wherever possible. When you have to type something, it appears in the book in **boldface**. Type it just as it appears. Use the same capitalization we do — a few systems care deeply about CAPITAL and small letters. Then press the Enter key. The book tells you what should happen when you give each command and what your options are.

When you have to choose commands from menus, we write File➪Exit, for example, when we want you to choose the File command from the menu bar and then choose the Exit command from the menu that appears.

Who Are You?

In writing this book, we made a few assumptions about you:

✔ You have or would like to have access to the Internet.

✔ You want to get some work done online. (We consider the term *work* to include the concept *play*.)

✔ You aren't interested in becoming the world's next great Internet expert, at least not this week.

How This Book Is Organized

This book has six parts. The parts stand on their own — although you can begin reading wherever you like, you should at least skim Parts I and II first to get acquainted with some unavoidable Internet jargon and find out how to get your computer on the Net.

Here are the parts of the book:

In Part I, "Welcome to the Internet," you find out what the Internet is and why it's interesting (at least why we think it's interesting). Also, this part gives you vital Internet terminology and explains concepts that help you as you read the later parts of the book. Part I discusses security and privacy issues and gives some thoughts about children's use of the Net.

For the nuts and bolts of getting on the Net, read Part II, "Internet, Here I Come!" For most users, by far the most difficult part of using the Net is getting to that first connection, with software loaded, configuration configured, and modem modeming or broadband banding broadly. After that, it's (relatively) smooth sailing.

Part III, "Web Mania," dives into the World Wide Web, the part of the Internet that has powered the Net's leap from obscurity to fame. We discuss how to get around on the Web, how to find stuff (which is not as easy as it should be), and how to shop online. We also wrote chapters on downloading music and video and managing your finances on the Internet.

Part IV, "E-Mail, Chat, and Other Ways to Hang Out Online," looks at the important Net communication services: sending and receiving e-mail, swapping instant messages, and chatting. You find out how to exchange e-mail with people down the hall or on other continents, how to use Internet-based phone and video conferencing programs, how to use instant messaging programs to chat with your online pals, how to use Twitter, and how to use e-mail mailing lists to keep in touch with people of similar interests. You're also briefed on avoiding and blocking online hazards, such as viruses and spam. Then we talk about virtual worlds, games, and simulations where many people (sometimes *very* many people) share the experience.

Part V, "Putting Your Own Stuff on the Net," talks about how to post all kinds of material on the Internet. Putting your writing, photos, and videos online is easier than ever because of the range of free Web services you can use, including blogs, which let anyone be an online journalist. If you want complete control over your Web site, we also give you an overview of how to create a Web site with your own domain name.

Part VI, "The Part of Tens," is composed of a compendium of ready references and useful facts (which, we suppose, suggests that the rest of the book is full of useless facts).

We stuck the glossary at the end of the book so that it's easy to find.

A cheat sheet that summarizes how to use the most important Web browsers and e-mail programs in this book is online at www.dummies.com/cheatsheet/internet.

Icons Used in This Book

Lets you know that some particularly nerdy, technoid information is coming up so that you can skip it, if you want. (On the other hand, you may want to read it.)

Indicates that a nifty little shortcut or timesaver is explained.

Gaack! We found out about this information the hard way! Don't let it happen to you!

Indicates something to file away in your memory archives.

What Now?

That's all you need to know to get started. Whenever you hit a snag using the Internet, just look up the problem in the table of contents or index in this book. You'll either have the problem solved in a flash or know where you need to go to find some expert help.

Because the Internet has been evolving for more than 30 years, largely under the influence of some extremely nerdy people, it wasn't designed to be particularly easy for normal people to use. Don't feel bad if you have to look up a number of topics before you feel comfortable using the Internet. Until recently, most computer users never had to face anything as complex as the Internet.

Feedback, Please

We love to hear from our readers. If you want to contact us, please feel free to do so, in care of

Dummies Press

10475 Crosspoint Blvd.

Indianapolis, IN 46256

Better yet, send us Internet e-mail at internet12@gurus.org (our friendly robot usually answers immediately; the human authors read all the e-mail and answer as much as we can), or visit this book's Web home page, at net. gurus.org. These e-mail addresses put you in contact with the authors of this book; to contact the publisher or authors of other *For Dummies* books, visit the publisher's Web site, at www.dummies.com, or send paper mail to the address just listed.

07512376033

Part I

Welcome to the Internet

The 5th Wave   By Rich Tennant

"I don't mean to hinder your quest for knowledge, however, it's not generally a good idea to try to download the entire Internet."

In this part . . .

The Internet is an amazing place. But because it's full of computers, everything is more complicated than it should be. We start with a look at what the Internet is and how it got that way. We tell you what's happening and what people are doing, and why you should care. We pay special attention to security problems, privacy issues, and family concerns — particularly the knotty question of what's the best way for kids to work with the Internet.

Chapter 1

What's So Great about the Internet, Anyway?

In This Chapter

▶ What, really, is the Internet?

▶ For that matter, what is a network?

▶ What is the Internet good for?

*I*t's huge, it's sprawling, it's globe spanning, and it has become part of our lives. It must be . . . the Internet. We all know something about it, and most of us have tried to use it, with more or less success. (If you've had less, you've come to the right place.) In this chapter, we look at what the Internet is and can do before we dive into details in the rest of this book.

If you're new to the Internet, and especially if you don't have much computer experience, *be patient with yourself.* Many of the ideas here are completely new. Allow yourself some time to read and reread. The Internet is a different world with its own language, and it takes some getting used to.

Even experienced computer users can find using the Internet more complex than other tasks they've tackled. The Internet isn't a single software package and doesn't easily lend itself to the kind of step-by-step instructions we'd provide for a single, fixed program. This book is as step-by-step as we can make it, but the Internet resembles a living organism mutating at an astonishing rate more than it resembles Microsoft Word and Excel, which sit quietly on your computer. After you get set up and practice a little, using the Internet seems like second nature; in the beginning, however, it can be daunting.

So, What Is the Internet?

The Internet — also known as the *Net* — is the world's largest computer network. "What is a network?" you may ask. Even if you already know, you may want to read the next couple of paragraphs to make sure that we're speaking the same language.

A computer *network* is a bunch of computers that communicate with each other. It's sort of like a radio or TV network that connects a bunch of radio or TV stations so that they can share the latest episode of *American Idol*.

Don't take the analogy too far. In *broadcast* networking, TV networks send the same information to all stations at the same time; in computer networking, each particular message is routed to a particular computer, so different computers can display different things. Unlike TV networks, computer networks are two-way: When computer A sends a message to computer B, B can send a reply back to A.

Some computer networks consist of a central computer and a bunch of remote stations that report to it (for example, a central airline-reservation computer with thousands of screens and keyboards in airports and travel agencies). Other networks, including the Internet, are more egalitarian and permit any computer on the network to communicate with any other computer. Many new wireless devices — cellphones, Palm handhelds, the BlackBerry, iPhones, and their ilk — expand the reach of the Internet right into our pockets. (Hands off our wallets!)

The Internet isn't really one network — it's a network of networks, all freely exchanging information. The networks range from the big, corporate networks to tiny ones (such as the one John built in his back bedroom, made from a couple of old PCs he bought at an electronics parts store) and everything in between. College and university networks have long been part of the Internet, and now high schools and elementary schools are joining in. Lately, the Internet has become so popular that many households have more than one computer and are creating their own little networks that they connect to the Internet.

What's All the Hoopla?

Everywhere you turn, you can find traces of the Internet. Household products, business cards, radio shows, and movie credits list their Web site addresses (usually starting with *www* and ending with "dot com") and their e-mail addresses. New people you meet would rather give you an e-mail address than a phone number. Everyone seems to be "going online" and "googling it."

The Internet affects our lives on a scale as significant as the telephone and television. When it comes to spreading information, the Internet is the most significant invention since the printing press. If you use a telephone, write letters, read a newspaper or magazine, or do business or any kind of research, the Internet can radically alter your worldview.

On networks, size counts a great deal: The larger a network is, the more stuff it has to offer. Because the Internet is the world's largest interconnected group of computer networks, it has an amazing array of information to offer.

When people talk about the Internet, they usually talk about what they can do, what they have found, and whom they have met. The number of available services is too huge to list in this chapter, but here are the Big Three:

- **Electronic mail (e-mail):** This service is certainly the most widely used — you can exchange e-mail with millions of people all over the world. People use e-mail for anything they might use paper (mail, faxes, special delivery of documents) or the telephone (gossip, recipes, love letters) to communicate — you name it. (We hear that some people even use it for stuff related to work.) Electronic *mailing lists* enable you to join group discussions with people who have similar interests and to meet people over the Net. Part IV of this book has all the details.

- **The World Wide Web:** When people talk these days about surfing the Net, they often mean checking out sites on this (buzzword alert) global multimedia hyperlinked database. In fact, people are talking more about the Web and less about the Net. Are they the same thing? Technically, the answer is "No." But practically speaking, the answer for many people is "Pretty close." We tell you the truth, the whole truth, and nothing but the truth in Part III of this book.

  Web sites can provide you with information ranging from travel information to how to raise chickens. You can also look at videos, listen to music, buy stuff, sell stuff, and play video games.

  The software used to navigate the Web is a browser. The most popular browsers now are Firefox and Internet Explorer. We tell you all about them in Chapters 6 and 7.

- **Instant messaging (IM-ing):** Programs such as Windows Live Messenger, Yahoo! Messenger, and AOL Instant Messenger let you send messages that "pop up" on the recipient's screen. We hear tales of nimble-fingered youth carrying on upward of 13 IM sessions simultaneously. Some Web sites also provide messaging services. We tell you about IM programs in Chapter 16.

Why Is This Medium Different from Any Other Medium?

The Internet is unlike any other communications media we've ever encountered. People of all ages, colors, creeds, and countries freely share ideas, stories, data, opinions, and products on the Net.

Anybody can access it

One great thing about the Internet is that it's the most open network in the world. Thousands of computers provide facilities that are available to anyone who has Internet access. Although pay services exist (and more are added every day), most Internet services are free for the taking after you're online. If you don't already have access to the Internet through your company, your school, your library, or a friend, you can pay for access by using an Internet service provider (ISP). We talk about some ISPs in Chapter 4.

One of the biggest changes in Net use in the past few years has been the move to ever smaller, lighter, and cheaper equipment to connect to it. *Netbooks* are small, cheap computers about the size and weight of this book that are mainly intended for connecting to the Net. If a netbook is too big for you, smartphones such as the Apple iPhone put a computer, and the Internet, in your pocket with an always-on connection.

It's politically, socially, and religiously correct

Another great thing about the Internet is that it is what one may call "socially unstratified." That is, one computer is no better than any other, and no person is any better than any other. Who you are on the Internet depends solely on how you present yourself through your computer. If what you say makes you sound like an intelligent, interesting person, that's who you are. It doesn't matter how old you are or what you look like or whether you're a student, business executive, or construction worker. Physical disabilities don't matter — we correspond with deaf and blind people. If they hadn't felt like telling us, we never would have known. People become famous (and infamous) in the Internet community as a result of their own efforts.

Does the Internet really reach every continent?

Some skeptical readers, after reading the claim that the Internet spans every continent, may point out that Antarctica is a continent, even though its population consists largely of penguins, who (as far as we know) aren't interested in computer networks. Does the Internet go there? It does. A few machines at the Scott Base on McMurdo Sound in Antarctica are on the Internet, connected by radio link to New Zealand. The base at the South Pole has a link to the United States. See the polar Webcam at www.usap.gov.

At the time of this writing, the largest Internet-free land mass in the world is probably one of the uninhabited islands in the Canadian arctic — Melville Island, perhaps. (You can look it up on the Internet.) We used to say New Guinea, a large jungle island north of Australia, until a reader there sent us e-mail in 1997 telling us about his new Internet provider. ***Note:*** If you live on Melville Island and you're online there, please e-mail us right away!

The Net advantage

The Internet has become totally mainstream, and you're falling further behind the curve — and at a faster rate — if you haven't yet gotten started. Increasingly, news gets out on the Internet before it's available any other way, and the cyberdeprived are losing ground.

Here are some of the ways people use the Internet:

- ✔ **Find information:** Many Web sites have information free for the taking. Information ranges from IRS tax forms that you can print and use to help-wanted ads, real estate listings, and recipes. From U.S. Supreme Court decisions and library card catalogs to the text of old books, digitized pictures (many suitable for family audiences), and an enormous variety of software — from games to operating systems — you can find virtually anything on the Net. You can check the weather forecast, view movie listings, find your childhood sweetheart, browse catalogs, and see school closings for anywhere in the world, from anywhere in the world.

  Special tools known as *search engines* and *directories* help you find information (and people) on the Web. See Chapter 8 to find out how to search for the information you need.

- ✔ **Stay in touch:** *Weblogs* (or *blogs*) let people and organizations distribute current information about themselves rapidly and easily. *Microblogs*, such as Twitter, combine the Net with mobile phone text messages to let people stay up to date anywhere, at any time.

✔ **Get an education:** Schoolteachers coordinate projects with classrooms all over the globe. College students and their families exchange e-mail to facilitate letter-writing and keep down the cost of phone calls. Students do research from their home computers. The latest encyclopedias are online.

✔ **Buy and sell stuff:** On the Internet, you can buy anything from books about beermaking to stock in microbreweries. And, you can make some cash by cleaning out your closets and selling your old junk on eBay. Software companies sell software and provide updates on the Net. Most software distribution is migrating to the Internet, where a customer can download and install programs without waiting for a CD to arrive. We talk about the relevant issues in Chapter 10.

✔ **Travel:** Cities, towns, states, and countries are using the Web to put up (or *post*) tourist and event information. Travelers find weather information, maps, and museum hours online, in addition to plane, train, and bus schedules and tickets. While you're at it, you can buy your airplane tickets, rent a car, and make your hotel reservations.

✔ **Use intranets:** Businesses have figured out that this Internet concept is truly useful, and they create their own, private networks — like mini-Internets. On these *intranets,* companies use Web pages for posting company information such as benefits, filing expense reports and time sheets, and ordering supplies. An intranet helps an organization provide information that employees can see from inside the company that folks on the outside can't see, including manuals, forms, videos of boring meetings, and, of course, endless memos. In some organizations, e-mail and intranets reduce the amount of paper wasted on this stuff.

✔ **Play games:** Internet-based multiuser games can easily absorb all your waking hours and an alarming number of what would otherwise be your sleeping hours. You can challenge other players who can be anywhere in the world. Many kinds of games are available on the Web, including such traditionally addictive games as bridge, hearts, chess, checkers, and go. In Chapter 17, we tell you where to find these games.

✔ **Find love:** People are finding romance on the Net. Singles ads and matchmaking sites vie for users. The Internet long ago grew beyond the original bunch of socially challenged 22-year-old nerdy guys and now has turned into the world's biggest matchmaker, for people of all ages, genders, preferences, and life situations.

✔ **Heal:** Patients and doctors keep up-to-date with the latest medical findings, share treatment experience, and give one another support around medical problems. We even know of some practitioners who exchange e-mail directly with their patients.

✔ **Invest:** People do financial research, buy stock, and invest money online. Some online companies trade their own shares. Investors are finding new ventures, and new ventures are finding capital.

✔ **Participate in nonprofits:** Churches, synagogues, mosques, schools, clubs, teen centers, and other community organizations put up pages telling Web users about themselves and inviting new people. The online church newsletter *always* comes before Sunday.

Okay, What Next?

If you're ready to jump on the Internet, first read Chapter 2 for some safety tips. If you have children (or grandchildren), read Chapter 3 about what kids should (and shouldn't) do online.

Done? Chapter 4 tells you how to get connected!

Where did the Internet come from?

The ancestor of the Internet was the *ARPANET,* a project funded by the Department of Defense (DOD) in 1969, as an experiment in reliable networking and to link DOD and military research contractors, including the large number of universities doing military-funded research. (ARPA stands for Advanced Research Projects Administration, the branch of the DOD in charge of handing out grant money. For enhanced confusion, the agency is now known as *DARPA —* the added *D* is for *Defense,* in case anyone had doubts about where the money was coming from.) Although the ARPANET started small — connecting three computers in California with one in Utah — it quickly grew to span the continent.

In the early 1980s, the ARPANET grew into the early Internet, a group of interlinked networks connecting many educational and research sites funded by the National Science Foundation (NSF), along with the original military sites. By 1990, it was clear that the Internet was here to stay, and DARPA and the NSF bowed out in favor of the commercially run networks that make up today's Internet. (And, yes, although Al Gore didn't invent the Internet, he was instrumental in keeping it funded so that it could turn into the Internet we know now.) Familiar companies such as AT&T, Comcast, Sprint, and Verizon run some of the networks; others belong to specialty companies, such as Level3 and Cogent. No matter which one you're attached to, they all interconnect, so it's all one, giant Internet. For more information, read our Web page at net.gurus.org/history.

Turn off the computer now and then

We can tell you from experience that when you're on the Net, the hands on the clock slow down and stop and you can spend more time online than you could imagine. For some people, it's impossible to go ten minutes without checking e-mail, dirty dishes are ignored while visiting just one more Web page, and it gets to the point where it could be Internet Addiction. Remember that the Net is a fine adjunct to real life — not a substitute.

As our friend and longtime Net user Jean Polly regularly says: The Internet is closing! Go outside and play!

Chapter 2

Is the Internet Safe? Viruses, Spyware, Spam, and Other Yucky Stuff

In This Chapter

▶ Taking a look at the dangers that lurk on the Net

▶ Protecting your online privacy

▶ Understanding how viruses can infect your computer

▶ Preventing spyware-makers from installing unwanted software on your PC

▶ Controlling how much junk e-mail you're stuck looking at

▶ Keeping yourself and your family safe online

*W*e like the Internet. It has been part of our lives — and livelihoods — for years. We'd love to tell you that all the stuff you may have read about the dangers of connecting a computer to the Internet is hype. We can't. The success of the Internet has attracted unsavory people who view you as a money tree ready to be plucked. (Nothing personal — they see everybody that way.) In a few countries, perpetrating Internet fraud is now a major part of the national economy.

Even if no one steals your money, information about your online activities can be gathered and result in a real loss of privacy. And, some people are trying to take over your computer so that they can use it for nefarious purposes. When a new computer is hooked up to the Internet, it's not a question of *whether* it will come under cyberattack, but when. And, the answer is measured not in months or days — but in hours or minutes.

When you combine the Internet with cellphones and global positioning systems (GPSs), privacy issues become even scarier. Cellphone providers can tell where you are whenever you have your phone with you. And, phones or other Internet-connected devices that contain a GPS can help you find your way around, but they can also report on your whereabouts.

Relax: The Internet doesn't have to be a dangerous place. Using the Internet is like walking around a big city — yes, you need to be careful, use some protection, and stay out of dangerous areas, but you can also safely take advantage of the wonders that the Net has to offer.

This chapter describes the types of issues that abound on the Internet:

✔ **Privacy issues** involve how much people can find out about you over the Internet.

✔ **Security issues** have to do with keeping control over which programs are running on your computer.

✔ Just plain **annoyance issues** include ending up with a mailbox full of *spam* (junk e-mail) or Web browser windows popping up with advertisements.

Throughout the rest of this book, we include instructions for staying safe by using a firewall, a virus checker, a spyware scanner, and some common sense. Chapter 3 talks about rules for letting kids use the Internet, and most of the suggestions make sense for grown-ups, too.

Privacy: Who's Who and What They Can Tell about You

Advances in technology are eroding the privacy that most of us take for granted. Innovations we use every day — credit cards, cellphones, electronic key cards, and automobile tollway transponders — allow our every purchase and movement to be tracked. The Internet is an extension of this trend. Much of what you do online can be watched and recorded — sometimes for innocent reasons and sometimes not.

All this is further compounded by the amount of publicly available information that is now conveniently available to a far *greater* public over the Internet. When paper records were kept by government officials and people had to visit the office and dig through the files for the specific information they wanted, a lot less information abuse was possible. Now the potential exists for anyone anywhere to access information about people hitherto unknown, and to gather information from various sources, including online directories. No longer are geography or time deterrents enough.

Some people worry that snoops on the Net will intercept their private e-mail or Web pages. That's quite unlikely, actually. The more serious problem is advertisers who build profiles of the sites you visit and the stuff you buy. Most Web ads are provided by a handful of companies, such as DoubleClick. com (Google), Advertising.com (AOL), and Razorfish (Microsoft), who can use their ads to determine that the same person (you) is visiting a lot of different Web sites. Using this information, these companies can create a profile. They say that they don't create these personal profiles, but they don't say they won't in the future.

Several techniques for gathering information about you as you use the Internet, or tricking you into providing information, are described in the next few sections.

Who is the party to whom I am speaking?

Although the Internet seems completely anonymous, it's not. People used to have Internet usernames that bore some resemblance to their true identities — their names or initials or some such combination in conjunction with their university or corporation names gave a fairly traceable route to real people. Creating a new e-mail address now takes just a few minutes, so revealing your identity is definitely optional.

Depending on who you are and what you want to do on the Net, you may, in fact, want different names and different accounts. Here are some legitimate reasons for wanting them:

- ✔ You're a professional — a physician, for example — and you want to participate in a mailing list or newsgroup without being asked for your professional opinion.

- ✔ You want help with an area of concern that you feel is private and you don't want your problem known to people close to you who may find out if your name is associated with it.

- ✔ You do business on the Internet, and you socialize on it. You may want to keep those activities separate.

Most Net activities can be traced. If you start to abuse the anonymous nature of the Net, you'll find that you're not so anonymous after all.

Safety first

The anonymous, faceless nature of the Internet has its downside, too. To protect you and your family, take these simple precautions:

- ✔ When posting information that appears on a public Web site (other than your own) or in any discussion venue, don't use your full name. This advice doesn't apply if you're working in a business context, such as posting information on your company's Web site.

- ✔ Never provide your name, address, or phone number to someone you don't know.

✔ Never believe anyone who says that he's from "AOL Tech Support," "eBay Fraud Prevention," "PayPal Administration," or some such authority and asks you for your password. No legitimate entity will ever ask you for your password.

✔ Be especially careful about disclosing information about kids. Don't fill out profiles that ask for a kid's name, hometown, school, age, address, or phone number, because they're invariably used for "targeted marketing" (also known as junk mail).

Although relatively rare, horrible things have happened to a few people who have taken their Internet encounters into real life. Many wonderful things have happened, too. We've met some of our best friends over the Net, and some people have met and subsequently married. We just want to encourage you to use common sense when you set up a meeting with a Net friend. A person you e-mail or swap instant messages with is still largely a stranger, and if you want to meet in person, take the same precautions you would on a first date with someone you don't know: Meet in a public place, perhaps with a friend along, and be sure that your family knows where you are and when you're planning to be back.

The Net is a wonderful place, and meeting new people and making new friends is one of the big attractions. We just want to make sure that you're as careful as you would be in the rest of your life.

Phishing for inphormation

Phishing is the fastest-growing Internet crime, and you're the target. The good news is that protecting yourself is easy when you and your family know how to spot the phish-hook.

Learn what phishing looks like. After you start using the Internet and receiving e-mail (as described in Chapter 13), there's an excellent chance that you'll receive a message like this one:

```
Subject: Ebay Important Warning

From: eBay Billing Department! <Service@eBay.com>

eBay Fraud Mediation Request

You have recieved this email because you or someone
had used your account to make fake bids at eBay. For
security purposes, we are required to open an
investigation into this matter.
```

```
THE FRAUD ALERT ID CODE CONTAINED IN THIS MESSAGE
WILL BE ATTACHED IN OUR FRAUD MEDIATION REQUEST FORM,
IN ORDER TO VERIFY YOUR EBAY ACCOUNT REGISTRATION
INFORMATIONS.

  Fraud Alert ID CODE: 00937614

Please access the following form to complete the
verification of your eBay account registration
informations:

http://www.eBay.com/cgi bin/secure/Fraud Alert ID CODE:
      00937614

If we do not receive the appropriate verification within
48 hours, then we will assume this eBay account is
fraudulent and will be suspended.

Regards, Safeharbor Department (Trust and Safety
Department), eBay Inc.
```

Sounds authentic and scary, doesn't it? Think you had better deal with this message right away? Better think again. You are the phish, and this message is the bait. That underlined text in the middle is the hook. Click it and soon an official-looking page appears that looks just like an eBay sign-in page. After you enter your username and password, another official-looking page asks for your credit card number, PIN, billing address, checking account details (complete with a helpful graphic so that you can find the right numbers on your personal checks), Social Security number, date of birth, mother's maiden name, and driver's license number. The page is smart enough to reject an invalid credit card number. If you fill in all the information and press Continue, you see a valid eBay page that says you've logged out. Then, who knows? The bad guys know enough about you to do anything from making a small purchase paid for by your credit card to full-scale identity theft that can take months or years to straighten out.

This message *did not* come from eBay. Millions of these types of messages are sent over the Internet every day.

Some clues might alert you. The misspelled words *recieved* and *informations* suggest that the author is someone whose English skills are limited. And, if you take the trouble to save the e-mail to a file and then print it, the under-lined link in the middle of the message looks like this:

```
<http://192.168.45.67/cgi_bin>http://www.eBay.com/cgi_bin/
      secure/Fraud Alert ID CODE: 00937614
```

The text between the angle brackets (< and >) is where the link really goes, to a Web site with a numeric address. (When we tried clicking the link two days after we got the mail, the Web site had already been shut down. Those eBay security folks are on the ball.)

Don't take the bait

Phishers have gotten a lot more skillful since the earliest phishes a decade ago, and now often have good editors and use a spell checker, so you can't rely on spelling and grammar mistakes, although they're dead giveaways when you spot them. Here are a few additional tips:

- ✔ Assume that every e-mail that leads you to a page seeking passwords or credit card numbers or other personal information is a phishing expedition.
- ✔ If the e-mail purports to be from a company you've never heard of, ignore it.
- ✔ If the message says that it's from a company with whom you have an account, go to the company's Web site by typing the company's URL into your browser (see Chapter 7), *not* by clicking a link in the e-mail. When you get to the company's Web site, look for a My Account link. When you log in there, if there's a problem, you should see a notice. If there's no way to log in and you're still concerned, forward a copy of the e-mail to the customer service department.

One trick phishers use to fool Internet users is *Web site spoofing* — tricking your browser into displaying one address when you're actually at another site. Some browsers allow a Web site to show only its main address so that it doesn't look so geeky. Phishers take advantage of this ability. Better Web browsers offer protection against Web site spoofing — they always show the actual Web address of the page you're on.

To summarize, make sure that your family knows this rule well: Never, *never, never* enter passwords, credit card numbers, or other personal information at a Web page you opened by clicking a link in an e-mail.

Web bugs track the ads you read

Ever since the World Wide Web became a household word (okay, three words), companies have increasingly viewed their Internet presence as a vital way to advertise their goods and services and conduct their business. They spend millions of dollars on their Web sites and advertising e-mail (the legitimate kind you actually asked for) — and want very much to know just how people use them. Small wonder that when you visit a site, companies can keep track of your actions as you go from link to link within the site. But they *really* want to know what you were doing before you entered their sites — and even more they want to know whether you read their mail. To gather this intelligence, they insert tiny images in mail messages that they call *Web beacons* and everyone else calls *Web bugs* that report your actions back to the mailer.

Most mail programs offer the option not to fetch any of the images in mail messages from unknown or untrusted senders, which stops Web bugs and also makes your mail reading faster.

Cookies aren't so bad

When you browse the Web (as described in Chapter 6), the Web server needs to know who you are if you want to do things that require logging in, putting items in a virtual shopping cart, or completing any other process that requires that the Web site remember information about you as you move from page to page. The most commonly used trick that allows Web sites to keep track of what you're doing is setting cookies. A *cookie* is a tiny file, stored on your computer, that contains the address of the Web site and codes that your browser sends back to the Web site every time you visit a page there. Cookies usually don't contain personal or dangerous information; they're mostly innocuous and — believe it or not — useful.

If you plan to shop on the Web (described in Chapter 10) or use other Web services, cookies make it all possible. When you're using an airline reservation site, for example, the site uses cookies to separate the flights you're reserving from the ones that other users are reserving at the same time. On the other hand, you might use your credit card to purchase something on a Web site and the site uses a cookie to remember the account with your credit card number. Suppose that you provide this information from a computer at work and the next person to visit that site uses the same computer. That person could, possibly, make purchases on your credit card. Oops.

Internet users have various feelings about cookies. Some of us don't care about them, and some of us view them as an unconscionable invasion of privacy. You get to decide for yourself. Contrary to rumor, cookie files cannot get other information from your hard disk, give you a bad haircut, or otherwise mess up your life. They collect only information that the browser tells them about. Your Web browser lets you control whether and when cookies are stored on your computer; see Chapter 7 for details.

The Web browser equivalents of Web bugs are *tracking cookies*. If several Web sites show ads from the same advertising network, the ad network can use cookies to tell whenever you're looking at one of their ads. By piecing together the information from many Web sites, these tracking companies get a clear picture of where you go online — and what you look at when you get there. Many are careful to provide only statistical information to their clients, but the potential for abuse is there. It's worth noting that U.S. courts set a lower standard of protection for "business records" gathered in this way than they do for personal papers stored in our homes. Fortunately, most Web browsers provide an option to reject *third-party* cookies, or cookies from anyone other than the source of the Web page itself; this makes tracking cookies go away.

We know where you are

Cellphones and GPSs don't make the privacy situation simple. Anyone with a cellphone can take pictures or video of you and e-mail them to friends or post them to the Web, which can be anywhere from innocent fun to citizen journalism to seriously creepy. (We've read news reports of people standing at the foot of stairwells and escalators and trying to take pictures up girls' skirts. Ewww.) Modern cellphones have built-in GPS receivers, primarily intended to provide your location if you call 911, but also potentially usable to track your location whenever the phone is on.

Security: How People Can Take Over Your PC

You can download and install software directly over the Internet, which is a wonderful feature. It's wonderful when you need a viewer program to display and print a tax form or when you want to install a free upgrade to a program that you purchased earlier. How convenient! We tell you all about it in Chapter 12.

However, other people can also install programs on your computer without your permission. Hey, wait a minute — whose computer is it, anyway? These programs can arrive in a number of ways, mainly by e-mail or your Web browser.

Google yourself

One big attraction of the Internet is *all that data out there* that is now quite easy to access. Some of that data is about you. If you have your own blog or a personal Web site (see Chapters 19 and 20), you expect that all the information you put up there is available for everyone to see — usually, forever. (We find stuff about ourselves from over 25 years ago.) Other people also put up information — newsletters, event listings, pictures from events, and other pictures, for example. Your online data trail may be longer than you think. If you haven't done it before, search the Web for your own name. Enter your name in quotes in the Google or Bing search box and press Enter. If you have a common name, you may need to throw in your middle initial or add the name of your town or school. (If you do this often, you're *ego surfing*.)

Viruses arrive by e-mail

Computer *viruses* are programs that jump from computer to computer, just as real viruses jump from person to person. Computer viruses can spread using any mechanism that computers use to talk to each other, like networks, data CDs, and DVDs. Viruses have been around computers for a long time. Originally, viruses lived in program files that people downloaded using a file transfer program or their Web browsers. Now, most viruses are spread by opening files that are sent by e-mail, as attachments to mail messages, although instant messaging (IM; see Chapter 16) is a popular alternative.

There was a time long ago when people in the know (like we thought we were) laughed at newcomers to the Internet who worried about getting viruses by e-mail. E-mail messages back then were just text files and could not contain programs. Then e-mail attachments were introduced. People could then send computer software — including those sneaky viruses — by e-mail. Isn't progress wonderful?

What viruses do

When a virus lands on your computer, it has to manage somehow to get executed. Getting *executed* in computer jargon means being brought to life; a virus is a program, and programs have to be run in order to start doing their nefarious work. After a virus is running, it does two things:

1. The virus looks around and tries to find your address book, which it uses to courteously send copies of itself to all your friends and acquaintances, often wrapped up in very convincing-sounding messages ("Hey, enjoyed the other night, thought this file would amuse you!").

2. Then the virus executes its payload, the reason the virus writer went through all that trouble and risk. (They do occasionally end up in jail.)

The *payload* is the illegal activity that the virus is running from your machine. A payload can record your every keystroke (including your passwords). It can launch an attack at specific or random targets over the Internet. It frequently sends spam from your computer. Whatever it's doing, you don't want it to do. Trust us. If your computer starts to act quirky or extremely sluggish, chances are, you've contracted a virus or 20.

In the good old days, virus writers were content just to see their viruses spread, but like everything else about the Internet, virus writing is now a big business, in many cases controlled by organized crime syndicates.

What you can do about viruses

Don't worry *too* much about viruses — excellent virus-checking programs are available that check all incoming mail before the viruses can attack. In Chapter 4, which describes getting connected to the Internet, we recommend installing a virus checker. After you install it, be sure to update it regularly so that you're always protected against the latest viruses.

Worms come right over the Net

A *worm* resembles a virus, except that it doesn't need to hitch a ride on an e-mail message. A worm just jumps directly from one computer to another over the Net, entering your computer by way of security flaws in its network software. Unfortunately, the most popular type of network software on the Net, the kind in Microsoft Windows, is riddled with security holes, so many that if you attach a nice, fresh Windows machine to a broadband Net connection, the machine becomes overrun with worms in less than a minute.

If you rigorously apply all security updates from Microsoft, they fix most of the known security flaws, but it takes a lot longer than a minute to apply them all. Hence, we strongly encourage anyone using a broadband connection to use a hardware *firewall,* a box that sits between the Net and your computer and keeps the worms out. If you have a broadband connection, you probably want to use an inexpensive device called a *router* to hook up your computers, anyway, and all routers include a firewall as a standard feature. See Chapter 4 for more information.

Spyware arrives via Web sites

Spyware (which includes *adware*) is like a virus, except that your computer catches it in a different way. Rather than arrive by e-mail, spyware is downloaded by your browser. Generally, you need to click something on a Web page to download and install spyware, but many people have been easily misled into installing spyware that purports to be a graphics viewer or another type of program they think they might want.

Know what spyware does

Spyware got its name from being frequently used for sneaky purposes, like spying on what you're typing. Sometimes, spyware gathers information about you and sends it off to another site without your knowledge or consent. A common use for spyware is finding out which sites you're visiting so that advertisers can display pop-up ads (described later in this chapter) that are targeted to your interests.

Targeted advertising isn't inherently evil. The Google AdSense program, for example, places ads on participating Web pages based on the contents of those pages. Targeted ads are worth more to advertisers because you're more likely to respond to an ad about something you're already reading about.

Spyware can also send spam from your computer, capture every keystroke you type and send it to a malefactor over the Net, and do all the other Bad Things that worms and viruses do.

Are Macs the solution?

We hear you Apple Macintosh users gloating as you read this chapter: "We don't have these problems. Why don't people just use Macs?" Mac users still have to put up with phishing and other forms of junk e-mail, and spyware has started to appear on Macs. But to date, almost none of the viruses or worms affects Macs, and the threat of spyware is lower than for PCs. Although this situation could change, we think that Mac users will always have an easier time on the Net. First, Macs are so scarce (compared to Windows machines) that it's not worth a virus writer's time to attack them — partly because this scarcity also makes it hard to spread Mac viruses. Most e-mail addresses in a Mac user's address book belong to Windows users anyway, so if a Mac virus makes copies of itself, the copies it mails out don't find nice, vulnerable homes. (Designing a virus that will run on *both* Windows and Macs is hard, even today.) Finally, the Mac OS X is designed to be more secure than Windows and is harder to infect.

Current Intel-based Macs can run Windows programs, or can even be set up to run native Windows, for applications that are Windows-only. We know of companies whose support staffs run *everything* on Macs — because they don't get infected. When employees need to run something on a PC, they do it in a window on the Mac screen. Cool.

Don't voluntarily install spyware

Lots of cute little free programs are available for download, but don't install them unless you're convinced that they're safe *and* useful. Most free toolbars, screen savers, news tickers, and other utilities are spyware in disguise. Besides, the more programs you run on your computer, the slower all your other programs run. Check with friends before downloading the latest program. Or, search the Web for the program's name (see Chapter 8) to find positive or negative reviews. Download programs only from reputable Web sites. Keep your computer free from software clutter.

Protect your computer from spyware

Spyware programs are often designed to be hard to remove — which can mess up your operating system. Rather than wait until you contract a bad case of spyware and then try to uninstall it, a better idea is to inoculate your computer against spyware. To block spyware, be careful about the screen elements you click. Install a spyware checking program that can scan your system periodically, such as the free Microsoft Windows Defender. See Chapter 4 for details.

Be aware that spyware can attack Macs and even phones

Macintosh computers aren't immune to spyware. (See the nearby sidebar, "Are Macs the solution?") The Macintosh operating system is inherently more secure than Windows, so few viruses and little spyware can attack it. However, a Mac user is just as likely as a PC user to be fooled into clicking a link to a free porn site that downloads spyware to your computer along with that sexy video. Even smartphones (like the iPhone or Palm Pre) can be infected with spyware, and although most spyware targets Windows, it also targets other kinds of computers and phones, so think before you click on all these devices.

Adware: Just another kind of spyware

Adware, a controversial type of software that many people consider to be spyware, is installed as part of some programs that are distributed for free. It watches what you do on your computer and displays targeted ads — even when you run other programs. We think that no users in their right minds would knowingly install a program that peppers them with ads — and we want laws to ban the practice, pointing out that adware often behaves like a parasite,

by obscuring or replacing ads from competing Web sites.

Before downloading a free program, make sure that you understand what the deal is. If you aren't sure, don't download it. Make sure that your kids know not to download free games, song lyrics, and the like — most are infested with adware. If you don't, before you know it, you'll have so many pop-up ads that you'll have to unplug your computer to shut it up.

Pop-up browser windows pop up all over the place

One of the worst innovations in recent decades is the *pop-up* window that appears on your screen unbidden (by you) when you visit some Web sites. Some pop-ups appear immediately, and others are *pop-unders,* which are hidden under your main window until you close the main window. The pop-ups you're most likely to see are ads for mortgages and airline tickets. (No, we don't give their names here; they have plenty of publicity already.)

Several mechanisms can make pop-ups appear on your computer:

- ✔ A Web site can open a new browser window. Sometimes this new window displays an ad or other annoying information. But sometimes the new window has useful information — some Web sites use pop-up windows as a sort of Help system for using the site.

- ✔ Spyware or other programs can display pop-up windows.

Luckily, Web browsers now can prevent most Web sites from opening unwanted new browser windows. See Chapter 7 to find out how to tell your browser how to display fewer pop-ups.

What's the secret word, Mr. Potter?

Everywhere you go these days, someone wants you to enter a password or passcode. Even Harry Potter has to tell his password to a magic portrait just to enter the Gryffindor dormitory (although there's apparently no security between the boys' and girls' wings). Security experts are nearly unanimous in telling us how we should protect all our passwords:

- ✔ Pick passwords that are long and complex enough that no one can guess them.

  Never use as a password a word that occurs in the dictionary. Consider sticking a number or two into your password.

- ✔ Never use the same password for different accounts.

- ✔ Memorize your passwords and never write them down.

- ✔ Change your passwords frequently.

- ✔ Check the strength of your passwords. This Microsoft site can help: `microsoft.com/protect/yourself/password/checker.mspx`.

This sound advice is intended for everyone — except ordinary human beings. Most of us have far too many passwords to keep track of and too little brain to store them in.

The perils of free Wi-Fi

Wi-Fi, the wireless way that your laptop can connect to the Internet, is available in many public places, including airports and coffee shops. As we explain in Chapter 4, when you use Wi-Fi to connect your computer to the Internet, you locate the network and click Connect and then start using the Internet. One of the first things you'll probably do is use your Web browser to check your e-mail or connect to your company's network, And, in the process, you type a password or two.

Can you trust the Wi-Fi network? How do you know that the Wi-Fi network isn't listening to what you type, including your passwords? Well, you don't.

Wi-Fi spoofing is surprisingly easy. A thief sets up a computer in an airport lounge or coffee shop by using the same Wi-Fi system identifier, and you connect to her Wi-Fi rather than to the real one. She monitors what you type and uses your passwords to send spam or empty your bank account or perform other nefarious deeds.

What's a traveling Internet user to do? Answer: Don't use free Wi-Fi unless you know for *sure* that it's legit. (For example, your kids' school or your company may provide free Wi-Fi on the school or company grounds.) If you absolutely must use public Wi-Fi to check your e-mail while you're on the road, here's what to do (advice courtesy of our friend Mark Steinwinter):

1. Before you leave on your trip, change your e-mail password (and any other password you plan to use).

2. While on your trip, limit your public Wi-Fi use to accounts whose passwords you just changed. Go ahead and use Web sites that don't require a password.

3. As soon as you get home, change your e-mail password again. You can change it back to what it was before your trip, or to another password. Just assume that a Bad Guy has the password you used on your trip, and never use this password again.

One common-sense approach is to use a single password for accounts where there's little risk of loss, such as the one you need in order to read an online newspaper. Use separate, stronger passwords for the accounts that truly matter (such as your online banking). If you feel you can't remember them all, write them down and keep them in a safe place, not on a PostIt note stuck to your monitor.

Our warning about not using a password that's in the dictionary — take that one seriously! Hackers managed to find a hole in our firewall one day, and we had stupidly left one password set to a normal English word (*weather,* if you must know). It took the hackers less than two hours to break into our computer, by simply having their computer type every English word until they found one that worked.

When making up a password, stick numbers and punctuation into words or glue two words together with some numbers or spell things backward. Use both capital and lowercase letters, too. If your kids are Fred and Susie and your house number is 426, how about Fred426susiE? Or Susie426dreF? Using the first letters of each word in a phrase is a good method, too. If your favorite song is "I Wanna Hold Your Hand," it wouldn't be that hard to remember a password like Iwhyh1963. You get the idea!

Over the years, we've ended up with so many passwords that we started storing them in a text file — which anyone with access to our PC could read! This idea is certainly one of the world's worst. If you have a lot of passwords and no way to remember them, consider using a password manager, which is designed to store your passwords in a safe place. Of course, you have to remember one password — for your password manager. We use KeePass, a freeware, open source program that you can download from `www.keepass.info` for PCs and Macs. See Chapter 12 to find out how to download and install programs.

Spam, Bacon, Spam, Eggs, and Spam

> *Pink tender morsel,*
> *Glistening with salty gel.*
> *What the hell is it?*
>
> — SPAM haiku, found on the Internet, sometimes credited to
> Christopher James Hume.

More and more often, we get unsolicited bulk e-mail (abbreviated UBE but usually called *spam*) from some organization or person we don't know. Spam is the online version of junk mail. Offline, junk mailers have to pay postage. Unfortunately, online, the cost of sending out a bazillion pieces of junk mail is virtually zilch.

E-mail spam (not to be confused with SPAM, a meat-related product from Minnesota and very popular in Hawaii) means that thousands of copies of an unwanted message are sent to e-mail accounts and even to instant message programs. The message usually consists of unsavory advertising for get-rich-quick schemes or pornographic offers — something you might not want to see and something you definitely don't want your children to see. Many spam messages tout worthless stocks that the spammers have bought and hope you'll buy at inflated prices. The message is *spam,* the practice is *spamming,* and the person sending the spam is a *spammer.* Phishing often involves spam, too.

Spam, unfortunately, is a major problem on the Internet because it's extremely cheap for sleazy advertisers to send. We receive hundreds or thousands of pieces of spam a day, and the number continues to increase. Spam doesn't have to be commercial (we've seen religious and political spam), but it has to be unsolicited; if you asked for it, it isn't spam.

Be careful with password hints

Web site operators are tired of dealing with customers who forget their passwords, so a new computer tool has emerged in the past few years — the password hint. When you create a new account, the friendly identity manager software asks for your username and new password. It then makes you select and answer a couple of security questions, such as "What's your favorite color?" or "What's your pet's name?"

Sometime in the future, you try to log in to that account — and find that you forgot that pesky password. No problemo! You're asked the security questions you picked; if you type the right answer, you're in. The problem is that a thief pretending to be you sees the same challenge. Rather than guess your password, all he has to guess is your favorite color (blue, maybe?) and figure out your pet's name (and did your kid post captioned photos of Rover on the school Web site as part of his third grade computer-literacy project?).

If you encounter one of these password hints when you sign up for an important account, pick questions whose answers an attacker can't glean by researching you. And, there's no rule that says you have to answer the security questions truthfully. You can pick a friend's pet, for example, or a color you detest, or you can say that your favorite color is Rover and your pet's name is Purple. You just have to remember your less-than-truthful answers to these questions.

Why it's called spam

The meat? SPAM might be short for *spiced ham.* Oh, you mean the unwanted e-mail? It came from the Monty Python skit in which a group of Vikings sing the word *spam* repeatedly in a march tempo, drowning out all other discourse. (Search for *Monty Python spam* at your favorite search engine and you'll find plenty of sites where you can listen to it.) Spam can drown out all other mail because some people receive so much spam that they stop using e-mail entirely.

Why it's so bad

You may think that spam, like postal junk mail, is just a nuisance we have to live with. But it's worse than junk mail, in several ways. Spam costs you money. E-mail recipients pay much more than the sender does to deliver a message. Sending e-mail is cheap: A spammer can send thousands of messages an hour from a PC. After that, it costs you time to download, read (at least the subject line), and dispose of the mail. The amount of spam is now about 20 times the amount of real e-mail, and if spam volume continues to grow at its alarming pace, pretty soon real e-mail will prove to be useless because it's buried under the junk. Another problem is that spam filters, which are supposed to discard only spam, can throw away good messages by mistake.

Not only do spam recipients have to bear a cost, but all this volume of e-mail also strains the resources of the e-mail servers and the entire Internet. ISPs have to pass along the added costs to its users. Spam volume doubled or tripled for many years, peaking in 2008, dropping back a bit in early 2009 when a few major spam sources were shut down, but is expected to keep growing quickly. America Online has estimated that more than 95 percent of its incoming e-mail is spam, and many ISPs have told us that as much as $2 of the $20 monthly fee goes to handling and cleaning up after spam. Spammers send 100 *billion* spam messages *every day*. And, as ISPs try harder to filter out spam, more and more legitimate mail is being mistaken for spam and bounced.

Many spam messages include a line that instructs you how to get off their lists, something like "Send us a message with the word REMOVE in it." Don't bother — they don't remove you from their lists, and you may well receive *more* spam now that they know your address is a good one. Reply to messages or click links to unsubscribe *only* if the messages are from lists that you remember subscribing to or from companies you have done business with.

What you can do about it

You don't have to put up with a lot of spam. Spam filters can weed out most of the spam you receive. See Chapter 14 to see how to use the spam filter that may already be built into your e-mail program or how to install a separate spam filtering program. Also visit www.cauce.org, the Coalition Against Unsolicited E-mail, the major grass roots antispam organization.

Safety: How to Keep Yourself and Your Family Safe

Viruses, spyware, phishing, pop-ups, spam — is the Internet worth all this trouble? No, you don't have to give up on the Internet in despair or disgust. You just have to put in a little extra effort to use it safely. In addition to the technological fixes we suggest (virus checkers, spyware scanners, and pop-up blockers), you need to develop some smarts about online security. Here's a quick checklist:

✔ **Develop healthy skepticism.** If it sounds too good to be true, it isn't true. No one in Africa has $25 million they will share with you if you help them get it out of the country, nor did you win a sweepstakes you never entered. As the old saying goes, there's a fool born every minute. Today's sucker doesn't have to be you.

✔ **Keep your computer's software up-to-date.** Both Microsoft and Apple have features that make this a more or less painless process. Use them. The latest software updates usually fix exploitable security flaws.

✔ **Use a firewall and keep it updated.** Your computer probably has firewall software built in. Make sure that your firewall is turned on. Some malware programs know how to turn off protective software, so check it every week or so. We recommend using a router — a device that lets you share Internet connections among several computers (whether wired or wireless) — because routers include built-in firewall programs that malware programs cannot disable or bypass. These units are so cheap that you should get one even if you have only one computer. (See Chapter 5 for details.)

✔ **Install virus-protection and spyware-protection software and keep it current.** Virus protection costs $25 per year or so. Pay it. Chapter 4 tells you how to install virus checkers and spyware scanners.

You must keep the virus-description files in your antivirus software updated — automatically if possible, and every week at least. (New viruses are launched every day.) The maker of your antivirus software should have a Web site from which you can download the updates; check your documentation.

✔ **Don't open an e-mail attachment unless it's from someone you know *and* you're expecting it.** Contact the sender if you aren't sure.

✔ **Don't click links in e-mail messages unless you're sure that you know where they lead.** If you click one and the site you end up at wants your password or credit card number or dog's name, close your browser window. Don't even think about giving out any information.

✔ **Pick passwords that are hard to guess, and never give them to anyone else.** Don't give them to the nice lady who says she's from the help desk or to the bogus FBI special agent who claims to need it for tracking down a kidnapped child. No one.

✔ **Be consistent.** If you share your computer with several family members or housemates, make sure that every one understands these rules and agrees to follow them.

For more tips about staying safe online, the U.S. government runs the OnGuard Online site at www.onguardonline.gov.

Chapter 3

Kids and the Net

. . . .

In This Chapter

▶ Recognizing good and not-so-good ways that kids use the Internet

▶ Getting wise to some concerns about the Internet

▶ Working up parental guidelines for using the Internet

▶ Looking at the Internet in schools

. . . .

Face it: Most kids are way more comfortable on the Internet than their parents (and grandparents) are. Schools assign kids to do research on the Web and e-mail information to other students or their teachers. Online games are designed for kids of all ages. Forbidding your kids from using the Net altogether is hopeless (unless they're younger than about 6), but you want to keep your kids safe. This chapter talks about what's great — and what's scary — about children and youth using the Internet.

With millions of kids online, a discussion about family Internet use is critical. (Obviously, if this isn't your concern, just skip this chapter and go to another one.)

Really Cool Ways Kids Use the Net

The Net is amazing. It can help kids with the things they have to do (homework) as well as with what they *want* to do:

> ✔ **Research homework assignments:** The Internet is an incredible way to expand the walls of a school. The Net can connect kids to libraries, research resources, museums, other schools, and other people. Kids can visit the American Museum of Natural History for information about anthropology and other natural sciences (at www.amnh.org, as shown in Figure 3-1) and the Sistine Chapel (www.vatican.va — click English and then Vatican Museums and then Online Tours); they can watch spotted newts in their native habitat; they can hear new music and make new friends. These days, many schools assume that kids have access to the Web, so parents had better be ready.

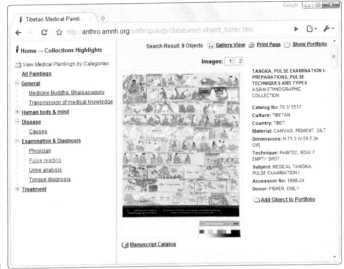

Figure 3-1:
Many
museums
have
interesting
information
online.

✔ **Make e-friends in other countries:** School projects such as the Global Schoolhouse connect kids around the world by working collaboratively on all types of projects. Its annual cyberfairs have brought together more than 500,000 students from hundreds of schools in at least 37 countries! Kids can find out more at the Global Schoolhouse Web site, `www.globalschoolnet.org/GSH`, where they can also subscribe to lots of mailing lists. (We explain in Chapter 6 how to reach these locations so that you can come back here later and help your kids follow up on them.)

✔ **Practice foreign languages:** Kids can visit online chat rooms, where they can try out their French or Spanish or Portuguese or Russian or Japanese or even Esperanto.

✔ **Pay for downloaded music:** Kids love music, and they can buy music over the Internet in several ways. (Adults can too, as it turns out.) The Apple iTunes music store, at `www.apple.com/itunes`, sells songs for about 99 cents. Other sites, such as `www.napster.com`, let you download as many songs as you like for a monthly fee. See Chapter 9 for details.

✔ **Write an encyclopedia article:** Wikipedia, at `en.wikipedia.org`, is a free online encyclopedia that anyone can contribute to. It's a useful research tool, but, even better, kids can add the material they found while researching those term papers to make Wikipedia even better. A worldwide team of volunteer writers and editors updates the material continually, and you — or your child! — can be one of them. (See Chapter 20 to find out what wikis are.)

✔ **Discover how to make Web sites:** A Web site can be as clever or as stupid as you like. You and your kids can post your stories or artwork for family and friends to admire. We explain how to do these things in Part V.

Whenever you or your kids search for a topic, you may see pages written by the world's greatest authority on that topic, a crackpot pushing a harebrained theory, a college kid's term paper, a guy on a bulletin board who thinks he's an expert, or, more likely, all of the above. Some Web sites are maintained by hate groups and push truly nasty venom. Being able to identify all those types of information is one of the most valuable skills that children (or anyone) can acquire.

So-So Ways Kids Use the Net

Here are some ideas that adults might consider a waste of time, but hey, we can't be serious all the time:

- ✔ **Play games:** Many popular games (both traditional — such as chess, bridge, hearts, and go — and video) have options that let kids compete against other players on the Internet. See Chapter 17, if you dare, but you may find yourself turning into a gamer!

- ✔ **Send IMs to friends:** Instant messaging (IM) is a cool way to get in touch — *instantly*. Wireless options are already happening in many parts of the world. We reveal all in Chapter 16.

- ✔ **Talk on a videophone:** Thanks to software such as Yahoo! Messenger and Skype, kids can see their friends while talking to them (not recommended on bad hair days). Chapter 16 talks about free video programs.

- ✔ **Create an online profile on a social networking site.** Web sites such as Facebook and MySpace enable people to create a page about themselves and then link to their friends. We have privacy and safety concerns about kids using these sites. See Chapter 18.

- ✔ **Shop:** What can we say? Internet shopping is like shopping at the mall, except that the Internet is always open and you don't have to hunt for a parking place. Kids can sell stuff too. Chapter 10 gets you started.

- ✔ **Role-play:** Any number of Internet sites let players pretend to be characters in their favorite science fiction or fantasy books. Chapter 17 describes virtual worlds on the Web.

Not-So-Good Ways Kids Use the Net

Make sure that your kids or grandkids stay away from these ideas, which will just get them into trouble — some of it serious:

- ✔ **Plagiarism:** That's the fancy word for passing off other people's work as your own. Plagiarizing from the Internet is just as wrong as plagiarizing from a book — and (for that matter) a lot easier for teachers to catch because teachers can use search engines, too.

- ✔ **Cheating:** Using translating software to do language homework is also no good. Besides, automated translations are still no substitute for the real thing.

- ✔ **Revealing too much personal information:** When chatting on the Net with people your kids don't know, they might be tempted to give out identifying information about themselves or your family, but it's dangerous — doing so can get them stalked, ripped off, or worse. Even revealing their e-mail addresses can invite unwanted junk mail. Some seemingly innocent questions that strangers ask online aren't so innocent, so we go into more detail later in this chapter about what to watch for.

- ✔ **Sharing copyrighted music and videos:** Now that kids can easily buy music online, they don't have much excuse for using file-sharing software to trade music or videos without permission. The music and movie industries are getting better at finding people who do that — and are taking legal action against them. It could cost you a lot of money.

- ✔ **Visiting porn and hate sites:** This advice is between you and your kids. Parents should make clear rules about what types of Web sites are acceptable, post them near the computer, and stick to them.

- ✔ **Pretending to be someone else online:** Kids should make up pseudonyms so that they don't have to use their real names. (This strategy can be one way to limit how much any stranger finds out.) But, pretending that you're a talent agent for *American Idol* or the latest reality show looking for a date is a bad idea.

- ✔ **Hanging out in adult chat rooms:** If kids pretend to be older than they are, they can get themselves *and* the chat room hosts into trouble.

- ✔ **Letting the Internet take over your life:** If the only thing your kids want to do after school is get online, it's time to set some limits. (Ditto for parents and their work!)

Truly Brain-Dead Things Kids Should Never Do

Here are some ideas that kids should *never* consider because they can lead directly into major trouble:

- ✔ **Meet online friends in person without telling a parent:** If a child or youth meets someone online and wants to meet that person face-to-face, fine — maybe. But parents need to take precautions! First, make sure that your kid tells you about the meeting so that you can decide together how to proceed. Second, no one (child, youth, or adult) should ever meet an online friend in a private place: Always arrange to meet in a public place, such as a restaurant. Finally, go to the meeting with your child, in case they have been completely misled. (You can lurk discretely nearby, so bring a book.)

✔ **Do anything illegal — online or off:** The Internet feels totally anonymous, but it's not. If kids or adults commit a crime, the police can get the Internet connection records from your Internet service provider (ISP) and find out who was connected over which modem on which day and at what time with which numeric Internet (IP) address, and they'll find you.

✔ **Break into other computers or create viruses:** This little escapade might have been considered a prank back in the 1980s, but the authorities have long since lost their sense of humor about it. Kids *have* gone to jail for it.

The Internet and Little Kids

We are strong advocates of allowing kids to be kids, and we believe that humans are better teachers than computers are. Now that you know our predisposition, maybe you can guess what we're going to say next: We are not in favor of sticking a young child in front of a screen. How young is too young? We believe that younger than age 5 is too young. At young ages, kids benefit more from playing with trees, balls, clay, crayons, paint, mud, monkey bars, bicycles, other kids, and especially older siblings. Computers make lousy babysitters. If your young children use computers, choose their programs and Web sites carefully, and limit their screen time.

We think that Internet access is more appropriate for somewhat older kids (fourth or fifth grade and older), but your mileage may vary. Even so, we think it's a good idea to limit the amount of time that anyone, especially kids, spends online. We (despite our good looks) have been playing with computers for 35 years (each), and we know what happens to kids who are allowed to stay glued to their computers for unlimited lengths of time — trust us, *it is not good.* Do you remember those old sayings "You are what you eat" and "Garbage in, garbage out"? What your brain devours makes a difference.

As human beings (what a concept), kids need to be able to communicate with other human beings. Too often, kids who have difficulty doing that prefer to get absorbed in computers — which doesn't help develop their social skills. Existing problems in that department grow worse, leading to more isolation. If you're starting to feel like your child is out of touch and you want to put the machine in its place (and maybe even encourage your child to get her life back), here are some quick self-defense tips:

✔ Keep a private log of all the time your child spends in front of the screen during one week. Then ask your child whether this is really how she wants to spend her life.

✔ Help your child find a hobby that doesn't involve a screen. Encourage him to join a team, form a band, or create some kind of art.

✔ Have your child set aside one computer-free day each week.

✔ Make your child have meals and conversations with actual human beings (that would be you and the rest of your family), face to face, in real time.

Surf Safe

Make sure your kids or grandkids know the safety rules for using the Net. Here are some basic guidelines for your kids to start with:

✔ **Never reveal exactly who you are.** Your child should use only his first name, and shouldn't provide a last name, an address, a phone number, or the name of his school.

✔ **Never, *ever*, tell anyone your password.** No honest person will ever ask you or your kid for it.

✔ **Be suspicious of strangers who seem to know a lot about you.** Maybe they say they're a friend of yours (the parent) who is supposed to pick up your kid after school or pick up a package from your house. Make sure your kid knows to never go with a stranger or let one into the house without asking a trusted (offline) adult first.

Here are a few more guidelines to help kids sidestep online trouble:

✔ **Think before you give your e-mail address to anybody.** Many Web sites ask users to register, and many require users to provide a working e-mail address that they verify by sending a confirmation message. Before you let your child register with a Web site, make sure that it's run by a reputable company from which you won't mind getting junk mail.

✔ **Never agree to talk to someone on the phone or meet someone in person without checking it out with a parent first.** Most people a kid can meet online are okay, but a few creepy types out there have made the Internet their hunting ground.

✔ **Don't assume that people are telling you the truth.** That "kid" who says he's your kid's age and gender and seems to share your child's interests and hobbies may in reality be a lonely 40-year-old. If your kids have younger siblings, impress upon them how important it is to watch out for the safety of their younger "sibs." They may not understand what a stranger is and believe that everything people tell them online is always true.

> ✔ **If someone is scaring you or making you uncomfortable — especially if the person says not to tell your parents —** *tell* **your parents.** If someone bothers your child, make sure she knows to ask you to talk to your Internet service provider. Remind your kid that she can always turn off the computer.

Sell, Sell, Sell!

If you spend a lot of time online, you will soon notice that everyone seems to be trying to sell you something. Kids, particularly those from middle- and upper-income families, are a lucrative target market, and the Net is being viewed as another way to capture this market.

Targeting kids for selling isn't new. Remember Joe Camel of the Camel cigarette campaign that many people claimed was aimed at kids? Some schools make students watch Channel One, a system that brings advertising directly to the classroom. If you watch TV, you know how TV programs for kids push their own lines of toys and action figures.

Kids should know that big company marketing departments have designed kid-friendly, fascinating, captivating software to help them better market to you. Delightful, familiar cartoon characters deftly elicit strategic marketing information directly from the keyboard in your home.

You should be aware of this situation and know what to do when someone on the Web is asking your kids for information. If your kids have access to credit cards, yours or their own, they can spend big bucks over the Internet. Beware of online stores where you have configured your Web browser to remember your passwords, because your kids will be able to waltz right in and start buying. And, your kids should be aware that if they spend your money online without permission, they're going to get into big trouble for it.

The Children's Online Privacy Protection Act (COPPA) limits the information that companies can collect from children under 13 (or at least, children who *admit* they're under 13) without explicit parental consent — which, by the way, we think parents should rarely give. We heard of one marketer who said he wanted to use the Net to create a personal relationship with all the kids who use his product. Ugh. We have names for guys who want relationships with kids, and they're not nice names.

The FTC (`www.ftc.gov/bcp/edu/pubs/consumer/tech/tec10.shtm`) has more useful information for teachers about COPPA and online privacy that's useful for parents, too.

Who's Online?

Lots of kids — and grown-ups — are putting up Web sites about themselves and their families. Social networking sites such as Facebook and MySpace (see Chapter 18) make it easy. We think that creating Web sites is cool, but we strongly encourage families who use the Net for personal reasons (distinct from businesspeople who use the Net for business purposes) *not* to use their full or real names. We also advise you and your children never to disclose your address, phone number, Social Security number, or account passwords in online social situations to anyone who asks for this kind of information — online or off. This advice applies especially when people who claim to be in positions of authority ask for them— for example, instant messages from people claiming that they're from America Online (AOL) tech support. They're not, as we detail in Chapter 2.

People with real authority *never* ask those types of questions. (For one thing, Internet service providers don't handle member accounts by using instant messages, and they never ask for credit card information by e-mail. It all makes a great case for knowing how your Internet service provider does work.)

More than ever, children need to develop critical-thinking skills. They have to be able to evaluate what they read and see — especially on the Web.

Regrettably, almost anyone with an e-mail address receives their share of junk e-mail (*spam*). This situation will only get worse until we have effective laws — as well as technology — against unwanted e-mail. In the meantime, remember this important rule: If an e-mail offer sounds too good to be true, it isn't true — and if an ad shows up from someone you don't know, that's also good evidence that it isn't true. See Chapter 14 for weapons on the war against spam.

The Internet in Schools

Some schools and libraries use software to filter Internet access for kids. A variety of filtering systems are available, at a range of costs and installation hassles, that promise to filter out inappropriate and harmful Web sites. It sounds good, but many kids are smart enough to find ways around rules, and extremely smart kids can find ways around software systems designed to "protect" them.

We believe that Internet filtering in schools isn't a good approach. Kids are quicker and more highly motivated and have more time to spend breaking into and out of systems than most adults we know, and this method doesn't encourage them to do something more productive than electronic lock-picking.

Checking out colleges on the Net

Most colleges and universities have sites on the Web. You can find a directory of online campus tours at www.campustours.com, with links to lots more info about colleges and universities.

After you're a little more adept at using the Net, you can use it to take a closer look at classes and professors to gain a better idea of what colleges have to offer.

Many institutions rely successfully on students' signed contracts that detail explicitly what is appropriate and what is inappropriate to use. Students who violate these contracts lose their Internet or computer privileges. We recommend the approach of contracts and consequences, from which kids can truly learn.

We don't think much of filtering software on home computers, for the same reason, but if you want to use it anyway, look at Windows Live Family Safety, part of the free Microsoft Windows Live software suite. (See Chapter 13 for download instructions.) It blocks Web sites that the parent specifies or that are in its built-in list, but it doesn't try to be sneaky. When it blocks, it says so and lets the kid send a note to the parent to ask to unblock the site. The service is free, so when you decide that you don't want it and turn it off, you haven't wasted any money.

Many schools use the Internet to post information that students can use in their classes, including a summary of the curriculum, upcoming assignments, and links to Web sites with useful resources. One such system is Moodle (at www.moodle.org) — ask your kids whether their teachers post assignments and resources online.

A few schools, such as the University of Phoenix (www.phoenix.edu), specialize in online education, but schools all over the world now offer online instruction, and some (such as MIT, at web.mit.edu) make all their course material available online for free. If the course is on the Net, it doesn't matter whether the school is across the street or across the ocean. You can find thousands of schools and courses in directories such as these:

```
www.petersons.com/distancelearning
www.online-colleges-courses-degrees-classes.org
```

A Few Useful Web Sites

Here are a few sites that may be useful for kids and parents (and grandparents).

These sites focus on education and parenting:

- **The Global Schoolhouse,** at `www.globalschoolnet.org/GSH`: An online meeting place for teachers, students, and parents
- **Great Web Sites for Kids,** from the American Library Association, at `www.ala.org/ala/alsc` (and then click Great Web Sites for Kids)
- **KidPub,** at `www.kidpub.com`: Book reviews by kids
- **FunBrain,** at `www.funbrain.com`: Educational games for kindergarten through eighth grade

These sites are just plain fun:

- **Yahoo! Kids,** at `kids.yahoo.com`: This Yahoo! Web portal is designed for kids.
- **Kids World,** at `northvalley.net/kids`: Find links to fun and interesting sites.
- **The Yuckiest Site on the Internet,** at `yucky.discovery.com`: It's just what it sounds like — the yuckier, the better!
- **The CIA Homepage for Kids,** at `https://www.cia.gov/kids-page`: You have to type the `https://` part (it's a secure site — that's what the *s* means) because it's, you know, the CIA.
- **Net-Mom** at `www.netmom.com`: The site is run by our friend Jean Polly, who has been looking for online resources for kids even longer than we have.
- **Sports Illustrated for Kids,** at `www.sikids.com`: This one highlights sports news and games.

Not just for kids: School on the Net

Your child's education, as well as your own, isn't over when you finish high school or college or (for those of us seriously dedicated to avoiding real life) graduate school. There's always more to learn. Nothing's quite like learning directly from a first-rate teacher in a classroom, but learning over the Net can be the next-best thing to being there — particularly for students who live far from school or have irregular schedules. You can now take everything online from high school equivalency exams to professional continuing education to college and graduate courses leading to degrees. Some courses are strictly online; others use a combination of classroom, lab, and online instruction.

Part II
Internet, Here I Come!

The 5th Wave
By Rich Tennant

"Awww, jeez — I was afraid of this. Some poor kid, bored with the usual chat lines, starts looking for bigger kicks. Pretty soon they're surfin' the seedy back alleys of cyberspace, and before you know it they're into a file they can't 'undo.' I guess that's why they call it the Web. Somebody open a window!"

In this part . . .

After you're ready to get started, where do you start? Probably the hardest part of using the Internet is getting connected. We help you figure out which kind of Internet service is right for you and help you get connected, with plenty of advice for broadband (fast), Wi-Fi (wireless), and mobile (smartphone) users.

Chapter 4

Assembling Your Gear and Climbing on the Net

"**G**reat," you say, "How do I connect my computer to the Internet?" The answer is "It depends." (You'll hear that answer perhaps more often than you'd like.) The Internet isn't one network — it's 100,000 separate networks hooked together, each with its own rules and procedures, and you can get to the Net from any one of them. Readers of previous editions of this book pleaded (they said other things too, but this is a family-oriented book) for step-by-step directions on how to get on, so we made this chapter as "steptual" as possible.

Here (drumroll, please) are those basic steps:

1. **Figure out which type of computer you have or can use.**

2. **Figure out which types of Internet connections are available where you are.**

3. **Sign up for your connection.**

4. **Set up your computer to use your new connection, and decide whether you like it.**

5. **Install the software you need to protect your computer from viruses and spyware.**

   See Chapter 2 for scary descriptions of the types of Internet dangers you need to protect yourself from.

You need four items to connect to the Internet:

- ✔ A computer, even a tiny computer, like a Palm or a phone or another handheld device

- ✔ A modem (a piece of computer equipment, which may be right inside the computer) to hook your computer to the phone line, cable system, or mobile phone system

- ✔ An account with an Internet service provider (ISP), to give your modem somewhere to connect to

- ✔ Software to run on your computer

We look at each of these items in turn.

If you have more than one computer to connect to the Internet, see Chapter 5. If your computer is a laptop, see the section in Chapter 5 about using your laptop or netbook at home and away.

Internet accounts are easy to use, but they can be tricky to set up. In fact, connecting for the first time can be the most difficult part of your Internet experience. Installing and setting up Internet connection software used to require that you type lots of scary-looking numerical Internet addresses, hostnames, communications-port numbers — you name it. These days, making the connection is much easier, partly because Internet software can now figure out most of the details itself, but mostly because all recent versions of Windows and Macs include setup software that can step you through the process.

What Kind of Computer Do You Need?

Because the Internet is a computer network, the only way to hook up to it is by using some kind of computer. But computers are starting to appear in all sorts of disguises — including in phones, MP3 music players, and toasters (okay, not really) — and they may well already be in your home, whether you know it or not.

Hey, I don't even have a computer!

If you don't have a computer and aren't ready or able to buy one, you still have some options.

A likely place to find Internet access is in your public library. Most libraries have added Internet access centers, with clusters of Internet-connected computers among the bookshelves. These computers tend to be popular, so call ahead to reserve time or find out which hours are less crowded.

Another option is your local cybercafé. You can surf the Net while sipping your favorite beverage and sharing your cyberexperience. If you want to check out the Internet, a cybercafé is a great place to try before you buy. Some have computers ready for you to use, whereas others require you to bring your own laptop (see the section about using your laptop or netbook at home and away, in Chapter 5, for laptop safety tips).

If you want to use the Internet from your very own home, you're stuck getting some kind of computer. Luckily, almost any newish computer can connect to the Internet, and you can get perfectly usable ones for less than $300.

Yup, I have this old, beige box in the closet

Almost any personal computer made since 1980 is adequate for *some* type of connection to the Internet. But unless you have a really good friend who is a computer geek and wants to spend a lot of time at your house helping you get online, it isn't worth fooling with that old clunker — unless, of course, you're looking for a reason for the geek to spend a lot of time at your house, but that's your business.

If you can afford it, we strongly encourage you to buy a new computer or at least one that isn't more than two years old. New computers come with Internet software already installed and are configured for the latest in Web technology. If you already own an older computer, you will spend more time and energy, and ultimately just as much money, just trying to get the thing to work the way you want. We think that it's best to buy a brand-new computer.

One problem with old computers is that they tend to run old versions of software. Any version of Windows older than Windows XP or any Mac system older than OSX is more hassle than it's worth to try to use.

Yup, I got a brand-new BitBucket 2010

Ah, you *do* have a computer. (Or maybe you're thinking about buying one.) Most Internet users connect by way of a broadband connection, or in a few areas where broadband isn't available, by the computer dialing over the phone line to an Internet service provider. When you first turn on your new computer, or when you run one of the Internet programs that comes installed, your computer offers to attempt to connect right then and there. First read the rest of this chapter. We have some warnings and some options we think you ought to consider first.

Yup, I'm getting a netbook

A new category of computer is on the scene, if you haven't noticed: the *netbook*. It's smaller and lighter than a laptop but bigger than a cellphone or handheld personal organizer. The netbook has a full keyboard, even if its keys are a little smaller than normal, and it's cheaper than most laptops — maybe the same price as an expensive phone (in the $200-$400 range). And, it has built-in Wi-Fi.

The first netbook was the ASUS Eee PC (sounds like a screech), and now laptop, phone, and other types of manufacturers have gotten into the game. For information on using a netbook, see Chapter 5.

Yup, I got this little BlackBerry, iPhone, or Palm

Modern mobile phones have itty-bitty screens and itty-bitty keypads, so industry groups devised a way to show itty-bitty Web pages on those screens and navigate around them. *Smartphones* (phones with Internet capabilities) are quite popular in Japan (where teenage girls use it to write novels one screen at a time), and have finally caught on in the United States. Unlike on your PC, a smartphone doesn't require special setup beyond what your phone company does when it sells you the phone.

However, you pay a lot extra for a smartphone. The phone itself costs several hundred dollars, and you also pay extra for Internet usage. On some plans, you can pay based on the amount of data you transfer, which can be several dollars per download. If you plan to do much browsing from your phone, call your phone company and sign up for a monthly data plan, which costs about $30 per month. With some smartphones (including the iPhone), you're forced to buy a monthly data plan.

Before getting a smartphone, consider whether you have a specific use in mind and be sure to try someone else's to see whether you can stand using its teeny screen. The Palm, the BlackBerry, and many other handheld models are designed to display text messages, e-mail, and simple Web pages on their small screens. Go to a cellphone store and ask to see a demonstration. If you get a smartphone and you want some tips, see the section in Chapter 5 about using your smartphone on the Net.

You don't need the Internet to send and receive text messages. You can even get information from some Web servers by sending a text message. For instructions, see the section in Chapter 8 about searching from your cellphone.

The Types of Internet Connections

If you use a computer at a library, at work, at a cybercafé, or at someone else's house, you don't need to worry about how it connects to the Internet because someone else has already done the work. But if you have your own computer, you have several options:

- ✔ Connect by using a fast phone line (DSL line).
- ✔ Connect by using your cable TV company.
- ✔ Connect by using AOL (America Online); AOL isn't the Internet, but it *connects to* the Internet.
- ✔ Dial in by using a regular phone line.

What's in an Account?

An Internet account — fast or slow — comes with

- ✔ **That all-important username and password:** You have to be able to connect, after all.
- ✔ **One or more e-mail addresses, each with its own mailbox:** Most accounts have from one to five e-mail addresses. If you have a family, each family member can have a separate address.
- ✔ **Webmail (a Web site where you can read your mail):** Webmail is useful when you want to check your mail and you're not at your own computer with your own e-mail program. You can use a Web browser to display your messages from any computer. See Chapter 13.

It should also come with a toll-free number that you can call for support. Every ISP has a Web site showing prices, sign-up instructions, and support information.

Speedy Connections: DSL and Cable Internet

The most popular way to connect, available almost but not quite everywhere, is a *broadband* (high-speed) connection. Broadband connections can provide greater *bandwidth* — that is, more data transferred in a specific amount of time — than older dialup phone connections. This type of connection can be extremely fast, several million bits per second, with downloads (in practice) often exceeding 300,000 bytes per second.

A word about usernames and passwords

Over a billion people are on the Internet. Because only one of them is you, it would be nice if the rest of them can't go snooping through your files and e-mail messages. For that reason — no matter which type of Internet account you have — your account has a user-name and a secret password associated with it.

Your *username* (or *user ID, login name, logon name,* or *screen name*) is unique among all the names assigned to your provider's users. It's usually also your e-mail address, so don't pick a name like *snickerdoodle* unless that's what

you want to tell your friends and put on your business cards.

Your password is secret and is the main thing that keeps bad guys from borrowing an account. Don't use a real word or a name. See "What's the secret word, Mr. Potter?" in Chapter 2 for ideas for passwords that you have some hope of remembering.

Never tell anyone else your password. Particularly don't tell people who claim to be from your ISP or your bank— they're not.

Broadband connections are now available and affordable by mere mortals in all but the most rural locations in the United States and Canada. (Even rural locations can connect using the same satellite that provides satellite TV.)

After you get used to having a broadband connection, you'll never be able to tolerate an old-fashioned dialup connection again. It's that good.

What is broadband, anyway?

There are two types of broadband Internet connections — DSL and cable:

- ✓ A *Digital Subscriber Line (DSL)* is a special phone line that you or your ISP orders from your local telephone company, usually shared with the same line that connects your regular phones.

- ✓ A *cable* Internet account is provided by your local cable TV company, using the same cable connection that brings you 250 brain-numbing TV channels.

DSL and cable Internet accounts have a lot in common: They're fast and they don't tie up your regular phone line. Some broadband accounts have a permanent connection that works a lot like a connection to a local network in an office. Others require you to log on each time you want to use the Internet. The ISP provides most of the equipment — for example, the modem — and often sends an installer to set it up with your computer. Ask your cable company whether it offers Internet access and ask your phone company whether it offers DSL. If yes is the answer to either question, get one or the other.

High-speed cable and DSL cost about $30 per month depending on your location, plus installation and the cost of the special modem you need, minus whatever discount you receive for buying a package of broadband and other types of services the provider supplies. You usually get the best price with a package combining Internet with some or all of its phone, cable TV, and mobile phone services.

A hidden cost in getting either cable or DSL Internet access is having to take a day off from work to wait for the installers, unless you feel brave enough to install it yourself. Sometimes it takes the installers two trips to get things working. Try to make the first appointment in the morning. Also, the cable company or phone company is usually also your ISP unless you pay extra, so you don't have a choice of ISPs. In theory, the phone company provides DSL access on equal terms to all ISPs — but, in practice, its own ISP somehow always seems to be more equal than the others.

Cable and DSL modems

To connect to a DSL or cable account, you use a DSL or a cable modem. The phone or cable company provides it (sometimes for a fee). Don't buy one yourself — you need a modem that's compatible with your provider's equipment, so smart Internauts get their DSL or cable modems from the ISP that provides their Internet service and then let someone there install it.

How your computer connects to the modem

DSL and cable modems connect to your computer in one of two-and-a-half ways:

✔ **Network adapter:** A *network adapter* (or *LAN adapter* or *Ethernet adapter* or *network interface card*) was originally designed for connecting computers into networks. If you have more than one computer in your home or office, you can use network adapters to connect the computers into a local-area network (LAN), as described in Chapter 5. A network adapter has an RJ-45 jack, which looks like a regular phone jack but is a little bigger, into which you plug your modem or network cable. Check the back and sides of your computer for holes that look like overgrown phone jacks. All modern PCs (and all Macs) have network adapters built in.

- ✔ **Wireless network adapter:** If your computer isn't located close to a phone or cable outlet or you have a laptop you carry around the house, you can use a wireless network, often called Wi-Fi. It works pretty much the same as a wired network, only without the wires (duh!). All laptops built in the past five years have built-in Wi-Fi. We cover the ins and outs of Wi-Fi in Chapter 5.

- ✔ **USB:** Almost all computers come with one or more *USB* (Universal Serial Bus, if you care) connectors, which are used for connecting all kinds of stuff to your computer, from mice to cameras to printers. A USB port looks like a small, narrow, rectangular hole.

Here's some information of interest only to people with very old computers: If your cable or DSL modem installer reports that your computer doesn't have the network adapter or USB port that's needed to connect your modem, don't panic. If the installer can't provide the needed adapter, contact a local computer store about adding a network card — it shouldn't cost more than $20. Desktop computers need PCI or PCI Express network adapters, which are printed circuit boards that you install by turning off the computer, opening the case, finding an empty slot, sliding the card in, screwing down the card, and closing up the computer. Laptops use various sorts of PC Card network adapters, which look like fat credit cards and just slide into a slot on the side of the laptop. Several different kinds of PCI and PC Card slots are available; if you buy a card, be sure that it fits the kind of slot your computer has.

Getting your DSL hooked up

DSL service is supposed to use your existing phone line and in-house wiring. But DSL often works better if the phone company runs a new wire from outside your building to where you use your computer. (Phone companies call this a *home run.*) For most kinds of DSL to work, you have to live within a couple of miles of your telephone central office, so DSL is unavailable in many rural areas.

DSL is available at different speeds. The higher speeds cost more (surprise, surprise!). The lowest speed, usually 640 Kbps, is adequate for most users.

If DSL service is available in your area, call either your phone company or an ISP to arrange for DSL service. Either it ships you the equipment to install yourself or a phone installer comes with a network connection box (a glorified modem) that you or the installer hook up to your computer. Some DSL modems connect to a network adapter or USB connector, some include a router (described in more detail later) which can also provide a Wi-Fi connection.

Getting your cable Internet hooked up

To sign up for a cable account, call your local cable company to open one. Unless you decide to install it yourself (which isn't all that hard), a technician comes and installs a network-connection doozus (technical term) where your TV cable comes into your house, installs a network adapter in your computer if it doesn't already have one (unlikely, these days), brings a cable modem (which can look like a junior laptop computer with a spike hairdo), and hooks them together. Magic.

If you have cable television, the cable is split, and one segment goes to your computer. If you don't have cable television, the cable company may have to install the actual cable before it can wire up your computer. When the technician goes away, however, you have a permanent, high-speed connection to the Internet (as long as you pay your bill, about $40 to $50 a month).

Do-it-yourself DSL

Hooking up your DSL modem shouldn't be tough. One side plugs into the phone line, the other side into your computer. How hard can that be? Well, a few little details are involved.

Avoiding the DSL buzz

One clever thing about DSL is that the DSL connection shares the same phone wires with your phone without tying up the phone line. You can tell that this is the case because on all the phones on the line with DSL, you may hear a loud buzz of Data Hornets swarming up and down your phone line. (Well, not really, but it can sound like it.)

To get rid of the buzz, you may need to install a *DSL filter,* which filters out the buzz, between the phone line and all your phones. Filters are available from your DSL ISP, but you can probably find them cheaper at stores like RadioShack. The ideal way to install a filter is to run a separate wire from the box where the phone line enters your house to the DSL modem, and to install one DSL filter in that box into which you plug the wire leading to all the phones. But life is rarely ideal, so most of us install a filter for each phone.

For the phone plug where your DSL modem is connected, you want a *splitter* filter with a filtered jack into which you plug a phone (the one you use to call tech support when your computer doesn't work) and an unfiltered or sometimes data-filtered jack for the DSL modem. For all other phones, the filter just plugs into the phone jack, and the phone cord plugs into the filter. For that tidy look, you can also get wall-phone filters (which fit between the phone and the wall plate that the phone is mounted on) and baseboard phone jacks with filters built in.

We assume that you have a DSL modem that connects to a network or USB connector. If you have a network connector, you need a *crossover network cable* that should have come with the DSL modem. (Regular, noncrossover cables plug into a router or network hub, not directly from a modem to a computer.) If you're using USB, you should have a USB cable with a flat connector on one end and a squarish connector on the other. Turn off and unplug both your computer and the modem from the wall socket, plug in the network or USB cable, and then plug everything back in. The modem also connects to the phone line with a regular phone cord. The phone and network jacks on the modem are similar, but the network connector is the bigger one. Your computer setup should look something like the one shown in Figure 4-1. The details may vary a little @md John's DSL came with filters that include the two-for-one adapter, and the modem includes a Wi-Fi router, so there's no cable to the computer.

Now you can skip ahead to the section "After the DSL or cable Internet installer." And be sure to read the nearby sidebar, "Avoiding the DSL buzz."

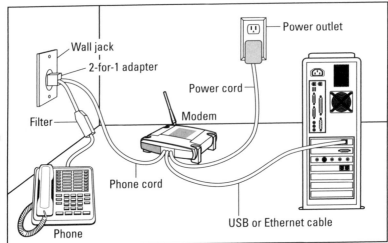

Figure 4-1: Your computer, connected to a DSL line.

Do-it-yourself cable modems

Connecting a cable modem is not unlike connecting a DSL modem, except that you connect it to your TV cable rather than to your phone line. If a TV is already attached to the cable, unscrew the cable from the TV and throw away the TV because you'll be having much too much fun with your Internet connection to waste time watching TV. (If you're not yet ready to throw away your TV, move it to another cable outlet or get a cable splitter, available at any store that sells cable accessories.) Screw the cable into the cable modem and plug the network or USB cable from the modem to the computer, just as we describe for a DSL modem in the previous section.

Fast, fibrous FiOS

Cable and DSL network speeds are limited by the old-fashioned copper wire they use. Fiber optics are much faster, and large telephone companies have been making and breaking promises to wire us up with fiber for about 20 years. According to Teletruth, a phone consumers' advocate, if Verizon had kept the promises that its predecessor Bell of Pennsylvania made in 1994, most Pennsylvania homes would be wired with 45-megabit fiber by now.

Verizon is finally sort of making good on its promises with *FiOS,* a fiber optic package that combines fairly fast Internet (not 45 megabits, though) with home Wi-Fi, phone, and TV. If you want fast Internet and high-definition TV and you're willing to sign up for at least a full year, it's not a bad deal, and costs $45 a month and more. But you might want to consider a few issues before signing up:

✔ Verizon has some odd rules about the connections it supports; in particular, it doesn't support wireless connections to Macs, only wired.

✔ There's no going back. The person who hooks up the fiber often physically rips out your old copper phone line so that you can't switch back without paying for a full new installation.

✔ It depends on your house power. Regular phone service powers your phone from the central office, so the phone company's large batteries and professionally maintained backup generators keep the phones working if the power fails. FiOS uses your house power to run your phones as well as your Internet and TV connections. It provides a battery that's supposed to keep your phone going for four hours if the power fails, but the battery lasts only two or three years, and if you don't remember to replace it (Verizon won't), you'll have an unpleasant surprise when the power fails.

After the DSL or cable Internet installer

The installer (which is you, if you installed the modem yourself) configures your computer to communicate with the Internet. Follow the instructions to connect to your account the first time; some DSL and cable modems come with a software CD you may need to use.

Chances are good, at this point, that you're on the Internet. You should be able to start up a Web browser, like Internet Explorer, and type the name of a Web site in the address box at the top (try our net.gurus.org). The Web page should appear momentarily. If you have a connection with a username, it may ask you whether to connect. (Well, yeah, that's the idea, but sarcasm is lost on machinery.)

If you still can't connect, you can try configuring Windows yourself.

Configuring Windows 7 to connect

Windows 7 detects an Internet connection if one exists, so you may not have to do a thing. It spots Wi-Fi or a connected DSL or cable modem and does the right thing. However, if you need to do it yourself, choose Start⇨Control Panel⇨Network and Internet⇨Network and Sharing Center⇨Set Up a New Connection or Network.

Configuring Windows Vista to connect

Windows Vista makes it slightly easier. If your network connects with a wired LAN connection and doesn't require a login or password (this includes most cable modems), Vista normally configures itself automagically, so you don't have to do any of this. For connections that do require a login, follow these steps:

1. **Choose Start⇨Connect To, and then click the little Set Up a Connection or Network link.**

   They still don't make it easy to find.

2. **For the Network Connection Type, choose Connect to the Internet and click Next.**

3. **Select Broadband (PPPoE).**

   We cover some of the other options for dialup and wireless later in this chapter and in Chapter 5.

4. **Enter the required information in the boxes.**

   In particular, enter the login name and password that your ISP gave you.

Configuring Windows XP to connect

To set up your connection using the Windows XP wizard, follow these steps:

1. **Choose Start⇨All Programs⇨Accessories⇨Communications⇨New Connection Wizard.**

   They sure don't make it easy to find.

2. **For the network connection type, choose Connect to the Internet and click Next.**

3. **Select Set Up My Connection Manually.**

   Choose either Connect Using a Broadband Connection That Requires a User Name and Password (if your ISP gave you a username and password) or Connect Using a Broadband Connection That Is Always On.

   If you're worried about your computer being connected to the Internet all the time, you can shut down your computer — when it's turned off, it's definitely hackproof! See the section "Essential Software to Keep Your System Safe," later in this chapter.

4. **Enter the required information in the boxes and accept the suggested check boxes, particularly the Internet firewall.**

Your PC communicates with the Internet by using the TCP/IP protocol, and you should see it listed in the Properties dialog box for the connection (in Windows XP). Don't fool with these settings unless you're sure that you know what you're doing!

Checking your DSL or cable connection

After you're connected, you can check the status of your connection:

✔ **Windows 7:** Display the Network and Sharing Center by choosing Start⇨ Control Panel⇨Network and Internet⇨Network and Sharing Center. Look in the View Your Active Networks section, shown in Figure 4-2.

✔ **Windows Vista:** Choose Start⇨Control Panel⇨Network and Sharing Center. Broadband connections appear in the upper part of the window.

✔ **Windows XP:** Choose Start⇨Control Panel⇨Network And Internet Connections⇨Network Connections. Broadband connections appear in the LAN or High-Speed Internet section.

✔ **Macs:** Use the TCP/IP Control Panel in OS 8 and OS 9. For OS X, choose System Preferences from the Apple menu and click the Network icon. Then select the TCP/IP tab.

Figure 4-2:
The
Network
and Sharing
Center in
Windows 7
shows
how your
computer
connects to
the Internet.

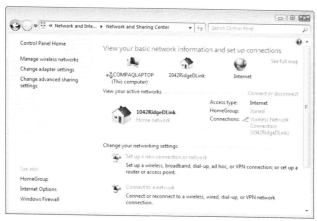

Dialing — the Old-Fashioned Way

A *dialup modem* connects to a normal, everyday phone line — using the same little plug (an RJ-11 jack) and phone wire. You can unplug a phone and plug in a dialup modem in its place. The problems with dialup are that the connection is s-l-o-w and that your phone line is tied up while you're online.

On the other side of the pond

The ISP situation in the United Kingdom is a little different from the one in North America. For broadband, British Telecom (BT) and many competitors provide DSL service with (by American standards) high speeds at a low price as long as you sign up for at least a year at a time. The government forced BT to let other companies share its equipment, so you can often get a better deal on phone and DSL from other companies, using the exact same phone line. Look, for example, at www.greenbee.com, from the John Lewis department store chain.

Cable modem service is also widely available, typically faster than BT and more expensive. You can also get wireless broadband from your mobile phone company, with a little *dongle* that plugs into a USB port on your PC, typically reasonably priced until you exceed the monthly usage cap at which the price rapidly becomes unreasonable.

Traditionally, all phone calls in the United Kingdom (UK) have been charged by the minute, including even local calls, which can make long dialup online sessions mighty pricey. As a result, the UK now has three different kinds of dialup ISPs:

✔ **Traditional:** These ISPs charge a modest monthly fee and provide access by way of either local numbers or national rate numbers. Unless you're sure that you won't spend much time online or your ISP provides another service you're using, such as Web hosting, this type probably isn't what you want.

✔ **Free:** These ISPs charge no monthly fee; they support themselves by splitting the per-minute charges with BT. (BT would rather not, but OFTEL, the regulatory agency of the telecom industry in Britain, insists.) If you just want to try out the Net, free ISPs are a good way to start. We don't recommend them for long-term use because the per-minute split is less lucrative than the ISPs hoped, and free ISPs have a disconcerting habit of going out of business on short notice. The tech support system also tends to be weak. (It's free. What do you want — your money back?)

✔ **Flat-rate:** These ISPs charge a monthly fee of about £20 but provide an 0800 or other number you can call without per-minute fees. Most dialup users find this choice the best because it makes the bill predictable. The largest flat-rate ISPs are AOL (yes, *that* AOL) and BT. Be warned that even though access is nominally unlimited, if you "camp" on the phone 20 hours a day, your ISP will invoke small print that you never noticed and cancel your account.

Depending on where you are and where your ISP is, your phone connection may be anywhere from wonderful to dreadful. If you try one ISP and keep getting slow or unreliable connections, try another.

Computers used to come with built-in dialup modems — examine your computer carefully for a phone jack and if you find one, plug a phone wire into it. Otherwise, you have to take your computer to the store and have someone install one. Don't confuse the phone jack with a wired Ethernet jack, which looks quite similar but is wider.

To use a dialup Internet connection, you sign up with an ISP for an Internet account. The features and services that one ISP offers are much like those of another. If you don't know what your local ISPs are, check the phone book or ads in the business section of your local paper.

If you're not careful, you can end up paying more for the phone call than you do for your Internet account. *Use an ISP whose number is a free or untimed local call* (that is, you're not paying by the minute). Nearly the entire continent is within a local call of an ISP; if you're one of the unlucky few, see whether your phone company has an unlimited long-distance plan.

Your ISP should give you information to set up your account: your username and password, its dialup phone number, and your e-mail address if it's different from your username. Here's how to set up your computer to dial up your ISP, depending on your version of Windows:

- ✔ **Windows 7:** Choose Start➪Control Panel➪Network and Internet➪ Network and Sharing Center➪Set Up a New Connection or Network.

- ✔ **Windows Vista:** Choose Start➪Connect To. In the window that opens, click the little Set Up a Connection or Network link. Click Set Up a Dial-Up Connection.

- ✔ **Windows XP:** Click the Start button and choose All Programs➪ Accessories➪Communications➪New Connection Wizard.

Enter the phone number as you would dial it on your phone, as 7, 10, or 11 digits. Unless you share your computer with someone you don't trust, select the check box to remember your password.

After your dialup account is set up, your computer should connect automatically whenever you use your Web browser or e-mail program. You can also connect at any time. In Windows 7, click the Networking icon on the taskbar (it looks like the connection bars on a cellphone). In Windows Vista and XP, choose Start➪Connect To, and then click the dialup connection and the Connect button. If you see a dialog box that asks for your ISP username and password, type them and then click Connect.

I'm In!

When you're connected to the Internet, you can monitor your connection or reconnect or disconnect. There's a Networking icon on the Windows taskbar; it's in the lower right corner of the screen, to the left of the digital clock. Here's where it is and what it does:

- ✔ **Windows 7:** A mobile phone-connection-bars Networking icon appears in the lower right corner of the screen. Click it to see what you're connected to. Click Open Network and Sharing Center at the bottom of its window to see more information (refer to Figure 4-2).

- ✔ **Windows Vista:** A two-computer-screen icon appears in the lower-right corner of the screen. Right-click the icon to see options.

- ✔ **Windows XP:** A two-computer-screen icon appears in the lower right corner of the screen. If you're connected by way of wireless, you see one computer screen with radio waves coming out of it. Double-click this icon to check the speed of your Internet connection.

If you use a broadband account, you never need to disconnect. We love being able to saunter up to our computers at any time to check the weather, our e-mail, a good buttermilk waffle recipe, or which movies Joe E. Brown was in, without having to wait while for our computer to reconnect.

If you dial in to the Internet, you eventually want to disconnect (hang up) so that you can use your phone line to talk to actual human beings. You can leave the rest of your programs (such as your Web browser and e-mail program) running even when you're not connected to the Net. To disconnect a dialup connection, double-click or right-click the Networking icon, which we just described, and choose Disconnect.

Essential Software to Keep Your System Safe

Okay, you're connected. Before you start surfing the Web, e-mailing, and instant messaging, you need to protect your computer from the Terrors of the Internet: viruses and spyware. Chapter 2 describes the concepts behind them, and now is the time to use protection.

Walling out the bad guys

A *firewall* is a barrier between your computer (or computers) and the Internet. In big companies, the firewall may consist of a computer that does nothing but monitor the incoming and outgoing traffic, checking for bad stuff. At your home or office, you have two good options:

- ✔ **Use firewall software built into Windows 7, Vista, and XP.** In Windows 7, choose Start➪Control Panel➪System and Security➪Windows Firewall (see Figure 4-3). In Windows Vista, click the little Security Center shield in the notification area at the bottom of the screen and then click Windows Firewall. In Windows XP SP2, choose Start ➪Control Panel➪Security Center or Start➪Control Panel➪Network and Internet Connections ➪Network Connections, right-click the icon for your Internet account, choose Properties from the menu that appears, click the Advanced tab, and look for the Internet Connection Firewall or Windows Firewall section.

If it's not already selected, select the check box to turn on Internet Connection Firewall. When that's done, your computers have basic protection from hackers.

✔ **Use a *router*, a small box that sits between your computer (or computers) and your broadband modem.** A router has one plug for a cable to your DSL or cable modem, several plugs (usually four) to which you can connect computers, and usually an antenna for wireless Wi-Fi connections. The router has firewall software running all the time. See Chapter 5 for how to use a router to connect more than one computer to one Internet account.

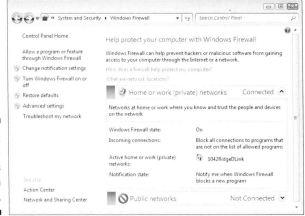

Figure 4-3:
Turn on the Windows built-in firewalls.

Even if you have only one computer that connects to the Internet, we recommend using a router. If your broadband provider didn't give you one they cost about $40 and we're sure that you'll want to hook up a second computer to the Internet before long. The firewall programs included in Windows 7, Vista, and XP work fine, too. Hey, why not use both?

A router is a particularly good idea if you have a broadband connection that is always on (that is, always connected). The router is always on, too.

No viruses need apply

Viruses are sneaky programs that arrive by way of e-mail or in downloaded programs, and immediately get up to no good. (See Chapter 2 for details.) You need to run a virus checker program all the time, and you need to update its list of viruses regularly so that the program can detect the latest viruses.

AOL isn't exactly the Internet, but it's close enough

America Online (AOL) provides two things:

✔ Dialup or high-speed access to the Internet

✔ AOL software that includes a Web browser, an e-mail program, and other features that give you access to their own, proprietary services (such as AOL chat rooms). Windows and Mac versions are available. You get an AOL e-mail address, too.

You can use one or both of these services. For example, you can connect to the Internet through DSL or cable Internet and use the AOL software to browse the Web and read your e-mail. You can use the AOL broadband service if it's available in your area, but use other programs for Web browsing and e-mail. Or, you can use AOL for everything.

If you want to sign up for an AOL account to connect to the Internet, call 1-800-827-3338 and ask for a membership. The introductory package has instructions and a disc containing the AOL access program. Follow the instructions to install the program and sign up for an account. You need a credit card to sign up if you want to use AOL to connect to the Internet. (The AOL Web site, mail, and instant messenger services are free.) For more information about how to use AOL, get *AOL For Dummies*, by John Kaufeld and Ted Leonsis.

Many virus checkers are available. The free AVG from `free.avg.com` isn't bad, particularly at the price. The big two commercial programs are McAfee VirusScan, which you can download from `www.mcafee.com`, and Norton AntiVirus, at `www.symantec.com`. These programs work fine, but are large and cost about $50 a year. If you have more than one computer on the Internet, consider F-Prot, at `www.f-prot.com`, because you have to pay for only one license (at $29 a year) to run the program on as many as five computers in your house. If you have several computers, note that Norton AntiVirus also has a 3-pack license.

Microsoft now has a virus checker named Windows Defender. It comes pre-installed with Windows Vista, and you can download it for free for use on Windows 7 or XP. It's at `www.microsoft.com/windows/products/winfamily/defender`. (See Chapter 12 to find out how to download and install programs.)

The commercial programs require that you pay annually for a subscription to updates. Do it — without updates to the list of viruses it's looking for, your program doesn't spot and block recent viruses. Some bundle the virus checker with other security packages so that you can get all the protection you need in one purchase.

Don't think that you're saving money if you don't subscribe to a virus-checking service. New viruses come out every day. Your virus checker can check for only the viruses it knows about. You need a service that updates your list of viruses to check for. It's like the FBI sending out new Wanted posters to the local police.

A good virus checker automatically connects to its home base over the Internet at least once a week and downloads updates to its virus lists. You may see a dialog box on your screen when this is happening. Your subscription usually lasts a year, and you should see warnings to update your subscription (that is, pay again) when your year is almost up.

For help with downloading and installing an antivirus program, see Chapter 12.

Detecting spyware

Spyware is a class of programs that sneak onto your computer, usually when you're browsing the Web, and run unbeknownst to you, doing God-knows-what. (See Chapter 2 for details.) A number of antispyware programs are available for free, although no single program seems to spot all types of spyware. We recommend that you run several antispyware programs from time to time, to sweep your hard disk and look for bad stuff.

Along with Windows Defender, which is built into Vista and is a free download for Windows 7 and Windows XP, the three free programs we use are

- ✔ **Ad-Aware Personal Edition,** at www.lavasoftusa.com. It's also free, although the developer wants you to buy the fancier paid version.

- ✔ **Malwarebytes Anti-Malware,** at www.malwarebytes.org.

- ✔ **Spybot Search & Destroy**, at www.safer-networking.org. It's shareware; donations are appreciated. Note that several unscrupulous programs have started using the word *spybot* in their names, so don't just use a search engine to find the program; type in your Web browser the address shown in this paragraph.

These programs (and many others) are also available for free download from www.download.com. For help with downloading and installing a spyware-checking program, see Chapter 12.

In addition, follow a few basic rules, which will make more sense after you read the later chapters of this book. (Don't worry: We mention them again in those later chapters, too.) Here they are:

- ✔ **Don't use Internet Explorer as your browser.** Most spyware is designed to use features of Internet Explorer to worm its way onto your computer. Instead, use Firefox or Chrome, as described in Chapter 6.

- ✔ **Don't use Internet Explorer within other applications.** For example, some e-mail programs have an option to use Internet Explorer to display messages that contain HTML (Web formatting). Turn off these options.

✔ **If you use Windows, turn on Automatic Updates, and download and install the updates it suggests.** Microsoft issues security fixes to Windows at least once a month. Windows 7 and Vista download and install updates automatically unless you turn off this feature. In Windows 7, you can ensure that Automatic Updates are on by choosing Start⇨Control Panel⇨System and Security⇨Windows Update. In Windows Vista, choose Start⇨Control Panel⇨Security⇨Windows Update. In Windows XP, choose Start ⇨ Control Panel⇨Security Center or Start⇨Control Panel⇨Performance and Maintenance⇨System. In the System Properties dialog box that appears, click the Automatic Updates tab. Choose the first or second option so that Windows lets you know when updates are available.

Our Favorite Internet Setup

You're probably wondering, "The authors of this book have used the Internet forever. What do they recommend as the very best way to connect to it?" Okay, you're probably not wondering that, but we wish you were. And we have the answer.

The best Internet setup (in our humble opinions) is this:

✔ A computer (Windows, Mac, or Linux — they're all good).

✔ A DSL or cable Internet account — broadband rocks! FiOS would be even better, but it isn't offered where we live.

✔ A *router*, to provide a firewall between your computer (or computers) and the Internet

You're Connected — Now What?

When you connect to your ISP, your computer becomes part of the Internet. You type stuff or click in programs running on your computer, and those programs communicate over the Net to do whatever it is they do for you.

You can run several Internet programs at a time, which can be quite handy. You may be reading your e-mail, for example, and receive a message describing a cool, new site on the World Wide Web. You can switch immediately to your Web browser program (usually Internet Explorer, Firefox, Safari, or Chrome), look at the Web page, and then return to the mail program and pick up where you left off. Most e-mail programs highlight *URLs* (Web addresses) and enable you to go straight to your browser by clicking the URL in your e-mail message.

Get rid of your Dell or Gateway software

Many computers come with Internet software created by the hardware manufacturers, designed to give you an easier Internet experience. Unfortunately, we find that these programs just give you a more *confusing* Internet experience because each program is renamed to add the name of the hardware manufacturer. (AOL used to do this, too.) If your Dell or Gateway or other new computer comes with Dell or Gateway or other Internet programs, we recommend that you ignore them and use the standard Windows stuff described in this book. The polite name for this stuff is *shovelware.*

You're not limited to running programs that your Internet provider gives you. You can download a new Internet application from the Net and begin using it immediately — your ISP just acts as a data conduit between your computer and the rest of the Net.

To find out more about using the Web, see Chapter 6. If you want to start off with e-mail, read Chapter 13. Or, just flip through the rest of this book to see what looks interesting!

Chapter 5

Connecting with Wi-Fi, Laptops, and Smartphones

*T*hese days, lots of families have more than one computer — perhaps one in the office, one in the family room, and one in their teenager's bedroom. Hey, one of us has one in the kitchen for our family's calendar and address book. And that's not to mention the road warrior laptop.

Luckily, you don't need a separate Internet connection for each computer. Instead, you can connect the computers into a network — with cables or through thin air with wireless Wi-Fi connections — and then set them up to share one Internet connection. This chapter shows you to set up both types of networks.

Maybe you already have a laptop, netbook, or smartphone or just got one — this chapter also talks about ways you can use them on the Internet both at home and on the road. If you set up Wi-Fi for your family or office, you can connect from almost all laptops, all netbooks, and many smartphones, too.

Just One Computer for Internet Access? Naah

Many years ago, back when computers were large, hulking things found only in glass-walled computer rooms, a wild-eyed visionary friend of ours claimed (to great skepticism) that computers would be everywhere, and would be so small and cheap that they would show up as prizes in cereal boxes. We're not sure about the cereal boxes, but it's certainly true that the last time we went to put an old computer in the closet, we didn't have room because of all the other old computers in there. Rather than let them rust in *your* closet, you may as well get some use out of them by connecting them all to the Internet.

With a broadband connection, it turns out to be pretty easy. No more arguing about who's going to use the phone line next! No more pouting from the computer users who didn't get the cable or DSL hookup! Everyone can send e-mail, receive e-mail, chat, and browse the Web — all at the same time.

To share an Internet connection, you connect your computers to each other in a local-area network and then you connect the LAN (rather than an individual computer) to the Internet. A *local-area network* (or *LAN*) is — drumroll, please! — a network entirely contained in one local area, like one building, and is connected by way of wires or wireless connections, with no phone lines within the LAN. Once the exclusive tool of businesses, LANs have become so cheap that they're showing up in homes. As long as your home is in one building, if you have some computers connected to each other, you have a LAN.

Figure 5-1 shows a typical home network: A cable or DSL modem connects to a *hardware router,* a device that connects your LAN to your Internet connection. Normally, you would connect your PC to a network hub (for a wired network) or an access point (for wireless) — but a hardware router has a hub or an access point built in. Then you connect the LAN to the rest of the computers around the house.

The computers on your LAN don't all have to be running the same version of Windows — or even running Windows. You can connect PCs, Macs, and Linux computers on the same LAN because they all speak the same networking protocol, the same protocol that the Internet itself uses (TCP/IP, if you were wondering).

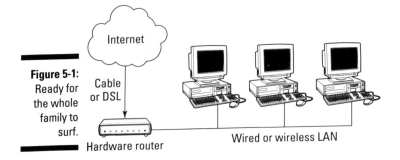

Figure 5-1:
Ready for
the whole
family to
surf.

Internet

Cable
or DSL

Hardware router

Wired or wireless LAN

First, Make a LAN

LANs come in two basic varieties: wired and wireless. In a wired network, a cable runs from each computer to a central box, whereas a wireless network uses radio signals rather than wires. Either way, you need a central box, which we talk about in a minute. If all your computers are in one room (or you're good at playing home electrician), a wired network is for you; otherwise, wireless is far easier to set up, although the pieces can be more expensive and the resulting network runs slower. Combos are also possible; most wireless equipment has a few jacks for wires to connect to the computers that are close enough to run cables.

The box in the middle — a hub, switch, or router

For any variety of current LAN, you need a special box that connects everything. Here are the main kinds of boxes you have to choose from:

- A *hub* is a book-size box with a bunch of jacks for network cables. It serves as a wired connection point that links all your computers into a LAN.

- A *switch* is the same thing as a hub, but it has a little extra circuitry to speed things up.

- An *access point* is the wireless equivalent of a hub, with a radio antenna or two and only one jack to connect to a wired network.

- A *router* is like a hub with the addition of Internet-connection smarts, like a firewall (as described in Chapter 4, in the section about walling out the bad guys).

Our advice is to go for a router; it's cheap ($40 to $80), and it saves you days of hair-tearing grief because it keeps most Windows worms out of your network. With a router, none of your computers needs to worry about connecting to the Internet — the router handles it.

Routers come in both wired and wireless versions. The wired versions have varying numbers of jacks, depending on how many computers you plan to connect to your wired LAN; the wireless ones have one jack for the cable to the modem, an antenna for the wireless network, and usually a few jacks for running wires to computers in the same room. For some perverse reason, wireless routers are usually cheaper than wired, even though the wireless ones include everything the wired ones do plus the wireless radio. So get a wireless router.

Setting up a router

A router invariably comes with a short Ethernet cable to connect the router to the cable or DSL modem, so connect your router to your modem, plug in both devices, and turn them on. An *Ethernet cable* (also known as *Category 5,* or *Cat 5*) looks like a fat phone cable, with little plastic connectors that look just like phone plugs but a little larger. (Even their technical names are a little larger; a phone connector is an *RJ-11 jack*, whereas an Ethernet connector is an *RJ-45 jack*.) Some ISPs provide a combined router and DSL modem, which has an RJ-11 jack for the DSL phone line rather than an incoming Ethernet jack.

Configuring routers for DSL connections that require a username and password

For the most part, routers take care of themselves, but if you have the kind of DSL connection that requires a username and password, you need to put those into the router. If your DSL connection doesn't require a username and password, you can probably just skip this section, although you can come back later if a program you're installing requires you to change the router's configuration. Setup instructions for routers are all the same in concept, but they differ in detail from one router to another — so you may have to (gack!) glance at the instructions that came with the router.

Because the router doesn't have a screen or keyboard that would enable you to configure it, you use a computer connected to the router instead, by way of a Web browser. The router has its own Web address, accessible only from the computers on your LAN; the address is usually a strange-looking, all-numeric creation. Even if you plan to have an entirely wireless LAN, the initial setup is a lot easier if you connect a PC (or Mac) to the router by using an Ethernet cable, at least for now, so that the router can figure out which computer it's supposed to be talking to. ("Hey, there it is, at the other end of that wire!") Follow these steps:

1. **Turn off the router and the PC (or Mac).**

   Computers are usually happier if you plug and unplug stuff while they're turned off.

2. **Plug an Ethernet cable into the network adapter on your computer and plug the other end into one of the jacks on the router.**

3. **Turn on the router and then turn on the computer.**

4. **Fire up your Web browser and type the address of the router's control page — its home page, with configuration settings.**

   Usually, this page is at `192.168.0.1` or `192.168.0.254` (special Web addresses reserved by the Internet powers that be for private networks like yours). If those Web addresses don't work, check the router's instructions.

5. **If your router's configuration page requires a username and password, check your router's manual to find out what it is and then type it.**

   If you lost the manual, don't panic: Often the username and password are printed on the bottom of the router. You see the configuration page for your router, something like Figure 5-2.

6. **If you have a broadband connection that uses a login and password, find the text box or field to enter your login name and password for your broadband connection.**

   Either follow the instructions in your router manual or try clicking the tabs or links on the page until you find boxes with names like Username and Password. Connections that use passwords may be called *PPPoE* (Point-to-Point over Ethernet, if you must know). Type them in.

7. **If you see a button or link named Save, Done, or OK, click it to make sure that the router saves your changes.**

   If you see no such button or link, don't worry.

Now your router knows how to log in to your DSL account.

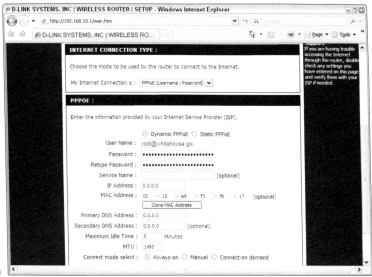

Figure 5-2: Your router doesn't have a screen, so you talk with it using your Web browser.

Connecting your LAN to the modem

Plug the router into your DSL or cable modem, turn on the modem (if it's not on yet), restart the router (by unplugging the power cord and plugging it back in), and verify that you can connect to the outside Internet. If you have a combined DSL modem and router, plug the phone line into its DSL jack. (Try a visit to our home page at net.gurus.org.) If that doesn't work, check the modem cable and ensure that both the username and password setup are correct if your Internet connection needs them. Most routers have reset switches that you can use to return them to their factory settings. It can take a long time, several minutes, for a DSL or cable modem to start the connection, so you might check the little lights to see whether the one that says WAN (for wide-area network) is lit yet.

You can configure a bunch of other router settings that you shouldn't need to worry about unless you're planning to do something fancy. The firewall part of the router watches the Internet traffic as it passes through and blocks the traffic it doesn't like. Routers let through Web pages, e-mail, instant messages, and other standard types of Internet communication, but if you're doing something special, like playing some types of online gaming, you may need to tell your router to allow additional types of data. If an online game or another program indicates that you need to "open a port" on your router, you need to return to this router configuration Web page to make some changes.

Wiring your computers into a LAN

After you have the router set up, if you want to create a wired LAN, you need wires. (Okay, you already knew that.) Specifically, LANs use Cat 5 Ethernet cable with RJ-45 connectors — it looks the same as the cable you use to connect your router to your modem. Cat 5 cable is available at any office supply store, electrical supply store, computer store, or even the occasional supermarket, and you can find it in varying lengths, from 10 feet to 50 feet or more. You need one cable to run from the router to each computer.

For each computer — PC, Mac, or whatever — plug one end of a Cat 5 cable into the computer's network adapter jack. (See the section in Chapter 4 about how your computer connects to the modem.) Plug the other end of the cable into the router.

After your computers are connected to the router and, indirectly, to each other, tell every computer about the LAN. Windows 7 and Vista make it easy — as soon as you plug in your network cable, Windows contacts the router and sets up your connection. (The most common problem: The cable isn't plugged in all the way at one end or the other.) If it doesn't, try these steps in Windows 7:

1. **Choose Start⇨Computer⇨Network.**

   You see a window showing the computers and networks that Windows thinks you're connected to.

2. **Click Network and Sharing Center.**

   You see the window shown in Figure 4-2, over in Chapter 4.

3. **Click Set Up a New Connection or Network if this is the first time, or Connect to a Network to connect to a network that already exists (such as someone else's LAN).**

In Windows Vista, try this:

1. **Choose Start⇨Network.**

2. **Click Network and Sharing Center to see which networks Windows thinks you're connected to.**

3. **Click the Diagnose and Repair link to help fix the most common problems.**

On every Windows XP computer on the network, follow this drill:

1. **Choose Start⇨All Programs⇨Accessories⇨Communications⇨Network Setup Wizard.**

2. **Follow the wizard's directions. When it asks what you want to do, choose the option labeled This Computer Connects through a Residential Gateway or through Another Computer on My Network.**

   The residential gateway is your router. On the next page, the wizard asks you to name your computer.

3. **When the wizard asks, give the computer a network name (such as PLAYROOM, OFFICE, or BOB).**

   When the wizard asks for the workgroup name, use the *same* name for all the computers on your LAN. (We use WORKGROUP. Windows may suggest MSHOME, which is fine too — just be consistent.)

If you connect a Mac to your LAN, it can probably see the LAN and work without your lifting a finger. If you do want (or need) to configure your network connection and you use Mac OS 9 or earlier, choose Apple⇨Control Panels⇨TCP/IP to access the TCP/IP control panel. Or, run the Internet Setup Assistant by choosing your hard disk and then the Internet folder and then Internet Setup Assistant. In Mac OS X, your network software is named Open Transport. To configure it, open the System folder and then the Control Panels folder and then the TCP/IP control panel.

For more details on setting up your LAN, see *Home Networking For Dummies,* by Kathy Ivens.

Forget the Wires — Go Wi-Fi!

If you have computers in more than one room in the house, using Wi-Fi is easier than snaking wires through the walls or basement.

Most laptop PCs have Wi-Fi built in. For computers that don't, you can get Wi-Fi PC cards, Wi-Fi doozits with USB connectors, and (less often) Wi-Fi add-in cards for desktop computers. Wi-Fi makers do a remarkably good job of adhering to industry standards, so you can expect anyone's 11b or 11g or 11n Wi-Fi equipment to work with anyone else's.

The main practical difference among Wi-Fi equipment is range. Wi-Fi components have one standard feature in common: laughably optimistic estimates of how far away they can be from other Wi-Fi equipment and still work. Bigger antennas bring you more range — as does more expensive equipment. Wi-Fi radio waves use the same band as 2.4GHz cordless phones, so you can expect roughly the same range — like a cordless phone, your Wi-Fi connection will probably work in most parts of your house but not down to the end of your driveway. If you have a normal-size house, normal Wi-Fi works fine. If you live in a $900,000 mansion, you might have to spring for the $100 Wi-Fi card rather than the $50 one.

Set a password, for Pete's sake!

You would probably notice if a random stranger walked into your house and plugged into your wired network. (At least, we like to think *we* would notice.) However, if you have a Wi-Fi network and a stranger is out on the street with a laptop scanning the area for unprotected wireless access points (a practice known as *wardriving*), he can connect to your Wi-Fi network and you can't easily tell. Some people don't care — at least until they realize that wardrivers can see *all* the shared files and printers on your LAN, and can send spam (and worse) through your network connection. You may well be able to hop on to your neighbors' Wi-Fi networks, and they on yours, which may or may not be okay, depending on how much you like your neighbors.

Fortunately, all Wi-Fi systems have optional passwords. Cryptographers laugh derisively at the poor security of Wi-Fi passwords, but they're adequate to make wardrivers and nosy neighbors go bother someone else. (If you have serious secrets on your network, don't depend on Wi-Fi passwords. A bad guy using a laptop and one of the widely available Wi-Fi password-cracker programs can gather enough data from your network to break any password in less than a week. If you need better cryptographic protection, it's available, but it's not exactly a do-it-yourself project to set up.)

Those creative Wi-Fi engineers created several flavors of passwords, too. Most new Wi-Fi equipment uses the secure password scheme Wireless Privacy Access (WPA). If all your Wi-Fi equipment can handle it, use WPA. WPA passwords can be almost any length, so you can pick something you can remember. (Don't use your last name or your address, which is likely to be the *only* information that a passerby might know about your house.) Some Wi-Fi equipment arrives configured with a network name and a random password, which you might as well use. A card is usually included with the network name and password printed on it to help you set up your PCs.

Older Wi-Fi equipment can't do WPA, and you may be stuck using the system named *WEP,* a term that allegedly means Wired Equivalent Privacy (which it's not). WEP passwords come in two sizes: 64 and 128 bits. Use 128 unless you have old equipment that can do only 64, in which case, 64 will do. (Your entire network has to use the same size.) The password can be represented as either a text string or a hexadecimal (base-16, also called *hex*) number — we leave it to you to choose which would be easier for you to type and remember. If you use 64-bit WEP, your password (in text format) must be exactly 7 characters long. For 128-bit WEP, you need a 13-character password. If you want to use a shorter password, pad it out with digits or punctuation.

The easiest way to set the password is to set it up at the same time you set up your network, as described in the next section.

Making the Wi-Fi connection

To create a Wi-Fi system, follow these steps:

1. **Get your router set up, and then set up your computers to connect to it.**

   See the section "Setting up a router," earlier in this chapter. Even if you plan to use an all-Wi-Fi network, to do the setup process, plug in one computer with a cable and use it to set up the Wi-Fi.

2. **Use your Web browser to display the router's control page (usually at** 192.168.0.1**) so that you can configure the router.**

3. **Find the page where you can configure the router's Wi-Fi settings.**

   What you click depends on your router. On our D-Link router, we clicked Setup and then Wireless Settings to open the page shown in Figure 5-3. Look for a page with settings about wireless, a network name, and wireless security.

4. **Give your network a name.**

   Every Wi-Fi network has a name. With typical machine imagination, your router suggests something like linksys (a router manufacturer) or dlink (another manufacturer) or default. We suggest something like FredsHouse so that any neighbors who happen on it know that it's you.

5. **Turn on Wi-Fi passwords and set one, as described in the preceding section.**

   Your router probably has lots of other options — such as MAC cloning (less pomological than it sounds, and nothing to do with Macintosh computers), all of which you can ignore.

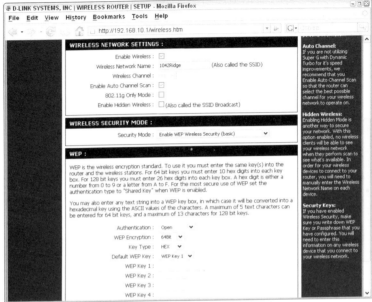

Figure 5-3:
Configuring
your router
to do Wi-Fi
with a
password.

6. **When your router is up and running and your computer can see the Internet (that is, you can display Web pages), you're done configuring the router for your Wi-Fi network.**

Now, at last, you can cut the cord and go wireless. You need to tell every PC which Wi-Fi network to use and what the password is. On Windows 7 and Vista, the setup is quick:

1. **In Windows 7, click the Networking icon in the lower right corner of the screen, to the left of the digital clock. In Windows Vista, choose Start⇨Connect To.**

   You see a window with a list of available networks, one of which is yours. If you have neighbors with Wi-Fi networks, it may show them, too, but don't use your neighbors' networks unless they give you permission.

2. **Double-click your network.**

   In a moment, you see a dialog box that asks for the security key or pass phrase.

3. **Enter the network password, exactly as you did on the router, and click Connect.**

   Windows retrieves network settings from the router, and in a few seconds you're online. If you have trouble typing the password, click the box to display the characters of the password (unless, we suppose, someone you don't trust is looking over your shoulder.)

Windows Internet Connection Sharing? Get a router!

Windows Vista and XP come with Internet Connection Sharing (ICS) — adequate built-in router software — but there's not much point in using it: You need a hub or router in order to connect your computers into a LAN anyway. With ICS, the computer running ICS must be awake and alert for any other computer to connect, and problems with that computer ("Rats! My game just crashed!") cause connection trouble for all the other computers. Who needs the hassle?

If you're using Windows XP SP2, the process is also fairly painless:

1. **Click Start⇨Connect To⇨Wireless Network Connection.**

2. **After your PC sniffs the airwaves for a moment, Windows shows you a list of available networks, including the one you just set up.**

3. **Click your network's name and then the Connect button at the bottom of the window.**

4. **Windows asks you to type the password, twice. Type the password, whether it's text or hexadecimal, exactly as you did on the router.**

5. **Click OK, and you should be online.**

Windows remembers the wireless setup; in the future, it connects automatically.

Using Your Laptop or Netbook at Home and Away

The whole point of having a laptop computer is to take it with you when you travel — and what fun is traveling with a computer if you can't use it to check your e-mail 17 times a day? Almost all laptops and absolutely all netbooks come with built-in Wi-Fi. After you set up your laptop or netbook on a home Wi-Fi network by following the instructions earlier in this chapter, you already know most of what you need to know to use it on other networks when you travel. All the information in this section about laptops applies to netbooks, too.

Home and office setup

Lots of people have laptops they take back and forth between home and the office. A lot of variables are involved in doing this successfully, depending on not only your particular laptop but also the networks you use at home and at the office. In general, however, this is how the various setups should work:

- ✔ If both home and the office have wired networks, your computer should work when it's plugged into either network. If your computer doesn't connect at work, talk to your network administrator.

- ✔ If your office has local shared files and printers and your house doesn't, or vice versa, Windows complains and sulks if it can't find them. As long as you don't try to print to a printer that's at the other place, though, you can go online just fine.

- ✔ If both the home and office networks are wireless, or one is wireless and the other is wired, set up each one as described earlier in this chapter, and your PC should automatically recognize whichever is available — that is, the network where you are.

Getting Wi-Fi with your latté

In olden days, people would go to a coffee shop and order cups of coffee, of which there was a maximum of two kinds, regular and decaf, and then chat with people sitting *right next to them*. Now, of course, that's hopelessly 20th century. We cruise into the coffee shop with our laptop, order a half-caf single-shot mocha cappuccino grande with 2 percent milk, cocoa drizzle, hold the sprinkles, and we put on our Bluetooth earpiece and talk or exchange messages with people thousands of miles away, utterly ignoring the losers at the next table. The magic of Wi-Fi makes this possible, as coffee shops install Wi-Fi *hotspots* (public areas with Wi-Fi Internet access) to which customers can connect.

The amount of effort needed to get online at your coffee shop varies from none to way too much. At some places, the management has enough confidence in its product to figure that if it can get you to stick around, you'll keep buying coffee, so Wi-Fi is free to customers. (The coffee shop where John is sometimes found is in this category.) You turn on your computer; choose the Start⟳Connect To command — if your computer doesn't look for a Wi-Fi network by itself; click the name of the shop's network when it appears; tell it that, yes, you really want to connect to that insecure network; and you're on. The next time you come back, your computer remembers the network and connects automatically.

Other places are less confident. A typical large chain — let's call it Ahab's — made the Wi-Fi a profit center, so you have to pay by the hour. This fee adds an extra, annoying step to the connection process, the one where you pay. After your computer is turned on, fire up your Web browser. No matter what your home page is, the network is set up so that your browser shows *its* home page, which allows you to make payment arrangements.

There are about as many ways to pay for Wi-Fi access as there are flavors of coffee. Maybe you buy or are given a ticket at the counter with a code number to enter. More likely, the coffee shop made a deal with one of the large, national mobile phone providers, T-Mobile or AT&T, that make a sideline of Wi-Fi. In this case, you pay with a credit card, either by the hour (at about $6 an hour) or by buying a package of hours. You sign up via your Web browser — the Wi-Fi network lets you connect to the sign-up page for free, but you have to sign up and pay to do anything else. If you plan to drink a great deal of coffee, you can sign up for a monthly flat-rate plan, or in some cases if you have mobile phone service from the provider, it tosses in a Wi-Fi account for cheap or free.

It's not hard to get into the Wi-Fi café biz, so you can also find lots of tiny providers. Many of them have reciprocal agreements and alliances, such that (for example) if you sign up with someone who belongs to the iPass group, you can use another iPass member's Wi-Fi hotspot.

Airports, hotels, and beyond

Coffee shops are hardly the only places that offer Wi-Fi. If you spend much time in airports (John does because he's on a lot of advisory boards), you find lots of Wi-Fi — with about the same options as in the coffee shops. The same two providers dominate, with a lot of little local ones as well. After a while, frequent travelers learn Wi-Fi folklore — say that there's free Wi-Fi in the airline club on the third level of the Pittsburgh airport, and even if you're not a member, you can use it if you sit in one of the chairs near the door.

Hotels, like cafés, treat Wi-Fi as either a service — like the ice machine on each floor — or a profit center, like your room's minibar full of overpriced beer. Some hotels still offer wired Internet connections (in which case a cable on the desk in your room plugs into your computer), and others go Wi-Fi. If you're at an ice-machine-style hotel, you may just be able to turn on your computer and go online with no fuss, or you may have to sign in through your browser, even though you don't have to pay. Some hotels with Wi-Fi give you a slip of paper with a login code when you register, to deter visitors who would otherwise sit in the lobby and use it for free. In minibar-style hotels, you have to log in through your browser. Most hotels put the charge on the room bill; some want your credit card number so that they can bill you separately. The typical charge is $10 per day, from noon to noon, but we've seen hourly rates, lower rates, and higher rates. Some hotels bundle the rate in a business package with long-distance phone calls and some other goodies.

If you encounter a problem with a hotel's Internet service, rarely does anyone at the hotel know anything about it, but they should be able to give you an 800 number you can call to talk to someone at the company that provides the service.

The mail problem

Wi-Fi connections in coffee shops, airports, and hotels sure are convenient, but remember: *They aren't private.* This is a particular problem when you send and receive e-mail, because you usually want your mail to be private *and* because your computer needs to send your network login and password over the Internet back to your mail server to pick up your mail. With a modest amount of advance planning, it shouldn't be hard to get your mail working securely on the road.

Snoops at the coffee shop

Although we think that a lot of concerns about Internet network security are overblown, one place where it's a real issue is on public Wi-Fi networks, like the ones in hotels and coffee shops. Those networks frequently have no passwords, which means that *anyone on that network can snoop on your network connection.* Even if everyone in the coffee shop seems nice, a snoop might be sitting in a car out by the curb. And in a hotel, of course, you have no idea who's in all the nearby rooms.

Fortunately, taking a few simple precautions will keep you safe. When visiting Web sites, make sure that any site where you type a password or other private info uses *SSL encryption:* The address starts with `https://`, and the little lock in the corner is locked. If the site doesn't have SSL encryption, wait until you get home. For advice on securing your mail program, see the section "The mail problem," a little later in this chapter. If you see a network named Free Public Wi-Fi, do *not* use it, because it is a password-stealing virus running on a nearby infected PC.

The simplest approach is webmail — a secure Web site where you can log in to read and send mail. It's worth checking to see whether your mail system offers optional webmail. If so, even if you don't use it at home, you might want to use it on the road, particularly if the webmail offers a secure server. To find out how Web-based mail works, see the section in Chapter 13 about the Web being a fine place to read your e-mail. Normally, we don't worry about secure Web sites (`https://` versus `http://`), but public Wi-Fi is one of the few cases where people might actually be snooping and the https security helps.

If you *really* want to be paranoid, create an account at Gmail, Hotmail, Yahoo! Mail, or another webmail site, use it during your trip, and then close the account when you get back home.

Using Your Smartphone on the Net

The newfangled, Internet-enabled *smartphone* is a tiny little computer that happens to have a phone antenna, a microphone, and speakers built in. Some types of phones can also communicate using Wi-Fi, which is faster than a phone connection and doesn't move data over the cellphone system (which you may pay for by the megabyte).

Like computers, which come primarily in Windows, PC, and Linux varieties, smartphones come in several flavors, based on which operating system they run. Most of these types of smartphone allow you to download additional programs (applications) from a Web site. Some applications are free, and others cost 99 cents or more.

The major types of smartphones are described in this list:

- ✔ **Android:** This system is *open source* (anyone can see the code and create compatible software). Because it's sponsored by Google, you can use your Google Apps (such as Gmail, Google Calendar, and Google Maps) on these phones. Android phones are available from HTC, Motorola, and Samsung, and Dell may climb on board, too. The T-Mobile G1 and G2 were the first widely available Android phones.

- ✔ **BlackBerry:** The BlackBerry was the first widely used smartphone that made it easy to send and receive e-mail. All BlackBerry phones are made by Research in Motion (RIM).

- ✔ **iPhone:** The iPhone is a beautiful thing, and its sleek design created a huge sensation when it debuted in 2007. All iPhones are made by Apple, and none (as of the end of 2009) has a keyboard. Figure 5-4 shows an iPhone displaying e-mail.

Figure 5-4:
Use your
smartphone
to read and
send e-mail,
browse the
Web, and
use other
Internet
services.

✔ **Palm webOS:** Palm made some of the first smartphones. Palm phones come in both Palm webOS (such as the Palm Pre) and Windows Mobile varieties.

✔ **Symbian:** This system is used by Nokia, Motorola, Samsung, and lots of phones in Japan.

✔ **Windows Mobile:** A variety of phones use a version of Windows designed for phones and other handheld devices. Windows Mobile phones are available from Palm, Samsung, and T-Mobile.

For each of these smartphone operating systems, you can buy a variety of different phones in different shapes and sizes. Some have little keyboards, some flip open, some have larger screens, some are bigger or heavier, some can connect to the Internet by way of Wi-Fi as well as by using the cellphone system — you get the idea. Shop around. New smartphone models are available every month.

All smartphones come with a Web browser and an e-mail program. (Otherwise, what's smart about them?) You can download other programs, including maps (Google Maps has a smartphone version), instant messaging (to communicate with AIM users, for example), and Internet games. Most can also play Internet audio and video files, so you can watch YouTube during your commute, preferably if someone else is driving.

Please don't call it a CrackBerry

One of the best innovations in e-mail, or the worst, depending on your point of view, is the *BlackBerry*. It's a combined mobile phone and e-mail device. Grown people in business suits nervously punch the Check Mail button every few seconds like trained lab rats, and when the entire BlackBerry system failed for a day in April 2007, you could hear the screams clear from the Arctic Circle to the Rio Grande. It was the first step in what has turned into the world of Web-enabled phones.

On the other hand, if you truly need to stay in touch every minute of every day, a BlackBerry is helpful. It can have its own e-mail address, or more often it receives copies of the same mail sent to your regular computer at work. You can read and send mail very much like you do on a regular computer, and with a little practice you can become surprisingly efficient at typing on the teensy keys and small screen. President Obama managed to talk his security staff into letting him keep his BlackBerry in the White House.

In most cases, each smartphone is available from and will work with only one carrier, so if you have preferences among carriers, you limit your choice of phones. Be sure you understand the monthly plan that comes with the phone and that the monthly data quota matches your usage. If you just check text mail a few times a day, an itty-bitty plan is enough, but if you plan to stream video an hour each way on your commute, you need an all-you-can-eat plan.

For much more information on smartphones and the mobile Internet, see *Mobile Internet For Dummies,* written and published by people you know and trust.

Part III
Web Mania

In this part . . .

No doubt about it, the Web is *the* happenin' place. For many people, the World Wide Web *is* the Internet. We explain what the Web is and how to get around, and we give you helpful tips about how to find truly interesting and useful stuff among the millions of clamoring Web pages. We take a break to listen to lots of online music and watch online videos. Then, relaxed and refreshed, we tell you about Web shopping and Web banking so that you can confidently spend and save your money online, and then we wrap up with ways to get free (and almost free) software and other downloadable stuff from the Web.

Chapter 6

Welcome to the Wild, Wonderful, Wacky Web

*P*eople now talk about the *Web* more than they talk about the *Internet*. The World Wide Web and the Internet aren't the same thing — the World Wide Web (which we call the Web because we're lazy typists) lives "on top of" the Internet. The Internet's network is at the core of the Web, and the Web is an attractive parasite that requires the Net for survival.

This chapter explains what the Web is and where it came from. Then it describes how to install and use some popular Web browsers, and how to use Web browsers to display Web pages. If you're already comfortable using the Web, skip to Chapter 7.

What Is the Web?

So what is the Web, already? The Web is a bunch of "pages" of information connected to each other around the globe. Each page can be a combination of text, pictures, audio clips, video clips, animations, and other stuff. (People add new types of other stuff every day.) What makes Web pages interesting is that they contain *hyperlinks,* usually called just *links* because the Net already has plenty of hype. Each link points to another Web page, and, when you click a link, your browser fetches the page the link connects to. (Your *browser* is the program that shows you the Web — read more about it in a couple of pages.)

The other important characteristic of the Web is that you can search it — all ten billion or so pages. For example, in fewer than ten seconds, you can find a list of Web pages that contain the phrase *domestic poultry* or your own name or the name of a book you want to find out about. You can follow links to see each page on the list to find the information you want. See Chapter 8 to see how to use a search engine to search the Web.

Linking up Web pages

Each page your browser finds for you can have more links that take you to other places. Pages can be linked to other pages anywhere in the world so that when you're on the Web, you can end up looking at pages from Singapore to Calgary, or from Sydney to Buenos Aires, all faster than you can say "Bob's your uncle," usually. Most of the time you're only seconds away from any site, anywhere in the world. This system of interlinked documents is known as *hypertext*.

Figure 6-1 shows a Web page (our Web page, in fact). Each underlined phrase is a link to another Web page.

Where did the Web come from?

The World Wide Web was invented in 1989 at the European Particle Physics Lab in Geneva, Switzerland, an unlikely spot for a revolution in computing. The inventor is a British researcher named Sir Tim Berners-Lee, who is now the director of the World Wide Web Consortium (W3C) in Cambridge, Massachusetts, the organization that sets standards and loosely oversees the development of the Web. Tim is terrifically smart and hard working and charming. (Margy met him through Sunday school — is that wholesome or what?)

Tim invented *HTTP* (HyperText Transport Protocol), the way Web browsers communicate with Web servers; *HTML* (HyperText Markup Language), the language in which Web pages are written; and *URLs* (Uniform Resource Locators), the addresses used for Web pages and most other information on the Net. He envisioned the Web as a way for everyone to publish and read information on the Net. Early Web browsers had editors that let you create Web pages almost as easily as you could read them.

For more information about the development of the Web and the work of the World Wide Web Consortium, visit its Web site, at www.w3.org. You can also read Tim's book, *Weaving the Web* (HarperOne, 1999). He was knighted in 2004 and became Sir Tim.

Links can create connections that let you go directly to related information. These invisible connections between pages resemble the threads of a spider web — as you click from Web page to Web page, you can envision the "web" created by the links. What's remarkable about the Web is that it connects pieces of information from all around the *planet,* on different computers and in different databases (a feat you would be hard pressed to match with a card catalog in a brick-and-mortar library).

Where's that page?

Before you jump onto the Web (boing-g-g — that metaphor needs work), you need to know about one more basic concept. Every Web page has an address so that browsers, and you, can find it. Great figures in the world of software engineering (one guy, actually, named Sir Tim Berners-Lee) named this address *URL,* or *Uniform Resource Locator.* Every Web page has a URL, a series of characters that begins with http://. (How do you say "URL"? Everyone we know pronounces each letter, "U-R-L" — no one says "earl.") Now you know enough to go browsing. For more entirely optional details about URLs, see the later sidebar "Duke of URL."

Reload

Back   Home   Address box

Figure 6-1: Underlined phrases on Web pages are links to other pages. (This page is displayed in the Firefox browser.)

Browsing to Points Unknown

Maybe you have some time to check out the Web for yourself. To do this, you need a *browser,* the program that finds Web pages and displays them on your screen. Fortunately, if you have any recent version of Windows, any recent Mac, any netbook, almost any other computer with Internet access, or a smartphone, you probably already have one.

Here are the most popular browsers:

- ✔ **Internet Explorer (IE)** is the browser that Microsoft has built into every recent version of Windows. About 75 percent of people use IE. The latest version is 8, shown in Figure 6-2, which comes with Windows 7 and is available as a free download for many earlier versions of Windows (at microsoft.com/ie) but not for the Mac. IE also runs on Windows Mobile smartphones. Previous versions of IE look a little different, but usually try to update themselves to the latest version, so you're likely to end up with IE 8 (or whatever comes after it).

- ✔ **Firefox** (refer to Figure 6-1) is the browser from the open source Mozilla project at www.mozilla.org. You can download Firefox for free for Windows, Macs, and Linux computers; the latest version as of late 2009 is version 3.5. Firefox is used by about 25 percent of Web users, runs faster than Internet Explorer, and is much, much less susceptible to spyware. See the nearby sidebar "Our advice: Switch from Internet Explorer to Firefox or Chrome."

- ✔ **Chrome,** shown in Figure 6-3, is from Google, the huge company responsible for the Google.com search site and lots and lots of free Web-based services. You can download it for free for Windows, Macs, and Linux at chrome.google.com. Google appears to have a plan for Chrome to become its own operating system, competing with Windows.

- ✔ **Safari,** shown in Figure 6-4, is the Apple browser for the Mac, iPhone, and iPod touch. Windows has a version, too, although we've never heard of anyone other than us using it. You can download the latest versions from apple.com/safari.

We describe Internet Explorer and Firefox in detail in this book, and we mention Chrome here and there. All browsers are similar, enabling you to view Web pages, print them, and save the addresses of your favorite pages so that you can return to them later. If you want to try a different browser, see the section "Getting and Installing a Browser," later in this chapter.

Back   Address box   Home   Refresh

Figure 6-2:
Your typical
Web page,
viewed in
Internet
Explorer 8.

Reload

Back   Address box

Figure 6-3:
The Google
Chrome
browser
displays
another
Web page.

Back   Address box   Reload

Figure 6-4:
Safari is the
Apple Web
browser.

Web Surfing with Your Browser

When you start your Web browser — Internet Explorer, Firefox, Chrome, Safari, or whatever — you see a window that displays one Web page, with menus and icons along the top. Figure 6-1 (shown earlier in this chapter) illustrates Firefox, Figure 6-2 shows Internet Explorer 8, and Figure 6-3 shows the Google Chrome browser. Other browsers look similar, but with different menus and icons along the top.

Which page your browser displays at startup — your *start page* — depends on how it's set up. Many ISPs arrange for your browser to display their home pages; otherwise, until you choose a home page of your own, IE tends to display a Microsoft page, and Firefox usually shows a Mozilla-branded Google search page. Chapter 7 explains how to set the start page to a Web page you want to see.

The main section of the browser window is taken up by the Web page you're looking at. After all, that's what the browser is *for* — displaying a Web page! The buttons, bars, and menus around the edge help you find your way around the Web and do things like print and save pages.

Here are some of the most important buttons and menus at the top of your browser window:

- **Back button:** Click to display to the last page you looked at, as described in the later section "Backward, ho!"

- **Reload or Refresh button:** Click to reload the page you're looking at now from the Web.

- **Home button:** Click to display your start page (or *home page*), as described in Chapter 7.

> ✔ **Address box:** Displays the Web address (URL) of the current page. You can enter the URL of a page to display, as described in the later section "Going places."
>
> ✔ **Search box:** Firefox, IE, and Safari have a *search box,* to the right of the address box, where you can type search terms. See Chapter 8 for details.

The rest of this chapter explains how to use these and other features of your browser.

Getting around

You need two simple skills (if we can describe something as basic as a single mouse click as a skill) to get going on the Web. One is to move from page to page on the Web, and the other is to jump directly to a page when you know its URL. Okay, we know that you aren't actually *moving* — your Web browser displays one page after another — but browsing feels as though you're cruising (or surfing, depending on which metaphor you prefer) around the Web.

Our advice: Switch from Internet Explorer to Firefox or Chrome

Internet Explorer, Firefox, and Chrome are free and downloadable from the Internet, but beyond that, they have some important differences.

The advantages of Firefox and Chrome

✔ Firefox and Chrome run faster. They're smaller and quicker. Chrome is even faster than Firefox.

✔ Firefox and Chrome don't use ActiveX controls, a feature of IE that spyware uses to infect your computer.

The advantages of Internet Explorer

✔ Some Web sites (mainly sites run by Microsoft itself) require Internet Explorer because they use ActiveX controls.

✔ If you use Windows, you already have IE because it comes bundled with Windows.

✔ A few add-ins work only with IE.

Any browser can display and print Web pages — don't get us wrong. However, we think that the security issue — avoiding spyware — trumps all other considerations hands down, and we recommend that you install Firefox or Chrome and use it except for the few Web sites that require Internet Explorer. You can have more than one browser installed at the same time — you can even have two or three running at the same time — so switching to Firefox or Chrome doesn't mean that you can never use Internet Explorer again.

If you decide to try Firefox, you can choose Help⇨For Internet Explorer Users to see a pageful of helpful information.

Duke of URL

The World Wide Web will eventually link together all the information in the known universe, starting with all the stuff on the Internet. (This statement may be a slight exaggeration, but not by much.) One key to global domination is to give everything a name so that no matter what a Web page link refers to, a Web browser can find it and know what to do with it.

Look at this typical URL:

```
http://airinfo.travel/
    index.phtml
```

The first item in a URL, the letters that appear before the colon, is the *scheme,* which describes the way a browser can get to the resource. Although ten schemes are defined, the most common by far is HTTP, which stands for HyperText Transfer Protocol, the Web's native transfer technique. HTTP is the language that your browser uses to request a Web page from the Web server on which it's stored, and that the Web server uses to send you back the page you want to see. (A conversation in HTTP can be translated into English as something like this: "I'd like a Web page, please." "Here it is. Enjoy!")

Although the details of the rest of the URL depend on the scheme, most schemes look similar. Following the colon are two slashes (always forward slashes, never backslashes) and the name of the host computer on which the resource lives; in this case, `airline. travel` (one of the many names of John's Internet host computer). Then comes another slash and a *path,* which gives the name of the resource on that host; in this case, a file named `index.phtml`.

Web URLs allow a few other optional parts. They can include a *port number,* which specifies, roughly speaking, which of several programs running on that host should handle the request. The port number goes after a colon after the host name, like this:

```
http://airline.travel:80/
    index.phtml
```

The standard `http` port number is 80, so if that's the port you want (it usually is), you can leave it out. Finally, a Web URL can have a *query part* at the end, following a question mark, like this:

```
http://airline.travel:80/
    index.phtml?chickens
```

When a URL has a query part, it tells the host computer more specifically what you want the page to display. (You rarely type query parts yourself — they're often constructed for you from fill-in fields on Web pages.)

When you type a URL into your Web browser, you can leave out the `http://` part because the browser adds it for you. Lazy typists, unite! When a Web address starts with www, you can usually leave that out, too.

Another useful URL scheme is `mailto`. A `mailto` URL looks like this:

```
mailto:internet12@gurus.org
```

That is, a `mailto` link is an e-mail address. Clicking a `mailto` URL runs your e-mail program and creates a new message addressed to the address in the link.

Moving from page to page is easy: Click any link that looks interesting. That's it. Underlined blue text and blue-bordered pictures are links, and sometimes other things are, too. Anything that looks like a button is probably a link. You can tell when you're pointing to a link because the mouse pointer changes to a little hand. Clicking outside a link selects the text you click, as in most other programs. Sometimes, clicking a link moves you to a different place on the same page rather than to a new page.

Backward, ho!

Web browsers remember the last few pages you visited, so if you click a link and decide that you're not so crazy about the new page, you can easily go back to the preceding one. To go back, click the Back button on the toolbar. Its icon is an arrow pointing to the left, and it's the leftmost button on the toolbar, as shown in Figures 6-1, 6-2, and 6-3. Or, press Alt+←.

Sometimes, clicking a link opens the new page in a new browser window or tab— your browser (IE or Firefox) can display more than one Web page at the same time, each in its own window or in tabs in one window. If a link opens a new window or tab, the Back button does nothing in that window.

Going places

Someone tells you about a cool Web site and you want to take a look. Here's what you do:

1. **Click in the Address box near the top of the browser window.**

   Figures 6-1, 6-2, and 6-3 show where the Address box is in IE, Firefox, and Chrome. Pressing F6 also gets you to the Address box.

2. **Type the URL in the box.**

   The URL is something like `http://net.gurus.org` — you just type `net.gurus.org`. Be sure to delete the URL that appeared before you started typing.

3. **Press Enter.**

Here are a few shortcuts:

  ✔ If the entire address in the Address box is highlighted, when you type, the new URL replaces what was there before. To highlight the entire old address, click in the Address box not once, not twice, but three times.

✔ You can leave the `http://` off the URLs when you type them in the Address box. Your browser can guess that part! Many Web addresses include a name that ends with .com, but not all do. See the later sidebar "Why .com?" for more information.

✔ When you start typing a URL, your browser helpfully starts guessing the address you might be typing, suggesting addresses you've already typed that start with the same characters. The browser displays its suggestions in a list just below the Address box. If you see the address you want on the list, click it — no point in typing the rest of the URL if you don't have to!

If you receive URLs in e-mail, instant messages, or documents, try clicking them — many programs pass along the address to your browser. Or, use the standard cut-and-paste techniques and avoid retyping:

1. **Highlight the URL in whichever program it appears.**

   That is, use your mouse to select the URL so that the whole URL is highlighted.

2. **Press Ctrl+C (⌘+C on the Mac) to copy the info to the Clipboard.**

3. **Click in the Address box to highlight whatever is in it.**

4. **Press Ctrl+V (⌘+V on the Mac) to paste the URL into the box, and then press Enter.**

Bad guys can easily create e-mail messages where the URL you see in the text of a message isn't the URL you visit; the bad guys can hide the actual URL. Keep this warning in mind if you receive mail that purports to be from your bank — if you click the link and enter your account number and password in the Web page that appears, you may be typing it into a Web site run by crooks rather than by your bank. See the section "Phishing for inphormation" in Chapter 2.

The best place to start browsing

You find out more about how to find things on the Web in Chapter 8, but for now, here's a good way to get started: Go to the Yahoo! News page. (Yes, the name of the Web page includes an exclamation point — it's very excitable.) To find Yahoo! News, type this URL in your browser's Address box and then press Enter:

```
news.yahoo.com
```

The Yahoo! Web site includes lots of different features, but its news site should look familiar — it's like a newspaper on steroids. Just nose around, clicking links that look interesting and clicking the Back button on the toolbar when you make a wrong turn. We guarantee that you'll find something interesting.

For information related to the very book you're holding, go to net.gurus.org. If we have any late-breaking news about the Internet or updates and corrections to this book, you can find them there. If you find mistakes in this book or have other comments, by the way, please send e-mail to us at internet12@gurus.org.

Why .com?

When you want to put information on the Internet with your own name on it, you register a *domain name* such as yahoo.com or wikipedia.org. A domain name for an ISP in the United States usually ends with a dot and a two- or three-letter code (which is the *top-level domain,* or TLD) that gives you a clue to what kind of outfit owns the domain name. The following list briefly explains which type of organization owns domains with which TLD codes:

✔ **Commercial organizations** typically own domain names ending in .com, such as google.com (the most popular Web search site, described in Chapter 8), aa.com (AMR Corporation, better known as American Airlines), greattapes.com (Margy's online video store), and taugh.com (John's hard-to-pronounce Taughannock Networks). Because "dot-com" has become a synonym for the Internet itself, lots of other organizations and even individuals have .com domains.

✔ **U.S. colleges and universities** typically own domain names ending in .edu (such as yale.edu).

✔ **Networking organizations** typically end with .net. These include ISPs, such as

comcast.net, and companies that provide network services.

✔ **Government organizations** in the United States typically own domain names ending in .gov. For example, the National Do Not Call Registry, run by the Federal Trade Commission, is at donotcall.gov.

✔ **U.S. military organizations** use domain names ending in .mil.

✔ **Nonprofits** and **special interest groups** typically own domain names ending in .org. For example, the Unitarian Universalist Association (where Margy works) is at uua.org.

✔ **Organizations in specific countries** frequently own domain names ending in two-letter country codes, such as .fr for France or .zm for Zambia. See our Web site (at net.gurus.org/countries) for a listing of country TLD codes. Small businesses, local governments, and K-12 schools in the United States usually end with the two-letter state abbreviation followed by .us (such as John's church Web site at unitarian.ithaca.ny.us).

Who makes up these TLDs?

An international group (the Internet Corporation for Assigned Names and Numbers, or ICANN, at `icann.org`) is in charge of TLDs (top-level domains). In 1997, ICANN proposed adding some extra, generic domains, such as `.firm`, `.arts`, and `.web`. After a lengthy detour through a maze of international intellectual-property politics, the first new domains (`.biz` and `.info`) appeared in 2001. The result is confusion that practically guarantees that, more often than not, `whatever.biz` and `whatever.info` are owned by the same group that owns `whatever.com`, and when they're owned by someone else, they're usually sleazy knockoffs. ICANN has since added these domain extensions:

- `.name`: Personal vanity domains
- `.pro`: Licensed professional doctors, lawyers, and accountants
- `.coop`: Co-ops
- `.museum`: Museums
- `.aero`: Air travel
- `.jobs`: Job offers

- `.travel`: Travel in general
- `.mobi`: For people using cellphones and other mobile devices
- `.asia`: For people in Asia
- `.cat`: For people in Catalonia (where Barcelona is)
- `.tel`: An online directory for Internet telephone users

None is widely used, although `.mobi` has a reasonable chance of success because of enthusiastic support from mobile phone companies. However, many Web sites have versions designed for smartphones (and other devices with small screens) with names that start with `m.`, like `m.yahoo.com`.

ICANN is planning to throw open the domain floodgates to anyone who fills out the application form and sends it in with a check for a modest $185,000 application fee. By the time you read this sidebar, lots more TLDs might exist. Even if they do, we doubt any of them will be important.

What not to click

The Web has some bad neighborhoods, and it's not always safe to click whatever you see. For example, clicking a link on a Web page can download and install a program on your computer, and that program might not be one you want to be running. So, exercise judgment when clicking. Here are some links *not* to click:

- Don't click ads claiming that you just won the lottery or a free laptop or anything else too good to be true.
- Don't click messages on Web pages claiming that your computer is at risk of some dire consequence if you don't click there. Yeah, right.

✔ Don't click OK in a dialog box that asks about downloading or installing a program, unless you're deliberately downloading and installing a program (as we describe in Chapter 12).

✔ Don't click any link that makes you suspicious. Your instincts are probably correct!

If one of these messages appears in a browser window, the safest thing is to close the window by clicking the X box in the upper right corner (or on a Mac, the red Close button in the upper left corner).

This page looks funny, or out of date

Sometimes, a Web page becomes garbled on the way in or you interrupt it (by clicking the Stop button on the toolbar or by pressing the Esc key). You can tell your browser to retrieve the information on the page again. Click the Reload or Refresh button (shown in Figures 6-1, 6-2, and 6-3) or press Ctrl+R.

Some people hardly ever close their browsers, which probably isn't a good idea for their long-term mental stability. (Naturally, we're not talking about anyone *we* know! Definitely not.) If you're such a person, however, remember that your browser *caches* pages — it stores the pages temporarily on your hard disk for quick retrieval. If you want to make sure that you're seeing an up-to-date version of a page, reload it.

Get me outta here

Sooner or later, even the most dedicated Web surfer has to stop to eat or attend to other bodily needs. You leave your browser in the same way you leave any other program: Click the Close (X) button in the upper right corner of the window (or on a Mac, the red Close button in the upper left corner) or press Alt+F4. Or, just leave the program running and walk away from your computer.

Browsing from Your Smartphone

Internet-connected phones — such as the iPhone and the BlackBerry and phones that run Android, Palm webOS, or Windows Mobile — can browse the Web, too. So can the iPod touch, if you have a Wi-Fi connection. Of course, you can see only teeny, tiny Web pages on their teeny, tiny screens, but phone-based browsing can still be incredibly useful, especially when you're looking for a good restaurant recommendation.

The iPhone and the iPod touch come with Safari (the Apple Web browser), Windows Mobile phones come with IE (the Microsoft Web browser), and Android phones come with Chrome (the Google Web browser). All these pint-size Web browsers have Back buttons and Address boxes and most of the same basic features as their larger siblings.

Some Web pages look great on smartphones, when the Web page designers create special versions that fit the small screens, dispensing with extraneous columns and graphics. Other pages are practically unreadable. As phone-based browsers become more popular, more Web sites will have sites customized for mobile devices. If you find a site that's unusable, try adding m. to the domain name or change the last part of the name to .mobi to see whether the site has a mobile version. For example, m.netflix.com is the spare, usable, version of the Netflix site designed for phones, and yahoo.mobi is the teeny screen version of Yahoo!.

Getting and Installing a Browser

Chances are, a browser is already installed on your computer. If you use Internet Explorer, we think you're better off installing either Firefox or Chrome, for speed and safety reasons. Fortunately, browser programs aren't difficult to find and install, and both Firefox and Chrome are free.

Even if you already have a browser, new versions come out every 20 minutes or so, and it's worth knowing how to upgrade because occasionally the new versions fix some bugs so that the browsers are better than the old versions. Microsoft gives away Internet Explorer, the Mozilla project gives away Firefox, and Google gives away Chrome, so you might as well upgrade to the current version.

Getting the program

To get or upgrade Firefox (for Windows or Mac or any of the other dozen computers it runs on), visit www.mozilla.com. To get or upgrade Chrome, go to chrome.google.com. To get or upgrade Internet Explorer, go to www.microsoft.com/ie. Use your current browser to go to the page and then follow the instructions for finding and downloading the program. You might also want to consult Chapter 12 for details.

Hey, how about us Mac users?

Macs have always been famous for their slick, easy-to-use software, and the Internet software is no exception. Macs come with a nice Web browser named Safari (refer to Figure 6-4). You use the ⌘ key rather than Ctrl for the keyboard shortcuts, and nearly all the rest of the keys work the way they do in the other browsers we describe.

Or, you can do what we do and use Firefox, which works very nicely on a Mac, just like it does on Windows with ⌘ rather than Ctrl. You can use Safari to visit www.mozilla.com to download and install Firefox and then use it instead of or alongside Safari.

If you're upgrading from an older version of your browser to a newer one, you can replace the old version with the new one. The installation program should be smart enough to remember your old settings and bookmarks (favorites). Some browsers automatically notify you when new versions are available, and you can just click Yes or Continue to download and install the new version. Updates to IE are included in the Microsoft Windows Update system, which is part of Windows.

Running a new browser for the first time

To run your new browser, click the browser's attractive new icon. If you use Windows, the default browser also appears at the top of the left column of the Start menu, too.

Your new browser will probably ask whether you want to import your settings — including your bookmarks and favorites — from the browser program you've been using. If you've already been using the Web for a while and have built up a list of your favorite Web sites (as described in Chapter 7), take advantage of this opportunity to copy your list into the new browser so that you don't have to search for your favorite sites all over again.

The first time you run IE, it might run the Internet or New Connection Wizard, which offers to help you connect to the Internet. If it does, see Chapter 4 for details.

Internet Explorer 8 asks whether you want to discover Web sites you might like based on sites you already have seen. You can turn the option on or off later by choosing Tools⇨Suggested Sites. IE8 also asks whether to use its *express* (recommended) settings, which set your search site to Windows Live Search, set IE8 as your default browser, and turn on accelerators for Windows Live Web sites. Go ahead and accept these express settings. To change them later, choose Tools⇨Options.

Chapter 7

Taking Your Browser for a Spin

*I*f you've read Chapter 6, you're all set to browse the Web. But to be an efficient, downright clever Internaut, you need to know about some other browser features, such as printing Web pages, displaying more than one Web page at the same time, and storing the addresses of Web pages you like to visit often. You also need to know how to handle spyware, an Internet menace we describe in Chapter 2. This chapter is your guide to these extra features and how you can make the most of them right away.

Saving Stuff from the Web

Frequently, you see something on a Web page that's worth saving for later. Sometimes it's interesting information, a picture or some other type of file, or even the entire Web page. Fortunately, saving stuff is easy.

There's not much point to saving an entire Web page. Web pages are usually made up of several files — one for the text, one for each picture, and sometimes other files, so your browser can't just save the page in a file. However, you can save images and text from a page.

If you want to remember a page and come back to it, *bookmark* it in your browser, as explained later in this chapter.

Saving text from a page

You can copy and paste text from a Web page into a word processing document or another type of file. Select the text with your mouse (click and drag the mouse over the text) and press Ctrl+C (⌘+C on the Mac) to save the text in your computer's clipboard. Then switch to the word processing or other program, position the cursor where you want the text to appear, and press Ctrl+V (⌘+V on the Mac) to paste it. Easy enough!

Saving an image

To save an image you see on a Web page, follow these steps:

1. **Right-click the image.**

2. **Choose Save Image As (in Firefox or Chrome) or Save Picture As (in Internet Explorer) from the menu that appears.**

3. **In the Save Image or Save Picture dialog box, move to the folder or directory in which you want to save the graphics file, type a filename in the File Name text box, and click the Save button.**

A note about copyright: Almost all Web pages, along with almost everything else on the Internet, are copyrighted by their authors. (A notable exception is U.S. federal government Web sites, which are all free of copyright.) If you save a Web page or a picture from a Web page, you don't have permission to use it any way you want. Before you reuse the text or pictures, send an e-mail message to the owner of the site. If an address doesn't appear on the page, write for permission to webmaster@*domain.com*, replacing *domain.com* with the domain name part of the URL of the Web page.

Printing pages

To print a page, click the Print button on the toolbar, press Ctrl+P, or choose File➪Print (in Firefox only). The browser has to reformat the page to print, which can take a minute, so remember that patience is a virtue. Fortunately, each browser displays a progress window to let you know how it's doing.

In Internet Explorer, click the down arrow to the right of the Print icon to choose Print (where you can select the printer), Print Preview (where you can see what you're going to print before you waste paper printing the wrong thing), or Page Setup (where you can set margins). Firefox has the same commands, but they're on the File menu (choose File➪Print, File➪Print Preview, and File➪Page Setup).

In Chrome, you can click the Control the Current Page menu (just to the right of the Address box) to find the Print command.

 If the page you want to print uses frames (a technique that divides the browser window into subareas that can scroll and update separately), click in the part of the window you want to print before printing. Otherwise, you might print only the outermost frame, which usually has just a title and some buttons.

Viewing Lots of Web Pages at the Same Time

When we're pointing and clicking from one place to another, we like to open a bunch of browser windows so that we can see where we've been and go back to a previous page by just switching to another window. Or, your browser can display lots of Web pages in one window, by using tabs (as explained in the section "Tab dancing," later in this chapter). You can also arrange windows side by side, which is a good way to, say, compare prices for *The Internet For Dummies,* 12th Edition (Wiley), at various online bookstores. (The difference may be small, but when you're buying 100 copies for everyone on your Christmas list, those pennies can add up. Oh, you weren't planning to do that? Drat.)

Wild window mania

To display a page in a new browser window, click a link with the right mouse button and choose Open in New Window (or Open Link in New Window) from the menu that pops up. To close a window, click the Close (X) button in the upper right corner of the window frame or press Alt+F4, the standard close-window shortcut. (On a Mac, click the red Close button in the upper left corner of the window.)

You can also create a new window without following a link: Press Ctrl+N. (Mac users should think "Alt" and "Apple" for "Ctrl.")

Tab dancing

Firefox, Chrome, and IE have *tabs,* which are multiple pages that you can switch among in a window. (IE 6 and earlier versions don't.) Figure 7-1 shows a Firefox window with three tabs. The names or addresses of the tabs are shown across the top of the browser window, below the browser's menu and toolbars, like old-fashioned manila folder tabs.

Short-attention-span tips

If you have a slow Internet connection, use at least two browser tabs or windows at the same time. While you're waiting for the next page to open in one tab or window, you can read the page that opened a while ago in the other tab or window.

If you have your browser begin downloading a big file, it displays a small window in the corner of your screen. You can click back to the main browser window and continue surfing while the download continues.

Warning: Doing two or three things at a time in your browser when you have a slow Net connection is not unlike squeezing blood from a turnip — only so much blood can be squeezed. In this case, the blood is the amount of data your computer can pump through your modem. A single download task can keep your Internet connection close to 100 percent busy, and anything else you do shares the connection with the download process. When you do two things at a time, therefore, each one happens more slowly than it would by itself.

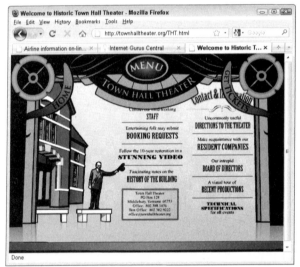

Figure 7-1:
A Firefox window with three tabs.

Just click a tab to show the page. Press Ctrl+T to make a new, empty tab. Click the X on the tab to get rid of it. (In Chrome, right-click the tab and choose Delete from the menu that appears, or hover the mouse over the tab and click the X when it appears.)

As with multiple windows, you can have one tab loading in the background while you're reading another tab, and little rotating arrows on the tab bar show you which ones are loading and which are ready. For most purposes, we find tabs more convenient than windows, but multiple windows are useful if you want to compare two Web pages side by side. You can use both tabs and windows; each window can have multiple tabs.

A Few of Your Favorite Things

You'll find some Web pages that you want to visit over and over again. (We've both visited the Google Web site thousands of times by now.) The makers of fine browsers have, fortunately, provided a handy way for you to remember those URLs, so you don't have to write them on the wall and type them again later.

The idea is simple: Your browser lets you add a Web address to a list on your computer. Later, when you want to go back, you just go to your list and pick the page you want. Firefox and Chrome call these saved Web addresses *bookmarks;* Internet Explorer calls them *favorites.*

Bookmarking with Firefox

Firefox has a Bookmarks choice on its menu where you can find all commands that relate to bookmarks. (That's logical enough, we think.) To bookmark a Web page — that is, to add the address of the page to your bookmarks — choose Bookmarks⇨Bookmark This Page or press Ctrl+D or drag the little icon at the left end of the Address box up to the Bookmarks menu item.

After you create a bookmark, it appears as an entry on the Bookmarks menu. To go to one of the pages on your bookmark list, just choose its entry from the menu.

If you're like most users, your bookmark menu grows and grows and crawls down your screen and eventually ends up flopping on the floor, which is both unattractive and unsanitary. Fortunately, you can smoosh (technical term) your menu into a more tractable form. Choose View⇨Sidebar⇨Bookmarks (or press Ctrl+B) to display the Bookmarks sidebar down the left side of the Firefox window, as shown in Figure 7-2. Then you can move, edit, and delete your bookmarks.

You can go to any bookmarked page by clicking its bookmark in the Bookmarks sidebar. (You can leave this sidebar open while you move around the Web, or close it by clicking the X in its upper right corner.) You can also organize your bookmarks into folders and rename your bookmarks with meaningful names— Web page titles can be long and uninformative.

In the Bookmarks sidebar, click Bookmarks Menu to see the list of your bookmarks. If you want to organize your growing list of bookmarks into folders, right-click Bookmarks Menu and choose New Folder to add a submenu. After you create a folder, you can drag bookmarks and folders up and down to where you want them in the Bookmarks sidebar. Drag an item to a folder to put it in that folder's submenu, and click a folder to display or hide that submenu. Because any changes you make in the Bookmarks sidebar are reflected immediately on the Bookmarks menu, you can easily fiddle with the bookmarks until you have them arranged as you like. Firefox starts out your bookmarks with pages that the Firefox developers want you to look at, but feel free to delete those pages if your tastes are different from theirs.

Figure 7-2:
Use the
Bookmarks
sidebar to
manage
bookmarks.

Creating one-click bookmarks in Firefox

Okay, you've got the Bookmarks menu, which is what you see when you click Bookmarks on the menu at the top of the window. You've got the Bookmarks sidebar, described in the preceding section. Wait — there's more! The Bookmarks toolbar is a row of buttons that usually appears just below the Address box. (If it isn't there, choose View⇨Toolbars⇨Bookmarks Toolbar to display it.) This row of buttons gives you one-button access to a bunch of Firefox developers' favorite Web sites. Wouldn't it be nice if your favorite Web sites appeared there instead? No problem! When you organize your bookmarks in the Bookmarks sidebar, drag your favorite sites onto the Bookmarks Toolbar folder in the sidebar — any sites in this folder automagically appear on the Bookmarks toolbar. Feel free to delete the bookmarks that come with Firefox — the only one we like is the Latest Headlines bookmark, which displays a menu of breaking news stories on the BBC Web site.

Storing favorites with Internet Explorer

Internet Explorer uses a URL-saving system similar to the one in Firefox, although it calls the saved URLs *favorites* rather than bookmarks: You can add the current page to your Favorites folder and then look at and organize your Favorites folder. If you use Windows, this Favorites folder is shared with other programs on your computer. Other programs also can add things to your Favorites folder, so it's a jumble of Web pages, files, and other elements. (To avoid insanity, most people use favorites only for Web pages.)

IE 8 has a Favorites icon — a gold star — just above the upper left corner of the Web page. To add the current page to your favorites, click the Favorites icon (or press Alt+C) and choose Add to Favorites from the menu that appears. The Add a Favorite dialog box, shown in Figure 7-3, displays the page name (which you can edit) and the folder in which the favorite will be saved. Click the Create In box to choose a folder, or click the New Folder button to make a new folder to contain the page's address. Click Add when you're ready to save the favorite.

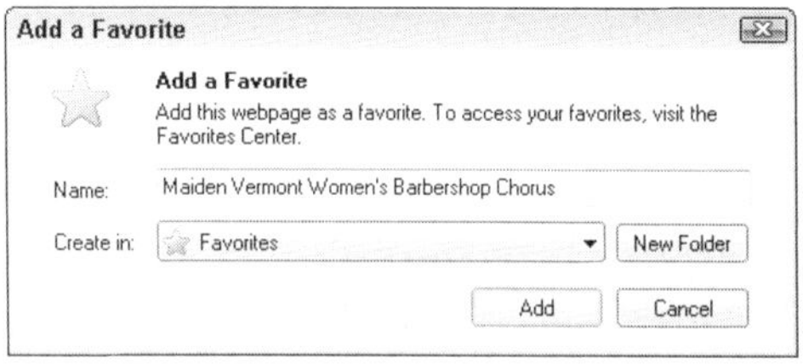

Figure 7-3:
Add a page
to your IE
favorites.

> **Add a Favorite**
>
> ⭐ **Add a Favorite**
> Add this webpage as a favorite. To access your favorites, visit the Favorites Center.
>
> Name: Maiden Vermont Women's Barbershop Chorus
>
> Create in: ⭐ Favorites ▾ [New Folder]
>
> [Add] [Cancel]

IE has a Favorites Explorer bar that looks like the Firefox Bookmarks sidebar, running down the left side of your browser window and showing you your favorites list. Click the Favorites icon (the gold star) to see the Favorites Explorer bar. Click a page name to display that page or click a folder to see (and click) the favorites that the folder contains.

If you want to reorganize your Favorites, just display the Favorites Explorer bar, click the down arrow to the right of Add to Favorites, and choose Organize Favorites. In the Organize Favorites window, shown in Figure 7-4, you can move favorites around, edit them, or delete them. To see what's in a folder, click it. When you're done organizing your favorite items, click Close.

Creating one-click bookmarks in Internet Explorer

 Have you noticed the Favorites (formerly Links) toolbar, which usually appears just below the Address box, to the right of the Favorites icon? (If it isn't there, click the Tools icon above the right corner of the Web page and choose Toolbars⇨Favorites to display it.) You might never want to visit any of the sites that appear by default on this toolbar, but you can put your favorite Web sites there instead. To add the current page to your Links toolbar, click the Add to Favorites Bar icon (a gold star with a green plus sign); an icon for the site appears on your toolbar. This feature is seriously handy for Web sites you visit often.

Figure 7-4:
Organizing
your
Internet
Explorer
favorites.

The Windows Live Toolbar

Windows *Live Essentials* is a bundle of free programs that Microsoft encourages Windows users to download. The "Windows Live Essentials" sidebar in Chapter 13 describes the whole package, but one of these programs affects how IE looks — the Windows Live Toolbar. After it's installed (from `download.live.com`), it appears just below the Address box. Some buttons require you to log in with your Windows Live ID, a free account you use to access various Microsoft services. The toolbar includes these cool boxes and buttons:

✔ **Live Search** is a search box that uses the Microsoft Bing search site (described in Chapter 8).

✔ **What's New** shows your new Windows Live Hotmail messages and other news updates.

✔ **Profile** opens the Microsoft attempt at a social networking site (described in Chapter 18), and **Share** enables you to share bookmarks with people in your network.

✔ **Mail** displays your Windows Live Hotmail account, if you use one (see Chapter 13).

✔ **Photos** and **Calendar** offer a photo album site and a sharable online calendar (see Chapter 18).

✔ **Map the Addresses on This Page** (the pin-in-a-map icon) shows a list of addresses it finds on the page and can display a map of every address.

✔ **Translate This Page** lets you choose a language and provides a translation, which isn't necessarily complete or totally correct, but gives you the general flavor.

If you decide that you don't want to waste your valuable screen space on the Windows Live Toolbar, click the X at its left end and click Disable on the dialog box that appears.

When you organize your favorites, drag your favorite sites and folders into the Favorites Bar folder — any sites in this folder automagically appear on the Links toolbar. Delete any sites in the Favorites Bar folder that aren't your favorites. You can also delete icons right from the Favorites toolbar; right-click one and choose Delete from the menu that appears.

Bookmarking (including one-click) with Chrome

Google Chrome has a clean, spare look with no menus and only a few icons to clutter its window. But the features we love are still there, including book-marks. To add the current page to your list of bookmarks, click the gold-star Bookmark This Page icon at the left end of the Address box. A Bookmark Added box pops up so that you can edit the name for the bookmark and choose which bookmark folder to put the Web page in. (Click Remove if you clicked this icon accidentally!)

 To edit your bookmarks, click the Customize and Control icon, the little wrench to the right of the Address box, and choose Bookmark Manager from the menu that appears. Or, press Ctrl+Shift+B — but who can remember that? You see the Bookmark Manager, shown in Figure 7-5. Click Organize to add folders into which you can drag your bookmarks.

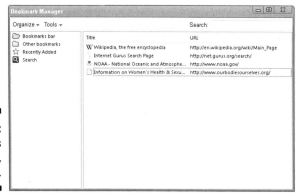

Figure 7-5:
Chrome has bookmarks, too.

When you drag a bookmark into the Bookmarks Bar folder, it appears (where else?) on the Bookmarks bar, between the Address box and the top edge of the Web page in the Chrome window. (If you don't see any bookmarks below the Address box, click the Customize and Control icon and choose Always Show Bookmarks Bar so that it has a check mark next to it.)

Filling In Forms

The Web isn't just for reading — it's for buying stuff, signing up for stuff, and expressing your opinion about stuff. To put your two cents into a Web page, you usually fill out a form that has boxes to type in, check boxes to select, and maybe other clickable stuff. Then you click a Submit button (or a button with another name) to send in the information you entered. Figure 7-6 shows a typical form.

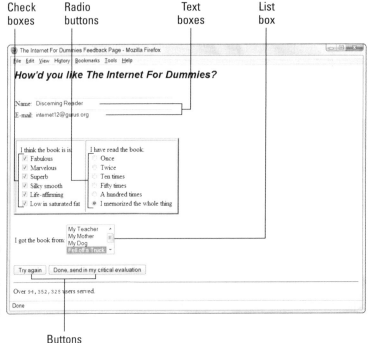

Check boxes   Radio buttons   Text boxes   List box

Figure 7-6:
Just fill out
a few forms.

Buttons

Little boxes all the same

Text boxes in a form are white, fill-in boxes in which you type, in this case, your name and e-mail address. *Check boxes* are little square boxes in which you check whichever ones apply (all of them, we hope, on our sample form). *Radio buttons,* the little round buttons, are similar to check boxes except that you can choose only one of them from each set. In Figure 7-6 (refer to the preceding section), you also see a *list box,* in which you can choose one possibility in the box. In most cases, you see more entries than can fit in the box, so you scroll them up and down. You can usually choose only one entry, though some list boxes let you choose more.

Your browser can keep a secret

When you fill out a form on a Web page, you may need to provide information that you prefer to keep private — your credit card number, for example. Not to worry! Browsers can *encrypt* the information you send to and receive from a *secure Web server.* You can tell when a page was received encrypted from the Web server by the little padlock icon at the right end of the Address box (in Chrome and IE) or in the lower right corner of the browser window (in Firefox). If the padlock doesn't appear, the page wasn't encrypted. To make it clearer, Chrome shows the whole Address box in yellow.

Typed-in data in forms on secure pages are almost always sent encrypted, making it impossible for anyone to snoop on your secrets as they pass through the Net. Encrypted pages are nice, but in practice, it's unlikely that anyone is snooping on your Web session anyway, encrypted or otherwise. The real security problems are elsewhere (refer to Chapter 2).

Firefox and Internet Explorer (IE) have the habit of popping up little boxes to warn you about the dangers of what you're about to do. They display a box when you're about to switch from encrypted to non-encrypted (or back again) transmissions. Most of these warning boxes include a check box you can select to tell the program not to bother you with this type of warning again. After you read the warning, select the check box so that your browser stops nagging you.

Forms also include buttons that determine what happens to the information you enter on the form. Most forms have two of these buttons: one that clears the form fields to their initial state and sends nothing, and one, usually known as the *Submit* button, that sends the filled-out form back to the Web server for processing.

Some Web pages have *search boxes,* which are one-line forms that let you type some text for which to search. Depending on the browser, a Submit button may be displayed to the right of the text area, or you may just press Enter to send the search words to the server. For example, the Google search page at `www.google.com` has a box in which you type a word or phrase; when you press Enter or click the Google Search button, the search begins. (See Chapter 8 to find out what happens!)

Remember the address!

Your browser can remember the entries, such as your name and address, that you frequently type into Web page forms. As you type, your browser may try to spot entries you made earlier and suggest the rest of the entry so that you don't have to type it. If a suggestion pops up from your browser as you're filling in a form, you can click the suggestion to accept it. If you don't like the suggestion, just keep typing.

Knowing Where to Start

When you run your browser, it displays your *start page*. Unfortunately, the people who make browsers usually don't pick pages that we particularly like. Why not tell your browser to start where *you* want to start? You may want to start at the Yahoo! page (www.yahoo.com), which we describe in Chapter 6; or Google (www.google.com); or Wikipedia (en.wikipedia.org for the English language encyclopedia); or the home page of your local newspaper. You can even start with more than one page by setting multiple start pages, and your browser can open each one in a separate tab.

 You can also specify a separate *home page*, which is the page you see if you click the Home icon in your browser. Firefox and IE have a Home icon automatically. If you use Chrome, you have to tell it to display a Home icon by clicking the Customize and Control wrench icon above the upper right corner of the Web page, choosing Options from the menu that appears, clicking the Basics tab if it's not already selected, clicking the Show Home Button on the Toolbar check box so that it contains a check mark, and clicking Close.

The following sections show you how to set both your start page and your home page. Most people set them to the same page (or pages) anyway.

Specifying where Firefox starts

Display the page that you want to use as your start page and home, and then follow these steps.

1. **Choose Tools⇨Options.**

   You see the Options dialog box, shown in Figure 7-7.

2. **Click the Main category icon, if it isn't already selected.**

   This category may already be selected, and its settings appear in the rest of the Options dialog box. The settings you're concerned with are in the Startup section.

3. **Set the When Firefox Starts option.**

   You can choose Show My Home Page (you set your home page in the next step), Show a Blank Page (make Firefox start faster), or Show My Windows and Tabs from Last Time.

4. **Set your home page(s) to the current page(s) by clicking (you guessed it!) the Use Current Pages button.**

5. **Click OK.**

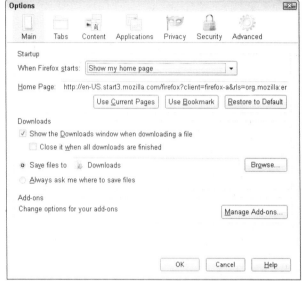

Figure 7-7:
Set a
favorite
Web site as
your start
page in this
dialog box.

You can set Firefox to display a bunch of pages when it starts up, each on its own, separate tab. For example, you might want to have Firefox open a weather-reporting page (such as Weather Underground at www.wunder ground.com), *The New York Times* (www.nytimes.com), or even something silly (like cuteoverload.com), every time you start Firefox. First display the Web pages you want to start with. Then choose Tools⇨Options, click Main, click Use Current Pages, and click OK.

Configuring Internet Explorer start and home pages

Display the page that you want to use as your start page and home page, and then follow these steps:

1. **Click the Tools icon above the upper right corner of the Web page and choose Internet Options from the menu that appears.**

   You see the Internet Options dialog box, shown in Figure 7-8.

2. **Click the General tab, along the top of the dialog box.**

   It's probably already selected, but we say this in case you've been look-ing around at what's on the other tabs.

3. **In the Home Page section, click the Use Current button.**

   The URL of the current page appears in the Address text box. To start with no page, click the Use Blank button.

4. Click OK.

IE also has a nifty command to add a page to your home set of tabs. Just above the top of the Web page, in the middle, is a Home icon. Click the down arrow to the right of the Home icon and choose Add or Change Home Page from the menu that appears. You can choose to use this page as your start page, or to add this page to the set of pages that IE displays when you start the program.

Telling Chrome what to display at start-up

Display the page that you want to use as your start page and home page, and then follow these steps:

1. **Click in the Address box and press Ctrl+C to copy the URL to your Clipboard.**

   You need to paste the address to set your home page. We consider this step to be dim design, and we're hoping that by the time you read this section, the Chrome home page setup has been improved.

2. **Click the Customize and Control wrench icon above the upper right corner of the Web page and choose Options from the menu that appears.**

   You see the Google Chrome Options dialog box, shown in Figure 7-9.

3. **In the On Startup section, choose Open the Home Page, Restore the Pages That Were Open Last, or Open the Following Pages.**

   If you choose the last option, you can click Use Current to set the current page as your start page (or one of several start pages, using tabs).

4. **Set your home page to the current page by choosing Open This Page, clicking in the box to its right, and pressing Ctrl+V to paste the URL from Step 1 into this box.**

   Wouldn't you think that Chrome would have a Use Current button here? Maybe soon.

5. **Click Close.**

Figure 7-9:
Chrome
options
include
setting your
start-up
page.

You might consider setting your home page to what Chrome calls its New Tab page. This page is pretty cool, actually — Chrome displays a bunch of tiny page pages, like thumbnail pictures of the pages, each with a title, showing the pages you've visited most often. It also shows bookmarks you've recently used and pages you've recently closed. Very useful! That's the home page we use.

Who Can Remember All Those Passwords?

Not us. Many Web sites ask you to enter a username and password. If you're buying something from an online store like Amazon.com, you create an account with a username and password that you enter every time you want to buy something. Amazon.com remembers your name, address, and credit card information as part of your account, so you don't need to enter it every time. If you want to read *The New York Times* online at www.nytimes.com, you create an account with a password, too. The account remembers what kinds of news you're interested in reading. After you use the Web for a while, you pile up a heap of usernames and passwords.

See the sidebar "What's the secret word, Mr. Potter?" in Chapter 2 for advice on choosing passwords and keeping track of them safely.

Web browsers offer to remember your usernames and passwords for you. Using this feature can be dangerous if other people use your computer or if you use a computer in a public place, like a library or an Internet café. But if you're the only person who uses your computer, you may want to let your browser do the work of remembering some, if not all, of your usernames and passwords.

When you see a Web page that asks for a username and password, your browser may pop up a little window that offers to remember the username and password you enter, similar to Figure 7-10. If you click Yes, the next time you arrive at the same page, your browser may fill in your username and password for you.

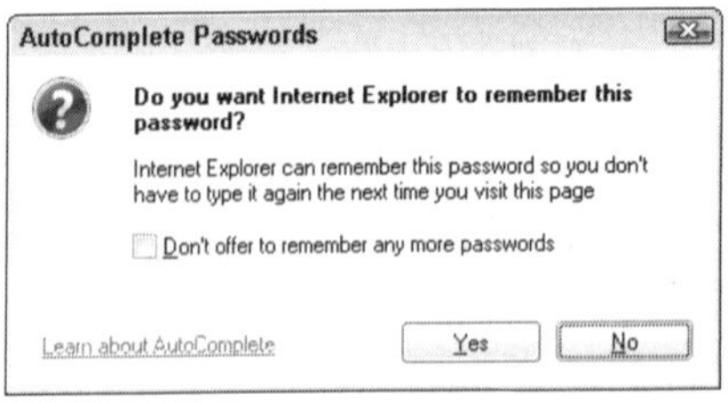

Figure 7-10:
Storing
passwords
in your
browser.

AutoComplete Passwords

Do you want Internet Explorer to remember this password?

Internet Explorer can remember this password so you don't have to type it again the next time you visit this page.

☐ Don't offer to remember any more passwords

Learn about AutoComplete   [Yes]   [No]

Depending on who else has access to your computer, you might let your browser remember only passwords to accounts that don't involve spending money or revealing personal information. For example, if we have an account at a Harry Potter fan site that enables us to participate in online discussions, the danger of having someone break into this account is a lot less daunting than the thought of someone hacking into an online bank account. Unless your computer is in a physically secure place, don't let your browser remember passwords that have any real power.

Storing passwords in Firefox

You can control whether and how your browser stores these passwords. In Firefox, follow these steps:

1. **Choose Tools⇨Options.**

   You see the Options dialog box, with a list of the categories of options across the top (refer to Figure 7-7).

2. **Click the Security category and look in the Passwords section.**

3. **Set the Remember Passwords for Sites check box.**

   Click it to clear the check mark if you want to turn off this feature (or click it again to turn it back on).

4. **If you want to see the list of usernames that Firefox has saved, click the Saved Passwords button.**

   You can review or delete usernames that Firefox is remembering for you. You can't see the passwords, but if you delete a username, the password goes, too. Click Close when you're done.

5. **Select the Use a Master Password check box to set a master password that you need to type only once, at the beginning of each Firefox session.**

   This option reduces the number of passwords you need to remember while maintaining some security.

6. **Click OK to close the Options dialog box.**

Storing passwords in IE

In Internet Explorer, remembering usernames and passwords is the job of the AutoComplete feature, which you set up by following these simple steps:

1. **Choose Tools⇨Internet Options.**

   You see the Internet Options dialog box (refer to Figure 7-8).

2. **Click the Content tab.**

3. **In the AutoComplete section, click the Settings button.**

   You see the AutoComplete Settings dialog box.

4. **Click the check boxes to control which kinds of entries IE stores.**

   IE doesn't show you a list of the passwords you saved, but you can turn the feature on and off by selecting the Ask Me Before Saving Passwords check box. The User Names and Passwords On Forms check box controls whether IE fills in your stored passwords on forms.

5. Click OK to close the AutoComplete Settings dialog box, and click OK again to close the Internet Options dialog box.

Storing passwords in Chrome

The Chrome settings for remembering passwords are more like those in Firefox. Follow these steps:

1. **Click the Customize and Control wrench icon and choose Options from the menu that appears.**

   You see the Google Chrome Options dialog box (refer to Figure 7-9).

2. **Click the Personal Stuff tab.**

3. **In the Passwords section, click Offer to Save Passwords or Never Save Passwords.**

4. **If you want to review the passwords that Chrome has already saved, click Show Saved Passwords.**

   You can't see the passwords, just the usernames, and you can remove any you don't want saved. Click Close when you're done.

5. **Click Close.**

Cookies Are (Usually) Your Friends

To enhance your online experience, browser makers invented a type of special message that lets a Web site recognize you when you revisit that site. They thoughtfully store this info, called a *cookie,* on your very own machine. See the section "Cookies aren't so bad" in Chapter 2 for a full description of cookies and how they compare to more serious security threats. You can control which sites can store cookies on your computer.

Usually, the Web site that sets a cookie is the only one that reads the cookie. However, *third-party cookies* can be set by one Web site and read by another. Third-party cookies are used by servers that deliver advertisements and those annoying pop-up and pop-under ads. We recommend that you accept most cookies but block third-party cookies.

Burning cookies in Firefox

Choose Tools➪Options, click the Privacy category, and look in the History section. If Remember History is selected, Firefox stores cookies. If you want more control over what it stores, change it to Use Custom Settings for History. This setting displays these cookie-related check boxes:

✔ **Accept Cookies from Sites:** We recommend that you leave this one selected.

✔ **Accept Third-Party Cookies:** Click this one to remove its check mark.

You can specify which sites can and cannot store cookies by clicking the Exceptions button. You can enter the Web addresses that you definitely trust with cookies (like the shopping sites you frequent) or that you don't trust (like advertising sites).

You can take a look at the cookies on your computer, too. Click the Show Cookies button and scroll down the list of sites. If you see one that you don't recognize or that sounds suspicious, click it and click the Remove Cookies button.

Exploring cookies in IE

Choose Tools➪Internet Options and click the Privacy tab. IE displays a slider that you can drag up and down to increase or decrease your level of privacy. By default, Internet Explorer sets your privacy level to Medium, allowing cookies except for third-party cookies. If you want to specify exactly how cookies are saved, click the Advanced button to see the Advanced Privacy Settings dialog box and then select the Override Automatic Cookie Handling check box. The options are

✔ **First-Party Cookies:** You can choose to accept or to block or to be prompted to choose, although this option gets tiresome quickly if you encounter a lot of cookies. Some sites can store three or more cookies *per page*. Choose Accept.

✔ **Third-Party Cookies:** Just say no to (that is, choose Block) third-party cookies.

✔ **Always Allow Session Cookies:** This check box lets through all *session* cookies, a type of cookie used to track a single instance of your visit to a Web site. These cookies are commonly used by shopping sites such as Amazon.com and are harmless. Select this option so that it contains a check mark.

Cookies and Chrome

Click the Customize and Control wrench icon, choose Options from the menu that appears, and click the Under the Hood tab in the Google Chrome Options dialog box that appears. Select the cookie setting labeled Restrict How Third-Party Cookies Can Be Used. (In our humble opinion, it's your best bet.)

If you want to see which cookies are stored on your computer, click the Show Cookies button to display the Cookies dialog box. You can see the Web sites that set the cookies, the names of the cookies, and their contents. (Most are boring.) If you don't like the looks of a cookie, click it and then click Remove.

Where Have You Been?

Browsers keep a *history list* of the Web sites you've been to. No, your browser isn't spying on you; the history list remembers pages you went to earlier, even days ago, so that you can find them again. You can see your history list, and return to any page on it by clicking it. Here's how:

- ✔ **Firefox:** The History command on the menu displays where you've been. You can also press Ctrl+H to display the list down the left side of your browser window, arranged by day. Close the history list by clicking the X in its upper right corner.

- ✔ **Internet Explorer:** The history list is associated with the Back and Forward buttons. Click the down arrow between the Forward button (the white, right-arrow icon) and the Address box, and IE displays the pages you've been to recently. You can choose History from the end of the list to display your history list down the left side of your browser window.

- ✔ **Chrome:** Click and hold the Back button and choose Show Full History from the menu that appears, or press Ctrl+H. You see a list of Web pages by day, with the time you viewed each page.

Oh, nowhere, really

Some of our readers have asked us how to clear out their browsing, presumably because they meant to type www.disney.com but their fingers slipped and it came out www.hot-xxx-babes.com instead. (It could happen to anyone.) Because some of the requests sounded fairly urgent, here are the gruesome details:

- ✔ **Firefox:** Choose Tools➪Clear Recent History. Choose how far back to forget (the default is the last hour) and click Clear Now.

- ✔ **Internet Explorer:** Click Safety (above the upper right corner of the Web page) and choose Delete Browsing History from the menu that appears. (Hmm, it's right at the top. There must be a lot of sloppy typists out there.) In the Delete Browsing History dialog box, clear all check boxes except the History check box (by clicking each one) and click Delete.

- ✔ **Chrome:** The history list (displayed by pressing Ctrl+H) is sorted by day, and next to each date is a Delete History for This Day link.

Your browsing is nobody else's business

If you're using someone else's computer, and especially if you're using a public computer in a library or Internet café, you should delete your browsing history and any other information about your session that might be stored on the computer. Otherwise, the next person to sit down at the computer might find your browsing history rather interesting, especially if the browser has thoughtfully stored the usernames and password you entered.

Here's how to delete your browsing information (history, cookies, and stored passwords):

- ✔ **Firefox:** Choose Tools⇨Clear Recent History, set the time range to Everything, and click Clear Now.

- ✔ **IE:** You can use InPrivate Browsing, by clicking Safety and choosing InPrivate Browsing. If you forgot to do that when you started browsing, choose Safety⇨Delete Browsing History, select all the check boxes, and click Delete.

- ✔ **Chrome:** You can browse incognito. (Don't forget your trench coat and fedora.) Click the Customize and Control wrench icon and choose New Incognito Window. Or, you can right-click any link or bookmark and choose Open Link in Incognito Window. If you forgot to go incognito, you can click the Customize and Control wrench icon, choose Clear Browsing Data, select all the check boxes, set the period to Everything, and click Clear Browsing Data.

Blocking Pop-Up Windows

Pop-up windows, as described in Chapter 2, are browser windows that open without your asking for them, usually at the command of the Web site you're viewing. Some Web sites display so many pop-ups that your computer becomes unusable until you can close them all. If you've encountered these sites, you'll be glad to hear that your browser can block most (though not all) pop-up windows.

No pop-ups in Firefox

In Firefox, choose Tools⇨Options to open the Options window and click the Content category, and you'll see the Block Pop-up Windows check box. We leave it selected.

Blocking all pop-ups makes a few Web sites stop working. In particular, some shopping sites pop up small windows in which you have to type credit card verification information. Online help sometimes appears in pop-ups, too.

Firefox thoughtfully includes an Exception button that lets you specify Web sites whose pop-ups are okay with you.

When a Web site tries to display a pop-up, you see at the top of the Web page a message saying "Firefox prevented this site from opening a popup window." Click the Options button and choose from the menu that appears:

- **Allow Popups from *Sitename*** puts this site on your Allowed list.

- **Enable Popup Blocker Options** displays the Allowed Sites dialog box so that you can edit your list of sites.

- **Don't Show This Message When Popups Are Blocked** continues to block pop-ups, without asking every time it blocks one.

Click the red X at the right end of the message to make the message go away.

Blocking pop-ups in Internet Explorer

Microsoft finally added a pop-up blocker in response to the growing popularity of Firefox. Choose Tools➪Pop-up Blocker to turn this feature off or back on. (We leave ours on.)

The IE pop-up blocker displays a "Pop-up blocked" message at the top of the Web page whenever it blocks a pop-up window, and clicking the message displays a similar set of options. You can tweak your pop-up blocking options at any time by choosing Tools➪Pop-Up Blocker➪Pop-Up Blocker Settings.

Chrome and pop-ups

Chrome includes a pop-up blocker, too. When it blocks a pop-up, you see a message in the lower right corner of the browser window. You can click the message and then choose the first option (the exact address of the pop-up) to display it, or choose Always Allow Popups to allow pop-ups from the site.

When Browsers Go Bad

If your browser looks odd, try these tricks:

- **If the Web page looks garbled,** click the Reload or Refresh icon (the circular arrow) to load the page again. Maybe it was damaged during its arduous trek across the Net.

- **If the whole top of the window is gone** — you have no window title bar or menu bar — you're in Full Screen mode. Press F11 to return to normal.

✔ **If the browser restarted and is telling you which fabulous new features it now has,** it probably just downloaded an updated version of the program and had to restart itself to complete the installation. Read the message appreciatively and then close the tab or window.

✔ **If some of your toolbars are missing,** you may need to give a command to bring them back. In Firefox, choose View⇨Toolbars; if a check mark doesn't appear to the left of one of the toolbars, choose the toolbar to put a check mark back in front of it and to redisplay that window component. In IE, choose Tools⇨Toolbars.

✔ **If the buttons on your toolbar aren't the buttons you're used to,** some helpful person (or interfering busybody) may have changed them when you weren't looking. In Firefox, right-click a blank place on the toolbar or menu bar, choose Customize from the menu that appears, click Restore Default Set, and click Done. In IE, right-click a blank place on the toolbar, choose Customize⇨Add or Remove Commands, click Reset, and click Close.

✔ **If the menu bar is missing in IE** — no File-Edit-View set of commands that you're probably used to, then hear this: Microsoft is abolishing the menu bar in all its programs. However, you can display it temporarily by pressing the Alt key. Or, put it back for good by right-clicking a blank place on the toolbar and choosing Menu Bar from the menu that appears.

✔ **If your browser is just acting weird,** close all your browser windows, take a few deep breaths, and run your browser again. If the situation is ugly, try restarting the computer. (Save any unsaved work first.)

✔ **If your browser, particularly IE, still looks strange,** especially if it's showing a lot of ads that you didn't ask for, your computer is probably infected with spyware. See Chapter 2 for a definition of spyware, and see the section in Chapter 4 about detecting spyware for advice on getting rid of it.

Getting Plugged In with Plug-Ins

Web pages with text and pictures are old hat. Now, Web pages have to have pictures that sing and dance or ticker-style messages that move across the page, or they have to be able to play a good game of chess with you. Every month, new types of information appear on the Web, and browsers have to keep up. You can extend your browser's capabilities with *plug-ins* — add-on programs that glue themselves to the browser and add even more features. Internet Explorer can also extend itself by using *ActiveX* controls, which are another (less secure) type of add-on program.

What are you to do when your browser encounters new kinds of information on a Web page? Get the plug-in program that handles that kind of information and glue it to the browser program. *Star Trek* fans can think of plug-ins as parasitic life forms that attach themselves to your browser and enhance its intelligence.

When you restart Firefox, maybe because it updated itself, it may display the Add-Ons window, showing a list of installed add-ons. (You can display this window at any time by choosing Tools➪Add-ons.) You can click Find Updates to update any add-on for which there's a newer version on the Web.

Two essential plug-ins

Here are just two useful plug-ins you may want to add to your browser:

- ✔ **Flash Player:** Plays both audio and video files in addition to other types of animations. Widely used on Web pages, it's available at `adobe.com/products/flashplayer`. Using Flash, you can view videos on YouTube (see Chapter 9). Flash can also play *streaming* sound and video files while you download them. Our favorite site with streaming audio is the National Public Radio Web site (`www.npr.org`), where you can hear recent NPR radio stories. Another favorite is the BBC at `www.bbc.co.uk` with news in 43 languages (really) and other BBC programs 24 hours a day.

- ✔ **Adobe Acrobat:** Displays Acrobat files formatted exactly the way the author intended. Lots of useful Acrobat files are out there, including many U.S. tax forms (at `www.irs.ustreas.gov`). You can find Acrobat at `get.adobe.com/reader`.

How to use plug-ins

After you download a plug-in from the Net, run it (double-click its icon or filename) to install it. Depending on what the plug-in does, you follow different steps to try it out — usually, you find a file that the plug-in can play and watch (or listen) as the plug-in plays it.

After you install the plug-in, you don't have to do anything to run it. It fires up automatically whenever you view a Web page containing information that requires the plug-in.

To confuse matters, Firefox also allows you to install add-in programs written in its own, special extension language. Go to `addons.mozilla.org/firefox` to find out more about them. Popular add-ons include programs to display maps or weather forecasts, see the inner workings of Firefox, or see price comparisons from other Web sites.

Chapter 8

Needles and Haystacks: Finding Almost Anything on the Web

"*O*kay, all this great stuff is out there on the Internet. How do I find it?" That's an excellent question and thanks for asking. Questions like that one are what make this country strong and vibrant. We salute you and say, "Keep asking questions!" Next question, please.

Oh, you want an *answer* to your question. Fortunately, quite a bit of (technical term follows) stuff-finding stuff is on the Web. More particularly, free services known as *search engines* and *directories* are available that cover most of the interesting material on the Web. There's even a free encyclopedia, written by Internet users like you.

You can search in dozens or hundreds of different ways, depending on what you're looking for and how you prefer to search. Search can take some practice because billions of Web pages are lurking out on the Net, most of which have nothing to do with the topic you're looking for. (John has remarked that his ideal restaurant has only one item on the menu, but it's exactly what he wants. The Internet is about as far from that ideal as you can possibly imagine.)

TIP

Search engine, directory — what's the difference?

When we talk about a *directory*, we mean a listing like an encyclopedia or a library's card catalog. (Well, like the computer system that *replaced* the card catalog.) A directory has named categories with entries assigned to them partly or entirely by human catalogers. You look up categories by finding one you want and seeing what it contains.

A s*earch engine,* on the other hand, periodically looks at every page it can find on the Internet, extracts keywords from them (all words except for *and, the,* and the like), and makes a big list. (Yes, it takes a lot of computers. Google has several hundred thousand of them.) The search engine then tries to figure out which pages are most important, using factors such as how many other sites link to that page, and gives each page a score. You use the search engine by specifying some words that seem likely, and

it finds all entries that contain that word, ranking them by their score.

We think of the index in the back of the book as a hard-copy equivalent of a search engine; it has its advantages and disadvantages, as do directories, which are more like this book's table of contents. Directories are organized better, but search engines are easier to use and more comprehensive. Directories use consistent terminology, and search engines use whichever terms the underlying Web pages use. Directories contain fewer useless pages, but search engines are updated more often.

Some overlap exists between search engines and directories — Yahoo! includes a directory and a search engine; Google, which is mainly a search engine, includes a version of the Open Directory Project (ODP) directory.

To provide a smidgen of structure to this discussion, we describe several different sorts of searches:

- **Built-in searches:** Topic searches that a browser does automatically, and why we're not always thrilled about it

- **Goods and services:** Stuff to buy or find out about, from mortgages to mouthwash

- **People:** Actual human beings whom you may want to contact, find out more about, or spy on

- **Topics:** Places, things, ideas, companies — anything you want to find out more about

To find topics, we use the various online search engines and directories, such as Google and Yahoo!. To find people, however, we use directories of people — and those are (fortunately) different from directories of Web pages. If you're wondering what we're talking about, read on!

Your Basic Search Strategy

When we look for topics on the Net, we always begin with a search engine, usually Google. (The word *google* has now been "verbed," much to the dismay of the Google trademark lawyers.)

You use all search engines in more or less the same way:

1. **Start your Web browser, such as Chrome, Firefox, or Internet Explorer.**

   Flip to Chapter 6 if you don't know what a browser is.

2. **Go to your favorite search engine's home page.**

   You can try one of these URLs (Web addresses): `www.google.com`, `www.yahoo.com`, or `www.bing.com`. We list the URLs of other search sites later in this section.

   Or, just click in the Search box in the upper right corner of your browser window, to the right of the Address box.

3. **Type some likely keywords in the Search box (either your browser's search box or the search box that appears on the search engine's home page) and press Enter.**

   After a delay (usually brief, but after all, the Web *is* big), the search engine returns a page with some links to pages that it thinks match your keywords. The full list of links that match your keywords may be way too long to deal with — say, 300,000 of them — but the search engine tries to put them in a reasonable order and lets you look at them a screenful at a time.

4. **Adjust and repeat your search until you find something you like.**

   One trick is to pick keywords that relate to your topic from two or three different directions, such as `ethopian restaurants trumansburg` or `war women song`. Think of words that would be on a page containing the information you want. After some clicking around to get the hang of it, you find all sorts of good stuff.

5. **If the search engine is producing results too scattered to be useful and you can't think of any better keywords, try Yahoo! Directory at `dir.yahoo.com` or Google Directory at `www.google.com/dirhp`.**

   When you see a list of links to topic areas, click a topic area of interest. In the directory approach, you begin at a general topic and become more and more specific. Each page has links to pages that become increasingly specific until they link to actual pages that are likely to be of interest.

The lazy searcher's search page

You may feel a wee bit overwhelmed by all the search directories and search engines we discuss in this chapter. If it makes you feel any better, so do we.

To make a little sense of all this stuff, we made ourselves a search page that connects to all the directories and search engines we use — call it

one-stop searching. You can use it, too. Give it a try at `net.gurus.org/search`.

In the not unlikely event that new search systems are created or some existing ones have moved or died, this page gives you our latest greatest list and lets you sign up for e-mailed updates whenever we change it.

Search, Ho!

Once upon a time in an Internet far, far away, lots of search engines and directories battled with each other to see which would be the favorite. Participants were AltaVista and Dogpile and lots of other sites you can find in earlier editions of this book. Well, it seems that the first pangalactic search war is pretty much over, with Google and Yahoo! the victors — at least for now. However, Microsoft is trying to mount a new campaign with its Bing search engine. Visit `net.gurus.org/search` for all the exciting developments.

Google, our favorite search engine

Our favorite Web search engine is Google. It has little (software) robots that spend their time merrily visiting Web pages all over the Net and reporting what they see. It makes a humongous index of which words occurred in which pages; when you search for something, it picks pages from the index that contain the words you asked for. Google uses a sophisticated ranking system, based on how many *other* Web sites refer to each page in the index. Usually, the Google ranking puts the best pages first.

The number-one reason a search doesn't find anything

Well, it may not be *your* number-one reason, but it's *our* number-one reason: A search word is spelled wrong or mistyped. John notes that his fingers insist on typing *Interent,* which doesn't find much — other than Web pages from other people who can't spell or type. Google

often catches spelling mistakes and helpfully suggests alternatives. We sometimes use a Google search to check the preferred spelling of words that haven't made it into the dictionary yet. (Thanks to our friend Jean Armour Polly, for reminding us about this problem.)

Refining your search

Using Google or any other search engine is an exercise in remote-control mind reading. You have to guess words that will appear on the pages you're looking for. Sometimes, that's easy — if you're looking for recipes for Key lime pie, key lime pie is a good set of search words because you know the name of what you're looking for. On the other hand, if you have forgotten that the capital of France is Paris, it's sometimes hard to tease a useful page out of a search engine because you don't know which words to look for. (If you try France capital, some search engines show you info about investment banking and Fort de France, which is the capital of the French overseas département of Martinique. Many people must ask this question, because Google takes pity on you and tells you at the top: "Capital: Paris.")

Now that we have you all discouraged, try some Google searches. Direct your browser to www.google.com. You see a screen like the one shown in Figure 8-1.

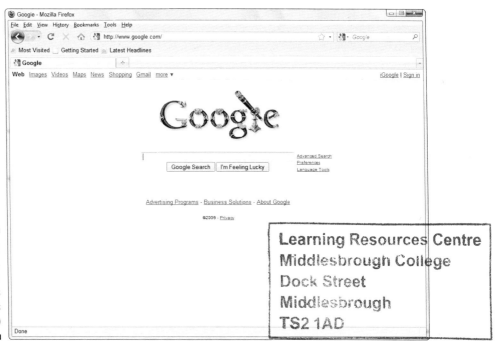

Figure 8-1: Google, classic style. (It was Galileo's birthday.)

Type some search terms, and Google finds the pages that best match your terms. That's "*best* match," not "match" — if it can't match all the terms, it finds pages that match as well as possible. Google ignores words that occur too often to be usable as index terms, both the obvious (ones such as and, the, and of) and merely routine (terms such as internet and mail). These rules can sound somewhat discouraging, but in fact it's still not hard to get useful results from Google. You just have to think up good search terms. Try that recipe example by typing *key lime pie* and clicking the Search button. You see a response like the one shown in Figure 8-2.

Your results won't look exactly like the ones shown in Figure 8-2 because Google will have updated its database since this book was published. Most of the pages that Google found do, in fact, have something to do with Key lime pie — some have good recipes. Google says it found 871,000 matches (yow!), but in the interest of sanity it shows you about 100 of them, 10 at a time. Although that's still probably more than you want to look at, you should at least look at the next couple of screens of matches if the first screen doesn't have what you want. Because the list includes a lot of restaurants with Key lime pie on the menu and a hair salon named Key Lime Pie, you can just narrow the search by adding the keyword `recipe`. Search engines are dumb; you have to add the intelligence. At the bottom of the Google screen are page numbers; click Next to go to the next page.

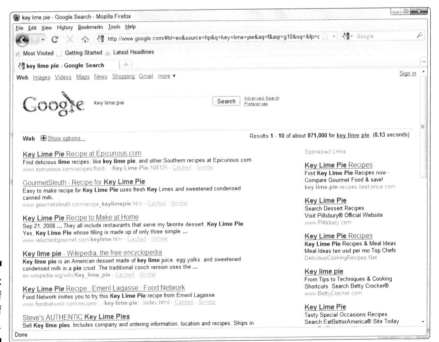

Figure 8-2:
Plenty of pages of pie.

The links in the right column and sometimes at the top of the results are "sponsored" links — that is, paid ads, ranked by how much the advertiser was willing to pay. Often, they're worth clicking, but remember that they're ads.

The I'm Feeling Lucky button searches and takes you directly to the first link, which works, well, when you're lucky.

Handy search engine targeting tips

Google makes it easy to refine your search even more specifically to target the pages you want to find. After each search, your search terms appear in a box at the top of the page so that you can change them and try again. Here are some tips on how you may want to change your terms:

✔ If two or more words should appear together, put quotes around them, as in `"Elvis Presley"`. You should do that with the pie search (`"key lime pie"`) because, after all, that's the pie's name, although in this example, Google is clever enough to realize that it's a common phrase and pretends that you typed the quotes anyway.

✔ Use + and – to indicate words that must either appear or not appear, such as `+Elvis +Costello -Presley` if you're looking for the modern Elvis, not the classic one.

✔ Capitalization doesn't matter. We use all lowercase for our search terms.

Even more Google options

Although Google looks very simple, it has plenty of other options that can be handy. You can

✔ **Get there from here.** Type a street address, and Google offers a link to a map. Type a person's name and a full or partial address, at least the state abbreviation, and Google gives you addresses and phone numbers. Type a phone number, and it often gives you the name and address. (Try typing *202-456-1414*). The information is all collected from public sources, but if you find this process a bit too creepy, look yourself up and if it finds you, it includes a link to a page where you can have your info removed.

✔ **Search Usenet for information.** *Usenet* is the giant collection of Internet *newsgroups* (online discussion groups) that has been around since before the Web. Simply click the Groups link above the Google search box. If a topic has been discussed in the past 28 years on Usenet (as it seems most topics have), this technique is the best way to find the messages about that topic. It's a useful place to find out how to fix computer problems — most likely, whatever question you have has been asked and answered on Usenet, and Google has all of it. (John found things there that he wrote in 1981.) To browse around Usenet newsgroups, start at `groups.google.com`. For a description of Usenet, see `net.gurus.org/usenet`.

✔ **Search for images and videos as well as for text.** Often, Google shows some relevant images or videos at the bottom of its search results. You can click any of them, or to see more images or videos, just click the Image or Videos links at the top of any Google search page. Google has no idea what each image or video is but looks at the surrounding text and the filename of the image or video and does a remarkably good job of guessing. If you search for a *key lime pie* image, you indeed see dozens of pictures of tasty pies, and a video search finds a lot of pie-preparation videos. The SafeSearch feature omits pictures of naked people and the like. If you turn it off, you can find some impressively unsafe pictures.

✔ **Read the news.** Google News (click the News link or start at news . google.com) shows a summary of current online news culled automatically from thousands of sources all over the world. ***Warning:*** If you're interested in current events, you can easily waste 12 hours a day following links from here.

✔ **Limit your search to documents in a specific language.** There's no sense in finding pages in a language you can't read, although Google has a subsystem that can try, with mixed success, to translate pages from certain other languages. Click the Language Tools link to the right of the search box.

✔ **Do painless arithmetic.** Google is even a calculator. Type *2+2* and Google says 2 + 2 = 4. It knows units, so if you type *4 feet 8.5 inches,* Google says 4 feet 8.5 inches = 1.4351 meters. It can also convert currencies.

Searching from your cellphone

Google isn't limited to the Internet; you can use it from any phone that can send and receive text messages. Google has a special five-digit phone number — 46645 (GOOGL) — that you can text from any phone that can send and receive text messages. Here's how:

1. **Compose a text message to the phone number 46645 (GOOGL).**

2. **In the text of the message, type a Google search command.**

   Here are some search commands you can use:

   • For driving directions, type the two addresses separated by *to.* For example, type *1600 Pennsylvania Avenue, Washington DC to 1 Fifth Avenue, New York, NY.*

   • For nearby restaurants, type the name or type of restaurant followed by the city and state or the zip code. For example, type *pizza Middlebury VT.*

   • For movie times, type the name of the movie followed by the city and state or zip code.

   • For help with other commands you can use, type *help.*

3. **Send the message.**

   Within a few minutes, you receive a text message back from Google with the results of your search.

See Google SMS, at sms.google.com, for more information. If your phone has a Web browser, you can use Google from it, too, the same way you visit any other Web page.

Bing!

Microsoft never cedes any part of the computer business without a struggle to the death, and Web search is no exception. After many false starts over many years, its new Bing search engine, shown in Figure 8-3, shows promise. Its basic operation is a lot like Google: You type some search terms and it finds you some Web pages. If you would rather see images or videos, look at the clickable Images and Videos links at the top of the page, just like Google. If you want maps and satellite images, use the Maps link, just like the one at Google. If you're looking for news stories, well, you get the idea. If imitation is the sincerest form of flattery, Google must be feeling extremely flattered.

Figure 8-3:
Bing, ready
to go, with
a bonus
geography
lesson.

Bing isn't exactly the same as Google. In most cases in its results, it suggests related searches you might want to try. The video search runs previews of the videos it found if you mouse over any of them, which is kind of cute. Its satellite images are different from Google's, so you might see a clearer view in one than the other. Overall, we don't find any overwhelming reason to prefer Bing, but it's worth a look.

A significant difference in Bing is that Microsoft has made it easy to embed Bing searches into other Web sites, including a split of the money from any ads in the search results, so you can expect to find Bing lurking in lots of places on the Net.

Google does more than search

Here are a bunch of other Web-based services that Google offers. (As far as we can tell, all these services are part of the Google Grand Plan for Global Domination, but the services are free and good, so we use them.)

You can find files fast on your own computer. Google offers Google Desktop, a program you can download to your PC that lets you do Google-like searches (while viewing Google-like ads) of the contents of your PC's hard drive. We find Google Desktop particularly useful for finding old files and e-mail messages that we're convinced are somewhere on our computers. Download it from `desktop.google.com`.

You can see a map of almost anywhere. At Google Maps, you type an address and see a map of the area or a satellite photo of the same area or both superimposed. Try it at `maps.google.com`. Or, if you're tired of hearing about Google all the time, try MapQuest, at `www.mapquest.com`, another excellent map site. Even cooler is Google Earth (at `earth.google.com`), which displays 3-D maps and images.

You can create and store word processing documents and spreadsheets. Why buy Microsoft Word or Microsoft Excel or WordPerfect when Google Docs & Spreadsheets can do the job? Go to `docs.google.com`, create a free Google account, and go to it. All you need is your browser. Neither the word processor nor the spreadsheet program is as powerful as PC-based programs such as Word and Excel, but for basic documents, they do the job. One of the nicest features is that you can share your documents and spreadsheets with your co-workers and friends so that they can see and edit the documents, too. For more information, see the section in Chapter 18 about sharing documents and calendars.

You can send and receive e-mail. We tell you about Google Mail (Gmail) in Chapter 13.

You can organize and display your digital photos. Google offers the Picasa program (at `picasa.google.com`), which helps you organize your photos, provides a photo editor, and enables you to upload them to your own photo Web site.

Google adds more features almost every week. To see what it's offering, start at `google.com`, click More, and choose Even More from the menu that appears.

Browsing with Directories

Sometimes a Web search just doesn't find what you're looking for. Coming up with the right search terms can be tricky if no specific word or phrase sums up what you want to know. This is the moment to try a Web directory. If you know in general but not in detail what you're looking for, clicking up and down through directory pages is a good way to narrow your search and find pages of interest.

Yahoo for directories!

Yahoo! (yes, the exclamation point is part of its name) is one of the oldest directories — and still a good one. Search for entries or click from category to category until you find something you like. Start at `dir.yahoo.com`. (At least the page name doesn't use an exclamation point.) As with all Web pages, the exact design may have changed by the time you read this section. A whole bunch of categories and subcategories are listed; click any of them to see another page that has even more subcategories and links to actual Web pages. You can click a link to a page if you see one you like, or click a sub-subcategory, and so on. Figure 8-4 shows the Yahoo! Directory page for Recreation & Sports.

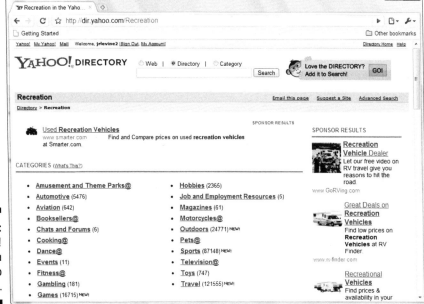

Figure 8-4:
Yahoo!
shows you
how to
have fun.

The 404 blues

More often than we want to admit, when you click a link from a search results page, you see — rather than the promised page — a message such as `404 Not Found`. What did you do wrong? Nothing. Web pages come and go and move around with great velocity, and the various Web search engines were designed as delivery vehicles (not garbage trucks), so they do a lousy job of cleaning out links to old, dead pages that have gone away.

At least the search engines are a bit better in this regard than the manual directories. That's because search engines have software robots (called *spiders* because they roam the Web) that revisit all indexed pages every once in a while and note whether they still exist. Even so, many lonely months can pass between robot visits, and a great deal can happen to a page in the meantime. Google *caches* (stores) a copy of most pages it visits, so even if the original has gone away, you can click the Cache link at the end of a Google index entry to see a copy of the page as it was when Google last looked at it.

(continued)

(continued)

Here are some other ways to chase down a tantalizing link that has wandered off into nowhere:

✔ The Internet Archive operates a nifty service, the Wayback Machine, that can retrieve older versions of Web sites. Enter your broken link in its search box at `www.archive.org`. (Yes, this site owns a lot of computers too.)

✔ Sometimes Web sites try to tidy up a bit and move their files around in the process. If the broken link is a long one — say, `www.frobliedoop.org/glompty-dompty/snrok/amazingtip.html` — try its shorter versions: `www.frobliedoop.org/glompty-dompty/snrok` or `www.frobliedoop.org/glompty-dompty` or

even `www.frobliedoop.org` to find clues to where they put that tip. Also try a Google search on just the filename, such as `amazingtip.html`. You might find a copy at another Web site.

✔ Finally, we should mention that Web sites sometimes shut down, because of either equipment failure or periodic maintenance. (Late nights, Sunday mornings, and major holidays are favorite times for the latter.) Your 404 link just might magically work tomorrow.

Bad links are all just part of life on the online frontier — the high-tech equivalent of riding your horse along the trail in the Old West and noticing that there sure are a lot of bleached-white cattle skulls lying around.

Early on, you could easily submit a Web page to Yahoo! by simply entering a description of the page and its Web address into the Submissions page and waiting a week or so for the editors to look at the new page. Submitting pages is now so popular that normal submissions take a long, long time (months) before anyone on staff looks at them, unless you pay them $299 a year for the "express" service. You can draw your own conclusions about how the fee affects what information gets into Yahoo! (and what doesn't).

For facts, try Wikipedia first

Wikipedia, at `en.wikipedia.org`, is an encyclopedia you can use for free over the Internet. The site looks like Figure 8-5. *Wiki* means fast in Hawaiian (actually, *wikiwiki* does, best known before the Internet as the name of the interterminal bus at the Honolulu airport), and Wikipedia has earned its name. The Wikipedia project, which started in 2001, has grown to more than 3 million articles in English, covering almost every conceivable topic, from the Battle of Dunkirk to *Dummies* books. Yes, it even has a Key lime pie article, where you read this: "Key lime pie is made with canned sweetened condensed milk, since fresh milk was not a common commodity in the Florida Keys before modern refrigerated distribution methods." Also, since 2006, it has been the Florida state pie.

If you're looking for the scoop on most topics, Wikipedia is a helpful place to start. You can search for article titles or article text. Words in the article body that are highlighted in blue link to other articles in Wikipedia. Many articles also have links to external Web sites that have more information on the topic. Articles are created and edited by a volunteer team of more than 300,000 active contributors. Wikipedia exists in dozens of other languages as well. (The en at the beginning of its Web address displays the English version. Check out `is.wikipedia.org` if you've ever wondered what the Icelandic language looks like.)

Figure 8-5: Anyone can edit the Wikipedia online encyclopedia.

Who pays for all this stuff?

You may be wondering who pays for all these wonderful search systems. Advertising supports all except two of them. On every page of most search systems, you see lots and lots of ads. It used to be that ad revenue was skimpy — hence the dot-com bust of 2000, — but then the search sites discovered an important secret: When you enter keywords, you're telling the search site something about your interests at the moment. That information turns out to be *extremely* valuable to advertisers. An automobile company might pay a lot to have its ad near the top of the results page when you search for `automobile` `dealer Kansas`. Some sites (notably, Google) auction off prime ad placement. Google marks all such ads as "sponsored links." Usually, they're on the right side of the results page, but sometimes they're on top with a colored background. (Surprise — this type costs more.) Other search sites may not be as scrupulous. Advertisers pay Google when you click their links.

Wikipedia works on the open source model. The vast majority of contributors are unpaid volunteers, but the substantial bills for running the site are paid by grants and donations. If you use Wikipedia much, you should kick in a few bucks.

The ten-minute challenge

Our friend Doug Hacker (his real name) claims to be able to find the answer to any factual query on the Net in less than ten minutes. We challenged him to find a quote we vaguely knew from the liner notes of a Duke Ellington album whose title we couldn't remember. He had the complete quote in about an hour but spent less than five minutes himself actually searching. How? He found a mailing list about Duke Ellington, subscribed, and asked the question. Several members replied in short order. The more time you spend finding your way around the Net, the more you know where to go for the information you need.

Anyone can edit most Wikipedia articles whenever they want. That might seem to be a prescription for chaos, but most articles are watched over by interested volunteers, and inappropriate edits are quickly reversed, so the overall quality remains remarkably high.

If the idea of editing encyclopedia articles on your favorite subjects sounds appealing, talk to your family first. Wikipedia can be extremely addictive.

Articles are supposed to reflect a neutral point of view (NPOV, in Wikispeak), but a few topics — such as abortion, creationism, and Middle East politics — are continually debated. Wikipedia isn't as authoritative as conventional works, like *Encyclopædia Britannica,* but its articles are usually up-to-date and to the point, with side issues dealt with by links to other articles. One particularly cool Wikipedia feature is its collection of comprehensive lists, `en.wikipedia.org/wiki/Category:Lists`, on all sorts of arcane subjects. One of our favorites is the list of countries with mains power plugs, voltages, and frequencies; type *Mains power systems* in the Search box to find it.

If you do a Google search on a topic, a Wikipedia article is likely to show up as one of the links Google returns. That link might be a good place to start reading.

The Usual Suspects: Other Useful Search Sites

After you surf around Yahoo!, Google, and Bing for a while, you may want to check out the competition. Here are some search Web sites that provide specialized types of searches:

✔ **About.com:** This directory (at `www.about.com`) has several hundred semiprofessional "guides" who manage the topic areas. The guides vary from okay to very good (Margy knows a couple of very good ones), so if you're looking for in-depth information on a topic, check About.com to see what the guide has to say. The site was purchased by *The New York Times* in 2005.

✔ **Bytedog:** Bytedog (`www.bytedog.com`) assembles the results of searches at other search engines and presents them in a ranked list with cute dog graphics (cuter than Microsoft's, if you ask us). It takes a few extra seconds to respond, but that's because it's filtering out bad links before you have to deal with them. Bytedog, which also includes a Web directory, is a project of a couple of students at the University of Waterloo, Ontario.

Finding People

Finding people on the Internet is surprisingly easy. It's so easy that, indeed, sometimes it's creepy. Two overlapping categories of people-finders are available: those that look for people on the Net with e-mail and Web addresses and those that look for people in real life with phone numbers and street addresses.

Looking for e-mail addresses

The process of finding e-mail and Web addresses is somewhat hit-and-miss. Because no online equivalent to the telephone company's official phone book has ever existed, your best bet is to type into Google a person's name and a few other identifying words (such as the town where the person lives and the company where the person works) to see whether any of the matches it finds includes an address. Finding addresses by searching used to be pretty easy, but in recent years, as spammers have taken to scraping every address they can find off the Web, a lot of Web sites now "munge" (obscure) or delete e-mail addresses.

You can search online all you want, but there's no substitute for calling someone up and asking, "What's your e-mail address?"

Googling for people

Type someone's name and address at Google (for the address, type at least the state abbreviation, but more is better), and it shows you matches from phone book listings.

If you're wondering whether someone has a Web page, use Google or Yahoo! or Bing to search for just the person's name. If you're wondering whether you're famous, use Google or Yahoo! or Bing to search for your own name to see how many people mention you or link to your Web pages. (If you do it more than once, you're *egosurfing*.) If you receive e-mail from someone you don't know, search Google for the e-mail address — unless the message was spam, the address is bound to appear on a Web page somewhere.

Using other people-search sites

Here are some other sites that search for people:

- **WhoWhere:** WhoWhere (`whowhere.lycos.com`) is an e-mail address directory. Although Yahoo! usually gives better results, some people are listed in WhoWhere who aren't listed in other places.

- **Yahoo! People Search:** You can search for addresses and phone numbers and e-mail addresses at `people.yahoo.com`. If you don't like your own listing, you can add, update, or delete it.

- **Yellow pages directories:** Quite a few "yellow pages" business directories, both national and local, are on the Net, at `www.superpages.com`, `www.yellow.pages.com`, and `www.infousa.com`. The directories in this list are some of the national ones. InfoUSA even offers credit reports and other unpleasantly intrusive information.

- **Canada 411:** Canada 411 (`canada411.com`) is a complete Canadian telephone book, sponsored by the major Canadian telephone companies. *Aussi disponible en français,* eh? For several years the listings for Alberta and Saskatchewan were missing, leading to concern that the two provinces were too boring to bother with, but they're all there now, proving that they're just as gnarly as everyone else.

We're from Your Browser, and We're Here to Help You

Every search engine wants to be your best friend, which no doubt by coincidence will increase its market share. (Who? Us? Opinionated?) To cement that friendship, browser makers go to great effort to arrange so that when you type some search words, the search happens on its own search engine rather than on anyone else's.

Internet Explorer, Firefox, and Safari all have a search box to the right of the address box, as shown in Figure 8-6.

If you type a word or phrase in a search box, your browser opens your preferred search engine and displays the results of a search on what you typed. Or, if you type in the address box an entry that doesn't look like an address, it pretends that you typed it in the search box and searches anyway. (Google Chrome has only one box where you type something, and it decides what you wanted.) How convenient is that! You can specify which search engine you want this feature to use:

- **Firefox:** Choose a search engine from its short list by clicking the search engine icon to the right of the address box (and to the left of the search box). Click the icon and choose another site. Or, choose Manage Search Engines to display a list of search engines that Firefox knows about and add your favorites.

- ✔ **Internet Explorer:** Choose Tools⇨Internet Options, click the General tab if it isn't already selected, and click Settings in the Search section.

- ✔ **Safari:** Click the little magnifying glass in the search box, where the menu will offer a choice between Yahoo! and Google.

- ✔ **Google Chrome:** Click the Customize (wrench) icon to the right of the address box, select Options, click the Basics tab if it's not already selected, and set Default Search to your favorite search site. Click the Manage button if you want to choose a site that isn't on the list.

Figure 8-6:
Shortcut
search
boxes in
Internet
Explorer,
Firefox, and
Safari.

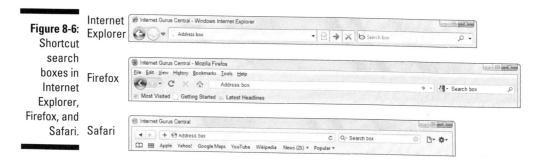

Too Many Toolbars

Every search engine vendor offers a *toolbar* that you can add to your browser. The *toolbar* is a bar above your browser's main window with a search box and some other stuff on it, such as links to relevant Web sites and sometimes browser tools such as pop-up blockers. Back when browsers were young and didn't have search boxes and built-in pop-up blockers, the toolbars were somewhat useful. These days, they're mostly a way to force another search-engine-specific search box into your browser, taking up space on your screen that would otherwise be available to look at Web pages (see Figure 8-7).

We generally recommend that you decline any invitations to install browser toolbars, because their value is marginal. If a specific toolbar has a specific feature you want that isn't otherwise available in your browser, such as the page rank display on the Google toolbar, it doesn't hurt to install it, other than losing that half-inch of screen real estate.

To get rid of unwanted toolbars in Internet Explorer, right click in a blank part of any menu or toolbar to open a menu where you can deselect the ones you don't want. To get rid of toolbars in Firefox, choose Tools⇨Add-Ons (which shows all add-ons, including the toolbars), click the one you don't want, and then click the Uninstall button that appears.

Getting the goods on goods and services

All commercial directories and search engines now offer shopping information to help get your credit card closer to the Web faster. Search results from Google and Bing have a Shopping link at the top, which opens a page full of links to items at online stores. You can find stuff for sale from all over, offering every conceivable item (and some inconceivable items). We tell you all the do's, don'ts, and how-to's in Chapter 10.

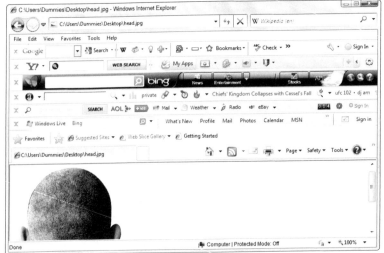

Figure 8-7:
Don't let this happen to you.

Making a Custom Start Page

Many sites want you to use them as your *start page* (the page your browser loads when it starts up, as described in Chapter 7). To encourage you to do so, these sites enable to you customize them to show all kinds of useful information just for you.

For example, if you create a free Google account, you can have a fancy, custom iGoogle page rather than the boring, plain one that most folks use. Click the Sign In link in the upper right corner of the Google page and create an account if you don't already have one (by clicking the Create an Account Now link). After you're logged in, go to `igoogle.com` if you don't see instructions for making a personalized home page. Your page can include a clock, calendar, weather report, news headlines, and other features.

Yahoo! provides similar features. (They even predate Google's by several years.) From `my.yahoo.com`, sign in and click Add Content to choose information to put on your My Yahoo! page, such as news headlines, stock prices, sports scores, Facebook updates, and other news. John likes My Yahoo! enough that he has made it his home page.

Chapter 9

Music and Video on the Web

A thousand years ago, when we wrote the first edition of *Internet For Dummies*, Internet content consisted almost entirely of text. (It was 1993, but it sure *feels* like a thousand years ago.) You could download a few archives of pictures, and there was this weird thing, the World Wide Web, that could mix together pictures and text on the same page, but for the most part, it consisted of text: People's connections were so slow, downloading pictures took so long, and computer screens were so fuzzy that we stuck to text. The pictures you could download were single images, such as cartoons and snapshots. Audio was nearly unheard of (so to speak), and video files were so bulky that even if you could find a clip and wait a week for it to download, it wouldn't fit on your computer's disk. By the late 1990s, Internet connections had sped up enough and screens had improved enough that pictures were normal fare — and audio was entering the mainstream enough that we put a sample voice message on our Web site, in case any of our readers had sound cards. (It's still there, at `net.gurus.org/ngc.wav`.)

Things have advanced a little since then. Ordinary users now have Net connections that run at several million bits per second — faster than the main backbones of the early 1990s — and computer disks have gotten enormous beyond imagining. Passing around audio and video over the Net has become practical and widespread. In fact, the amounts of available audio and video are now so vast that you could spend your entire life looking at online commercials without ever finding anything worth watching. This chapter tries to bring a little order to the vast wasteland of online media.

To avoid writing *audio and/or video* a hundred more times in this chapter, henceforth we use the concise (albeit imprecise) term *media* to refer to them.

Seven Ways to Get Media and One Way Not To

You can get your media fix in approximately ten zillion different programs and formats. Fortunately, they fall into a modest number of categories: free, streaming, rented, purchased, shared, and outright stolen.

Receive it as a gift

The simplest approach is to download media offered for free and then play it. Visit www.nasa.gov/multimedia, where NASA has lots of free little movies on topics ranging from dust storms on Mars to how a roller coaster ride feels like taking off in the space shuttle. You can also find independent movies and videos from producers more interested in letting people see their work than in charging for it. Visit epitonic.com for an eclectic collection of music by artists, some well known and some obscure, released so that people can listen to it and make their own mixes.

Borrow it

Even on a broadband connection, downloading a whole media clip can take a while. Rather than download first and play later, *streaming* media downloads as it plays, thereby re-creating (in a complex digital manner) the way that radio and TV have worked since the 1920s. As with TV and radio, after it's streamed, it's gone — and if you want to play it again, you have to stream it again. Streaming audio can work over a dialup connection, but streaming video needs a broadband connection.

Most streaming media is provided *on demand:* You click a link and they send you whatever it is, sort of like a jukebox. Alternatively, sometimes streaming media is a single program to which you can listen in and hear what's playing at any moment. Not surprisingly, it's named *Internet radio,* and in many cases the audio stream is an actual radio program, such as our local public radio stations at `wrvo.fm` (click Listen Live) in upstate New York and `www.vpr.net` (click Listen Online) in Vermont. We say more about Internet radio later in this chapter.

Rent it

A great deal of music isn't available for free, but it's available for cheap. Services such as Real Networks Rhapsody (`www.real.com/rhapsody`) offer monthly subscriptions that let you listen to large libraries of recorded music. Napster (`www.napster.com`) charges about $5 per month for unlimited streaming music and five MP3 downloads each month that you can play on your MP3 player or cellphone. You pay a fixed monthly fee, and then you can click songs from a catalog to play them and to make and share playlists of your favorites.

These rental services have enormous catalogs of music, and each one claims to be the largest. They really *are* large: While checking out Rhapsody, we were finally able to do a side-by-side comparison of Desi Arnaz's muscular late-1940s version of *Babalu* and his mentor Xavier Cugat's more elegant 1941 recording. (You'll just have to decide for yourself which one you like better.) However, when you stop paying rent, your music vanishes — remember, you never owned it.

You can find video-rental Web sites too — not just for renting a DVD but also for downloading the video over the Internet and watching it on your computer. For example, Netflix, at `www.netflix.com`, is known for its DVD-rental-by-mail service, but you can also download videos on demand. Not all its DVDs are available for download, but for the ones that are, you see a Play button on the Web site. Blockbuster, at `www.blockbuster.com`, lets you rent or buy downloaded movies. Note that Blockbuster works with only Internet Explorer, not with Firefox, Safari, or Chrome.

Buy it

Apple iTunes makes buying music easy. Go to `www.apple.com/itunes` to listen to the first little bit of any song in its catalog. If you like it, you can buy your own, permanent copy (for 99 cents) that you can copy to your iPod, play on your computer, or burn on a CD. You don't have to be a Mac user to use iTunes; you can play the tunes by using the Windows version of the iTunes program. (See the section "Organizing your music with iTunes," later in this chapter.) It's no surprise that people buy in droves, making iTunes the biggest online music store. Likewise, many more Web sites sell music either from a Web store or as an add-on to a rental service, most for about the same price as iTunes.

Amazon.com (www.amazon.com), the world's largest bookstore, also sells downloadable tunes in MP3 format.

Already own it

You probably own a whole lot of digital music in the form of music CDs. Copying your music CDs to your computer is known as *ripping*, and it's easy to do. Windows Media Player, iTunes, and other music programs can copy all tracks from a CD and put the songs into your music library so that you can play them from your computer (without the CD) or copy them to your MP3 player. See "Copying music from your own CDs," later in this chapter.

Share it

The original version of Napster was the first well-known music exchange service, allowing members to download MP3 music files from each other for free. The system was the first large-scale *peer-to-peer* (*P2P*) information exchange, where people exchange files with each other rather than download them from a central library. Eventually, the big record labels sued and shut it down because most of the material that people exchanged was in flagrant violation of the music's copyright. Napster was later reincarnated as a site for music rental and free online music streaming — but no free downloading.

Two current popular file-sharing systems are BitTorrent (www.bittorrent.com) and LimeWire (www.limewire.com), which have thus far been able to fly under the legal radar. Each one is much like what Napster was — a network from which you can download music for free, a certain amount of which is provided against the wishes of the owners of said music. While you're downloading music from other people's computers, they are in turn downloading music from you, so they can significantly slow down your computer and your Internet connection. The music industry insists that these folks are morally reprehensible, but particularly with BitTorrent, people use it to share large amounts of entirely legal and legitimate material along with the dodgy stuff.

Subscribe to it

You can subscribe to audio programs over the Internet. A *podcast* is an audio file distributed over the Net for listening to on an iPod or another type of MP3 player or any computer with speakers. Many radio shows are available as podcasts; go to www.npr.org to find many of them. Lots of organizations and people make podcasts, too. See the section "Subscribing to podcasts with iTunes," later in this chapter, for instructions.

Downloads for the post-literate

Not all downloadable audio files contain music. A thriving niche market exists for what used to be called "talking books." You can download books and magazines and just about anything else you might otherwise read, as well as radio programs you might have missed. Although listening to downloaded books on your computer works fine — and it can be an essential tool for the visually impaired — it's kind of pointless if you can read the paper book faster than you can listen to it (and kick back on the patio while you're at it). But if you drive to work or go jogging, a talking book on CD in the car player (or copied to the MP3 player or iPod on your belt) is just the ticket.

The largest source of talking books is Audible. com (www.audible.com). You can buy individual books for book-like prices or subscribe and listen to one or two books a month cheaper than you can by paying individually. Either way, the

books you buy are yours to keep. They provide a reasonably nice program that you can download and install to keep track of the files for the books you bought and then burn them to CDs (*lots* of CDs — about 15 for a full-length book). Audible has also made deals with many other media programs, so you can find an Audible plug-in for iTunes that lets you copy your books to an iPod, as well as a plug-in for Windows Media Player for all the MP3 devices it handles, and so forth.

Audible usually offers a trial subscription with a couple of free books, and its catalog includes public-interest stuff (such as presidential inaugural speeches) available for free if you want to try it out. ***Warning:*** John tried it out and ended up inventing errands that involved driving to faraway stores so that he could listen to the last CD of *The DaVinci Code*. On the other hand, Margy's husband survived a long commute thanks to his Audible subscription.

Steal it — um, no

Plenty of pirated stuff is still on the Net, and probably always will be. We expect that our readers, because they're of good moral character, wouldn't want to look for it, but if you do, you have to do so without our help.

What Are You Listening With?

The three most popular programs used for playing Web-based online media are Windows Media Player, Real Player, and Apple iTunes. The first two include separate player programs and plug-ins for Web browsers so that Web pages can embed little windows that show movies or play music. You eventually have to install all three if you want to handle all the links you click. All three work pretty well.

iTunes

`www.apple.com/itunes`

iTunes, shown in Figure 9-1, has become insanely popular because you have to use it if you have an iPhone or iPod. In addition to playing and organizing music, iTunes, from Apple, is the way to load music from your computer onto iPods and iPhones. You may have heard of it as a music store and a way to organize music, but iTunes can play all sorts of media, including videos. iTunes supports streaming video as well as audio in most popular formats.

Ripping CDs to your computer and keeping your music organized in iTunes are described later in this chapter.

Figure 9-1:
You can use
iTunes to
buy music,
rip and
burn CDs,
organize
songs into
playlists,
subscribe
to podcasts,
and maybe
even wash
the dishes.

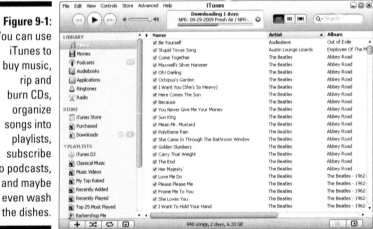

Windows Media Player

`www.microsoft.com/windows/windowsmedia`

Microsoft has its own streaming audio and video formats, and it bundles a player for them with Windows. The Windows Media Player program, shown in Figure 9-2, can play files in Advanced Systems Format (with the extension `.asf` or `.asx`), in addition to most other formats. More recent versions added useful new features, so if you don't have Media Player version 11 or later, it's worth your time to visit Windows Update or the Media Player site to download it. (Media Player itself may nag you to upgrade if you have an older version.)

Figure 9-2:
Organizing
your
music with
Windows
Media
Player.

Click the Library tab on the left side of the Media Player window to see which audio and video files you have. Click Media Guide to browse links to popular music. When you put an audio CD into your computer's CD drive, it displays the list of tracks on the CD and you can click Rip CD to *rip* (copy) tracks from the CD to your hard drive and to your Windows Media Player library. You can also burn music CDs by clicking the Burn tab.

RealPlayer

www.real.com

Another system for playing streaming media files, the kind you borrow or rent, is RealPlayer. Files in the Real format have the extension .ra or .ram. To play RealAudio files, you need the RealPlayer program, which you can download from www.real.com. The RealAudio player also handles RealVideo, which shows smallish moving pictures to accompany your sound.

Okay, How about Some Music?

Two hot activities on the Internet are downloading and exchanging music files with your friends in the MP3 file format. MP3 stands for *MP*EG level *3* (acronyms within acronyms — how technoid) and is simply the soundtrack format used with MPEG movies. Because that format is widely available and does a good job of compressing music to a reasonable size for downloading, it has been adopted by music lovers on the Net. As you may already have guessed, MP3 players (similar to iPods and little, less-expensive devices from Sandisk and Rio) can play MP3 files, too, which is the main reason for their popularity. Many mobile phone models can play MP3 files, too.

You can play MP3 files by using many different programs, including iTunes, RealPlayer, and Windows Media Player. This section explains how to use iTunes to organize music, subscribe to podcasts, make playlists, and listen to radio stations over the Internet because all the programs are fairly similar. If you use Windows Media Player or RealPlayer, you get the general idea.

Naturally, Microsoft has the competing file format WMA, with the extension .wma. Real Player and iTunes can also handle WMA.

Copying music from your own CDs

You already own tons of music on those racks of CDs that will soon be obsolete. You can rip (copy) the tracks from an audio CD by using iTunes. When you put an audio CD into your computer's CD drive, iTunes asks whether you want to import the tracks into you iTunes library. Click Yes to begin copying. iTunes looks up the CD using an online database so that you can see the titles of the tracks and even the album artwork.

When you rip music from CDs, you can specify which format to store the files in. We use the MP3 format because the files are smaller than some other formats and because every music player can handle MP3s. In iTunes, choose Edit➪Preferences, click the General tab if it's not already selected, click the Import Settings button, click the Import Using option and set it to MP3 Encoder. You can also choose the quality, where you trade off file size against sound quality.

Organizing your music with iTunes

Apple iTunes (www.apple.com/itunes) lets you buy legal, downloaded songs for a reasonable price, from 99 cents apiece and up, based on popularity. Both Mac and Windows users can buy and play songs from iTunes by downloading the free iTunes program, which is excellent for keeping your songs organized even if you don't have an iPod or buy from the iTunes store.

Making playlists

In iTunes, you can organize your music into playlists, which are your own, customized albums. One playlist can be music you like to listen to while washing the dishes, and another playlist might be for your fabulous oldies collection. Or, each user of your computer can have her own playlists. You can have as many playlists as you like. (Margy has one playlist of the baritone parts she needs to learn for her women's barbershop group, Maiden Vermont, and another playlist of instrumental jazz, 1960s rock, and Hindu chanting to listen to at work.)

You create a new playlist by choosing File⇨New Playlist or by pressing Ctrl+N. You can name the playlist whatever you want and then drag in music from your library. Dragging a song from the library to a playlist doesn't remove it from the library or copy the file — you can put the same song into multiple playlists, and all the while it continues to be stored in your general iTunes library just once.

Subscribing to Podcasts

Podcasts are audio magazines that deliver MP3 files of talk or music directly to your computer (see the section "Subscribe to it," earlier in this chapter). Radio programs, companies, musicians, comedians, and just plain people produce podcasts about a huge variety of different subjects, everything from "The Twilight Saga" to the stock market.

Subscribing to podcasts on the Web

Several Web sites provide directories of podcasts, including Podcast.com and PodcastAlley.com. They enable you to find podcasts by topic, subscribe to them, and listen to them from the Web site.

Or, go to the Web site of the program you want to subscribe to. National Public Radio at www.npr.org originates dozens of podcasts.

Subscribing to podcasts with iTunes

To subscribe to a podcast, click the iTunes Store link in iTunes and then click the Podcasts link. When you find a podcast that looks interesting, you can click an episode to listen to it on the spot or click the Subscribe button to receive all future episodes automatically. Most podcasts are free, and iTunes downloads the latest episodes every time you start the program.

Playing Music and Podcasts

If you want to listen to music or podcasts while you're sitting in front of your computer, you're all set — fire up iTunes, RealPlayer, or Windows Media Player and listen. But we hear that some people actually have lives and want to listen to music in other places.

You can buy a portable MP3 player — an iPod, a cheaper alternative from Sandisk or Rio, or a phone that includes an MP3 player — and take thousands of MP3 cuts to listen to while you jog, travel, or just hang out. It's similar to a Walkman, but you don't need tapes or CDs. You hook your MP3 player to your computer whenever you want to download new tunes. These players can hold *weeks* of music and podcasts. The most popular is the ubiquitous Apple iPod, but lots of other players are cheaper and work fine. Only iPods can play M4P (copy-protected) music and only files to which you own a license. Or, check whether your mobile phone can play MP3 files.

More threats and promises

Folks ripping their favorite tunes from CDs and e-mailing them to their 50 closest friends comprise a hideous threat to the recording industry, not to mention that they're violating copyright law. (The previous hideous threats, for readers old enough to remember, were cassette tapes and home VCRs, which totally destroyed the music and movie industries. What — they didn't? Uh, well, *this* time it's different because, um, just because it is.) The industry's efforts to shut down Web sites that offer ripped songs for free downloading has been moderately successful, but private e-mail is hard to stop.

The recording industry came up with the Secure Digital Music Initiative, a music file format of its own. The SDMI was intended to let you download but not share music. It flopped, partly because it had technical defects quickly analyzed and reported by enterprising college professors and students and partly because nobody wanted crippleware music. The recording industry has been filing lawsuits against the most visible music sharers, on the peculiar theory that if it threatens and sues its customers, their attitudes will improve and they will buy more stuff. Maybe someday the industry will figure out, as Apple did, that if it sells decent music at reasonable prices and lets customers listen to it the way they want to, people will pay for it.

There's CDs, and then there's CDs

Although all CDs look the same, they don't all play the same. Normal audio CDs contain a maximum of about 74 minutes of music and work on every CD player ever made. When you burn a CD-R (the kind of CD you can write to only once), you're making a normal audio CD. Because blank CD-Rs are cheap (about 20 cents apiece if you buy them in quantity), the main disadvantage of this approach is that you end up with large stacks of CDs.

MP3 files are much smaller than audio CD files, so if you burn a CD full of MP3s, you can put about ten hours of music on each disc. DVD players and many recent CD players can play MP3 CDs. If you're not sure whether your player can handle MP3 CDs, just make one on your computer and try it in your player. It doesn't hurt your player, although you might see some odd error messages. Although rewritable CD-RWs don't work in normal CD players, players that can handle MP3 CDs can usually handle CD-RWs. Again, if you're not sure, try it; it doesn't hurt anything if it doesn't work.

Listening to Internet Radio

If you like to listen to music while you work, check out real radio stations or Internet-only radio stations. Most radio stations now *stream* their talk and music on the Internet in addition to broadcasting it over the air. Go to a radio station's Web site and click the Listen Now or similarly named link — for example, we're listening to a show about backyard chickens at `wbur.org` as we write this section. Many radio stations have MP3 players built into their Web sites.

Tuning into a station

Like real radio stations, Internet-only stations offer a mix of music and talk and sometimes commercials. Unlike real (broadcast) radio stations, they're extremely cheap to set up, so lots and lots of people do — providing lots of quirky little niche stations run by people all over the world. You listen to them in a streaming program, usually iTunes, Real Player, or Windows Media. Most are available for free, some require a subscription, and some have a subscription option to make the ads go away.

If you use iTunes, click the Radio link in iTunes to get started. You see a menu of different types of stations, and after choosing one, you can peruse stations from across the country at your leisure for free. Double-click a station to listen to it.

To get started, here are some directories of Internet radio stations:

 ✔ `music.yahoo.com` — Yahoo! Music and then click Radio⇨Radio Station Guide.

✔ shoutcast.com — SHOUTcast Radio, from AOL, gives you a choice of its own SHOUTcast Radio Mini Player or your existing player.

✔ www.live365.com — Live 365 Internet Radio streams several thousand stations with every possible kind of music

Either way (broadcast radio or Internet-only radio), you can listen to talk and music from all over the United States — or the world.

Making your own station

Every radio station — Internet or broadcast — chooses a range of styles of music to play. Why should you be limited to the musical tastes of existing radio stations? Instead, you can create your own musical mix, including music you don't even own!

Enter Pandora Radio, at www.pandora.com (shown in Figure 9-3). As its Web site states, it's a new kind of radio station, one that plays only music you like. Type the names of a musician or group or the name of a song, and Pandora finds, in its huge musical database, music that's similar to what you specify. You can't play the exact song you want, but you can play similar music, displaying information about the artist and album. When Pandora guesses wrong about what it thinks you like, you can click the thumbs-down icon to kill the song. When it guesses right, click the thumbs-up icon to tell it to play more songs like that one.

Figure 9-3: Make your own radio station at Pandora.

You can name your "radio station" and have several stations for different kinds of music — maybe one for while you're working and another to pay bills by. You can also share your radio station with other people so that they can listen to the mix you have created.

Jango, at www.jango.com, and last.fm (at last.fm — no .com) work like Pandora.

Watching Movies on the Net

Now that most people have fast Internet connections, watching video over the Net has become possible and popular. You can watch short videos at YouTube, television shows, or entire movies or upload your own videos for others to watch.

Older Web browsers, such as Firefox before version 3.5, can't play videos — you need to get a player program. You also need a reasonably fast computer to display movies in anything close to real time. Flash, the most widely used player, plugs into your Web browser. iTunes, RealPlayer, and Windows Media Player also handle movies (and are described earlier in this chapter).

The YouTube thing

Probably the largest Internet video phenomenon is YouTube (www.youtube.com). It's a site like Google (which owns YouTube), but rather than an Internet search engine for information at large, it's only for videos. On YouTube you can find everything from *Saturday Night Live* clips to previews for upcoming movies to strange homemade Lego flicks. According to *The New York Times*, people post more than 100 million videos on YouTube every *day*. Unfortunately, Google is losing an amazing amount of money on YouTube every day because few advertisers want their ads displayed alongside such a weird and unpredictable collection of videos.

In the search box, you can type a word or phrase related to the video you're looking for and YouTube displays a list of links of possible videos, as shown in Figure 9-4. Click the image or title to play the video. Video-playing software is embedded in the Web site, so you don't need anything but an Internet connection to watch videos on YouTube (see the later sidebar "Too many video file formats"). If you see a video you like a lot and want to share with your 50 closest friends, you can click the Share link below the video to e-mail a link, post a tweet on Twitter (see Chapter 19), or write it on your Facebook wall (as described in Chapter 18). The e-mail arrives with a link to the YouTube page that has the video on it.

Google has formed its own niche in the world of Internet movies with Google Video (video.google.com), a site similar to YouTube. Because Google now owns YouTube, the two sites are morphing into one. Other YouTube-like Web sites include Metacafe (www.metacafe.com) and MSN Video (video.msn.com).

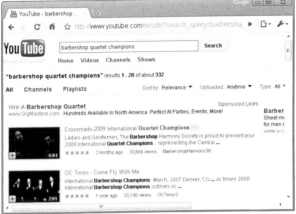

Figure 9-4:
Millions of
weird and
occasionally
wonderful
videos are
available on
YouTube.

Putting the "you" in YouTube

You can upload a video to YouTube as long as it's on your computer, you
own the copyright (YouTube deletes stolen videos), it isn't defamatory or
pornographic, and it's no longer than ten minutes. To upload, follow these
steps:

1. **Create a free YouTube account by clicking the Create Account link in
   the upper right corner of any YouTube page.**

   Or, sign in to your existing account. If you have a Google account, use it.

2. **Click the Upload button.**

   Or, click the Post a Video Response link below an existing video.

3. **Select the video file on your computer and follow the instructions.**

   You can choose whether to make the video public or private, name the
   video, and specify which category it's in. YouTube uploads your video and
   converts it to the Flash format for streaming. Uploading can take a while
   (10 to 20 minutes) depending on the speed of your Internet connection.

After your video is on YouTube, you can share it with your friends.

If a video is public on YouTube, it's really, really public. Think twice about
including personally identifying information about yourself or your kids unless
the video is something you're truly proud of.

Too many video file formats

The original standard digital-movie format is Moving Picture Experts Group (MPEG). MPEG was designed by a committee down the hall from the JPEG committee that defined file formats for scanned photos and (practically unprecedented in the history of computer standards efforts) was designed based on earlier work. MPEG files have the extension `.mpeg` or `.mpg`.

Microsoft, responding to the challenge of emerging standards that it didn't control, created its own formats. Audio/Visual Interleave (AVI) format is for nonstreaming video, with the extension `.avi`. Advanced Streaming Format (with the extension `.asf` or `.asx`) is for both streaming audio and video data.

All these formats are being replaced by Flash because it's what YouTube uses — files that end with `.flv` and a few variations. The Flash player (a free download from `get.adobe.com/flashplayer`) plugs into your Web browser and plays streaming video in several qualities, including one that's similar to HD television.

Watching TV

Missed your favorite television show? Didn't record it on your TiVo? You might be able to catch it on Hulu, at `www.hulu.com`. It's supported by ABC, Fox, NBC, and others, so it shows entire episodes, not ten-minute clips, and copyrighted shows aren't liable to be deleted, as they are on YouTube. YouTube has responded with YouTube Shows, at `www.youtube.com/shows`, which is different from the regular YouTube site; like Hulu, it has commercial video, with no amateur uploads.

Blip.tv (at `blip.tv` — no ".com" at the end) hosts shows you may never have heard of because they're made by independent creators. Link TV (at `www.linktv.org`) shows educational programs from around the world.

Two Web sites offer advertising-supported, professional-quality videos on your PC: Joost (pronounced "juiced," we imagine) at `www.joost.com` and BabelGum (from Italy) at `www.babelgum.com`. The sites are new, so check their selection of shows and how many ads they're throwing at you.

Watching movies

You can stream movies from the Web, although usually not for free (at least, not legally). If you have a Netflix account to read DVDs by mail, you can stream videos from its Web site (www.netflix.com) without paying anything extra. Netflix has a huge inventory of DVDs, and many of them are also available for streaming. On the Web site, you add movies to your queue if you want to watch them later or receive the DVD by mail. Or, click the Watch Instantly tab to find a movie and watch it now.

Blockbuster, whose lunch Netflix was eating when Netflix began its DVD rental business, retaliated with an online service at www.blockbuster.com that is quite similar to Netflix.

Amazon.com offers a Video On Demand service, which enables you to stream movies for a fee. You can save movies for later after you pay for them, or you can watch a previously purchased video again. Choose the Movies Music & Games department and then click Video On Demand.

Sharing media around the home and dorm

Microsoft Windows 7 has a new feature that lets you set up all your computers, at least the ones running Windows 7, as a *HomeGroup* that can easily share resources on all your computers and other networked devices. Open Windows Media Player, switch to the Library page, and click Stream⇨Turn On Media Streaming. If your computer isn't already in a HomeGroup, it goes through the process to join an existing group and set one up. After you do that, the Library page shows an icon for the libraries of everyone else, on your computer and others, who has turned on media streaming, and you can play their stuff just like you can play your own. You're also supposed to be able to play from your computer onto networked players and other devices; if your Windows 7 computer can see them on the network, it sets up icons so that you can access them.

You also have the option to allow streaming to the Internet, which we do *not* recommend because, unless you set up your system file protections very carefully, you can allow random strangers on the Net into your computer. We expect the most enthusiastic use of network media streaming will be in "homes" that are college dormitories, where everyone in the dorm is already on the same network, so now they can all share each other's music at the click of a mouse.

Chapter 10

More Shopping, Less Dropping

· ·

In This Chapter

▶ Discovering the pros and cons of shopping online

▶ Using your credit card online without fear

▶ Shopping step-by-step

▶ Finding the lowest price

▶ Finding airline tickets, books, clothes, computers, food, and mutual funds online

· ·

The Internet is the world's biggest bazaar, with stores that carry everything from books to blouses, from DVDs to prescription drugs, from mutual funds to musical instruments, and from plane tickets to, uh, specialized personal products. (Don't read too much into that one.) Shopping online is convenient — no parking or standing in line — and you can compare prices easily. But is online shopping safe? Well, we've bought all kinds of products online, and we're still alive to tell the tale.

Shopping Online: Pros and Cons

Here are some reasons for shopping on the Net:

✔ Online stores are convenient and open all night, and they don't mind if you aren't wearing shoes or if you window-shop for a week before you buy something.

✔ Prices are often lower online, and you can compare prices at several online establishments in a matter of minutes. Even if you eventually make your purchase in a brick-and-mortar store, the information you find online can save you money. Shipping and handling is the same as you pay for mail order, and you don't have to drive or park.

✔ Online stores can sometimes offer a better selection. They usually ship from a central warehouse rather than have to keep stock on the shelf at dozens of branches. If you're looking for an item that's hard to find — for example, a part for that vintage toaster oven you're repairing — the Web can save you weeks of searching.

✔ Sometimes, stuff just isn't available locally. (The authors of this book live in small rural towns. Trumansburg, New York, is a wonderful place, but if you want to buy a new toaster, you're out of luck. And Margy couldn't find a harmonium anywhere in the Champlain Valley.)

✔ Unlike malls, online stores don't have Muzak. (A few Web sites play background music, but we don't linger on those sites.)

On the other hand, here are some reasons that you shouldn't buy everything on the Net:

✔ You can't physically look at or try on stuff before you buy it, and in most cases, you have to wait for it to be shipped to you. (We haven't had much luck buying shoes and pants online, f'rinstance.)

✔ Your local stores deserve support so that they'll be there when you need something right now or need their help in picking something out.

✔ You can't flirt with the staff at a Web store or find out the latest town gossip.

The Credit Card Question

How do you pay for stuff you buy online? Usually, you pay by credit card, the same way you pay for anything else. Isn't it incredibly, awfully dangerous to give out your credit card number online, though? Well, no.

When you use plastic at a restaurant, you give your physical card with your physical signature to the server, who takes it to the back room, does who-knows-what with it, and then brings it back. Compared with that situation, the risk of sending your number to an online store is pretty small. A friend of ours used to run a restaurant and later an online store and assures us that there's no comparison: The online store had none of the credit card problems that the restaurant did.

Many books (including earlier editions of this one) made a big deal about whether a Web site has a security certificate, which means that it shows a little lock in the corner of the Web browser window. The lock is nice to have, but the problem it solves, bad guys snooping on the connection somewhere between your PC and the seller's Web site, isn't a likely one unless you're using a wireless network connection. We think you should worry more about whether a store selling something is run well enough that it actually ships you what you bought.

Take a credit card number — any number

One of the cleverer innovations in online banking is *virtual* credit cards. If you want to place an online credit card order with a merchant you don't entirely trust, first visit your bank's Web site and tell the bank how much the order will cost, and on the spot, it may be able to concoct a brand-new card number. Then you return to the merchant's site and order with that card number rather than with your regular number. As soon as the merchant places the charge, your bank links the new number to the merchant, so even if the merchant leaks the number, it's no good to anyone else. The number's credit limit is the amount you set when you created it, so if the merchant tries to overcharge you, the bank says no. You can also create virtual numbers that are good for a set number of charges, for subscriptions that require regular payments.

Different banks use different names for this service. Citibank and Discover call it *virtual numbers*. Bank of America calls it *ShopSafe*. Ask your bank whether it offers this service.

John found that virtual numbers also work for phone orders and mail orders and any other type of charge where you don't use your physical card. Because he's paranoid, he uses virtual numbers for everything from his electric bill to his college alumni association. *Don't use them for buying plane tickets or reserving hotel rooms, though, because you often have to show a real card with the number at the check-in desk.*

Credit cards and debit cards look the same and spend the same, but credit cards bill you at the end of the month whereas debit cards take the money right out of your bank account. In the United States, consumer protection laws are much stronger for credit cards. The important difference is that in case of a disputed transaction, *you* have the money if you used a credit card but *they* have it if you used a debit card. Use a credit card to get the better protection, and then pay the bill at the end of the month so that you don't owe interest.

If, after this harangue, you still don't want to send your credit card number over the Internet, most online stores are happy to have you call in your card number over the phone (although, likely as not, an operator halfway around the globe then enters your credit card number by using the Internet). If you're one of those fiscally responsible holdouts who doesn't do plastic, send a check or money order.

Cookie alert

You may have heard horrible stories about the cookies that Web sites reputedly use to spy on you, steal your data, ravage your computer, inject cellulite into your hips while you sleep, and otherwise make your life miserable. After extensive investigation, we have found that most cookies aren't bad; when you're shopping online, they can even be quite helpful. (See the section "Cookies aren't so bad" in Chapter 2 for more info about cookies.)

A *cookie* is no more than a little chunk of text that a Web site sends to a PC with a request (not a command) to send the cookie back during future visits to the same Web site. The cookie is stored on your computer in the form of a tiny snippet of text. That's all it is. For online shopping carts, cookies let the Web server track the items you have selected but not yet bought, even if you log out and turn off your computer in the interim. Stores can also use cookies to keep track of the last time you visited and what you bought, but they can keep that data on their own computers, so what's the big deal? (If you don't want Web sites to store cookies on your computer, you can prevent them; see how in Chapter 7.)

Paying at the Store

Buying stuff at an online store isn't much different from buying it at a regular store. In the simplest case, a store sells only one item per Web page, as shown in Figure 10-1. To buy the item, you visit the page, you see the item, and you enter the payment and shipping details, and then the store sends the item to you.

Most stores hope you will buy several items at a time, so they use *shopping carts* instead. Margy runs the little online kids' videotape store Great Tapes for Kids at www.greattapes.com. Originally, it had a single order page with an order form listing every tape in her rapidly expanding catalog. When the Great Tapes order form got hopelessly large, John reprogrammed it to provide a shopping cart to help track the items people order. (John will do practically anything to avoid writing.)

As you click your way around a site, you can toss items into your cart, adding and removing them as you want, by clicking a button labeled something like Add Item or Buy Now. When you have the items you want, you visit the virtual checkout line and buy the items in your cart. Until you visit the checkout, you can always take the items out of your cart if you decide that you don't want them, and at online stores they don't become shopworn, no matter how often you do that.

Figure 10-2 shows the Great Tapes for Kids shopping cart with two items in it. When you click the Proceed to Checkout button, the next page asks for the rest of your order details, much like the form shown earlier, in Figure 10-1.

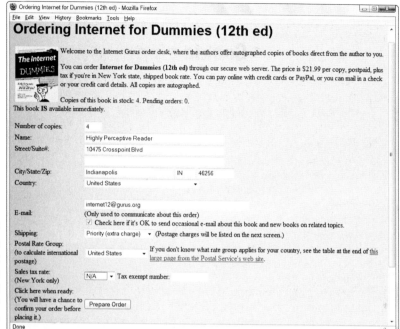

Figure 10-1:
You just
can't have
too much
quality
literature.

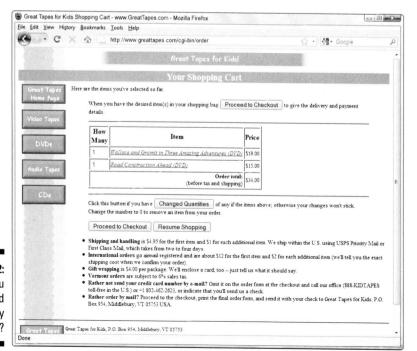

Figure 10-2:
Have you
finished
your holiday
shopping?

Some stores even have the online equivalents of layaway plans and gift registries. For example, some Web shopping sites let you add items to a wish list that you can share with your friends so that you or someone else can buy the item for you later. Some sites offer gift certificates, too, for shopping online.

How Little Do You Want to Pay?

As little as possible, of course. About 15 minutes after the second online store appeared, someone realized that you could look at the stores to find who charges how much for which item and then report back on your own Web site. Price comparison sites work really well *if* you can exactly identify what you want to buy. For books, consumer electronics, computers, and computer parts, it's always worth a look. But if you're looking for khaki pants, no two pairs are the same, and most of us would rather pay an extra ten bucks to avoid a pair that makes us look like a spandex-wrapped potato.

Comparison sites now work two ways. One is to visit store sites and "scrape" the prices. The other is to make a deal with interested stores and let them upload their prices directly, typically in return for a commission when users click through. Both methods work okay, but we have occasionally seen comparison sites showing different prices from the ones you see if you visit the store site directly. Here are a few of our favorites:

- ✔ **Google Product Search** (`www.google.com/products`) is the latest incarnation of the Google price-comparison site that was originally named Froogle. Stores upload prices, but Google doesn't charge them. (The search pages have ads on the right.) The searching is helpful, but the inventory is spotty.

- ✔ **ISBN.NU** (`isbn.nu`) checks prices for new books at a dozen online stores and tells you which one has the best price. The site scrapes the prices and then uses the stores' affiliate programs to get paid.

- ✔ **MySimon** (`www.mysimon.com`) compares prices from a wide variety of online stores, finding its information about high-tech products from CNET and about nontechnical products from Shopping.com.

- ✔ **Nextag** (`www.nextag.com`) also covers a wide range of products, but we would decline their offer to help you shop for online degrees.

- ✔ **Pricegrabber** (`www.pricegrabber.com`) has good coverage of everything from musical instruments to computer parts.

Up, Up, and Away

We buy lots of airline tickets online. Although the online travel sites aren't as good as the very best human travel agents, the sites are now better than most agents and vastly better than bad travel agents. Even if you have a good agent, online sites let you look around to see your options before you get on the phone. Some airlines offer on their own Web sites some cheap fares that aren't available any other way. The airlines know that it costs them much less to let the Web do the work, and they pay you (in the form of a hefty discount) to use the Web.

The theory of airline tickets

Three giant airline computer systems in the United States — Sabre, Galileo/Worldspan (two formerly separate systems that are merging), and Amadeus — handle nearly all airline reservations in the United States. (The sites are known as _CRSs,_ or computer reservations systems, or _GDS,_ for Global Distribution System.) Although each airline has a "home" GDS, the systems are all interlinked so that you can, with few exceptions, buy tickets for any airline from any GDS. Some low-price, start-up airlines are available by way of GDS, and others — notably, Southwest and Jet Blue — don't participate in any of these systems but have instead their own Web sites, where you can check flights and buy tickets.

In theory, all the systems show the same data; in practice, however, they get a little out of sync with each other. If you're looking for seats on a sold-out flight, an airline's home system is most likely to have that last, elusive seat. If you're looking for the lowest fare to somewhere, check all four systems (using different travel Web sites) because a fare that's marked as sold out on one system often mysteriously reappears on another system. Also check Orbitz (www.orbitz.com) which has direct-connect access to many airlines, bypassing GDS altogether.

Some fare categories are visible only to travel agents and don't appear on any Web sites, particularly if you aren't staying over a weekend, so check with a good agent before buying. On the other hand, many airlines offer some special deals that are _only_ on their Web sites and that agents often don't know about. Confused? You should be. We were.

The confusion is even worse if you want to fly internationally. Official fares to most countries are set by way of the IATA cartel, so computer systems usually list IATA fares for only international flights. If you need to buy tickets sooner than a month ahead, you can often find entirely legal *consolidator tickets* for considerably less than the official price, so an online or offline agent is extremely useful for finding the best price. International airlines also have some impressive online offers, most notably from Cathay Pacific, which usually has a pass that includes a ticket from the United States to Hong Kong and then unlimited travel all over Asia.

Here's our distilled wisdom about buying tickets online:

- ✔ Check the online systems to see which flights are available and the range of prices. Check sites that use different GDSs. (We list some sites at the end of this section.)

- ✔ After you find a likely airline, check that airline's site to see whether it has any special Web-only deals. If a low-fare airline flies the route, be sure to check that one, too.

- ✔ Check prices on flights serving all nearby airports. An extra 45 minutes of driving time can save you hundreds of dollars.

- ✔ Check with a travel agent (by phone, e-mail, or the agent's Web site) to see whether he can beat the online price, and buy your tickets from the agent unless the online deal is better.

- ✔ For international tickets, do everything in this list and check both online and with your agent for consolidator tickets, particularly if you don't qualify for the lowest published fare. For complex international trips, such as around the world, agents can invariably find routes and prices that the automated systems can't.

- ✔ If you bid on airline tickets at a travel auction Web site, make sure that you already know the price at which you can buy the ticket so that you don't bid more.

Before looking at online agents, check out ITA Software (www.itasoftware.com). This company produces the fare search engine used by Orbitz and many airline sites. ITA's own site has a version that just searches and doesn't try to sell you any tickets, with more search options than most of its clients offer.

If you hate flying or would rather take the train, Amtrak and VIA Rail Canada offer online reservations (at www.amtrak.com and www.viarail.ca). If you're visiting Europe, you can buy your Eurailpass online at www.raileurope.com or check schedules and fares for most European railways at the German railways site at www.db.de (click the small English link near the right center).

Major airline ticket sites, other than individual airlines, include

- ✔ **Expedia** (www.expedia.com): The Microsoft entry into the travel biz is now a part of the Interactive media empire.

- ✔ **Hotwire** (www.hotwire.com): This multi-airline site offers discounted leftover tickets and rental cars and hotels.

- ✔ **Orbitz** (www.orbitz.com): Orbitz is the high-tech entry into the travel biz, now an independent company, with most airlines' weekly Web specials.

- ✔ **Travelocity** (www.travelocity.com): Travelocity is the Sabre entry into the travel biz. Yahoo! Travel and the AOL travel section are both Travelocity underneath.

Fare-comparison sites abound, including Kayak (www.kayak.com), Mobissimo (www.mobissimo.com), and Sidestep (www.sidestep.com). We don't find any of them comprehensive enough to depend on, but they're worth a look if you want to try to find that elusive last cheap seat.

More about online airlines

Because the online airline situation changes weekly, anything more we print here would be out of date before you read it. One of the authors of this book is an air travel nerd in his spare time; to see his current list of online airline Web sites, Web specials, and online travel agents, visit airinfo.travel.

Even More Places to Shop

Here are a few other places for you to shop on the Web. We have even bought stuff from most of them.

Auctions and used stuff

You can participate in online auctions of everything from computers and computer parts to antiques to vacation packages. Online auctions resemble any other kind of auction in at least one respect: If you know what you're looking for and know what it's worth, you can find some decent values; if you don't, you can easily overpay for junk. When someone swiped our car phone handset, at eBay we found an exact replacement phone for $31, rather than the $150 the manufacturer charged for just the handset.

Many auctions — notably, eBay (as shown in Figure 10-3) — also allow you to list your own stuff for sale, which can be a way to get rid of some of your household clutter a little more discreetly than in a yard sale. The PayPal service (www.paypal.com), now owned by eBay, lets you accept credit card payment from the highest bidder by e-mail. (See Chapter 11 for more information about PayPal.)

Online auction sites include

- ✔ **eBay** (www.ebay.com): This auction site is the most popular one on the Web, and people flock there to sell all sorts of stuff, from baby clothes and toys to computer parts to cars to the occasional tropical island. You can sell stuff, too, by registering as a seller. eBay charges a small commission for auctions, which the seller pays. Searching the completed auctions at eBay is also a terrific way to find out how much an item is worth — you can see what people end up paying for items. If you're thinking of selling that rare Beanie Baby, search the completed auctions for the bad news that it's worth slightly less than it was when it was new.

- ✔ **Half.com** (www.half.com): This division of eBay is more like a consignment shop than an auction. Sellers list used items they want to sell at a fixed price, such as books (including textbooks), CDs, movies, video games, electronic equipment, and trading cards. eBay keeps saying that it'll merge this site into its main eBay site, but it never does.

- ✔ **Priceline.com** (www.priceline.com): This site sells airline tickets, hotel rooms, rental cars, and a grab bag of other items. Mostly like anyone else, you tell it what you want and it tells you the price. It still also has its famous reverse auction where you can specify a price for what you want and Priceline then accepts or rejects it.

Books, music, and more

You can't flip through the books in an online bookstore as easily as you can in person (although Amazon.com comes close by offering a selection of pages from many books). However, if you know what you want, you can get good deals.

Here are some top sites:

- ✔ **AbeBooks:** This site, formerly Advanced Book Exchange, offers the combined catalogs of thousands of secondhand booksellers at www.abebooks.com. You pay the same as you would in a used-book shop (plus shipping, of course), and you save hours of searching. Whether you're looking for a favorite book from your childhood or a rare, first-edition *For Dummies* book, this site is worth visiting.

Figure 10-3:
You can find
just about
anything
for sale on
eBay.

✔ **AddALL:** AddALL (`www.addall.com`) is another good used-book site offering titles from thousands of used-book stores as well as a price-comparison service for new books.

✔ **Amazon.com:** One of the great online-commerce success stories (at `www.amazon.com`) sprang up from nothing — if you call several million dollars of seed money nothing — to become one of the Net's biggest online stores. Amazon.com has an enormous catalog of books and CDs and a growing variety of other junk, much of which can get to you in a few days. It also has an affiliates program in which other Web sites can refer you to their favorite books for sale at Amazon, creating sort of a virtual virtual-bookstore. Amazon sells most books at less than list price, and in most cases also has used copies from independent sellers. It also has DVDs and used books and just about everything else from pogo sticks to underwear.

✔ **Barnes and Noble:** Barnes & Noble (`www.bn.com`) is the biggest book-store chain in the United States, and its online bookstore is big, complete, and well done. You can even return online purchases at any of its stores. It also has a large selection of music.

✔ **J&R Music World** (`www.jr.com`): The online presence of one of New York's largest music stores has a huge selection of music CDs. You can also buy a stereo to listen to your new CDs and a refrigerator to keep appropriate beverages at hand.

✔ **Powell's Books:** The country's largest independent (nonchain) bookstore has a correspondingly large Web site (`www.powellbooks.com`) offering new and used books. We like its e-mail newsletter with new and rediscovered books and author interviews.

Clothes

This section points out a few familiar clothing merchants with online stores. Directories such as Open Directory Project (ODP, at `www.dmoz.org`) and Yahoo! (at `dir.yahoo.com`) have hundreds of other stores both familiar and obscure:

✔ **Lands' End:** Most of this catalog is online (`www.landsend.com`), and you can order anything you find in any of its individual printed catalogs along with online-only discounted overstocks. It also has plenty of the folksy blather that encourages you to think of the company in terms of a few folks in the cornfields of Wisconsin rather than a corporate mail-order colossus belonging to Sears Roebuck. (It's both.)

✔ **REI:** This large sports-equipment and outdoor-wear co-op is headquartered in Seattle. Members get a small rebate on purchases. The whole catalog is online (`www.rei.com`), and you can find occasional online specials and discounts.

✔ **Eddie Bauer:** This site (`www.eddiebauer.com`) has way more stuff than is available in its stores. (John gave up on the stores about the third time they said, "Oh, you have to order that from the Web site.")

✔ **The Gap:** This site (`www.gap.com`) has the same stuff you find in its stores, but for people of unusual vertical or horizontal dimension, it also has jeans in sizes the stores don't stock, as well as links to Banana Republic and Old Navy, its upscale and downscale divisions.

Computers

When you're shopping for computer hardware online, be sure that the vendor you're considering offers both a good return policy (in case the computer doesn't work when it arrives) and a long warranty.

Here are a few well-known vendors:

✔ **Apple Computer:** The Apple site (`store.apple.com`) has lots of information about Macintosh computers, and now it offers online purchasing of iPods and iPhones, too.

- **Best Buy:** This site (www.bestbuy.com) is the online version of the ubiquitous big-box store. Orders can be shipped, or you can pick them up at your local store.

- **CDW:** CDW (www.cdw.com) has a good selection of hardware and software, and we've found it to be reliable.

- **Dell Computers:** This site has an extensive catalog with online ordering and custom computer system configurations (www.dell.com).

- **PC Connection and Mac Connection:** For computer hardware, software, and accessories, PC and Mac Connection (www.pcconnection.com and www.macconnection.com) is one of the oldest and most reliable online computer retailers. And, you can get overnight delivery within the continental United States even if you order as late as 2 a.m.!

Food

To show the range of edibles available online, here are some of our favorite places to point, click, and chow down:

- **Cabot Creamery:** This site (www.cabotcheese.coop) sells some of the best cheddar in Vermont. (Don't tell anyone that a lot of the milk comes from New York.)

- **Bobolink Dairy:** A recovering software nerd and his family in rural New Jersey make and sell their own cheese — a rich, gooey, French-style cheese. Its URL (www.cowsoutside.com) refers to cows out in the pasture rather than tied up in the barn.

- **Gimme Coffee:** This site (www.gimmecoffee.com) features highly opinionated coffee from the wilds of upstate New York. Gimme Coffee has online orders and lots of advice on what to do with your coffee after it arrives; follow the Gimme Locations link to find pictures of the place John goes when he's in need of literary inspiration, also known as *caffeine.*

- **Gaspar's** (www.linguica.com): If you weren't aware that Portuguese garlic sausage is one of the four basic food groups, this site will fix that problem. Oddly, online orders incur steep shipping charges, but phone or fax orders are shipped free, so we print and fax the order form. Also check out the competition at www.amarals.com and www.furtados.com.

- **The Kitchen Link:** Search this site (www.kitchenlink.com) for the perfect recipe and then shop for the ingredients.

- **Peapod:** Peapod (www.peapod.com) lets you shop for groceries online and then delivers them to your home. You have to live in an area that the parent grocery chains serve — the northeast and the Chicago area. If you live somewhere else, Netgrocer (www.netgrocer.com) delivers nonperishables by rather pricey overnight express, and perishables in a limited area near its New Jersey headquarters.

An online shopper's checklist

Here are some questions to keep in mind when you're shopping online. Astute shoppers will notice that these questions are the same ones to keep in mind wherever you're shopping:

- Are the descriptions clear enough to know what you're ordering?

- Are the prices competitive, with other online stores *and* with mail-order and regular retail?

- Does the store have the products in stock, or does it offer a firm shipping date?

- Does the store have a good reputation?

- Does the store have a clearly written privacy policy that limits what it can do with the data it collects from you?

- Can you ask questions about your order?

- How can you return unsatisfactory goods?

Chapter 11

Banking, Bill Paying, and Investing Online

*O*nce upon a time, money was substantial stuff that glinted in the sun and clinked when you dropped it on the table. Investments were engraved certificates that you kept in your safe-deposit box if they worked out, and used as bathroom wallpaper if they didn't. Well, that was then. Now, money and investments are mere electronic blips scampering from computer to computer, and if you do any banking or investing, one of the computers they scamper through might as well be yours.

You can do just about any banking online that doesn't require physically handling pieces of paper, which means everything except depositing checks and withdrawing cash. For those tasks, you have to use an ATM or, if you're truly retro, physically visit a bank branch and talk to a human being. But we help you avoid that last option as much as possible.

Going to the Bank without Ever Leaving Home

Nearly every bank in the country now offers online banking. They don't do it to be cool; they do it because online banking is vastly cheaper for them than

ATMs or tellers. Because both you and your bank have a strong interest in making sure that the person messing around online with your accounts is *you,* the sign-up process is usually a bit complicated — the bank either calls you to verify that you signed up or mails you a paper letter specifying your password. After you're signed up, you visit the bank's Web site and log in with your new user name or number and password. Each bank's Web site is different, but they all show you an account statement along the lines of the one from John's bank, shown in Figure 11-1.

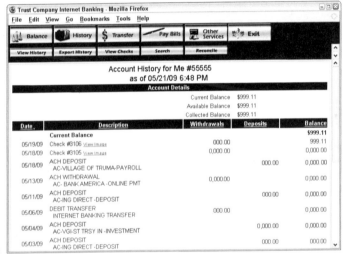

Figure 11-1: A week of bank action, give or take a few details.

As you can see, deposits and withdrawals look like they do on printed statements you receive in the mail. If you click the View Image link next to a check number, it shows you a picture of the canceled check. The Automated Clearing House, or ACH, lines are described in the nearby sidebar "ACH! It's better than a check!"

If you use an accounting program such as Quicken or Microsoft Money, banks invariably offer a way to download your account info into your program. Look for a link labeled Download or Export. In Figure 11-1, it's the small Export History button, near the upper left corner.

Details differ, but beyond the capability to check your statement, banks all offer roughly the same services, including transfers and bill-paying.

Chapter 11: Banking.

ACH! It's better than a check!

For the past 150 years or so, the usual way to move money from one person's account at a bank to a second person's account at another bank has been for the first person to write a check and give it to the second person, who takes it to her bank and deposits it. (At least, that's the system in the United States — in Europe, the first person writes out a bank transfer and gives it to his bank to set up the payment.) Now that we're in the computer age, we have a high-tech replacement for this process: ACH transfers.

Automated Clearing House, or *ACH,* transfers can do anything a check can do. Rather than print payroll checks, companies can use ACH to deposit money directly into employees' bank accounts. The U.S. government uses ACH to make Social Security payments. You can use ACH to pay bills or to move money between accounts at different banks. For most purposes, ACH transactions are better than paper checks because they're faster and more reliable.

To identify the account to use for an ACH transfer, you need to provide the *routing number* that identifies the bank and the account number at that bank. The easiest way to find the routing number for your own checking account is to look at the line of funny-looking numbers printed along the bottom of one of your checks. The routing number consists of nine digits, usually printed at the left end of the line. The account number also appears on that line, and a check number (which ACH doesn't use) may appear, too. Savings accounts also work for ACH transfers; to find the routing number, look at a check from the same bank or call the bank and ask.

You may be wondering, "Can anyone who knows my account number suck money from my account by using ACH?" Yes, but when you receive your statement, you can challenge any bogus ACH transaction just as you can challenge a forged check and get your money back. In practice, ACH is safe and reliable, and we use it for our own accounts all the time.

Transferring money between bank accounts

If you have more than one account at a bank, a checking and savings account, some CDs, or a mortgage, you can usually move money from one account to another. In the account shown earlier, in Figure 11-1, the line that says Internet Banking Transfer indicates that money has been transferred from the checking account to a mortgage account, to make the monthly mortgage payment. To get a better idea of how this transaction works, here are the steps for transferring money from a checking account to a mortgage account (again, specific steps vary among banks):

1. **Click the Transfer button (or whatever your bank's Web site calls it).**

2. **Enter the amount you want to transfer in the box labeled Amount (or similar wording).**

3. **Select the account that the transferred money is coming from, generally from a list of possible From accounts.**

4. **Select the account number that the transferred money is going to, generally from a list of possible To accounts.**

5. **Click the button labeled Transfer or Do It (or similar wording) — it's done.**

It's that easy. Most banks handle transfers within the bank the same day; at John's bank, you can enter a transfer as late as 7 p.m., which is handy when you remember at dinnertime that the mortgage is due today.

Many banks also let you make transfers to and from accounts at *other* banks, using ACH. To set up the transfers, you provide the other bank's routing code and account number. Depending on the bank, it may require you to provide a voided check from that account, verify that the account name is the same as your account name, or make a couple of tiny deposits into the account and ask you how much they were. After you set up a transfer, it resembles a transfer within your own bank: You specify the accounts and the amount and then click. You can also transfer money between your bank and your mutual fund or brokerage account. In Figure 11-1, for example, the ACH deposits from ING Direct are from another bank, and the ACH deposit from VGI-ST TRSY is from a Vanguard mutual fund.

Transfers to other banks have two important differences: time and price. Even though the transfer is handled entirely electronically, it takes anywhere from two days to a week for the money to show up at the other end, depending on the other bank. The time it takes for any particular bank is consistent, so if the transaction took three days the last time, expect it to take three days the next time. If you must have the money available so that you can write checks on it, allow a week and keep an eye on your balances until you've made enough transfers to know how long they take.

The price for transfers varies from zero to two bucks, with no consistency among banks. A transfer can be started from either the sending *(push)* or receiving *(pull)* end; often, Bank A charges you a dollar if you tell it to *send* money to Bank B, but if (instead) you tell Bank B to *receive* exactly the same amount of money from Bank A, it's free. All else being equal, pushing gets the money there faster.

You can use PayPal to move money from just about any bank account to any other bank account for free. It's a handy way to make online transfers (and we describe it later in this chapter).

Paying bills online

Writing checks is *so* 20th century. Now you can pay most of your bills online. In many cases, you can arrange for automatic payments from your bank account for routine monthly bills. (In Figure 11-1, *Bank America* refers to the MasterCard bill.) We've arranged for payments for credit cards, the electric and gas companies, and mobile phones — a typical mix. Most banks offer a *bill-pay* service, using one of a handful of specialized companies in this field. Some banks provide bill-pay for free, some charge, and some provide it for free as part of a package. Even if your bank doesn't offer bill-pay, utility and credit card companies often can arrange for you to pay their bills automatically from your checking account.

Each of these companies has its own procedure. We use a credit card example to show how this process usually works. Figure 11-2 shows the online payment page at American Express. When logged in to its Web site, you set up payments by entering for your bank account the routing code and account number that ACH needs. (See the preceding sidebar, "ACH! It's better than a check!") After the payment info is set up, you visit the Web site and specify how much you want to pay and when, and the bill is paid from your bank account. Usually, you get credit the same day, which is a big help to avoid paying credit card interest when you remember at the last minute that the bill is due. Some cards, including American Express, also offer the option to pay every month automatically on the due date, just the thing for thrifty card users who pay off the bills every month.

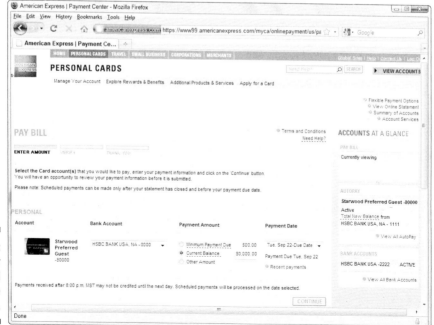

Figure 11-2: Pay your credit card bill with one click.

How safe are these banks, anyway?

When you open a bank account in person, you visit the bank and then look around to see that the bank looks like a bank, with tellers, people in suits, and a vault, which is good — or, you see a couple of people in a Winnebago with card tables and some money in cooler chests, which is bad. When you visit a bank's Web site, it's hard to tell a good one from a bad one. But it's not hard to do a little research.

Every real bank in the United States is a member of the Federal Deposit Insurance Corporation (FDIC). The FDIC has a nice-looking Web site at www.fdic.gov that has, among other things, detailed reports on each member bank. On the home page, click the Deposit Insurance link near the upper left corner, and then click Bank Find, at the top of the list. On that page,

you can search by name or location. For example, to check out ING Bank, enter its full name (**ING bank, fsb**, as it says on its home page) and search. (For this particular bank, an alternative route to the same information is to click the FDIC icon on the bank's home page.) Either way, you see a reassuring page indicating that yes, it's insured. For more info, click Financial Information to see the bank's latest balance sheets. In this case, it says that the bank has $68 billion in assets and $5.7 billion in capital. Sounds like a bank to us.

Credit unions (joining one isn't a bad idea if you're eligible) are insured by the National Credit Union Association at www.ncua.gov. You can search for the name of your credit union to check its status.

Figure 11-3 shows the bill payment service from John's bank. To set it up, you pick the companies to pay and then enter your account number and the name and address of the company if the bank doesn't already have it on file. Some bill-pay systems offer the option of *electronic presentment*, in which you see your bill on the Web rather than receive it by paper mail. You also tell the system which bank account you want to pay the bills from. Then, to pay your bills each month, you just visit the bank's Web site and enter the amounts to pay and the date. The bank automatically moves the money out of your account on the date for each payment. Some banks offer recurring payments so that you can tell it to pay the same amount every month.

If the payment service knows the payee's bank account info, it uses ACH to pay. Otherwise, the service prints an old-fashioned paper check and mails it.

Taking advantage of other online bank services

Because doing business over the Web is much cheaper than doing it in person, banks are putting all sorts of other services online. Visit your bank's Web site to see what it offers. Some of the services we've seen offered are

✔ Loan applications

✔ New accounts

✔ Retirement accounts

✔ Checkbook-balancing calculators

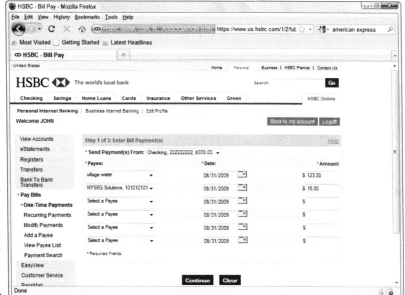

Figure 11-3:
Point, click,
and pay
the water
and electric
bills.

Checking out a few recommended banks

These days, any bank you pass while driving down the street offers online banking, but some specialist banks do everything online. Although it's possible to do all your banking online, we prefer to have our main account at a local bank, where we can drop by and argue with the staff, and use an online bank for a high-interest savings account that you can't get at a local bank.

To give you a flavor of what's available, here are two banks we use and recommend:

✔ **HSBC Direct:** A British bank that is, by some measures, the largest bank in the world (www.us.hsbc.com)

✔ **ING Direct,** www.ingdirect.com: A large Dutch bank also with subsidiaries all over the world (not as large as HSBC, but still big)

Both have U.S. subsidiaries that offer online accounts with better interest rates than most competitors and no minimum balances. HSBC has lots of physical offices, but for the high-interest online account, you have to sign up online. ING has an office in Wilmington, Delaware, that we walked past one time, but we didn't see any reason to go in.

To open an account at either bank, you fill out a form on its Web site, including the ACH info about your existing checking account to link to your new HSBC or ING account. After it's set up, you can move money back and forth between the accounts as needed. (Money you put into your ING account has to stay there for a week before you can get it back. The HSBC account limits you to six withdrawals per month. Accounts at other banks have similar rules.) Both also offer checkless checking accounts, certificates of deposit, mortgages, home equity loans, and retirement accounts. HSBC, a full-service bank, offers everything else a bank offers, all available online if you want it.

We've used both these banks quite happily, but we give the nod to HSBC because it pays slightly more interest and gives you an ATM card you can use for withdrawals anywhere and deposits at HSBC branches. If you travel a lot, you pay no withdrawal fee at any HSBC machine anywhere in the world.

Trying out combo banking

If you have an account with a stockbroker, such as the ones we list later in this chapter, it generally offers a check-writing option, which makes it act like a checking account, usually at very low cost. If you don't have a local bank you like, this option can be a good one.

Dealing with Credit Cards

Just about every credit card in the country offers online access for the same reason that bank accounts do — online transactions are a lot cheaper for them than calls to the 800 number.

Online credit card services start with applying for the card. Search Google for credit cards, and you find a phantasmagoria of offers. They change daily, but you can look for various goodies — no annual fee, bonuses and rebates, and low interest rates. Most of the sites that appear to compare cards are in fact selling one bank's cards, so treat their claims of unique and superior features with skepticism.

After you have your card, typical online conveniences include these:

✔ Check your balance and recent transactions.

✔ Pay your bill from your checking account.

✔ Apply for a credit line increase.

✔ Ask for copies of sales slips for charges you don't recognize, or challenge ones you think are bogus.

✔ Download account information into Quicken and other personal finance programs.

✔ Manage rebate and bonus programs related to the cards.

Different credit-card-issuing banks have somewhat different versions of these services, but it's difficult to compare them without getting the credit card first. For example, some banks let you set up automatic payments to pay each bill in full on the due date, getting the maximum use of your money without paying interest. At others, you have to visit their Web sites each month to schedule the month's payment. Some have single-use card numbers, some don't. We would make a list of features, but it would be out of date before it was printed, so visit some bank Web sites to see what they're offering. (We compared two different banks in the tenth edition of this book, but then they merged, keeping the worst features of each. Sigh.)

Pay Your Pals with PayPal

Credit cards are easy to use — if you're *spending* money. Until recently, it has been all but impossible for individuals (rather than companies) to receive payments by credit card. Even small businesses found it expensive and time consuming to accept credit card payments. PayPal (www.paypal.com) has changed all that, and also provides an easy way to move money among accounts at different banks.

PayPal is a boon to individuals who sell at auction sites like eBay (which owns PayPal), but it has many other uses, too. PayPal makes it easy to start a small business on the Web: Small organizations can use PayPal to collect payments for events such as dinners and amateur theater, nonprofits can accept donations, and it's just about the only way to make payments to individuals in other countries without paying a service charge larger than the amount you're paying.

If you plan to accept PayPal for your business, be sure to heed PayPal's warnings regarding shipping *only to verified buyer addresses.* Be sure to comply carefully with all the fine print to protect yourself against fraud. Most first-time sellers learn the hard way that it's they who pay the cost of fraud — and even the cost of their customers' innocent errors. The PayPal fraud rate is lower than that of most credit card fraud, but it's a case of *merchant beware* — know your customer and take appropriate steps to safeguard your transactions.

PayPal offers the following services, but you have to observe a few rules:

- ✔ To send money, you have to have a PayPal account. An account is easy (and free) to open.

- ✔ After you open an account, you can send money to anyone who can receive e-mail. If that person doesn't already have a PayPal account, she opens one when "cashing" your e-mail. The money you send can come from the balance in your PayPal account or from a bank account or credit card that you link to your PayPal account.

- ✔ After you have money in your account, you can use it to pay other people, move it to your linked bank account, or spend it with a debit card linked to your PayPal account.

- ✔ Individual accounts are free, but there are limits on the size and type of payments you can accept. The limits for payments from bank accounts tend to be higher than those from credit cards.

- ✔ Check the list of fees carefully. Payments marked Personal are generally free. Everything else has about a 3 percent fee.

- ✔ Premier accounts have a much higher limit on accepting payments, but are charged a fee on each payment they receive.

The folks at PayPal encourage you to provide them with your bank account number so that when you pay somebody, PayPal can take the money directly. That way, they don't have to pay the credit card companies, and you can move any money you receive into your account with minimum hassle.

Be careful about giving your bank-account information to *anyone.* A variety of criminals send out huge numbers of notices, claiming to be from PayPal and claiming that you "must" provide them with your account number and password right away to clear up an account problem. Don't fall for it. PayPal will *never* ask you for your password or account information in an e-mail message — or anywhere other than on its Web site (at `https://www.paypal.com`).

When you first tell PayPal to link your account to a bank account, PayPal verifies your bank account number by making two random deposits of less than a dollar. You then have to tell it the amount of the deposits to complete your registration. You can link several bank accounts to your PayPal account and then move money out of one account into PayPal, wait a few days for the transaction to be complete, and then move the money out of PayPal and into a different account — all for free.

If you leave money in your PayPal account, it pays interest at a decent rate — but because PayPal is not a bank, your money is safer in your bank account. (Most U.S. bank accounts are insured, whereas PayPal accounts are not.) We recommend that you only leave money in PayPal that you're planning to use within a few days. If you're fortunate enough to need to keep a significant balance in an online account, ING Direct and HSBC (described earlier in this chapter) are real banks with deposit insurance and pay about the same as PayPal. Open an account at either one and then link your PayPal account to your HSBC or ING Direct account, as well as to your main bank account.

Investing Your Money Online

If you invest in mutual funds or the stock market (something that's difficult to avoid these days unless you anticipate dying at an early age), you can find a remarkable range of resources online. An enormous amount of stock information is also available, providing Net users with research resources as good as professional analysts had before the advent of online investing.

The most important thing to remember about *all* online financial resources is that everyone has an ax to grind — and wants to get paid somehow. In most cases, the situation is straightforward; for example, a mutual fund manager wants you to invest with her funds, and a stockbroker wants you to buy and sell stocks with him. Some other sites are less obvious: Some are supported by advertising, and others push certain special kinds of investments. Just consider the source (and any vested interests they may have in mind) when you're considering that source's advice.

Mutual funds

Mutual funds are definitely the investment of the baby boomer generation. The world now has more mutual funds than it has stocks for the funds to buy. (Kind of makes you wonder, doesn't it?) Most fund managers have at least descriptions of the funds and prospectuses online, and many now provide online access so that you can check your account, move money from one fund to another within a fund group, and buy and sell funds — all with the money coming from and going to your bank account by way of ACH.

Well-known fund groups include

- **American Century:** A broad group of funds at `www.american century.com`
- **Fidelity Investments:** The 500-pound gorilla of mutual funds; specializes in actively managed funds at `www.fidelity.com`

✔ **Vanguard Group:** The other 500-pound gorilla; specializes in low-cost and index funds at `www.vanguard.com`

The online brokers listed in the following section also let you buy and sell mutual funds, although it almost always costs less if you deal directly with the fund manager.

Stockbrokers

Most well-known, full-service brokerage firms have jumped onto the Web, along with a new generation of low-cost online brokers that offer remarkably cheap stock trading. A trade that may cost $100 with a full-service firm can cost as little as $8 with a low-cost broker. The main difference is that the cheap firms don't offer investment advice and don't assign you to a specific broker. For people who do their own research and don't want advice from a broker, the low-cost firms work well. For people who need some advice, the partial- or full-service firms often offer lower-cost trades online, and they let you get a complete view of your account whenever you want. The number of extra services the brokerages offer (such as retirement accounts, dividend reinvestment, and automatic transfers to and from your checking account) varies widely.

Online brokers include

✔ **Charles Schwab:** The original discount broker (`www.schwab.com`) offers somewhat more investment help than E-Trade and TD Ameritrade, but at a slightly higher price. Kathleen Sindell, the author of *Investing Online For Dummies,* recommended this site to us.

✔ **E-Trade:** This low-cost, no-advice broker (`www.etrade.com`) also offers bank accounts, credit cards, boat loans, and just about every other financial service known to humankind.

✔ **Smith Barney:** This full-service broker (`www.smithbarney.com`) offers online access to accounts and research info. It's a subsidiary of Citigroup, one of the largest banks in the world, which may or may not be a good thing.

✔ **TD Ameritrade,** `www.tdameritrade.com`: The low-cost, limited-advice broker, which is affiliated with Toronto-Dominion Bank, one of the largest Canadian banks. It has good online research tools.

Most fund groups, including the ones in the preceding list, have brokerage departments — which can be a good choice if you want to hold both individual stocks and funds.

Portfolio tracking

Several services let you track your portfolio online. You enter the number of shares of each fund and stock you own, and the service can tell you — at any time — exactly how much they're worth and how much money you lost today. Some of them send by e-mail a daily portfolio report, if you want. These reports are handy if you have mutual funds from more than one group or both funds and stocks. All the tracking services are either supported by advertising or run by a brokerage that hopes to gain your trading business:

- ✔ **Google Finance:** (www.google.com/finance) offers multiple portfolios with a minimalist Google style. Google is at the moment the only site that offers real-time as opposed to 20-minute delayed stock quotes, for people who think they can beat the market.

- ✔ **MSN MoneyCentral:** (moneycentral.msn.com) This service also has portfolios and lots of information, although we find it cumbersome to set up and more of a pain to use than My Yahoo!. To use all its features, you have to use Internet Explorer.

- ✔ **Smart Money:** (www.smartmoney.com) The online face of *Smart Money* magazine lets you track portfolios and read news stories. Although the site wants you to subscribe to the magazines, the free portfolio tracker isn't bad.

- ✔ **My Yahoo!:** (my.yahoo.com) Enter multiple portfolios and customize your screens with related company and general news reports. You can also see lots of company and industry news, including some access to sites that otherwise require paid subscriptions. It's advertiser supported, comprehensive, and easy to use. We stock market junkies particularly like the streaming updates that continually update stock values in flickers of red (bad) and green (good).

Budgeting Tools

Sites to help spend, pay, and invest your money are useful, assuming that you have money to spend, pay, and invest. Toward that end, some Web sites help you make and follow a budget. They link to your bank and credit card accounts so that they can track the money coming in and out and let you know how reality compares to your budget. We've found some significant bugs in the ones we've tried that made them misreport our financial situation, so check their numbers before you trust them. However, if your finances are simple (and all in one currency), these sites can be useful for categorizing your spending and comparing it to your budget. Here are two:

✔ **Mint.com** tracks your budget against your bank accounts, with occasional offers from their sponsors. It's strong in budgeting tools, suggestions about how your budget compares with its other million users, warnings of upcoming bills, and lots of pretty charts and graphs.

✔ **Quicken.com** is the online version of the popular Quicken personal finance package. The Web site isn't as glitzy as Mint.com, but account setup is easier and the overall site is easier to use if you don't want all the helpful Mint.com advice.

(Quicken has bought Mint.com, so these two sites may end up merging.)

Chapter 12

Swiping Files from the Net

. . . .

In This Chapter

▶ Using your Web browser to download files

▶ Downloading and viewing pictures

▶ Installing software you swiped from the Net

▶ Scanning downloaded files for purity and wholesomeness

▶ Downloading other types of files

. . . .

*T*he Internet is chock-full of computers, and those computers are chock-full of files. What's in those files? Programs, baby pictures, adult pictures, sounds, movies, documents, spreadsheets, recipes, *Anne of Green Gables* (the entire book and several of its sequels) — you name it. Some of the computers are set up so that you can copy some of the files they contain to your own computer, usually for free. In this chapter, we tell you how to find some of those files and how to copy and use them.

What Is Downloading?

Downloading means copying files from a computer Up There On The Internet "down" to the computer sitting on or under your desk. *Uploading* is the reverse — copying a file from your computer "up" to a computer on the Internet.

You probably won't be surprised to hear that you can download and upload files in three different ways:

- ✔ **Click a link on a Web page.** Web browsers can download files, too. In fact, they do it all time when they download Web pages so that you can see them.

- ✔ **Participate in a file sharing service.** Because these services are of dubious legality, and tend to install spyware on your computer, we don't recommend them. File-sharing services include LimeWire and BitTorrent.

    ✔ **Run a file transfer program.** *FTP* stands for File Transfer Protocol, an older (but still widely used) way that computers transfer files across the Internet.

You can also transfer files by attaching them to e-mail messages sent to other e-mail users, which we discuss in Chapter 13.

By far the easiest way to download files is by using your Web browser — clicking links is our favorite method of finding and downloading files.

How you download a file and what you do with it after you have it also depends on what's in the file. This chapter describes how to download pictures, programs, and other files using your Web browser. If you want to download music and video, refer to Chapter 9.

Downloading Pictures

High-quality digitized pictures; a large fraction of all the bits flying around the Internet is made up of them. About 99.44 percent of the pictures are purely for fun, games, and worse. We're sure that you're in the 0.56 percent of users who need the pictures for work.

The most commonly used graphics formats on the Net are GIF, JPEG, and PNG. A nice feature of these file formats is that they do a fair job of compression internally, so quality is high even in files that aren't too humongous.

Dozens of commercial and shareware programs on PCs and Macs can read and write graphics files. Firefox, Google Chrome, and Internet Explorer can display them as well; just choose File⊅Open from the menu. The buttons and icons on Web pages are usually stored as GIF files, too.

To download a picture from the Web, follow these steps:

1. **Display the picture in your Web browser.**

2. **Right-click the picture and choose Save Image As or Save Picture As from the menu that appears.**

   A small number of Web sites disable right-clicking pictures to prevent you from saving them. Oh, well!

3. **In the dialog box that appears, tell your browser where to save the picture on your computer.**

   You can choose the folder where you want to put it and the filename to use.

4. **Click Save.**

That's all it takes!

 Graphics files have special filename extensions that identify which graphics format the file is in. When you download a picture, you can change the name of the file, but *don't* change the extension. Common extensions are GIF; JPEG or JPG; TIFF or TIF; and PNG.

Art Ain't Free

As plentiful as art is on the Internet, consider this: Somebody had to work to create every one of those images. Some artists want to control what happens to their work, or even be paid for it. (What a concept.)

 Just because a picture is on a Web page doesn't mean that no one owns it. Nearly all graphics on Web pages are copyrighted, and it's not legal to use the picture without getting permission from the copyright owner. No one will sue you for storing a picture on your computer (so far as we know — we're not lawyers) but don't plan on using downloaded graphics in your own Web site or publication without getting permission. Unless a picture comes from a site that specifically offers pictures as reusable *clip art* (art you can clip and use), you have to get permission to reuse the picture for most purposes — even to upload it to your own, noncommercial Web page.

To find clip art sources, search for *clip art* or *clipart* — and include a word or phrase describing what you need a picture of. Some of the images you're shown are free, and some require a subscription or payment per picture. We like `www.clipart.com`, which requires a subscription fee but offers a mountain of clip art and photos you can legally download and reuse.

Downloading Programs

Lots of the programs that this book recommends can be downloaded from the Web, often for free. This section describes the process for downloading programs and getting them running.

Sticking with the plan: Download, install, and run

When you download a program, you transfer a file from a computer on the Internet to your computer. But the program is still trapped inside the file — you usually need to take additional steps to let it out. The file you download is usually an installation program, which you run to install the actual program. While you're at it, you'd be wise to scan the program for viruses before running it.

All these steps are described in the following pages — just keep reading!

Finding programs to download

The first step in downloading a program is to find it. In some cases, you already know the Web address where the file is available for download. For example, in Chapter 6 we recommend that you avoid Internet Explorer because it's a target for viruses and spyware. (Chapter 2 describes what we mean by viruses and spyware.) We suggest that you switch to Firefox, which is a free download from the Web site www.mozilla.com, or Google Chrome, which you can download for free from chrome.google.com.

In other cases, you may hear about a program but not know where to find it. Google is your friend — search for the program's name and you will probably find its source.

Another good source for downloadable programs is a software library, such as CNET at www.download.com (for freeware, described in the following sidebar, "Free and not-quite-free-ware") and www.shareware.com (for shareware). Libraries include recommendations and reviews, and they scan their programs for viruses and other bad stuff.

Free and not-quite-free-ware

Some software is free — it's freeware. *Freeware* is available for download for free with no strings attached. Firefox and Google Chrome are freeware, as are many of the programs at the TUCOWS software library at www.tucows.com.

When the authors ask for donations if you like their programs — on the honor system — it's *shareware*. You can download and install a program for free, just like freeware, but if you keep using it, you should make a donation to its author. (If you don't, don't expect the program to be updated in the long run!) The site from which you download shareware should specify the requested donation. You can usually also choose Help from the program's menu to find out how to make a donation.

Some downloaded programs are *trialware* or *crippleware*, which are time-limited or otherwise-limited versions of the program. You can use the downloaded program for free, but if you want the real, complete program, you need to pay for it. The program itself tells you its limitations, its price, and how to pay. Some programs don't limit their features, but they display ads unless you pay — a reasonable trade-off.

Viruses and spyware can be contained in any program, so don't run an executable file unless you're sure that you know what's in it! Stick with the software libraries we recommend in this chapter because they scan their files for viruses and spyware. Or, download programs directly from the software organization. (For example, get Firefox from www.mozilla.com and Google software from google.com.)

Downloading a program file

Before you start downloading, make a folder to store all your downloaded program files, like this:

✔ Windows 7 comes with a folder named Downloads. To open it, choose Start⇨Documents and click Downloads.

✔ Windows Vista comes with a Downloads folder in your user folder.

✔ In Windows XP, to create a Downloads folder in My Documents, choose Start⇨My Documents, choose File⇨New⇨Folder from the menu, and name the new folder Downloads.

✔ On a Mac, in Finder, open Places, your username, and Downloads.

Downloading a program file over the Web is easy:

1. **Click a link to the file, frequently a link that says either Download or the name of the program.**

   Your Web browser asks you what to do with the file. If it's a program (in Windows, a file with the extension .exe) or a Zip file (with the extension .zip), the most reasonable thing for you to do is to save it in your Downloads folder and then install it at your leisure.

2. **Click Save.**

   Depending on which browser you use, downloading looks a little different. In Firefox, you may see a Downloads window that shows your progress. In Google Chrome, a message at the bottom of the window may appear and warn you that you're downloading a program, and if you're not sure that it's a safe program, it could do a lot of damage. Assuming that you trust the source of the program, go ahead. Internet Explorer may block the download when it sees an executable file arriving; follow the directions to click the message and choose Download File. Sometimes, other download manager programs appear, too.

3. **When the download has finished, decide what to do next.**

   Your browser may display a message or window showing that the file is ready to install — read on.

Scanning for Viruses

We warn you about viruses in Chapter 2 and encourage you in Chapter 4 to install a virus checker. Chapter 14 describes how to configure your virus checker and how to tell your e-mail program not to run programs you receive by e-mail. As you can tell, we take viruses seriously, and we think you should, too.

We all know that you practice safe software: You check every new program you get to make sure that it contains no hidden software viruses that may display obnoxious messages or trash your hard drive. If that's true of you (no fibbing, now), you can skip this section.

The rest of you — make that all of us, these days — should run a virus-scanning program at regular intervals and keep it updated. You never know what naughty piece of code you may otherwise unwittingly download to your defenseless computer!

Run your virus checker after you have obtained and run *any* new piece of software. Although the Web and FTP servers on the Internet make every effort to keep their software archives virusfree, nobody is perfect.

Installing the program

Okay, now you have the downloaded program file and you know that it's safe to proceed. However, most downloaded programs are still trapped in an installation file — they aren't ready to use yet. For example, when you download Firefox, you get a file with a name like `Firefox Setup 3.5.2.exe`. (The .exe at the end tells you that it's a program; it's short for *exe*cutable.) That's not Firefox; it's the Firefox Setup program, which *contains* Firefox.

If you just downloaded the program file, your browser may be waiting breathlessly to install it:

- ✔ **In Firefox,** the Downloads window shows the filename, ready to click when the download is finished.

- ✔ **In Google Chrome,** the name of the file appears at the bottom of the Chrome window, along with a Show All Downloads link to see anything else you've downloaded recently.

- ✔ **In IE,** you see a Download Complete window with a Run button.

Uncompressing and unzipping files

Most downloadable software on the Internet is in a compressed format to save storage space on the server and transmission time when you download the file. Most software is *self-installing* — the file is (or contains) a program that does the necessary uncompressing and installing. Self-installing Windows files have the extension .exe or .msi, and non-self-installing compressed files have the extension .zip.

To install a self-installing file, just double-click the file to run it — and skip to the later section "Installing the program." If a file is compressed, you need a program to open and uncompress it. Files with the file extension .zip identify compressed files (these files are, amazingly, *Zip files*). If you use Windows 7, Vista, or XP or a modern Mac, they all pretend that Zip files are folders. Just double-click the Zip file to see what's inside it. For older versions of Windows, programs such as WinZip (downloadable from www.winzip.com) can unzip and zip things for you. Users of older Macs may need the StuffIt program, from my.smithmicro.com/mac.

If none of these buttons or windows is visible (maybe you're getting around to installing the program a couple of days after downloading it), double-click the name of the setup program in My Computer or Finder. The file should open itself and walk you through a wizard-style set of windows to collect any needed setup info — and then install itself. If you're using Windows 7 or Vista, a box pops up and asks whether you're an administrator to complete the installation. If you're sure that you trust the source of the program, click OK. The setup program probably creates an icon for the program on your desktop. In Windows, it may also add the program to your Start menu.

A small number of simple programs don't come with an installation program — you just get the program itself, and after it's unzipped, you need only run the program you extracted from the Zip file. To make the program easy to run, you need an icon for it. You can create your own icon or menu item for the program. In Windows, follow these steps:

1. **Run either My Computer or Windows Explorer and select the program file (the file with the extension .exe or occasionally .com or .msi).**

2. **Use your right mouse button to drag the filename out on the desktop or into an open folder on the desktop.**

   An icon for the program appears.

Downloading the old-fashioned way with FTP

Back before the Web was even invented, the Internet was up and running. (And yes, then-Senator Al Gore was a major player in getting the funding that made the Internet possible.) When you wanted to download a file, you used an FTP program — File Transfer Protocol. You needed to know the name of the server on which the file was stored and in which folder it was stored.

If you want the retro FTP experience, see `net.gurus.org/ftp` to read how FTP used to work — and still does.

Web browsers can download files by FTP automatically; if you see a URL that starts with `ftp://`, that's an FTP download, which works just like any other Web download.

Another method is to choose Start➪Programs or Start➪All Programs, find the menu choice for the program, hold down the Shift key, drag the menu choice to the desktop, and release the Shift key. Windows copies the menu choice as an icon on the desktop.

To run your new program, you can just click or double-click the icon (depending on how you have Windows configured — try clicking first, and if nothing happens, double-click). Cool!

Configuring the program

Now you can run the program. Hooray!

You may have to tell the program, however, about your Internet address or your computer or who-knows-what before it can do its job. Refer to the text files (if any) that came with the program — or choose Help from the program's menu bar — to see more information about how to configure and run your new program. The Web site from which you got the program may have some explanations, too.

Downloading Other Types of Files

If you want to download almost any type of file — such as a Word document, a spreadsheet, or a database — you can follow these steps:

1. **Find the file on the Web.**

   Search the Web for it, as described in Chapter 8.

2. **Follow the instructions on the Web page to download the file.**

   This step usually just means clicking a Download button.

3. **When your browser displays a Save or Save As dialog box, choose where to put the file.**

   If you have created a Downloads or Downloaded Files folder, put it there. Or, put it in the folder where you want the file to end up.

4. **Check the file for viruses.**

   See the section "Scanning for Viruses," earlier in this chapter, for details.

5. **Unzip the file if necessary (which it usually isn't).**

   If the file is large or you're downloading a group of files, the file or files may be compressed into a Zip file. See the "Uncompressing and unzipping files" sidebar, earlier in this chapter, to find out how to uncompress the file.

6. **Open the file with its matching program.**

   If you downloaded a Word document, open it in Word (or, maybe OpenOffice, a nice freeware office suite you can download from www. openoffice.org.) If you aren't sure which kind of file you have, or which program opens it, display the filename in My Computer or Finder and double-click the filename. If you have a program installed that can open the file, your computer should run the program and open the file automatically.

Your files are ready to use!

Some File Types and What to Do with Them

The name of a file — in particular, its *extension* (the end of the name after the last period) — usually gives you a clue about the type of file it is. Although people usually try to be consistent and follow the conventions for filename extensions, file naming isn't a sure thing. Windows uses the extension to specify which program to use to open a file, so you may sometimes have to rename a file to an extension that will persuade Windows to use the right program. For example, if you double-click a file with the extension DOC, Windows runs Microsoft Word, OpenOffice, or WordPad (which all are associated with the DOC file extension) to open the file. If you rename a Word document to end with the extension GIF, Windows no longer knows that the file contains a document.

Hundreds of kinds of files exist, maybe thousands. Fortunately, they fall into some general categories:

✔ **Executable:** Files you can execute, or run; in other words, programs. In Windows, these programs have the extension `.exe` or sometimes `.msi`. Executable programs are widely available for downloading for PCs and Macs; see the section "Downloading Programs," earlier in this chapter, to find out how to install them safely.

✔ **Compressed:** Archives, Zip files, SIT files, and other compressed files, encoded in a special way that takes up less space but can be decoded only by the corresponding *uncompressor.* Windows compressed files end with ZIP and appear as compressed folders. Mac compressed files are decoded by using StuffIt. (See the sidebar "Uncompressing and unzipping files," earlier in this chapter.)

✔ **Graphics:** See "Downloading Pictures," earlier in this chapter.

✔ **Audio and video:** Files that contain pictures and sounds encoded in computer-readable form. Graphics files on Web pages are usually in GIF or JPEG format. Audio files can be in WAV (Windows audio), RAM (RealAudio), MP3 (music), WMA (Windows Media Player), or other formats. Video files contain digitized movies, in AVI, MPEG, or WMV format. Audio and video files — files that contain digitized sound and movies — can be found all over the Web, ranging from songs to radio shows to recorded books to full-length movies. For all kinds of music and video on the Web, refer to Chapter 9.

✔ **Plain text:** Files that contain text, believe it or not, with no formatting codes. Text files contain readable text with no word-processor-style formatting codes. (What did you expect?) Sometimes, the text is human-readable text, such as the manuscript for the first edition of this book, which we typed into text files. Sometimes, the text is source code or data for computer programs. On PCs, text files usually have the file extension `.txt` (or no extension). You can look at these files by using Notepad, WordPad, or any word processor. Mac text files also often have the TXT file type. Read text files on a Macintosh with TextEdit or any word processor.

✔ **PDF:** Portable Document Format files (with the extension `.pdf`) are formatted documents, ready to view and print. The most popular program that displays and prints PDF files is Acrobat Reader. If your computer doesn't already have it, you can download it from `adobe.com/products/acrobat`. Several free or cheap PDF creators are now available; we recommend the Pdf995 Printer Driver, at `www.pdf995.com`. You usually can't edit a PDF file, but when you print it, it looks great, and some PDFs are forms you can fill out and print. The IRS offers tax forms as PDFs at `www.irs.gov/formspubs`.

✔ **Formatted text documents:** Formatted text documents are frequently stored in Microsoft Word (DOC) or Rich Text Format (RTF) format. Unfortunately, different versions of Word store different types of DOC files; RTF is slightly more standard. OpenOffice Writer uses the extension `.sxw`. Most word processing software can recognize a competitor's format and make a valiant effort to convert the format to something usable so that you aren't tempted to buy the other product. Windows comes with the WordPad program, which can open many Word documents.

✔ **Entire books:** You can download entire books and read them on your PC, reader (Amazon Kindle or Sony Reader), or smartphone. Unfortunately, too many competing formats for books exist. Books that are copyrighted usually have to be purchased, are copy-protected in some way, and need a special reader; for example, you can buy Kindle-formatted books at Amazon.com and read them by using its Kindle Reader program. Books out of copyright (like the thousands of classics that you've been meaning to read) can be downloaded for free from Project Gutenberg, at `gutenberg.org/catalog`, in a variety of formats. (Margy has downloaded *War and Peace* and hopes to finish reading it on her iPhone before the year 2025. John is working on *Ben-Hur*.)

✔ **Data:** Any other type of file. You can handle Excel (`.xls`) and PowerPoint (`.ppt`) files similarly, by opening them in the application.

Part IV

E-Mail, Chat, and Other Ways to Hang Out Online

The 5th Wave   By Rich Tennant

PRINCIPAL'S OFFICE

"He should be all right now. I made him spend two and a half hours on a prisoners' chat line."

In this part . . .

Now we turn to the part of the Internet that *very* slightly resembles talking on the phone because you're talking (or typing) to other people. We start with e-mail, one of the oldest but still most useful Net services, for one-to-one conversations *and* discussions among larger e-mail communities. You'll find advice about how to use e-mail and how to keep safe from e-mail-borne spam and viruses. We finish with faster-paced modern alternatives, such as instant messages, online chat, Twitter, Internet phones, and the wild world of online gaming.

Chapter 13

It's in the Mail: Sending and Receiving E-Mail

In This Chapter

▶ Dissecting the anatomy of an e-mail address

▶ Mastering the maze of mail servers 'n' stuff

▶ Choosing an e-mail program

▶ Setting up e-mail on your smartphone

▶ Sending e-mail

▶ Receiving e-mail

▶ Finding e-mail addresses

*E*lectronic mail, or *e-mail,* is without a doubt the most popular Internet service, even though it's one of the oldest and least glitzy. Although e-mail doesn't have the flash and sparkle of the World Wide Web, more people use it. Every system on the Net supports some sort of mail service, which means that no matter what kind of computer you're using, if it's on the Internet, you can send and receive mail. Even some systems that aren't technically on the Internet — think mobile phone — can do e-mail.

Regardless of which type of mail you're using, the basic tasks of reading, sending, addressing, and filing mail work in much the same way, so skimming this chapter is worthwhile even if you're not using any of the mail programs we describe here.

Young whippersnappers are alleged to think that e-mail is for old people, and that the cool way to send messages is by using text messages on their phones, instant messaging (covered in Chapter 16), or messages within Facebook or another social networking site. However, e-mail is still *the* way that businesses communicate with each other and with customers, and that most people send messages over the Internet. Not everyone is on Facebook, LinkedIn, or whatever the new Web site is, but almost everyone who has ever used the Internet has an e-mail address. Don't worry: E-mail is still cool! (And anyway, nearly all those sites send you mail when someone sends you a message, so you just need to check your mail, not all umpteen Web sites, to see what's new.)

What's My Address?

Your *e-mail address* is the cyberspace equivalent of a postal address or a phone number. When you send an e-mail message, you type the addresses of the recipients so that the computer knows where to send it.

Before you can do much mailing, you have to figure out your e-mail address so that you can give it to people who want to get in touch with you. You also have to figure out some of their addresses so that you can write to them. (If you have no friends or plan to send only anonymous hate mail, you can skip this section.)

E-mail addresses have two parts, separated by an @ (the *at*-sign). The part before the @ is the *username* or *mailbox,* which is, roughly speaking, your personal name. The part after that is the *domain.*

The domain part

The domain (the part after the @) indicates where your mailbox is stored. Mailboxes usually live in one of four places:

- ✔ **Your Internet service provider (ISP):** If you sign up for a DSL account at Verizon, the domain is `verizon.net`. If you use AOL, it's `aol.com`.

- ✔ **Your school, employer, or other organization:** If you attend Tufts University (Go, Jumbos!), the domain is `tufts.edu`. If you work for Microsoft, it's `microsoft.com`.

- ✔ **Your own domain, such as gurus.org:** (That's one of ours.) You can own your domain name, as described in Chapter 20. You need to arrange for your domain to live somewhere, which is probably where your mail-boxes will be stored, too.

- ✔ **A Web-based e-mail service, or *webmail:*** If you don't have an ISP (say, you connect from the public library), all is not lost. Years ago, some genius had the idea of creating a Web site where you can sign up for an e-mail account and then log in to read and send messages. Your e-mail mailbox lives on the Web site's mail servers, and you use your browser, rather than a regular e-mail program, to read and send messages. Many

Web sites now provide free mailboxes — try one out at Google Gmail, www.gmail.com, Windows Live Hotmail (formerly just Hotmail) at mail.live.com, Yahoo! Mail at mail.yahoo.com, or AIM Mail at web-mail.aol.com. See the later section "The Web Is a Fine Place to Read Your E-Mail" to find out how to sign up for a webmail account.

Even if your ISP or employer offers mailboxes, you may want to sign up for a webmail account. Some of us prefer to separate our work-related e-mail from our personal ones. Another advantage of webmail is that if you change ISPs, your e-mail address doesn't change. When our local cable Internet company changed its domain from verizon.net to myfairpoint.com, all its customers had to let their friends know about their new e-mail address, and many chose to switch to a webmail address instead.

The username part

Your *username* is the name assigned to your particular mailbox. You can write to the president of the United States at president@whitehouse.gov, for example. The president's username is president, and the domain that stores his mailbox is whitehouse.gov — reasonable enough.

If you're lucky, you get to choose your username; in other cases, ISPs standardize usernames and you get what you get. You may choose (or be assigned) your first name as your username — or your last name, your initials, your first name and last initial, your first initial and last name, or a completely made-up name. At the major webmail sites, all obvious usernames have already been taken, so you may need to get creative, by adding numbers or other information to create a username that's not already in use.

Many organizations assign usernames in a consistent format for all users, most often by using your first and last names with a dot (.) between them or your first initial followed by the first seven letters of your last name. In these schemes, your e-mail address may resemble elvis.presley@bluesuede.org or epresley@bluesuede.org. (If your name isn't Elvis Presley, adjust this example suitably. On the other hand, if your name *is* Elvis Presley, please contact us immediately. We know some people who are looking for you.)

When you sign up with an ISP, the provider creates a mailbox for each of your usernames. Although some ISPs offer only one username with each Internet account, many ISPs offer as many as five mailboxes with five different usernames for a single account so that each person in your family can have a mailbox.

Whaddaya mean you don't know your own address?

It happens frequently — you know the e-mail address you requested for your new account, but you're not absolutely positive that it was approved. Before you give out your address to everyone you know, test it out by sending a message to a friend or two. Tell them to reply to your message when they receive it and to let you know which address your message came from. Or, send yourself a message and use your e-mail login name as the mailbox name. Then examine the return address on the message.

Better yet, send a message to *The Internet For Dummies* Mail Central, at `internet12@gurus.org`, and a friendly robot will send back a message with your address. (While you're at it, tell us whether you like this book, because we authors read that mail and write back when time permits.) If you're planning on testing your e-mail repeatedly and don't care whether we read your message, send it to `test@gurus.org`.

Don't share an e-mail address with other people, unless they're *very* close friends. Many Internet services use your e-mail address as your personal identifier, send a message to your address to confirm your identity, and assume that anyone with access to your account is you. Webmail addresses are free, so if you don't already have your own e-mail address, get one.

Putting it all together

Whenever you set up a mail program, you need to enter information about your e-mail mailbox. People switch mail programs from time to time (new versions often come out with swell new features), so write in Table 13-1 your e-mail address and other info that your ISP, employer, or school or another e-mail provider gave you (and fold down the corner of this page so that you can find it again later). Capitalization never matters in domains and rarely matters in usernames. To make it easy on your eyes, therefore, most domain and mailbox names in this book are shown in lowercase. (Don't worry about the parts of the table you don't understand right away — we explain later in this chapter what *servers* are.)

Table 13-1   **Information Your Mail Program Needs to Know**

	Description	*Example*
Your e-mail address _____	Your username followed by @ and the domain name.	`internet12@gurus.org`
Your e-mail password _____	The password for your e-mail mailbox (usually the same as the password for your account).	`dum3myBook`
Your incoming (POP or IMAP) mail server _____	The name of the computer that receives your e-mail messages. (Get this name from your ISP; skip it if you use webmail or AOL.)	`email.gurus.org`
Is your incoming mail server POP or IMAP? __ POP __ IMAP __ Webmail __ AOL	Which protocol your server uses, and which your e-mail program needs to use to retrieve your mail; doesn't apply to webmail or AOL.	
Your outgoing (SMTP) mail server _____	The name of the computer that distributes your outgoing mail to the rest of the Internet (often the same as the POP or IMAP server). Doesn't apply to webmail or AOL.	`smtp.gurus.org`

And I Would Read My Mail How?

How you read and send e-mail depends on which kind of e-mail account you have:

- **Mailbox at your ISP or school or your own domain:** Most ISPs expect you to use a *mail program* to read your e-mail — a program that displays incoming messages and allows you to send messages. You can use any of a long list of mail programs, including Thunderbird, Outlook, Windows Mail, Eudora, Mail.app, or Entourage, as well as mail programs on your smartphone. We talk about the most popular mail programs in the rest of this chapter. Most of these providers also have webmail options; see the next section.

- **Corporate account:** If you use e-mail at work, your organization may use a different type of mail server: Microsoft Exchange. In addition to providing mail services, Exchange also provides shared calendars, to-do lists, and other nifty features. The most popular program that works with all Exchange features is Microsoft Outlook, so your organization probably insists that you use it, despite its security flaws. To read about Outlook, see *Outlook 2010 For Dummies* by Bill Dyszel. Exchange provides a Web-based system, too; see the next section.

- **AOL:** If you use an AOL account to connect to the Internet, you get as many as seven mailboxes as part of the AOL service. If you have a very large family, for example, you can sign up for as many free AOL email accounts as you like. You have three options for using AOL mail:

  - *The AOL e-mail program:* Most people who connect to the Internet via AOL read and send e-mail from the same AOL program they use to connect to their account. Click the Read icon on the toolbar or any little mailbox icon you can find.

  - *Another mail program:* You can use almost any Windows or Mac mail program. These mail programs tend to have better features for reading and filing messages than does AOL's own software. We recommend that you use Thunderbird, which we describe later in this chapter.

  - *Your Web browser:* Your third option is to do mail from the AOL Web site at www.aol.com, which has the advantage that you can use any Web browser from any computer. See the next section.

- **Webmail:** The whole point of webmail is that you can read it on (drumroll, please) the Web. Any Web browser will do, as described in the next section.

If you want to read your e-mail on your smartphone, see the section "Reading Your E-mail on Your Smartphone," later in this chapter.

The Web Is a Fine Place to Read Your E-Mail

No matter which type of e-mail account, you have, even if you normally use an e-mail program like Thunderbird or Outlook to read your messages, check whether your ISP or other mailbox provider has a Web-based mail system. On a webmail system, you can read your mail from any computer on the Internet, including computers at your friends' houses, public libraries, and Internet cafés. For example, if you have a cable Internet account with Comcast, you can use its Web site to read and send messages at any computer on the Net; go to comcast.net and click the Email link.

To find out whether your ISP provides webmail, go to its Web site and look around or write to its support e-mail address. Most ISPs have a Mail or similar link on their home pages. You log in with the same mailbox name and password that you may have jotted down in Table 13-1.

A cool thing about webmail systems such as Yahoo! Mail, Gmail, AIM Mail, and Hotmail is that you can read and send messages from any computer on the Net. Your mailbox is stored on the webmail server, and any computer with a Web browser can access it — you can check your mail from a friend's computer, at a cybercafé, or from the computer at the public library. Of course, no one can read your messages, or send messages as you, without typing your password. One downside is that reading and sending messages tends to be slower with webmail than with an e-mail program because you have to wait for a new Web page to open every time you click a new message.

Setting up a webmail account

If you don't have a webmail account and you want one, follow these steps:

1. **Using your Web browser, go to the webmail service's Web site.**

   Try Google Gmail at www.gmail.com, Windows Live Hotmail at mail.live.com, Yahoo! Mail at mail.yahoo.com, or AIM Mail at webmail.aol.com. See Chapter 6 for help starting your Web browser.

2. **Look for a link named Click Here to Get a Free E-Mail Account or Create Account or similar wording and follow the instructions to create your account.**

   They don't ask anything too nosy. Be sure to click the links to read the *terms of service* (rules of the game) and *privacy policy* (what they plan to do with the information you give them).

3. **In Table 13-1, write down your e-mail address and your password.**

   Your e-mail address ends in @gmail.com, @hotmail.com, @live.com, @yahoo.com, or @aim.com, depending on which service you chose.

You'll end up with a username and password that you can use for other services provided by these Web sites. You're ready!

Reading webmail

You can read webmail — where else? — on the Web, whether your mailbox is at one of the webmail sites listed in the previous section or is hosted by your ISP. Almost every ISP has a Web site where you can read your mail.

To access your webmail mailbox, go to the Web site and log in:

1. **Go to the same Web site where you created your account.**

   If you created a webmail mailbox at AIM Mail (webmail.aol.com), Google Gmail (www.gmail.com), Windows Live Hotmail (mail.live. com), or Yahoo! Mail (mail.yahoo.com), log in at that Web site. If your mailbox is provided by your ISP, employer, or school or another organization, go to its Web site.

2. **Sign in with your new username and password.**

   You see a Web page that may have ads and news and all kinds of other information, but somewhere is an Inbox link or other link for reading and sending mail. For example, Figure 13-1 shows the part of the Comcast home page where you can log in to myComcast to read your mail.

Figure 13-1:
Log in, read
e-mail.

3. **Click the Inbox or other mail-related link.**

   You see your inbox, which might look something like Figure 13-2. You may not have any e-mail yet, or you may have a welcome message from the webmail service. If so, you see the sender and subject line of the message.

4. **Click the message to read it.**

   Then you can click the Reply, Forward, or Delete buttons or links to deal with the message.

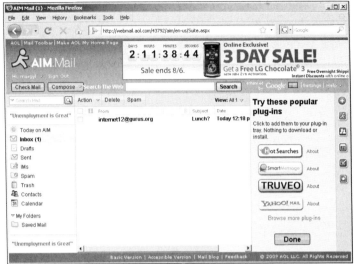

Figure 13-2:
Reading
mail in AIM
Mail.

Sending e-mail with webmail

To send an e-mail message using webmail, follow these steps:

1. **Sign in.**

   See Steps 1 and 2 in the previous section to find out *where* to sign in.

2. **Click the Compose button or New button or any link that seems to be about writing and sending a message.**

   Your browser displays a form with boxes for To (the address) and Subject and a large, unlabeled box for the text of the message, as shown in Figure 13-3.

3. **Type one or more addresses in the To box.**

   If you want to send your message to more than one address, separate each address with a comma.

4. **If you see a Cc box, you can enter addresses there, too.**

   The Cc (carbon *copy*, for you historians) is for people to whom the message isn't directly addressed but who might want to be aware of your message.

5. **Type a subject line in the Subject box.**

6. **Type your message in the big box.**

7. **Click the Send button.**

   If you want to check your spelling first, which is the polite thing to do, look for a Spelling or Spell Check button to click before clicking Send.

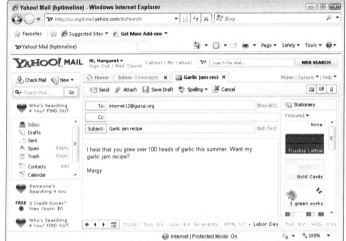

Figure 13-3:
Sending
mail from
Yahoo! Mail.

Be sure to log out from the webmail site when you're done reading and sending mail, especially if you're using a friend's computer or a computer in a public place. Otherwise, someone else can come along and read or send messages using your account.

Reading Your E-Mail on Your Smartphone

Regular old cellphones can't send or receive e-mail, but so-called *smartphones* can. (To find out what a smartphone is, see the section in Chapter 4 about getting a little Blackberry, iPhone, or Palm.) Here are some tips for reading and sending mail depending on which kind of smartphone you have:

✔ **BlackBerry:** You get an e-mail address at Blackberry.com when you set up your phone. Ask your phone store to help.

✔ **iPhone:** An iPhone can read and send mail from one or several accounts. Tap Settings➪Mail Contacts Calendars➪Add Account. You see a list of popular mail providers, including Microsoft Exchange (used by many corporations and other organizations), MobileMe (see the following sidebar, "Mobile who?"), Gmail, Yahoo! Mail, and AOL. If your mail is somewhere else, tap Other⤳Add Mail Account and enter your name, your e-mail address, your e-mail password, and a name for the account. Tap Save. Tap IMAP or POP, fill in the names of your incoming (IMAP or POP) and outgoing (SMTP) mail server, and tap Save.

✔ **Palm:** If your phone uses the Palm webOS, the process is something like this (but your phone store can probably help you if it doesn't work): Open Email and tap Sign In. Tap Add an Account and enter your e-mail address and password, and tap Sign In again. Now you can open Email anytime you want to read or send messages. You can set up more than one e-mail account so that you can check your business and personal accounts.

✔ **Windows Mobile phones:** If your phone runs Windows Mobile (a teeny-tiny, slow version of Windows), you can read and send e-mail from one or more accounts. Press the Start button and choose Messaging to start the e-mail program. To set up a new account, press Menu, choose Tools⤳New Account, enter your e-mail address, and follow the instructions on the screen.

If you see an option similar to Leave Messages on Server, we recommend that you select it. If you have a choice between POP and IMAP as the account type, choose IMAP. (These two types of mail servers are described in the next section of this chapter.) Although checking e-mail on a phone is cool, you *also* want to be able to check it on your computer!

If you don't have a smartphone, you aren't necessarily out of luck. Other service providers (such as US Cellular) offer proprietary Web browsers that can retrieve webmail. Check with your cellphone provider.

Mobile who?

Apple offers the MobileMe server (at www. me.com), where you can set up an @me.com e-mail address, an online calendar, and an online contacts list (address book). You can see them on any PC or Mac and on your iPhone. The service looks slick, but it costs $99. You can do the same thing for free by using a Gmail account (which includes a contacts list) and Google Calendar — all three are usable from any Web browser and iPhone. MobileMe also includes an online file storage area, a photo gallery, and (our favorite part) a Find My Phone feature, which can show your phone's location on a map. However, it doesn't seem to be able to tell you which couch cushion it's under.

Reading Your E-Mail in a Mail Program

Although reading your mail on the Web is convenient, it's usually slower than using a *real* mail program. Mail programs have more features than many web-mail sites, too. Many mail programs are available. Many businesses and other organizations use Outlook, which comes with Microsoft Office. Our favorite free mail program is Thunderbird, from the same people who make Firefox, an excellent free Web browser.

If you want to use a mail program (we sure do!), you need to figure out which mail servers it uses for sending and receiving mail, choose a program (download it if you don't already have it), and set it up. This section walks you through the process.

Mail servers galore

If you use a mail program to read your e-mail, one of the things you have to set in your mail program is the *incoming mail server,* which holds your mail until your mail program picks it up. (AOL and webmail users can skim this section.)

IMAP: Mail anywhere and everywhere

When you use POP to pick up your mail, the messages are downloaded to your PC and stored there and are deleted from your mailbox on the mail server. If, like most people, you build up large files of saved messages, the saved messages are on your PC and accessible only from your mail program on that PC. Often that's good enough, but if you read your mail in more than one place (say, at home and at work), it can be a pain if you're one place and the saved message with a crucial work-related item (a recipe for Killer Tequila Nachos, for example) is in the other. IMAP solves this problem by storing all your mail on a mail server so that you can access it from any mail program, and

you have the same set of mailboxes no matter which computer you use. Many mail systems offer both IMAP and webmail, in which case you see the same mail in your mail program as you see in the webmail.

To use IMAP, you need a broadband connection at each of the places you read your mail, because IMAP is rather sluggish on dialup and your mail provider has to offer IMAP service. Because all your mail folders are on your ISP's computer, see how much mail you're allowed to store there because folders can get pretty big. One or 2 megabytes is tight, whereas 100 megabytes should be plenty unless you mail around a lot of video files.

The usual way to pick up mail is known as _POP_ (Post Office Protocol, sometimes also written as _POP3_ because it's version 3). All ISPs offer POP as the standard way to receive your mail. (If you have broadband, you'll like the IMAP alternative, described in the following sidebar.) To send mail, your mail program reverses the process and sends messages to your _outgoing mail server_ (or _SMTP server,_ for the badly misnamed Simple Mail Transfer Protocol).

Write the names of your incoming (POP or IMAP) and outgoing (SMTP) mail servers in Table 13-1. If you don't know what to write, ask your ISP or whichever organization hosts your e-mail mailbox. With luck, your mail program has the server names set automatically, but when the setup gets screwed up, you'll be glad that you know how to restore its settings.

If you want to use a mail program (like Thunderbird or Outlook) to read AOL or webmail, here are the mail servers they provide:

✔ **AOL** has its own mail system, so AOL users don't use POP, IMAP, or SMTP servers when they're using AOL's own software. However, AOL provides a POP server (`pop.aol.com`), an IMAP server (`imap.aol.com`), and an SMTP server (`smtp.aol.com`) in case you want to use another mail program. Use your AOL username and password to connect.

✔ **AIM Mail** (at `mail.aol.com`) is free webmail that you can sign up for even if you don't have an AOL account. It has the same POP, IMAP, and SMTP servers as AOL's mail.

✔ **Windows Live Hotmail** (at `hotmail.com` or `mail.live.com`) doesn't do POP, IMAP, or SMTP. Microsoft Windows Live Mail program can connect directly to a Hotmail account, or if you use Outlook, the mail program that comes with Microsoft Office, you can download the Microsoft Office Outlook Connector to read your Hotmail mail from Outlook. (From `microsoft.com/downloads`, search for _Microsoft Office Outlook Connector._)

✔ **Yahoo! Mail** (at `mail.yahoo.com`) provides Web-based accounts, but if you sign up for its premium Yahoo! Plus service at $20 per year, it also provides a POP server (`pop.mail.yahoo.com`) in case you want to use a mail program rather than your browser to read your mail. It may also add IMAP support for use from smartphones. The free program YPOPS (at `ypopsemail.com`) works to give you POP and SMTP for a free Yahoo! Mail account.

✔ **Gmail** (at `gmail.com`) provides POP (`pop.gmail.com`), IMAP (`imap.gmail.com`), and SMTP (`smtp.gmail.com`) servers for all its users. You enable them by clicking Settings at the top of any Gmail page, clicking Forwarding and POP/IMAP, and clicking either Enable POP or Enable IMAP. If you use IMAP, enter your entire e-mail address (including the @ gmail.com) as your username and change the port from 143 to 993. Then choose SSL as the connection type. For your outgoing mail, you need to change the port for the SMTP server from 25 to 587 and choose TLS as the connection type.

Windows Live Essentials

Windows 7 doesn't come with all the free programs that earlier versions of Windows did. The reason might be the Microsoft response to various antitrust suits, in which the makers of competing programs (other Web browsers, e-mail programs, and chat programs, for example) pointed out that Microsoft took advantage of sales of Windows itself to push its other products. Or, maybe Microsoft had other reasons.

Instead, Windows 7 encourages you to download the Windows Live Essentials package, which includes several Internet-related programs:

- Windows Live Mail, described in this chapter
- Windows Live Toolbar, an add-on to the Internet Explorer Web browser, described in Chapter 7. It includes a Mail button that displays your Hotmail inbox page in your browser.
- Windows Live Messenger, an instant messaging program described in Chapter 16
- Windows Live Photo Gallery, a photo-editing and -organizing program described in Chapter 18
- Windows Live Writer, a blogging program described in Chapter 19
- Windows Live Family Safety, an Internet filtering program described in Chapter 3

You don't have to have Windows 7 to use these programs; they work with Windows XP (with Service Pack 2) and Windows Vista, too. To download Windows Live Essentials, follow these steps:

1. Go to `download.live.com` and click Download. (In Windows 7, you can also choose Start⇨Getting Started⇨Go Online to Get Windows Live Essentials.)

2. Save the file in your Downloads folder.

3. Open or run the file you just downloaded.

4. Choose which Windows Live Essential programs you want to download. You can download others later.

5. During the installation, the program asks to set Live Search as your default search provider; Chapter 8 describes ways to search the Web. We recommend deselecting this option because you might prefer another search site.

6. The installation program asks to make MSN your browser's home page, which we doubt you will enjoy, so deselect that one, too.

7. Finally, the installation program suggests that you sign up for a Windows Live ID. This free account gives you a Hotmail webmail mailbox and lets you participate in instant messaging. You can click Sign Up now, or you can sign up at any time at `signup. live.com`.

See Chapter 12 for more information about downloading and installing software from the Internet.

Which mail program do you like?

You can easily make a specific e-mail program do what you want — after all, dealing with mail is what these programs are for. We picked the two most popular e-mail programs to show you the ropes:

✔ **Thunderbird:** The people at the Mozilla Foundation who created Firefox, the Web browser we describe in Chapter 7, have also written the excellent, free e-mail program Thunderbird. It works with regular Internet accounts as well as with AOL accounts and some webmail accounts. Refer to Chapter 12 to find out how to download and install Thunderbird.

✔ **Windows Live Mail:** Windows Live Mail is part of Windows Live Essentials (see the sidebar of that name, earlier in this chapter).

✔ **Windows Mail:** Windows Vista comes with Windows Mail. Windows XP (and earlier versions) came with the mail program Outlook Express, which looks similar to Windows Mail. *Note:* Despite the similar name, Outlook Express is unrelated to Outlook, the mail program included with the Microsoft Office package.

Before you can use your mail program, you need to tell it two things:

✔ **Where your mailbox is stored:** Usually on a POP or IMAP server at your ISP

✔ **Where to send outgoing mail:** Usually to the same or another mail server at your ISP

Follow the instructions in the following sections to get your mail program up and running. Later sections describe how to send and receive mail with each program.

Setting up Thunderbird

The Mozilla Foundation, which creates free, open source software, has written Thunderbird to complement its excellent Firefox browser. This chapter describes Thunderbird 2. To download it and set it up, follow these steps:

1. **Download and install Thunderbird from www.mozilla.com.**

   Chapter 12 describes how to download and install programs; follow its procedures.

2. **Start Thunderbird by clicking the desktop icon or choosing Start⇨All Programs⇨Mozilla Thunderbird⇨Mozilla Thunderbird.**

   The first time you run Thunderbird, the Account Wizard runs, asking for your name, the type of e-mail account you have (POP or IMAP), your e-mail address, and your mail servers (incoming and outgoing), as described in the earlier section "Mail servers galore."

3. **Type your name, e-mail address, incoming mail server, and outgoing server, copying the information from Table 13-1.**

   When you're done, you see your new account in the Account Settings window, which you can close.

If you need to change your e-mail account information later or set up Thunderbird to work with a different e-mail account, choose Tools⊅Account Settings. To run the Account Wizard again, click New Account. To change the settings for an existing account, choose the account, click the settings categories below the account name, and change the settings that appear.

The Thunderbird window looks like the one shown in Figure 13-4. A list of your mailboxes (mail folders) appears in the upper left corner. To the right is a list of the messages in that mailbox and the text of the selected message.

Figure 13-4: Thunderbird displays mail folders to the left, messages to the (upper) right, and the selected message to the lower right.

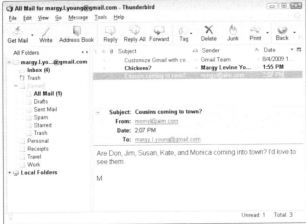

Setting up Windows Live Mail

You can download Windows Live Mail along with any other Windows Live Essentials programs you might want to use. Follow these steps:

1. **Follow the steps in the "Windows Live Essentials" sidebar, earlier in this chapter, to download Windows Live Mail.**

   You can download other Windows Live programs, too, if you want them.

2. **Choose Start⊅Windows Live Mail.**

   You see the Add an E-Mail Account window, shown in Figure 13-5.

3. **Enter your e-mail address, password, and name and click Next.**

   Or, if you want to sign up for a free Hotmail account, click the link.

4. **Enter the specs for your incoming mail server and outgoing server, copying the information from Table 13-1.**

If you have an account at any of the popular webmail systems (including Hotmail, Yahoo! Mail, AOL, and Gmail), you can skip this step because the system already knows how to set it up. Windows Live Mail downloads the folders and mail from the mail server.

5. **If the program displays a list of your folders (usually just Inbox, Trash, and a few other folders, unless you've created more), click OK.**

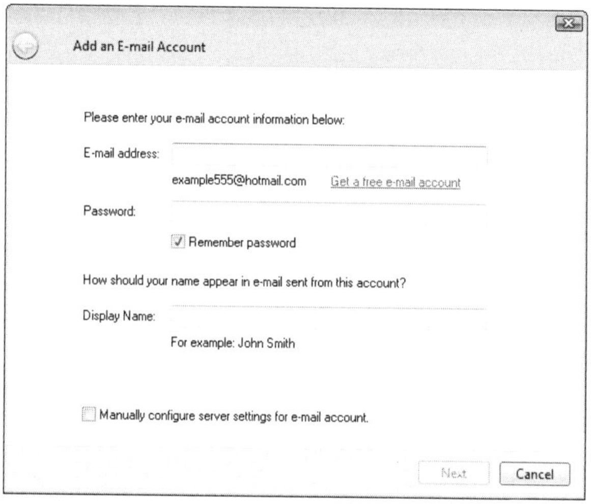

Figure 13-5: Adding an account to your Windows Live Mail program.

The Windows Live Mail layout looks a little different from the other mail programs, with a lefthand column of tasks and features, a middle column that lists your messages, and a righthand column that shows the selected message, as shown in Figure 13-6.

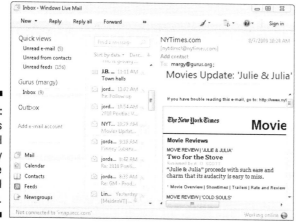

Figure 13-6: Windows Live Mail can display multiple e-mail accounts.

Setting up Windows Mail

Windows Vista comes with Windows Mail already installed. (If you still use Windows XP and Outlook Express, it's similar.)

To run Windows Mail, choose Start@–>Windows Mail. The first time you run Windows Mail, the Internet Connection Wizard wakes up and asks some questions: Most of the answers you should already have written in Table 13-1. When prompted, type your name, e-mail address, incoming (POP or IMAP) mail server, outgoing (SMTP) mail server, username, and password. Click Next after filling in the information that the wizard requests, and then click Finish when the wizard says that you can leave.

When you finish, you see the Windows Mail window. The layout is similar to Thunderbird's, displaying the Folders and Contacts lists, a message list, and the selected message.

If you need to add or change your e-mail accounts later, choose Tools↪ Accounts from the menu. Click the Mail tab if it's not already selected. You can edit an account by clicking it and clicking the Properties button. Add an e-mail account (mailbox) by clicking the Add button.

Sending Mail Is Easy

Whether you use an e-mail program or webmail, sending messages is easy enough that we show you a few examples rather than waste time explaining the theory. It works much the same way in all e-mail programs.

Follow these steps to write an e-mail message and send it off:

1. **Click the Write icon (in Thunderbird), the New button (in Windows Live Mail), or the Create Mail icon (in Windows Mail), or press Ctrl+N.**

   A window (the Compose or New Message window) opens. In webmail, your composition area appears in the Web browser.

2. **Fill in the recipient's address (or recipients' addresses) in the To box.**

   You can send this message to more than one person at a time by entering more than one To address. This feature works a little differently in different programs. In Thunderbird, press Enter (rather than Tab) to move down a line to enter another address. In Windows Live Mail, just type a comma or semicolon between the addresses. In Windows Mail, press Tab.

   Remembering people's e-mail addresses is annoying (or, for those of us at a Certain Age, just plain impossible). See the section in Chapter 15 about keeping track of your friends to find out how to add people to your address book and use it when sending messages.

3. Add any Cc or Bcc addresses that you want the messages to go to.

See the later sidebar "CC and BCC" if you're wondering what we're talking about. In Thunderbird, after you enter an address, click the To button next to the address and select Cc or Bcc from the list that drops down. In Windows Live Mail, click Show Cc & Bcc to see boxes in which you can enter those addresses in the New Message window. In Windows Mail, choose View➪All Headers.

4. Type the subject in the Subject box.

Make it specific. If you want help, don't type `Help!` as the subject. Type *Need help getting my cat not to spit out his pills.*

Press Tab to move to the message box.

5. Type the message in the big box.

The cursor should be blinking in the *message area,* the large, empty box where you type the message.

6. Click the Send icon or button to send the message.

In Thunderbird, you can also press Ctrl+Enter or choose File➪Send Now. In Windows Live Mail and Windows Mail, you can press Alt+S.

7. If the message isn't sent right away, tell your mail program to send all waiting messages by clicking the Get Mail icon (in Thunderbird) or the Send/Receive icon (in Windows Mail). In Windows Live Mail, press F5.

When you send a message in which you use formatting (such as boldface or italics, by using the toolbar buttons in the Compose window), Thunderbird may ask whether you really want to send the message using formatting. See the sidebar "To format or not to format," later in this chapter, to find out when to send formatted messages.

Cc and Bcc

The term *carbon copy* should be familiar to those of you who were born before 1965 and remember the ancient practice of putting sheets of carbon-coated paper between sheets of regular paper to make extra copies when using a typewriter. (Please don't ask us what a typewriter is.) In e-mail, a *carbon copy* is simply a copy of the message you send. All recipients, on both the To and Cc lines, see who's receiving the message — unless a recipient's e-mail address is typed in the Bcc field instead. *Blind carbon copies* (Bccs) are copies sent to people without putting their names on the message so that the other recipients are none the wiser. You can figure out why you may want to send a copy to someone but not want everyone to know that you sent it.

To format or not to format

Years ago, someone got tired of e-mail's plain, unformatted appearance. Once almost all computers could display boldface, italics, different fonts, and different font sizes, why not use them in e-mail? And formatted e-mail was born.

Very old e-mail programs may not be able to display formatted e-mail. All the programs described in this chapter, including webmail, can. The formatting usually takes one of two forms: *MIME,* in which the formatted text is sent like an attached file with the message, and *HTML,* in which Web page formatting codes are included in the text. If your mail program can't display formatted mail and you receive a formatted message, you see all kinds of gobble-dygook mixed in with the text of the message, rendering it unreadable.

A big problem is that any HTML-formatted mail can potentially contain viruses, hostile Web pages that take over the screen, and other annoying or dangerous content. Some people turn off HTML mail, both the nice mail that you send and the nasty kind, to avoid having to deal with the nasty kind.

Boldface, italics, and color can add emphasis and interest to your messages although they're no substitute for clear, concise writing. Some people (including John) prefer mail without formatting. To be sure that a message doesn't have any of that tatty-looking formatting, do this in the New Message or Compose window when you're writing your message:

- ✔ **Thunderbird:** Choose Options⇨Format⇨Plain Text Only

- ✔ **Windows Live Mail:** Press Alt to display the hidden menus, and then choose Format⇨Plain Text.

- ✔ **Windows Mail:** Choose Format⇨Plain Text.

Spell-checking your message is a good idea; avoid the embarrassment of spotting your typos only after it's too late to fix them. You can ask your mail program to check the spelling in your message before you send it. Click the Spell icon to see which typos your program finds. In Thunderbird, you can also press Ctrl+K or choose Options⇨Check Spelling; in Windows Mail, press F7 or choose Tools⇨Spelling.

After your mail program sends a piece of e-mail to the outgoing mail server, you can't cancel it!

Mail Coming Your Way

If you send e-mail, and in most cases even if you don't, you most likely receive it also. The arrival of e-mail is always exciting, even when you receive 200 messages a day. (It's exciting in a depressing kind of way, sometimes.)

A helpful feature of mail programs (not webmail) is that you can compose mail while you're offline. On the other hand, when you want to check your mailbox for your most current messages, you have to connect to the Internet. Webmail users have to be online to do anything.

Reading your messages

To check your e-mail in almost any e-mail program, follow these steps:

1. **Start your e-mail program if it's not already running.**

   If you use webmail, start your Web browser and go to your webmail Web site.

2. **If your program doesn't retrieve mail automatically, select the Check Mail, Sync, or Send/Receive button on the toolbar to retrieve your mail.**

   If you have a full-time Internet connection, your mail program may retrieve your mail automatically, in which case you only have to start the program to fetch your mail. In addition, if you leave your mail program running, even hidden at the bottom of your screen as an icon, it may automatically check for new mail every once in a while. Most mail programs can even pick up mail while you're reading or sending other messages.

   The program may play a tune or display a message when you receive messages. The mail appears in your inbox (usually in a window or folder named In or Inbox), showing one line per message. If you don't see it, double-click the In or Inbox mailbox in the list of mailboxes that usually appears on the left side of the window.

3. **To see a message, double-click the line or click the line and press Enter.**

   You see the text of the message, along with buttons for replying, forwarding, and deleting the message.

4. **To stop looking at a message, click the Close (X) button in the upper right corner of the message window (the standard way to get rid of a window) or press Ctrl+W or Ctrl+F4.**

   On a Mac, click the red Close button in the upper left corner.

Here are some tips for displaying your inbox in specific e-mail programs:

- ✔ **Thunderbird:** To display your inbox, click your e-mail address, account name, or Inbox in the Mail Folders list.

- ✔ **Windows Live Mail:** If you've clicked Calendar (to see an appointment calendar), Feeds (to see articles from newsfeeds or blogs to which you have subscribed), or Newsgroups (to participate in online discussion groups, described on the Web at net.gurus.org/usenet or groups.google.com), you may need to click Mail to return to the Mail part of the program.

To tell Windows Live Mail to check for new messages, click the Sync button on the toolbar, just to the right of the Delete button. If you don't see it, your Windows Live Mail window is too narrow (ours usually is); make your window wider.

✔ **Windows Mail:** If you don't see your inbox, double-click the Local Folders item in the Folders list.

You can do lots of other tasks with messages (such as reply, save, and forward), which we discuss in Chapter 15.

Deleting messages the quick-and-easy way

You don't have to read every single message before you delete it; sometimes, you can guess from the sender's name or the Subject line that reading the message would be a waste of time. If you subscribe to mailing lists (which we describe in Chapter 16), certain topics may not interest you.

Buttons on the e-mail program's toolbar at the top of its window let you dispose of your mail. First, click once to highlight the message. Then (in most mail programs) click the Trash or Delete button on the toolbar to discard the message.

In webmail, on the Web page that displays each message is some kind of Delete button. Some webmail systems have a check box on the Web page that lists all messages in your inbox folder, and a Delete button at the bottom of the list. To delete a bunch of messages, select their check boxes and then click Delete.

One-click surfing

Most e-mail programs display Web addresses as links. That is, if the text of a message includes a Web address (such as `http://net.gurus.org`), the address appears underlined and perhaps in blue. Just click the link to display the page in your browser.

When you send messages, you don't have to do anything special to display a Web address as a link — the recipient's mail program should do it automatically.

When you delete a message, most e-mail programs don't throw it away immediately. Instead, they file the message in your Trash or Deleted Messages mailbox or mail folder, or just mark it as deleted. From time to time (usually whenever you close the e-mail program), the program empties your trash, truly deleting the messages. Until then, you can undelete it if you deleted it by mistake.

To Whom Do I Write?

As you probably have figured out, one teensy detail is keeping you from sending e-mail to all your friends: You don't know their addresses. In this section, you find out lots of different ways to look for addresses. Start out with the easiest, most reliable way to find out people's e-mail addresses:

Call them on the phone and ask them.

Pretty low-tech, huh? For some reason, this technique seems to be absolutely the last thing people want to do. (See the nearby sidebar "Top ten reasons *not* to call someone to find an e-mail address.") Try it first. If you know or can find out the phone number, this method is much easier than any of the others.

Another way to find a person's e-mail address is by using an online directory. Wouldn't it be cool if an online directory listed everybody's e-mail addresses? Maybe, but the Internet doesn't have one. For one thing, nothing says that somebody's e-mail address has any connection to her name. For another, not everybody wants everybody else to know his e-mail address.

Another approach is to go to a search engine, such as Google (www.google.com) or Yahoo! Search (www.yahoo.com), and type the person's full name, enclosed in quotes. You see a list of pages that include the name — of course, many people may have the same name if your friend is named Allen Johnson or Bob Smith. Or, try Yahoo! People Search at people.yahoo.com, which enables you to search by name and state. Try searching for your own name and see what you find!

If you're in contact with someone by way of Facebook or another social networking site (described in Chapter 18), you can send them messages through that site to ask for an e-mail address.

Top ten reasons *not* to call someone to find an e-mail address

10. You want to surprise a long-lost friend.

9. You want to surprise a long-lost *ex*-friend who owes you a large amount of money and thinks that she has given you the slip.

8. Your friend doesn't speak English. (That happens — a majority of Internauts are outside the United States.)

7. You don't — or your friend doesn't — even speak. (That happens, too — networks offer a uniquely friendly place for most people with handicaps; nobody has to know or care whether someone has a disability.)

6. It's 3 a.m. and you need to send a message right now or else you'll never get to sleep.

5. You don't know the phone number and, because of an unfortunate childhood experience, you have a deathly fear of calling directory assistance.

4. The pay phone takes only quarters; nobody around can break your $100 bill.

3. Your company has installed a new phone system, no one has figured out how to use it, and no matter what you dial, you always end up with Dial-a-Prayer.

2. You inadvertently spilled an entire can of soda into the phone and can't wait for it to dry out to make the call.

1. You called yesterday, didn't write down the answer, and forgot it. Oops.

Chapter 14

Keeping Your Mail Safe from Viruses, Spam, and Wi-Fi Snoops

. . . .

In This Chapter

▶ Protecting yourself from viruses by e-mail

▶ Dealing with spam (it's not just for breakfast any more)

▶ Considering who might read your messages

▶ Securing your mail against wireless snooping

. . . .

*O*kay, maybe you know how to send and receive e-mail. If you do, it's time to have a little chat about e-mail safety. If you've used e-mail, you probably have already seen spam and maybe even viruses. Take a look at Chapter 2 for definitions of these e-mail-borne menaces. This chapter describes how to protect yourself from them. Listen up.

I Think I've Got a Virus

A virus arrives on your computer as an attachment to an e-mail message. (Refer to the section in Chapter 2 about viruses arriving by e-mail for a description of how viruses work.) In most mail programs, programs contained in attachments don't run until you click them — so *don't* open programs that come from people you don't know. Don't even open attachments from people you *do* know if you weren't expecting to receive them. Many successful viruses replicate themselves by sending copies of themselves to the first 50 people in an address book. Many viruses look like they come from someone who knows you.

It used to be that only an attachment that looked like a program (for example, a file with the filename extension `.com` or `.exe`) could contain a virus. Then the bad guys (aided by software written without security in mind) came up with ways to hide viruses in word processing documents, PDF files (print-ready formatted documents, described in the section in Chapter 12 about files and what to do with them), and even pictures.

In addition to taking care not to run viruses by opening attachments, you should set up your virus checker and mail program to catch as many viruses as possible and not to run them inadvertently. The following sections explain how.

Configuring your virus checker

In Chapter 4, we tell you to install a virus checker as soon as you connect your computer to the Internet, but this topic is so important that we tell you again. You need to pay for a virus checker — and you need to pay annually to keep your subscription current for updates to the list of viruses that the checker checks for. (The free ClamWin at `www.clamwin.com` looks promising but isn't ready for prime time yet.) The many good virus checkers include

- AVG, at `free.avg.com`
- F-Prot, at `www.f-prot.com`
- McAfee VirusScan, at `www.mcafee.com`
- Norton AntiVirus, at `www.symantec.com`
- Windows Defender, at `www.microsoft.com/windows/products/winfamily/defender` (If you use Windows 7 or Vista, you already have it.)

After your virus checker is installed, look at its configuration settings to make sure that the program downloads updates regularly. You can set up the program to connect to the Internet and download updates automatically. Most programs check for updates at least weekly. If you have an always-on Internet connection and you leave your computer on all the time, you can configure your program to check in the middle of the night so that it never disturbs you during the day. If you turn off your computer when you're not using it or if you have a dial-up Internet account, you need to remember to run the program's update function regularly.

Most virus checkers look for viruses in two ways:

- Check e-mail messages as they arrive.
- Scan your whole computer (your hard disk) for viruses.

We recommend that you turn on both these options.

You can also configure what your virus checker does when it finds a virus in a file. You usually have options like these:

- ✔ **Disinfection:** Throws away the virus but keeps the rest of the file
- ✔ **Quarantine:** Moves the file to a safe place on your computer
- ✔ **Deletion:** Just kills the file

We recommend that you set your virus checker to delete virus files. Infected files are unlikely to contain anything you want, and we can't see any reason to leave them lying around your hard disk.

Configuring your mail program against viruses

Depending on which mail program you use, you may need to tell it about your virus-checker.

Webmail (at least, the big, popular ones, such as Yahoo Mail!, Hotmail, Gmail, and AIM Mail) includes virus-checkers, although you should still install and run one on your own computer.

Thunderbird was designed to resist viruses: It doesn't use Internet Explorer to display formatted e-mail messages (as some other mail programs do), and it doesn't automatically open attachments. If you're running a third-party virus filter, such as the ones listed in the previous section, choose Tools⇨ Options in the main window, click the Privacy button at the top of the options window and then the Anti-Virus tab, and be sure that the Allow Anti-Virus Clients to Quarantine Individual Messages check box is selected.

Checking security settings in Windows (Live) Mail

Windows Mail (which comes with Windows Vista) may use Internet Explorer to display messages, which can run viruses: We recommend that you check the Microsoft site www.windowsupdate.com weekly for the latest bug fixes or follow the directions there to set Windows Update to do it automatically.

Windows Live Mail (downloadable as part of Windows Live Essentials, described in Chapter 13) includes a virus-checker and spam filter, too.

If you use either of these programs, check its security configuration. Here's how:

1. **In Windows Mail, choose Tools⇨Options. In Windows Live Mail, click the Menus icon on the toolbar and choose Safety Options.**

   You see the (Safety) Options dialog box, shown in Figure 14-1.

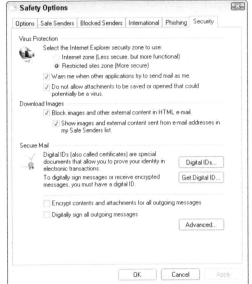

Figure 14-1: Windows Mail and Live Mail have virus protection settings.

2. **Click the Security tab.**

   The Virus Protection and Download Images sections both deserve your attention.

3. **Set the Internet Explorer security zone to Restricted Sites Zone.**

   If you work in a corporation and expect to receive programs in e-mail from co-workers, you may need to change this setting; talk to your system administrator. For the rest of us, this setting is the safest.

4. **Make sure that the Warn Me When Other Applications Try to Send Mail As Me check box is selected. (Click it if it doesn't contain a check mark.)**

   If your computer is infected with a spyware or virus program that tries to use your computer as a spam-sending machine, this setting may prevent it.

5. **Select the Do Not Allow Attachments to Be Saved or Opened That Could Potentially Be a Virus so that it contains a check mark.**

   If you expect to receive programs, Excel spreadsheets, Word documents, or Access databases, you need to turn off this setting because all these types of files can contain viruses. Start out with it turned on, though.

6. **Select the Block Images and Other External Content in HTML E-Mail check box.**

   Images in e-mail may be Web beacons, which we describe in Chapter 2. Web beacons aren't viruses, but we don't like them anyway.

7. **Click OK.**

Chain letters: Arrrrrggghhh!

One of the most obnoxious things you can do with e-mail is pass around chain letters. Because all mail programs have forwarding commands, you can send a chain letter along to hundreds of other people with only a few keystrokes. Don't do it. Chain letters are cute for about two seconds, and then they're just annoying. After 20 years of using e-mail, we've *never* received a chain letter worth passing along. That's **NEVER!** (Please excuse the shouting.) Don't pass them along, okay? No, they don't destroy your computer, but they're just *annoying*.

A few chain letters just keep coming around and around, despite our best efforts to stamp them out:

✔ **Make big bucks with a chain letter:** These letters usually contain lots of testimonials from people who are now rolling in dough, and they tell you to send $5 to the name at the top of the list, put your name at the bottom, and send the message to a zillion other suckers. Some even say, "This isn't a chain letter." (You're supposedly helping to compile a mailing list or sending reports or something — your 100 percent guaranteed tipoff that it's a chain letter). Don't even think about forwarding it. These chain letters are illegal in the United States even when they say that they aren't, and, besides, they don't even work. (Why send any money? Why not just add your name and send it on? Heck, why not just replace all names on the list with yours?) Think of them as gullibility viruses. Send a polite note to the sender's postmaster to encourage her to tell users not to send any more chain letters. If you don't believe that they're illegal, see the Postal Service Web site at `www.usps.com/postallaw/_txt/RANDReport.txt`.

✔ **Big company will send you cash for reading e-mail:** This one has circulated with either Disney or Microsoft as the designated corporation. The message claims that the company is conducting a marketing test and that you can win big bucks or a trip to Disney World for sending along the message. Some claim that a sick child will receive one cent for each person you forward the message to. Yeah, right. A variation says that something interesting but unspecified will happen when you forward it; we suppose that's true if having all your friends find out you're a sucker is interesting. This chain letter isn't dangerous; it's just a waste of time — yours and everyone to whom you send it.

✔ **Hideous virus will wreck your computer:** Occasionally, these are true; generally they're not, and when they are true, they tend to be about viruses that have been around since 1992. If you run software that's subject to viruses, look at the vendor's Web site and at the sites belonging to antivirus software makers for some more credible reports, downloadable updates, and antivirus advice. Some of the apparent virus warnings are themselves viruses. If a message shows up saying, "Install this patch from Microsoft immediately to keep viruses out," it's not a patch; it's a virus.

Get This Spam Outta Here!

Spam is unsolicited bulk e-mail, and we describe its history and sources in detail in Chapter 2. But you probably don't care about details — you just want it to go away.

One approach to spam is to ask your computer to figure out which messages are spam and then either trash them or put them in a separate folder so that you can trash them yourself. This seems like the perfect solution. The problem is how to get your computer to know what is spam and what is not. Many techniques are available, but none is perfect. Here are a few of the most common types:

- ✔ **Blackhole list:** A number of organizations circulate lists of Internet addresses that they consider to be sources of spam. Most ISPs subscribe to one or more of these blackhole lists and block all messages from listed sites. These ISPs block spam for you, at least the spam that comes from these Internet addresses. That's not all the spam, but it can catch about ¾ of it, which is a good start.

- ✔ **Content-based filter:** These filters look for words or phrases in the e-mail that are common in spam. They also note certain formatting errors that spammers seem to make often. Each text match earns a score. If a message scores above a certain threshold, it gets trashed. For example, messages with the word *Viagra* or the phrase *mortgage rate* are much more likely to be spam than other messages are.

- ✔ **Bayesian filter:** The mathematician Tom Bayes died 208 years before the Internet was born, but his groundbreaking work in statistics now helps computers figure out what is spam by being shown examples of messages that are spam along with others that are not. Many e-mail programs have built-in Bayesian filters. In your e-mail program, you might have noticed a button or menu option labeled something like This Is Junk. As you read your e-mail, you tell it which messages are spam. After a while, the program starts guessing based on the examples you give it and redirects suspected spam into a Junk or Trash mailbox so that you don't have to read it. However, you do need to check the spam mailbox from time to time because the Bayesian filter may guess wrong and move in good messages with the bad.

All these methods make mistakes that let through some spam and block the occasional legit message. To reduce the latter problem, some e-mail systems *whitelist* senders who are listed in your e-mail address book, telling the filters that you always want to see messages from those senders — perhaps your boss or your significant other. Whitelists don't help you receive messages from long-lost friends or people who just changed their e-mail addresses because their ISPs got bought out.

Filtering spam in webmail

The major webmail sites try to identify spam and move it to a Junk or Spam folder. (In Gmail, you may need to click a "More" link to see the Spam folder.) Take a look in this folder from time to time to look for any real messages that might accidentally have gotten marked as spam. (In the technical jargon, it's known as "mixing the ham with the spam.")

When reading your incoming mail, if you see spam messages, you can mark them as spam, which helps the webmail service identify these messages in the future. From the list of messages, select the message and click the Spam, Report Spam, or Junk icon or link.

You can configure how aggressively your webmail service looks for spam. In Yahoo Mail!, click Options⇨Mail Options and click Spam to see the Spam settings shown in Figure 14-2. In AIM Mail, click Settings and then Spam Controls. In Hotmail, click Options⇨More Options⇨Filters and Reporting. (As of late 2009, Gmail doesn't have spam controls you can set.) You can control how stringently the system filters out spam and what it does with suspected spam.

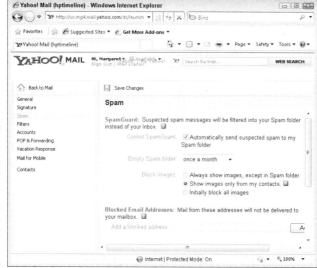

Figure 14-2: Yahoo! Mail provides spam filtering, as do most other webmail services.

Filtering spam in Thunderbird

Thunderbird 2 contains a Bayesian filer that works pretty well after you give it some examples of what your spam looks like.

Telling Thunderbird to start filtering

First, set up your spam-filtering configuration settings, like this:

1. **Choose Tools⇨Account Settings. In the new window, click Junk Settings under your e-mail account.**

   You see the Junk Settings dialog box, shown in Figure 14-3.

Figure 14-3:
Configuring
Thunderbird
to can your
spam.

2. **Select the Enable Adaptive Junk Mail Controls for This Account check box if it's not already selected.**

3. **Select the check box labeled Do Not Mark Mail As Junk If the Sender Is in Personal Address Book if it doesn't already contain a check mark in it.**

   Usually, people you know don't spam you.

4. **Click to select the Move New Junk Messages To check box if it doesn't already contain a check mark. Choose where to move your spam.**

   The default setting is a Junk folder, which sounds good to us.

5. **Clear any check mark from the Automatically Delete Junk Messages Older Than ___ Days check box.**

   Until your filter is well trained, don't let Thunderbird delete suspected spam before you have a chance to review it. It's terribly embarrassing to tell someone that you threw away their important message because your program thought it was spam.

6. Click OK.

> If you have set up more than one account, repeat this set of steps for each account in the Account Settings window.

Now Thunderbird is ready to distinguish the spam from the ham — the bad messages from the good. As you read the messages in your Inbox folder, every time you receive a spam message, click the Junk button on the toolbar. The message vanishes from your inbox, and Thunderbird analyzes the words in the message and makes a note that they're likely to appear in spam. The more spam messages you mark with the Junk button, the more Thunderbird knows about what spam looks like.

Checking your Junk folder for real mail

From time to time (every week or so), open the Junk mail folder (or whatever folder you told Thunderbird to put suspected spam into in Step 4 in the previous section). The Junk mail folder appears on your list of folders, below your Inbox, Templates (form letters you send out), and Sent folders. Click the Junk folder to see the list of messages. You don't need to open each message — reviewing the sender names and subjects is usually enough to find any good messages mixed in there.

If you see a good message in your Junk folder, select it and click the Not Junk button on the toolbar. (It's where the Junk button usually is — the button turns into Not Junk when you open the Junk folder.) This button tells Thunderbird to look at this message and to adjust the filters accordingly. Then drag the message back into your Inbox. When you're sure that all messages in your Junk folder are indeed junk, delete them. An easy way to do it is to click the first message and then scroll down and Shift+click the last message — now all the messages in the Junk folder are selected. Press the Del key or click the Delete button on the toolbar to trash them.

Filtering spam in Windows (Live) Mail

Neither Windows Live Mail (which comes with Windows Live Essentials) nor Windows Mail (which comes with Vista) have Bayesian filters, but they have a number of other spam-fighting features:

- ✔ **Junk E-Mail Options:** You can adjust the built-in spam filters.

- ✔ **Blocked Senders list:** If you receive a message from anyone on this list, the message goes right into the trash.

- ✔ **Safe Senders list:** Messages from people on this list *don't* get marked as spam, even if the message looks like spam.

The following sections describe how to use these features.

Configuring your junk e-mail options

To configure the built-in junk mail filter, follow these steps:

1. **In Windows Live Mail, click the Menu icon and choose Safety Options. In Windows Mail, choose Tools➪Junk E-Mail Options. Click the Options tab if it isn't already selected.**

   You should see the Safety Options or Junk E-Mail Options window.

2. **Select Low to pick the normal junk filter setting.**

   You can try High, but we find that it catches too much nonspam.

3. **Click the Phishing tab.**

4. **Select Protect My Inbox from Messages with Potential Phishing Links if it's not already set.**

   This feature is useful, but it raises some privacy concerns. Because it checks any Web URLs in the message against a list of known phishing sites maintained by Microsoft, the link information in your mail is sent to Microsoft for checking.

5. **Click OK.**

You can use the Safe Senders and Blocked Senders tabs to list addresses of people whose mail you always and never want, respectively. On the Options tab of this window, click Safe List Only to accept mail only from people listed on the Safe Senders tab. This setting is way too restrictive for adults, but is appropriate for children, so you can set up a list of the friends and relatives from whom you expect them to be receiving mail.

The International tab lets you block mail from addresses from certain top-level domains (the part of the e-mail address after the last dot) and in certain language encodings. We don't recommend the domain blocking, which tends to block more mail than you want, but if you don't speak Korean (or Arabic, Chinese, Greek, Vietnamese, or another language in the list) and don't know anyone in Korea, you can somewhat safely tell it to block mail encoded as Korean. Don't tell it to block US_ASCII or Western European or else you'll block most of your real mail.

Blocking messages by sender

In Windows Live Mail, right-click the message in the message list and choose Junk E-Mail➪Add Sender to Blocked Senders List. If you've opened the message in a separate window, click Junk.

In Windows Mail, open the message and choose Message➪Junk Email➪Add Sender to Blocked Senders List.

The message you opened is still in your inbox; the program will block *future* messages, but doesn't do anything about this one. Just delete it! Blocking by sender is occasionally useful to deal with real people who send mail that is never interesting (see the sidebar on chain letters) but useless for spam since spammers never use the same address twice.

Viewing your Blocked Senders list

You can look at or edit the Blocked Senders list later, in case you add a friend accidentally or you want to type a bunch of spammer addresses. In Windows Live Mail, click the Menu icon and choose Safety Options. In Windows Mail, choose Tools⇨Junk E-Mail Options from the menu bar in the main window. Click the Blocked Senders tab to see the list of senders you have blocked. Messages from any addresses on this list are shunted straight to your Deleted Items folder.

You can add more addresses to your Blocked Senders list by clicking the Add button and typing or pasting the address in the dialog box that appears. If you decide to accept messages from an address after all, you can delete it from the list by choosing the address and clicking Remove.

Blocking messages from entire domains

The Blocked Senders list can include entire domains. (A *domain* is the part of an e-mail address after the @.) For example, if you don't want to receive *any* mail from the White House, you can block all messages that come from `anything@whitehouse.gov`. Follow these steps to block all messages from an entire domain:

1. **Display the Blocked Senders list, as described in the preceding section.**

2. **Click the Add button.**

   You see the Add Sender dialog box.

3. **Type the domain name and click OK.**

   (In Windows Mail, leave the Mail Messages radio button selected.) When you click OK, the new entry appears on your Blocked Senders list.

Reviewing your spam

From time to time, be sure to look through the messages that have been identified and filed as spam. Perfectly innocent messages may have been mislabeled as spam.

To look in your Junk E-mail folder, click it on the folder list. The list of messages in that folder appears. Scroll through the messages; the unread messages appear in bold. (Spam you never saw should all appear in bold.) If you see any good messages, select each one and click Not Junk to put them back in your Inbox.

Sneaky ways that spammers evade filters

Spammers are smart — if they weren't, outraged Internet users would have shut them down long ago. Every time spam filterers come up with another way to spot spam, spammers change what they send out. It's like a sped-up version of e-mail evolution.

Here are some tricks that spammers use to prevent your filters from catching their junk messages:

✔ **Funky capitalization:** Most mail filter programs look for the exact capitalization you specify. If your filter looks for `spammers rus.com` on the From line, you don't catch messages from `SpammersRus.com` or `spaMmersruS.com`.

✔ **No text:** Many spam messages contain almost no text — just a graphical image of text. When text is sent as a graphical image, filters can't read the text to spot the phrases you're looking for.

✔ **Wrods Speled w.r.0.n.g:** People are remarkably good at making sense of garbled text, so it's not hard to garble text enough to defeat filters and remain legible to people.

✔ **Hidden bogus codes:** E-mail messages can contain HTML formatting codes, which are enclosed in <angle brackets>. These formatting codes can create bold (using the <b> code) and italic (using <i>) text in your messages. However, lots of codes have no meaning in HTML, such as <m> and <n>, so your e-mail program ignores them when displaying messages. However, if these meaningless codes are sprinkled in your messages, your filters are prevented from finding the words you have flagged. For example, a filter that's looking for `make money` doesn't match a message that contains `ma<m>ke mon<n>ey`.

What else can I do?

The Internet grew from a need for the easy and free flow of information, and everyone using it should strive to keep it that way. Check out these Web sites for information about spam and how to fight it technically, socially, and legally:

✔ **Coalition Against Unsolicited Commercial Email:** Antispam laws, at `www.cauce.org`

✔ **Fight Spam on the Internet!:** A spam overview, at `spam.abuse.net`

✔ **Internet and E-mail Policy and Practice:** John's highly geeky blog, at `weblog.johnlevine.com`

✔ **Network Abuse Clearinghouse:** A complaint-forwarding database for e-mail abuse, at `www.abuse.net`

One-click surfing, but no phishing

Most e-mail programs convert URLs (Web site addresses) in your e-mail messages into links to the actual Web sites. You don't have to type these addresses into your browser. All you have to do is click the highlighted link in the e-mail message and — poof — your browser opens and you're at the Web site. If your e-mail program has this feature (all programs mentioned in this chapter do), URLs in e-mail messages appear underlined and in blue — a nice feature.

Unfortunately, this feature is abused by phishers. *Phishing* is sending faked e-mail that claims to be from your bank or another official organization to trick you into revealing personal information, and we describe it in Chapter 2. If you click one of these links and it opens a Web site that asks for a password or credit card number or the like, don't give it any information!

Thunderbird, Windows Live Mail, and Windows Mail have phish detection features. The features aren't perfect, but if either one says that a link looks phishy, you probably shouldn't click it.

We believe that spam is not just a technical problem and that only a combination of technical, social, and legal solutions will work in the long run. In the meantime, every ISP now does at least some spam filtering on incoming mail, and many let you "tune" their filters. Check with your ISP for the specific services it provides.

How Private Is E-Mail?

Relatively, but not totally. Any recipient of your mail may forward it to other people. Some mail addresses are actually mailing lists that redistribute messages to many other people. We've gotten misrouted mail in our `internet12@gurus.org` mailbox with details of our correspondents' lives and anatomies that they probably would rather we forget. (So we did.)

If you send mail from work or to someone at work, your mail isn't private because companies have the right to read all employee e-mail that passes through their systems. You and your friend may work for companies of the highest integrity whose employees would never dream of reading private e-mail. When push comes to shove, however, and someone is accusing your company of leaking confidential information and the corporate lawyer says "Examine the e-mail," someone reads all the e-mail. (This situation happened to a friend of ours who was none too pleased to find that all his intimate correspondence with his fiancée had been read.) E-mail you send and receive is stored on your disk, and most companies back up their disks regularly.

If anybody wants to read your mail, it's not hard to do. The usual rule is not to send anything you wouldn't want to see posted next to the water cooler or perhaps scribbled next to a pay phone.

Secure That Mail

If you have a laptop and you use it to read your e-mail in public Wi-Fi hotspots, you may have a security problem. (Refer to the section in Chapter 5 about getting Wi-Fi with your latté to find out what we mean by *Wi-Fi* and *hotspot*.) Public Wi-Fi setups allow anyone connected to the same hotspot (that is, anyone in the same café or area of the airport) to eavesdrop on what you type, including potentially seeing your e-mail username and password.

Fortunately, most mail programs and mail servers let you use a secure connection, the same kind that secure Web pages use, for incoming and outgoing mail. Setting up the secure connection can be a little tricky, but you have to do it only once.

Secure webmail — or maybe not

You'd think that webmail services would use secure Web sites, but you'd be wrong in some cases. If you use Gmail, you can click Settings and scroll down the list of General settings until you see the Browser Connection setting; set it to Always Use Https (the secure version of the HTTP Web browsing protocol).

Secure mail with Thunderbird

To set up secure mail in Thunderbird, follow these steps:

1. **Choose Tools⇨Account Settings.**

   You see the Account Settings window, with a list of your mail accounts on the left.

2. **Click Server Settings under your incoming mail account.**

   You may have to click the little + sign next to your account's name to see the Server Settings option.

3. **Select the Use Secure Connection (SSL) check box.**

4. **Click Outgoing Server (SMTP) at the bottom of the left column.**

   If you have several accounts set up, you may have to scroll down to find it.

5. **Click Edit.**

6. **Under Use Secure Connection, select TLS.**

7. **Click OK.**

Now check your mail and try sending yourself a message. If it doesn't work, your mail provider may not offer secure mail, or it may offer it in a nonstandard way, and you have to call for help.

Secure mail with Windows Live Mail

To set up secure mail in Windows Live Mail, follow these steps:

1. **Right-click the account name in the left column (for example, Hotmail) and choose Properties from the menu that appears.**

   You see the Properties dialog box for that account.

2. **Click the Advanced tab, shown in Figure 14-4.**

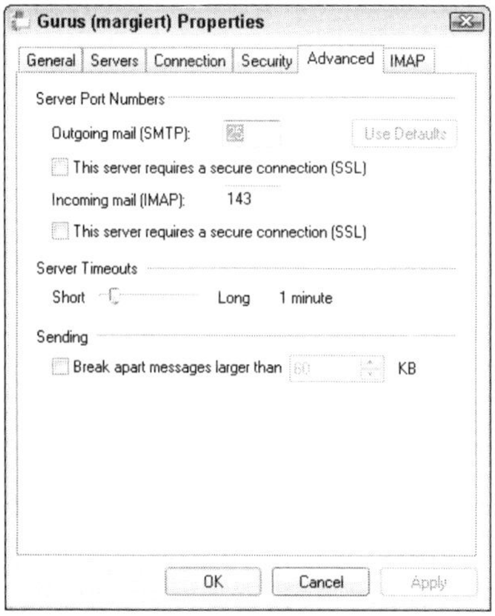

Figure 14-4: Configuring a Windows Live Mail account to use a secure connection.

3. **Select both Secure Connection (SSL) check boxes.**

   If the check box isn't checked, click it.

4. **Change the Outgoing Mail (SMTP) port number to 465.**

5. **Change the Incoming Mail (IMAP) port number to 993, or the Incoming Mail (POP3) port number to 995.**

6. **Click OK to save your settings.**

Secure mail with Windows Mail

To set up secure mail in Windows Mail, follow these steps:

1. **Choose Tools➪Accounts.**

2. **Click the name of your mail account in the window that opens, and then click Properties.**

3. **In the window that opens, click the Advanced tab.**

    There's a Security tab, but that's not the one you want here.

4. **Select the check boxes labeled This Server Requires a Secure Connection (SSL) for both incoming and outgoing mail.**

5. **Click OK.**

Now check your mail and try sending yourself a message, clicking the Send/ Receive button to make Windows Mail connect to the server. If it doesn't work, your mail provider may not offer secure mail, or may offer it in a non-standard way, and you have to call for help.

Chapter 15

Putting Your Mail in Its Place

In This Chapter

▶ Following the rules of e-mail etiquette

▶ Responding to mail

▶ Keeping an e-mail address book

▶ Forwarding and filing mail

▶ Sending and receiving exotic mail and mail attachments

▶ Sorting and filtering your messages

*A*fter you get used to using e-mail, you start sending and receiving enough messages that you had better keep it organized. This chapter describes how to delete, reply to, forward, and file messages in Thunderbird, Windows Live Mail (which comes with Windows Live Essentials), Windows Mail (which comes with Windows Vista), and webmail systems such as Yahoo! Mail, Gmail, AIM Mail, and Hotmail. (Refer to Chapter 13 to find out how to get started using these programs.)

After you read (or decide not to read) an e-mail message, you can deal with it in a number of ways, much the same as with paper mail. Here are your usual choices:

✔ Throw it away (as described in Chapter 13).

✔ Mark it as spam (as described in Chapter 14) so that your program and sometimes your mail provider can learn to identify spam before you even have to see it.

✔ Reply to it.

✔ Forward it to other people.

✔ File it.

You can do any or all these things with each message. If you don't tell your mail program what to do with a message, the message usually stays in your mailbox for later perusal.

A Few Words from the Etiquette Ladies

Sadly, the Great Ladies of Etiquette, such as Emily Post and Amy Vanderbilt, died before the invention of e-mail. Here's what they may have suggested about what to say and, more important, what *not* to say in e-mail.

E-mail is a funny hybrid, something between a phone call (or voice mail) and a letter. On one hand, it's quick and usually informal; on the other hand, because e-mail is written rather than spoken, you don't see a person's facial expressions or hear her tone of voice.

A few words of advice:

- ✔ When you send a message, watch the tone of your language.
- ✔ Don't use all capital letters — it looks like you're SHOUTING.
- ✔ If someone sends you an incredibly obnoxious and offensive message, as likely as not it's a mistake or a joke gone awry. In particular, be on the lookout for failed sarcasm.

Flame off!

Pointless and excessive outrage in e-mail is so common that it has a name of its own: *flaming*. Don't flame. It makes you look like a jerk.

When you get a message so offensive that you just *have* to reply, stick it back in your inbox for a while and wait until after lunch. Then . . . don't flame back. The sender probably didn't realize how the message would look. In about 20 years of using e-mail, we can testify that we have never, ever, regretted *not* sending an angry message (although we *have* regretted sending a few — ouch).

When you're sending e-mail, keep in mind that the person reading it will have no idea what you *intended* to say — just what you *did* say. Subtle sarcasm and irony are almost impossible to use in e-mail and usually come across as annoying or dumb instead. (If you're an extremely superb writer, you can disregard this advice — but don't say that we didn't warn you.)

Another possibility to keep in the back of your mind is that it's technically easy to forge e-mail return addresses. If you get a totally off-the-wall message that seems out of character for the person who sent it, somebody else may have forged it as a prank. (No, we don't tell you how to forge e-mail. How dumb do you think we are?)

Smile!

Sometimes, a :-) (a *smiley* or an *emoticon*) can help clarify your meaning. It means "This is a joke." (Try tilting your head to the left if you don't see why it's a smile.) In some communities, <g> or <grin> serves the same purpose. Here's a typical example:

```
People who don't believe that we are all part of a warm,
caring community who love and support each other are no
better than rabid dogs and should be hunted down and shot.
:-)
```

We feel that any joke that needs a smiley probably wasn't worth making, but tastes differ.

For more guidance about online etiquette, see our `net.gurus.org/ netiquette` Web page.

BTW, what does IMHO mean? RTFM!

E-mail users are often lazy typists, and abbreviations are common. Here are some of the most widely used:

Abbreviation	What It Means
AFAIK	As far as I know
BTW	By the way
FWIW	For what it's worth
IANAL	I am not a lawyer, (but. . . .)
IMHO	In my humble opinion
LOL	Laughing out loud
ROTFL or ROFL	Rolling on the floor laughing
RSN	Real soon now (that is, any time in the next century)
RTFM	Read the manual — you could have and should have looked it up yourself
TIA	Thanks in advance
TLA	Three-letter acronym (for a three-letter acronym)
YMMV	Your mileage may vary

Back to You, Sam: Replying to Mail

Replying to mail is easy: Choose Message➪Reply in Thunderbird or click Reply in Windows Live Mail or choose Message➪Reply to Sender in Windows Mail. Pressing Ctrl+R (⌘+R on the Mac) works in some mail programs, too. In webmail, you usually see a Reply button.

After you open the reply message, ask yourself two important questions:

✔ **To whom does the reply go?** Look carefully at the To line, which your mail program has filled out for you. Is that who you thought you were addressing? If the reply is addressed to a mailing list, did you truly intend to send a message to the entire list, or is your reply of a more personal nature, intended only for the individual who sent the message? Did you mean to reply to a group? Are all the addresses that you think you're replying to included on the To list? If the To list isn't correct, click it and edit it as necessary.

Occasionally, you may receive a message that has been sent to a zillion people and their addresses appear in dozens of lines in the To section of the message. If you reply to a message such as this one, make sure that your reply isn't addressed to the entire huge list of recipients.

Some mail programs have a separate Reply to All command or button that addresses your reply to the people that the message was from *and* the people who received copies of the message (the "To" people and the "Cc" people). Thunderbird, Windows Live Mail, and Windows Mail all have a Reply All button on their toolbars,

✔ **Do you want to include the content of the message to which you're replying?** Most mail programs include the content of the message to which you're replying, usually formatted to show that it's a *quotation* or *quoted text.* Edit the quoted text to include just the relevant material, so as not to bore or confuse the recipient with unrelated stuff. If you don't provide some context to people who get a great deal of e-mail, your reply makes no sense, so including part of the original message can be helpful. If you're answering a question, include the question in the response. You don't have to include the entire text, but give your reader a break. She may have read 50 messages since she sent you mail and may not have a clue what you're talking about unless you remind her.

When you reply to a message, most mail programs fill in the Subject field with the letters *Re:* (short for *regarding*) and the Subject field contents of the message to which you're replying. Type your message above the quoted text from the original message and click Send.

Keeping Track of Your Friends

After you begin using e-mail, you quickly find that you have enough regular correspondents that keeping track of their e-mail addresses is a pain. Fortunately, every popular e-mail program provides an *address book* or *contacts list* in which you can save your friends' addresses so that you can send mail to Mom, for example, and have it automatically addressed to `chairman@exec.hq.giantcorp.com`. You can also create address lists so that you can send mail to `family`, for example, and it goes to Mom, Dad, your brother, both sisters, and your dog, all of whom have e-mail addresses.

All address books let you do the same things:

- ✔ Save in your address book the address from a message you have just read.
- ✔ Use addresses you have saved for outgoing messages.
- ✔ Edit your address book.

Some address books also provide space for you to store other information about your friends and coworkers.

Who's who

Click the Address Book or Contacts icon or link to see your address book. (In Windows Mail, it looks like a little flag.) Most programs open a new window for your contacts list. Figure 15-1 shows the Windows Live Mail contacts list for a Hotmail webmail account. In most address books, you double-click a contact to edit the person's information.

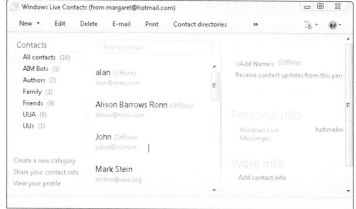

Figure 15-1: Your contacts list (or address book) remembers e-mail addresses so that you don't have to.

Here's how to add people to your address book:

- ✔ **Thunderbird:** Click New Card and fill out the form. To edit an entry, select it and click the Properties button on the toolbar. You can also create a *list* — that is, an address book entry that sends a message to a bunch of people (for example, the members of a committee or of your family). To create a mailing list for your use, click the New List button, which creates an empty list, and then type the addresses you want.

  When you're reading a message, you can add the sender's address to your address book by clicking the sender's name or address on the From line and choosing Add to Address Book from the menu that pops up.

- ✔ **Windows Live Mail:** Click Contacts to see your contacts list, and then click New to create a new contact. Fill out the information and click Add Contact. When you're reading a message and want to save the sender's name in your contacts list, right-click the person's name and choose Add to Contacts or Add Sender to Contacts from the menu that appears.

- ✔ **Windows Mail:** Click the New Contact button and fill in as much info as you want in the Properties window that opens. To add an e-mail address, type it in the E-mail box and then click the Add button to the right of that box. After you enter the contact info (the name and one e-mail address are plenty), click OK. To change an entry, just click it in the Contacts window, and a Properties window opens, where you can change it.

  To add an address from a message in a mailbox, right-click the person's name or address in the list of messages and then choose Add Sender to Contacts from the menu that appears.

- ✔ **Webmail:** Click the Contacts, Contact List, Addresses, or Address Book link to display your address book. Click the Add Contact, Create Contact, or New button or the little plus sign or similar icon or link to add someone. Fill out the form that appears, and be sure to enter a *nickname* for the person: You can type the nickname when addressing an e-mail message rather than type the person's whole e-mail address. The form may include fields for the person's postal address and phone numbers, but you can leave them blank. Then click the Save or Save Contact button. (These instructions are approximate because webmail sites change their designs all the time.)

Addressing messages the easy way

Composing a message is when you really want to use your address book, because who can remember all those weird e-mail addresses your friends pick? When you're writing a new message (or replying to or forwarding a message, as described later in this chapter), here's what to do:

✔ **Thunderbird:** Just start typing the person's name in your new message. As soon as Thunderbird sees a name that begins with the same letters as an address book entry, it displays the person's name. If more than one entry matches, you see a list you can choose from.

✔ **Windows Live Mail and Windows Mail:** Click the little flag or book icon to the left of the To, Cc, or Bcc line, and a Select Recipients window opens. Double-click the one or ones you want, and then click OK to return to the message.

✔ **Webmail:** Webmail systems provide several ways to address a message to someone in your address book. In Yahoo! Mail, you can display a list of your contacts. When composing a message, try typing the person's nickname to see whether a matching entry appears in the window of address book entries or click the To or Cc button to see a list of contacts from which to choose.

Hot Potatoes: Forwarding Mail

You can forward e-mail to someone else. It's easy. It's cheap. Forwarding is one of the best things about e-mail and at the same time one of the worst. It's good because you can easily pass along messages to people who need to know about them. It's bad because you (not *you* personally, but, um, people around you — that's it) can just as easily send out floods of messages to recipients who would just as soon not hear *another* press release from the local Ministry of Truth or another joke that's making the rounds. Think about whether you will enhance someone's quality of life by forwarding a message to him. If a message says "forward this to everyone you know," do everyone you know a favor and delete it instead.

Forwarding a message involves wrapping the message in a new message of your own, sort of like putting sticky notes all over a copy of it and mailing the copy and notes to someone else.

Forwarding mail is almost as easy as replying to it: Select the message and click the Forward button on the toolbar or choose Message➪Forward. Pressing Ctrl+L (⌘+L on the Mac) also works in Thunderbird, and Ctrl+F forwards in Windows Live Mail and Windows Mail. In webmail systems, a Forward button usually appears when you view a message. The mail program composes a message that contains the text of the message you want to forward; all you have to do is address the message, add a few snappy comments, and send it.

The text of the original message appears at the top or bottom of the message, usually formatted as quoted text and preceded by a line that specifies whom the original message was from, and when. You then get to edit the message and add your own comments. (See the nearby sidebar "Fast forward" for tips about pruning forwarded mail.)

Fast forward

Whenever you're forwarding mail, be sure to delete uninteresting parts. All the glop in the message header is frequently included automatically in the forwarded message, and almost none of it is comprehensible, much less interesting, so get rid of it.

The tricky part is editing the text. If the message is short (a screenful or so), you probably should leave it alone:

```
>Is there a lot of demand for
   fruit pizza?
>
I checked with our research
   department and found
   that the favorite
   pizza toppings in the
   18-34 age group are
   pepperoni, sausage,
   ham, pineapple, olives,
   peppers, sauerkraut,
   hamburger, and broccoli.
   I specifically asked about
   prunes, and they found no
   statistically significant
   response.
```

If the message is long and only part of it is relevant, you should, as a courtesy to the reader, cut it down to the interesting part. We can tell you from experience that people pay much more attention to a concise, one-line e-mail message than they do to 12 pages of quoted stuff followed by a two-line question.

Sometimes it makes sense to edit material even more, particularly to emphasize a specific part. When you do so, of course, be sure not to edit to the point where you put words in the original author's mouth or garble the sense of the message, as in the following reply:

```
>I checked with
>our research department and
   found that the
>favorite pizza toppings ...
   and they
>found no statistically
   significant
>response.
```

This version of the original message is totally misleading — it twists the original text. Sometimes, it makes sense to paraphrase a little — in that case, put the paraphrased part in square brackets, like this:

```
>[When asked about prunes on
   pizza, research]
>found no statistically
   significant response.
```

People disagree about whether paraphrasing to shorten quotes is a good idea. On one hand, if you do it well, it saves everyone time. On the other hand, if you do it badly and someone takes offense, you're in for a week of accusations and apologies that will wipe out whatever time you may have saved. The decision is yours.

Cold Potatoes: Saving Mail

Saving e-mail for later reference is similar to putting potatoes in the fridge for later. (Don't knock it if you haven't tried it — day-old boiled potatoes are yummy with enough butter or sour cream.) Lots of your e-mail is worth saving, just as lots of your paper mail is worth saving. Lots of it *isn't*, of course, but that's what the Delete icon is for.

You can save e-mail in a few different ways:

✔ Save it in a folder full of messages.

✔ Print it and put it in a file cabinet with paper mail. (Spare a tree; don't use this method.)

The easiest method usually is to stick messages in a folder. E-mail programs usually come with folders named In (or Inbox), Outbox, Sent, and Trash, and perhaps others. But you can also make your own folders.

People use two general approaches in filing mail: by sender and by topic. Whether you use one or the other or both is mostly a matter of taste. For filing by topic, it's entirely up to you to come up with folder names. The most difficult part is coming up with memorable names. If you aren't careful, you end up with four folders with slightly different names, each with a quarter of the messages about a particular topic.

Gmail takes a different tack — it saves all your mail in one huge folder. When you want to find an old message, you search for it by sender or by some text in the message. This method sure saves filing!

You can save all or part of a message by copying it into a text file or word processing document. Select the text of the message by using your mouse. Press Ctrl+C (⌘+C on a Mac) or choose Edit⇨Copy to copy the text to the Clipboard. Switch to your word processor (or whatever program in which you want to copy the text) and press Ctrl+V (⌘+V on the Mac) or choose Edit⇨Paste to make the message appear where the cursor is.

Filing messages with Thunderbird

Thunderbird lists your mail folders down the left side of the window, starting with Inbox. Thunderbird provides folders named Inbox, Unsent Messages, Drafts, Sent, and Trash, but you can create your own folders. If you have a *lot* of messages to file, you can even create folders within folders to keep things organized. To make a new folder, follow these steps:

1. **Choose File⇨New⇨New Folder.**

   You see the New Folder dialog box.

2. **Type a name for the folder in the Name text box.**

   Make one named Personal, just to give it a try.

3. **Set the Create As a Subfolder Of drop-down box to the folder name in which you want the new folder to live.**

Usually, you want your folder to be a subfolder of Local Folders, so set it to Local Folders and click Choose This for the Parent. Or, choose another folder; for example, you can have a folder named Personal, and inside that can be a folder for each friend you receive messages from.

4. **Click OK.**

The new folder appears on the list of folders on the left side of the Thunderbird window. You can see the list of message headers for any folder by clicking the folder name.

You can save a message in a folder by dragging the message to the folder name — easy enough. Or, right-click the message, choose Move To from the menu that appears, and choose the folder from the list that appears.

When you compose a message, you can tell Thunderbird to save a copy of your message in a folder. While writing the message, choose Options⇨Send a Copy To and then choose a folder.

Filing messages with Windows Live Mail and Windows Mail

You start out with folders named Inbox, Outbox, Sent Items, Drafts, Deleted Items, and Junk E-Mail. To make a new folder:

- ✔ In Windows Live Mail, click the little down arrow next to the New button and choose Folder.
- ✔ In Windows Mail, choose File⇨Folder⇨New or File⇨New⇨Folder.

Either way, give the folder a name and choose which folder to put this new folder in. (You can have folders within folders — very convenient.)

Move messages into a folder by clicking a message header and dragging it over to the folder name or by right-clicking the message on the message list and choosing Move to Folder.

Filing messages with webmail systems

Webmail systems change every time the company decides to redesign the Web site, but here's how the popular webmail system worked the last time we checked.

Your folders appear in the list of folders down the left side of your browser window, under the My Folders heading. Your folders include names like Inbox, Sent, Draft, Spam, and Trash. Click a folder name to see the messages in that folder. To save a message in a folder, drag it from the list of messages into the new folder, like in a real mail program. To create a new folder, click the Add link to the right of My Folders, or in Hotmail, click Manage Folders and then click New.

With Gmail, rather than put mail into folders, you label it. All the mail with the same label acts sort of like a folder. Click the Labels button and choose from the list. If you're creating a new label, click the Labels button, choose Manage Labels, scroll down to the Create a New Label box, type a name, and click the Create button.

Handling Exotic Mail and Mail Attachments

Sooner or later, just plain, old, everyday e-mail isn't good enough for you: Someone will send you a picture you just have to see, or you will want to send a video clip of Fluffy to your new best friend in Paris. To send stuff other than text through the mail, a message uses special file formats. Sometimes the entire message is in a special format, and sometimes people *attach* things to their plain text mail. The usual format for attaching files to messages is *MIME,* or Multipurpose Internet Mail Extensions. The programs we describe in this chapter can send and receive files attached with MIME, as do most e-mail programs on the planet — only a few, very old e-mail programs can't.

When you receive a file that's attached to an e-mail message, your mail program is responsible for noticing the attached file and doing something intelligent with it. Most of the time, your program saves the attached file as a separate file in the folder you specify. After the file has been saved, you can use it just like you use any other file. If you see a picture in a message and you're not sure where it's saved, most programs let you right-click the picture and choose Save Image As to put the picture in the folder of your choice.

These types of files are often sent as attachments:

✔ Pictures, in image files

✔ Word processing documents

✔ PDF files (printable, viewable formatted documents)

✔ Sounds, in audio files

✔ Movies, in video files

✔ Programs, in executable files

✔ Compressed files, such as zip files

E-mail viruses usually show up as attachments. If you receive a message with an unexpected attachment, even from someone you know, **DON'T OPEN IT** until you check with the sender to make sure she sent it deliberately. Viruses often suck all the addresses from a victim's address book so that the virus can mail itself to the victim's friends. Some kinds of attachments can't carry viruses — notably, GIF and JPG images. Refer to Chapter 14 for details.

Your ISP or webmail service may place a limit on the size of your mailbox (the place on its server where your messages are stored until you pick them up). Google Gmail and Yahoo! Mail have high limits, so other mail systems have been increasing their limits to match, but you may still run into a size limit if someone sends you a truly gigantic file, such as a video file. One way to shrink the size of attached files is to zip them first. Read the sidebar in Chapter 12 about uncompressing and unzipping files if you receive a zipped file (with the file extension .zip).

When you receive a picture as an attachment, it's sometimes so large that all you see in your message window is one corner of a picture that would measure about 4 feet by 6 feet if viewed in its entirely, as shown in Figure 15-2. When this happens, right-click the picture and save it as a separate file, and then view it using another program.

Figure 15-2: Pictures can show up looking enormous in your program.

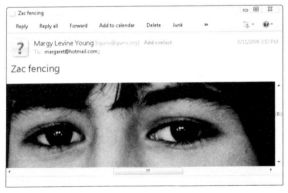

Thunderbird attachments

To attach a file to the message you're composing, click the Attach button or choose File⇨Attach. Then select the file you want to send. Or, just drag the file from an Explorer window or the desktop into the message composition window. You can insert a picture directly into the text of the message by positioning the cursor where you want the picture to appear, choosing Insert⇨Image, and specifying the filename.

For incoming mail, Thunderbird displays any attachments that it can display itself (Web pages and GIF and JPEG image files). For other types of attachments, it displays a little description of the file, which you can click. Thunderbird then runs an appropriate display program — if it knows of one — or asks you whether to save the attachment to a file or to configure a display program, which Thunderbird then runs in order to display the attachment.

Windows Live Mail and Windows Mail attachments

In Windows Mail, create a new message and then attach a file to the message by clicking the Attach button. (In Windows Mail, the Attach button, which looks like a paper clip, might be off the right side of the toolbar — make the Composition window wider to display it.) Then select the file to attach. Or, just drag the file into the New Message window. Then send the message as usual.

When an incoming message contains an attachment, a paper-clip icon appears in the message on your list of incoming messages and in the message header when you view the message. Click the paper clip to see the filename — double-click and you may be able to see the attachment.

Microsoft has "solved" some chronic security problems by making Windows Mail refuse to show you certain attachments, including a lot of benign ones, such as attached text messages and PDF files. You can sort of fix this problem by choosing Menu⇨Safety Options (in Windows Live Mail; the Menu icon is to the left the question-mark icon) or Tools⇨Options (in Windows Mail). Then click the Security tab and deselect Do Not Allow Attachments to Be Saved or Opened That Could Potentially Be a Virus. Now the program lets you open your attachments, although of course when someone *does* send you a virus, it cheerfully opens that one, too.

Webmail attachments

To attach stuff with most webmail sites, compose a message as usual. Then click the Attach button and select the file. (You might need to click Browse first, to find the file.) Your Web browser, amazing beast that it is, copies the file right off your hard drive and sends it to the Yahoo! Mail system to include in your message. When the file is done uploading, the filename appears just below the subject line. Send the message as usual.

Corresponding with a robot

Not every mail address has a live person behind it. Some addresses belong to mailing lists (which we talk about in Chapter 16), and some are *robots* (or *mailbots*) — programs that automatically reply to messages. Mail robots are a common way of subscribing or leaving a mailing list, and for the occasional other arcane purpose. You send a message to the robot (usually referred to as a *mailbot* or *mail server*), it takes some action based on the contents of your message, and then the robot sends back a response. If you send a message to internet12@gurus.org, for example, you receive a response telling you your e-mail address. See Chapter 16 for more details on mailing lists.

When you receive a message with attachments, a paper clip may indicate that a file came along for the ride. If it's a picture, the browser usually displays the picture directly in the message, or you might have to click a Show Images button. The filename of the attached file also appears, and you can click it, or a View or Download link, to open or save the file.

Teaching Your E-Mail Program to Sort Your Mail

After you begin sending e-mail, you probably will find that you receive quite a bit of it, particularly if you put yourself on some mailing lists (see Chapter 16). Your incoming mail becomes a trickle, and then a stream, and then a torrent, and pretty soon you can't walk past your keyboard without getting soaking wet, metaphorically speaking.

Fortunately, most mail systems provide ways for you to manage the flow and avoid ruining your clothes. (Enough of this metaphor already.) Thunderbird can create *filters* that can automatically check incoming messages against a list of senders and subjects and file them in appropriate folders. Windows Mail has Message Rules, which can sort your mail automatically. Most other mail programs (and a few webmail systems) have similar filtering features. If you sort mail into separate mailboxes for each mailing list or other category, you can deal with it a lot more efficiently.

For example, you can create filters that tell your mail program, "Any message that comes from the CHICKENS-L mailing list should be automatically filed in the Cluck mail folder." Figure 15-3 shows this type of filter in Thunderbird.

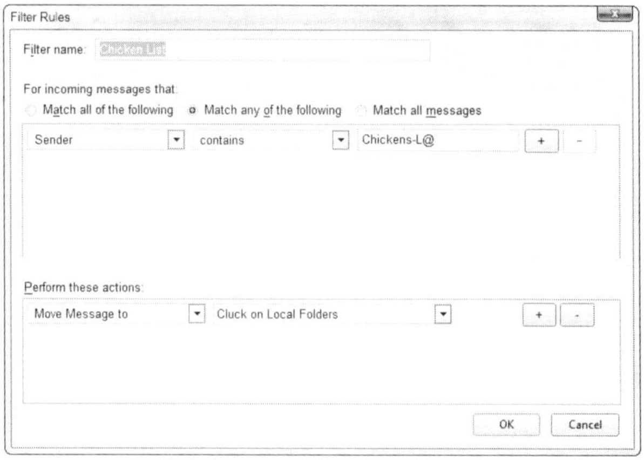

Figure 15-3:
Moving
poultry-
related
messages to
a separate
folder for
immediate
attention.

You can create filters to highlight messages from particularly interesting friends, or delete certain messages (you know the ones we mean) so that you never have to see them. You first choose a condition, which enables the program to identify messages based on the From line, Subject line, or message body. Then you select an action, which is usually to move the message to a folder. (Remember that Trash is a folder.) Here's how to make a filter or message rule for the main e-mail programs we discuss in this book:

- ✔ **Thunderbird:** Choose Tools➪Message Filters to display the Message Filters window, where you can see, create, edit, and delete filters. Click New to create a new filter, and then specify a filter name (for your own reference), how Thunderbird can match incoming messages to this filter, and what to do with messages that match. Or, click the To or From address in a message and choose Create Filter from Message to make a filter for mail sent to or from that address.

- ✔ **Windows Mail and Windows Live Mail:** Choose Tools➪Message Rules➪Mail. (You may have to tap the Alt key to see the menu bar so that you can select Tools.) The bottom part of the window that opens shows a description of what to the filter will do. Because you haven't yet told it what messages to look for or where to move the message, clickable placeholders appear in the description. Click each one to enter the words to match and the folder to use. Then click OK. This method is a lot simpler in practice than it is to describe; try making a rule to move messages with *pickle* in the subject line into a folder named Pickles and you'll get the hang of it.

- ✔ **Yahoo! Mail:** Click the Options button on the Yahoo! Mail Web page and then the Mail Options entry on the menu that drops down, and then click the Filters heading. You can create, edit, or delete your filters.

All this automatic-sorting nonsense may seem like overkill, and if you receive only five or ten messages a day, it is. After the mail starts flowing, however, dealing with it takes much more of your time than it used to. Keep those automated tools in mind — if not for now, then for later.

Chapter 16

Typing and Talking on the Net

- -

- -

*I*nternet e-mail is pretty fast, usually arriving in less than a minute. But sometimes that's just not fast enough. Instant-message (IM) systems let you pop up a message on a friend's screen in a matter of seconds. You can also tell your instant-message program the usernames of your friends and colleagues so that the program can alert you the instant that one of your buddies comes online and you can instantiate an instant message to them. (Excuse us, this gives us a headache. Wait just a moment while we get some instant coffee. Ahh, that's better.)

The good thing about instant messages is that you can stay in touch with people as fast as by talking to them on the phone. The bad thing about instant messages is that they also offer an unparalleled range of ways to annoy people. AOL Instant Messenger, discussed later in this chapter, has about two features to send and receive messages, and about 12 features to reject, denounce, erase, and otherwise deal with unwanted messages. (This may say more about AOL users than about the technology, of course.)

Gregarious people can chat with a whole bunch of people at once, by either typing at the same time, like a party line, or sending messages to each other by e-mail or Web forums.

Of course, even better than typing messages to another person is talking right out loud. If your computer has a microphone and speakers, you can use IM or other systems to talk to people over the Net — even groups of people — with no toll charges. If you connect a digital video camera (or *Webcam*) to your computer, your friends can even see you as you talk or type. It's not hard to do!

AIMing to Chat via Text

Instant messaging (IM) lets you type short messages that appear in a window on someone else's computer. It's faster than e-mail but slightly less intrusive than a phone call — whoever heard of people having their secretaries screen their IMs?

This chapter describes how to use the most popular IM system: AOL Instant Messenger. Google Chat, Windows Live Messenger, and Yahoo! Messenger work similarly, and have similar features. Skype, a voice-over-Internet program described in "Internet Phones and Voice Chat," later in this chapter, also includes IM chat.

AOL Instant Messenger (*AIM,* for short) is one of the simplest chat systems around. All it does is let you type messages back and forth. This chapter describes AIM version 7. If you use AOL, you can use either the separate AIM program we describe here, the AIM part of the regular AOL program, or AIM Express, which runs in a Web browser window. (They all do the same things although the windows are a little different.)

Instant-message programs open a new window when one of your buddies sends you a message. If you have a program that blocks pop-up windows in your browser, IM windows aren't affected because popup-blockers block only Web browser pop-ups.

Taking AIM

If you're an AOL user, you're already set up for instant messages. If not, you have to install the AIM program. AOL subscribers can also run the AIM program and use their AOL screen names when they're logged in to another kind of Internet account.

AOL, hyperaggressive marketing organization that it is, has arranged for AIM to be bundled with a lot of other packages. If you don't have it, visit www.aim.com and follow the directions on the Web page to download it. (See Chapter 12 to find out how to download and install programs from the Internet.) We recommend choosing the custom installation, which enables you to decline the various parasitical programs that arrive with AIM.

When you install the program, you have to choose a screen name — which can be as long as 16 letters (be creative so that yours doesn't collide with one of the 40 million names already in use) — and a password. You also have to enter your e-mail address. AOL, refreshingly, doesn't want any more personal information. The e-mail address you give has to be real; AOL sends a confirmation message to that address, and you must reply or else your screen name is deleted. Normally, AIM runs in the background whenever you're online. If it's not running, click the AIM icon on your desktop.

The first time you use AIM, you enter your AIM or AOL screen name, as shown in the left part of Figure 16-1. Type your screen name and password and click Sign On. If you want to use AIM every time you're online, select the Remember My Password and Automatically Sign Me In boxes before signing on. After you sign in, you see the AIM window, shown on the right side of Figure 16-1.

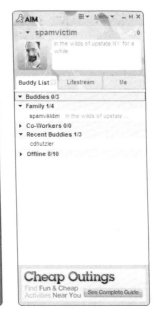

Getting your buddies organized

First you create your Buddy List, and then you can send messages.

When AIM opens, you see your *Buddy List*; that is, other AIM users you like to chat with. The window shows which of your many buddies is online now (everyone who's not listed in the Offline category). What? None of your pals appears? You should add your friends' AOL or AIM screen names to your Buddy List.

In the AIM window, choose Menu➪Add to Buddy List➪Add Buddy or press Ctrl+D to display the New Buddy window. (The Menu button is in the upper right corner of the window.) Enter an AIM username, a nickname to use for your friend or coworker, and (optionally) a cellphone number (preceded by +1 for U.S. numbers) and e-mail address. (AIM can send IMs as text messages to cellphones.) Click the Buddy Group button to choose which group to put your new buddy in. AOL provides a few groups, but you can also make your own, by choosing Menu➪Add to Buddy List➪ Add Group. Click Save to add your friend as a buddy.

Which instant-message system should I use?

Unfortunately, most instant-message systems don't talk to one another. Because the goal of all these systems is to help you stay in touch with your friends, use whichever one they use. If you're not sure who your friends are, AOL Instant Messenger is a good bet because it's easy to set up and works automatically with any AOL user; it's the same system that AOL uses internally. AIM, Google Chat, Windows Live Messenger, and Yahoo! Messenger have similar features because when one adds something, the others tend to follow suit. All are free; support text, voice, and video; and allow more than two people to chat. (We've held meetings on Yahoo! Messenger with six people on voice and two on video and everyone typing snide comments at the same time.) Windows Live Messenger is preinstalled on Windows XP and easy to install on Windows Vista and Windows 7.

The bottom line: Use whichever system your friends use. If you're message-mad or you have friends on more than one system, you can run more than one messaging program at the same time. While we were writing this chapter, we had AOL Instant Messenger, Windows Live Messenger, and Yahoo! Messenger all running at the same time. It was an awful lot of blinking and flashing, but it worked.

Better yet, use a program that speaks all three IM languages. We know of and like two, both free. They are Pidgin, at www.pidgin.im, and Trillian, at www.trillian.im, and they simultaneously handle every IM system you ever heard of. Trillian requires that you set up an account with it (separate from the accounts with the IM systems you're using) and tries to install a bunch of extra applications and toolbars when you install it; say No unless you're sure you want them. A Pro version has more features for $25 per year. Pidgin is plain old-fashioned freeware — no ads, no registration, no begging. Adium from www.adiumx.com is the Mac version of Pidgin.

You can drag a buddy from one group to another in the Buddy List or get rid of a buddy (by clicking the buddy and then pressing Del).

Getting buddy-buddy online

To send a message to someone, double-click the buddy's name to open a message window, type the message, and click the Send button or press Enter. AIM pops up a window (shown in Figure 16-2) on the recipient's machine and plays a little song, and you and your buddy can type back and forth. When you're done, close the message window.

Figure 16-2:
Chatting
using AIM.

Making noise and pictures with AIM

After you establish a conversation using AIM, you can switch to voice or video (assuming that both parties have computers equipped with microphones and speakers and, for video, a camera). Click the little camera icon and pick Audio or Video. Your friend sees a window asking whether he wants to make a direct connection with you. If your friend accepts the invitation, you can chat using the microphone and speakers on your PC. Click Disconnect when you're done talking. See the section "Adding Voices and Faces," later in this chapter, for more about both voice and video on AIM.

Buzz off

AOL evidently has a lot of ill-mannered users, because AIM has a system for warning and blocking users you don't like. If someone sends you an annoying message, you can choose Menu⇨Block or Menu⇨Report This User in the chat window.

What if someone IMs you when you aren't online? You can tell AIM to show you your missed messages by pressing F7 or choosing Menu⇨Settings in the AIM window, which displays the Setting – Buddy List window. Click the Offline IM tab, select the settings you want, and click Save. AIM can save as many as 40 offline messages for as long as two weeks.

You can fine-tune whom you let send messages to you: Choose Edit⇨Settings and then click the Privacy tab. You can limit messages to people on your Buddy List, permit access to specific people, or block specific people. You can also add or delete people from your Block List. We recommend choosing Only Buddies on My Buddy List unless you like being contacted by total strangers at inconvenient moments.

Some obvious rules of messaging conduct

Sending someone an instant message is the online equivalent of walking up to someone on the street and starting a conversation. If it's someone you know, it's one thing; if not, it's usually an intrusion.

Unless you have a good reason to expect that the other person will welcome your message, don't send instant messages to people you don't know who haven't invited you to do so. Don't say anything that you wouldn't say in an analogous situation on the street.

Most instant-message programs allow you to send and receive files. Unsolicited files from people you don't know are always spam, viruses, or both. Most virus checkers don't monitor file transfers via an IM program.

The messages you send with AIM and other chat programs may appear to be ephemeral, but anyone in the conversation can easily store the messages. Most IM programs have a log feature that saves the series of messages in a text file, which may be embarrassing later. In AIM, you control your own logging by choosing Edit⇨Settings and clicking the IM Logging tab.

Finally, if someone tells you to give a series of commands or to download and install a program, don't do it. And never tell anyone any of your passwords.

The more the merrier — chatting with a group

AIM doesn't limit you to chatting with one person at a time. You can have several chat windows open at the same time, and have separate chats in each window. It can make you crazy, though, keeping track of a bunch of conversations, but teenagers do it every day.

An alternative is to have one chat window for more than just one other person. In a chat window, you can press Alt+C or choose Menu⇨New Group Chat and type the screen names of people you want to invite into a group chat window. AIM opens a new tab in your chat window and sends invitations to your buddies, and, assuming that they click Accept, you're all in!

You can control whether your multiple chats appear in separate windows or as separate tabs in one window. Choose Menu⇨View⇨Group IMs in One Window to switch between separate windows and tabs in one window.

AIM on your phone

You can tell AIM to forward messages to your cellphone by way of text message. Choose Edit➪Settings, and then click the Mobile tab. Click Register a Phone Number to display the sign-up page in your Web browser. AIM sends a text message to your phone with a code that you must type on the registration page, to prove that the phone is truly yours.

Or, use Windows Live Messenger

Someone at Microsoft noticed that instant messaging was a niche in which the company didn't have the dominant program, and so they decided to issue everyone a copy of theirs. Windows XP comes with Windows Messenger (which used to be named MSN Messenger), whereas Windows Vista and Windows 7 have Windows Live Messenger Download command on the Start menu, which installs Messenger as part of the Windows Live package.

We don't see the advantage of Windows Live Messenger over the other instant-message programs, but one nice thing is that it interconnects with Yahoo! Messenger, so you can chat with people who use either system. (Or, you can use Adium, Pidgin, or Trillian to talk with people on all the major systems. See the earlier sidebar "Which instant-message system should I use?") It supports voice and video, along with sending text messages to cellphones. Windows Live Messenger also has a nice Sharing Folder feature that allows you and a friend to share photos and other files.

Versions are available for Windows and Macs. If your friends use Windows or Yahoo! Messenger, you can download it from `get.live.com/messenger`. See Chapter 12 to find out how to download and install programs. We recommend that you decline all other programs that come along with Windows Live Messenger, by deselecting their check boxes during installation.

After Windows Live Messenger is installed, you can run it by choosing Start➪Windows Live➪Windows Live Messenger. You sign in with your free Windows Live ID (previously known as a .NET Passport), if you created one; this account is the same one you use to read Hotmail, a type of webmail account described in Chapter 13. The program, shown on the left side of Figure 16-3, works similarly to AIM, with a buddy list (contact list) and chat windows. You add people to your contact list by specifying their Windows Live e-mail address at Live.com or Hotmail.com or their Yahoo! e-mail address at Yahoo.com. Then right-click a contact name and choose how to contact them — IM, e-mail, voice call, or video call (if you have a Webcam). You can also make phone calls from your computer, but the calls aren't free.

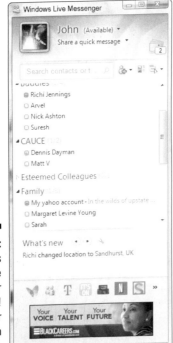

Figure 16-3:
Windows Live Messenger and Yahoo! Messenger look much like AIM.

Or, use Yahoo! Messenger

Yahoo!, the popular Web site, has its own instant-message program, named Yahoo! Messenger. It pioneered multiperson voice and video chats back in 2001. We've held six-person voice-and-video conference calls using Yahoo! Messenger for a total cost of $0. Yahoo Messenger can communicate with Windows Live Messenger, so there's no reason to install both programs, and it also has a photo-sharing feature. Yahoo! Messenger can make and receive voice calls to real telephones, although it costs money. You can also use Yahoo! Messenger to join Yahoo! chat rooms, described in the section "Look Who's Chatting," later in this chapter.

To get the program, go to messenger.yahoo.com and follow the directions to download and install the program. If you don't already have a Yahoo! account, which is also used for Yahoo! Mail and other Yahoo! services, you have to create one before you can log in.

Instant messaging away from home

Most IM systems let you send and receive messages from a Web browser, which is handy if you're at the library or a café that has public computers. The Web version usually doesn't have all the goodies of the downloadable programs, but it's fine to exchange a few text messages.

For AIM, visit `www.aim.com` and click the AIM Express button. For Windows Live Messenger, log in to `www.hotmail.com` and click the Messenger button near the upper right corner to open a menu that lets you sign in and view your contacts. For Yahoo! Messenger, it's `webmessenger.yahoo.com`, or there's a Messenger module you can add to `my.yahoo.com`. Google and Facebook chat are Web based.

Yahoo! Messenger, shown on the right side of Figure 16-3, looks and acts much like AIM. Choose Contact⇨Add a Contact to add your friends who use Yahoo! or Windows Messenger. Then you can right-click a contact and choose how you want to communicate with them — chat, send a text message to their cellphone, leave a voice message, call their telephone number — you name it. After you're chatting, you can click the Conference button to add other people or choose Actions⇨View Webcam to view each other's Webcams.

And there's Google Chat

Every Google Gmail account includes Web-based chat that can also connect to AIM users. Visit `www.gmail.com` and log in to your Gmail account, and on the left side is a list of other Gmail users in your address book. (If you just see the word *Chat* or your own name, click it to expand the list.) The ones with colored dots are online, so click one to open a little chat window and start typing. If you have an AIM account, you can click Options at the bottom of the chat user list and sign into AIM. Google has an optional voice and video add-on for Windows and the Mac. Choose Options⇨Voice and Video to open a page where you can download the voice and video plug-in. After you've done that, a little camera marks people who can do multimedia chat.

Google Chat uses an open standard known as Jabber or XMPP, so you can chat with anyone who has an account on any Jabber system. Google doesn't offer a separate chat program (it doubtless thinks that its Chrome Web browser, in which you can display the Gmail window, is plenty good) but you can use any Jabber/XMPP client, including Adium, Pidgin, or Trillian.

Facebook has chat, too

👤● Chat (**42**) Facebook (the social networking site described in Chapter 18) has chat built into its Web site, so you can chat with any Facebook user who's online. Because Facebook users often are online just about constantly to fiddle with their pages and keep track of their friends, the chances of finding someone online for a chat are pretty good. In the lower right corner of every Facebook Web page is a little chat icon showing the number of your friends who are online. Click it to see a list of potential chat-ees, pick a friend, and start typing. If someone chats with you, your Facebook page pops up a little chat window. Like Google, Facebook doesn't offer a separate chat program, but Pidgin (with an optional add-in) or Trillian will do.

Skype does chat as well as phone calls

Although Skype is best known for voice chatting (see the sidebar "The hype about Skype"), it also has an easy-to-use chat feature. Open the Skype window and click any of your online contacts, and you can type messages in a chat subwindow in the lower right area. During Skype phone calls, you can conveniently type information into the chat box or cut and paste Web addresses that you want your friends or associates to look at.

Abbreviations and smileys

Typing is way slower than talking, so when people IM (or participate in online chat, described later in this chapter), they tend to abbreviate wildly. Many chat abbreviations are the same as those used in e-mail. Because IM is live, however, some are unique. We also list some common *emoticons* (sometimes called *smileys*) — funky combinations of punctuation used to depict the emotional inflection of the sender. If at first you don't see what they are, try tilting your head to the left. Table 16-1 shows you a short list of chat abbreviations and emoticons.

Table 16-1	IM and Chat Shorthand		
Abbreviation	*What It Means*	*Abbreviation*	*What It Means*
AFK	Away from keyboard	RL	Real life (opposite of RP)
A/S/L	Age/sex/location (response may be 35/f/LA)	ROTFL	Rolling on the floor laughing

Abbreviation	What It Means	Abbreviation	What It Means
BAK	Back at keyboard	RP	Role playing (acting out a character)
BBL	Be back later	TTFN	Ta-ta for now!
BRB	Be right back	WB	Welcome back
CYBER	A chat conversation of a prurient nature (short for *cybersex*)	WTG	Way to go!
FTF or F2F	Face to face	:) or :-)	A smile
IC	In character (playing a role)	;)	A wink
IGGIE	To set the Ignore feature, as in "I've iggied SmartMouthSam"	{{{{bob}}}}	A hug for Bob
IM	Instant message	:(or :-(	Frown
J/K	Just kidding	:'(	Crying
LTNS	Long time no see	O:)	Angel
LOL	Laughing out loud	}:>	Devil
NP	No problem	:P	Sticking out tongue
		*** or xox	Kisses
OOC	Out of character (an RL aside during RP)	<----	Action marker that appears before a phrase indicating what you're doing (<----eating pizza, for example)
PM	Private message (same as IM)	WTF?	What the heck?

In addition to using the abbreviations in the table, chatters sometimes use simple shorthand abbreviations, as in `If u cn rd ths ur rdy 2 chat.`

Adding Voices and Faces

If you don't want to talk with or see people while you chat — that is, if you don't mind being limited to typing back and forth with your friends — skip this section. If you do want the audiovisual goodies, read on. You can use a Webcam with AIM, Google Chat, Skype, Windows Live Messenger, and Yahoo! Messenger.

Say what? Hooking up the sound

Almost every computer comes with speakers, which are connected to a *sound board* inside the computer. These speakers produce the various noises that your programs make (such as the AOL "You've got mail!" announcement). Most laptops have built-in microphones, and most desktop computers also have jacks for microphones, or a microphone built right into the monitor. (Check your computer manual or ask almost any teenager for help with this.)

If you don't have a microphone, you can get one that works with almost any computer. A mike should cost less than $20 at your local computer or office supply store. While you're there, also check the prices on computer headsets that have both headphones and a mike, because both you and the people you are talking to will sound much better over a headset than on the computer's built-in speakers.

To test your mike and speakers on a Windows machine, run the Sound Recorder program; try recording yourself and playing it back:

1. **Choose Start➪All Programs➪Accessories➪Entertainment➪Sound Recorder or Start➪All Programs➪Accessories➪Sound Recorder**

2. **Click the red Record button to start recording, and the square Stop button to stop.**

   Talk or sing or make other noises between your Start and Stop clicks.

3. **Click the triangular Play button to hear what you just recorded.**

   Click Record again to add to the end of your recording. Choose File➪New to start over and throw away the sound you recorded.

4. **Choose File➪Save to save it as a WAV (audio) file.**

   We like to make WAV recordings of our kids saying silly things and then e-mail them (the recordings, not the kids) to their grandparents.

You can adjust the volume of your microphone (for the sound coming into the computer) and your speakers or headphones (for the sound coming out) by choosing Start➪All Programs➪Accessories➪Entertainment➪Volume Control or clicking the Volume Control icon on the right side of the Windows taskbar. If a volume control for your microphone doesn't appear, choose Options⇨Properties, select the Microsoft check box so that a check mark appears, and click OK.

If you want to test how voices from the Net sound on your computer, type the URL net.gurus.org/ngc.wav into your browser and see what happens. You may need to click an Open or Open with Default Application button after the sound downloads.

If you can record yourself and hear the recording when you play it back, you're ready for Internet-based phone calls or chats!

Many Webcam-related sites are, um, not, shall we say, family friendly. If you want to test your Webcam with a total stranger, don't be surprised to see parts of the stranger that you weren't expecting to see.

I see you!

If you want other people to be able to see you during online conversations, consider getting a *Webcam*. This small digital video camera can connect to a computer. Some laptops, such as the MacBook, have built-in Webcams above their screens; otherwise, you have to buy one. Webcams come in many sizes and shapes, and prices run from $30 to $300. More expensive Webcams send higher-quality images at higher speeds and come with better software. On the other hand, we've had great luck with a $36 Webcam for chatting with friends and participating in videoconferences.

Most Webcams connect to your computer's USB port, a little rectangular plug on the back of the computer. Some cameras connect to special video-capture cards, which you have to open your computer to install.

If you own a digital video camera for taking video of your family and friends, you may be able to connect it to your computer for use as a Webcam. Check the manual that came with the camera.

Viewing your chat buddies

When chatting in AIM with one other person, if both you and your friend have Webcams set up, you can switch them on for use in your chat. Make sure that AIM knows about your Webcam; choose Edit⇨Settings, click the Enhanced IM tab, and see whether the camera appears in the Video setting. (It may just say Default Device.)

To switch on your Webcams, click the Video button at the bottom of the chat window. You see a message while AIM sets up the connection, and then your buddy's image appears! You can choose Actions in the video window to control the size of the video image.

Getting Webcams working with Google Chat, Skype (described in the next section), Windows Live Messenger, or Yahoo! Messenger works much the same way as with AIM.

Internet Phones and Voice Chat

For about a decade, Internet phones were just around the corner. If you have a broadband Net connection, you're now rounding that corner. No Internet phenomenon would be complete without an arcane abbreviation, so this one is VoIP, for Voice over Internet Protocol, pronounced either "V-O-I-P" or to sound like a dripping faucet.

Some kinds of VoIP use a microphone and headphones plugged into the computer, but you can also plug a regular phone into a *terminal adapter,* or TA.

Easy VoIP with Skype

The freeware VoIP service Skype is owned by eBay and located in Luxembourg, a tiny country in Europe whose main attraction is that it's not anywhere else. You download and install Skype on your computer from www. skype.com, set up a free account, and start using it to talk to other Skype users. You can use your computer's built-in speakers and microphone, a headset with headphones and a microphone, or a handset (which is like a phone handset) plugged into your computer. Skype voice quality over most broadband is very good, much better than that of a normal phone. You can also buy Skype phones that work like regular cordless phones, except that calls are made by using Skype.

Skype isn't limited to talking to other Skype users. You can set up a SkypeOut account to which you add money — from a credit card or as a bonus included with certain computer headsets — and you can then call any normal phone in the world and pay by the minute. Rates are quite low, about 2 cents per minute for the United States, Canada, and Europe, and do not depend on where you're using Skype — only where you're calling. John once called home using his laptop by way of a Wi-Fi connection in a hotel lobby in Argentina for 2 cents rather than the dollar a minute it would have cost from a pay phone. You can also use SkypeIn — a real phone number for your Skype phone so that people can call you — for a monthly fee.

Skype lets you have conference calls of as many as five people and any combination of Skype users and SkypeOut calls to regular phones. It includes an IM feature for typing with your friends while talking to them (or even when you're not talking to them). And, it has a chat feature with SkypeMe, in which you set up a profile, set your online status to SkypeMe, and invite people to call. Skype users live all over the world, so with luck you may make some new faraway friends.

Using a regular phone for VoIP

If you want to use a regular phone for VoIP, setting up VoIP phone service is moderately complicated, not unlike setting up regular phone service. You visit a VoIP provider's Web site and go through the signup process, which includes giving your payment info and picking your phone number, which can be either where you live or anywhere you want people to be able to call you as a local call. Most VoIP companies can also *port* your existing phone number away from your old phone company so that you don't have to change your number. (If you later hate your VoIP company, you can port it back, or to a different VoIP company.) The company then ships you the TA, which you plug into your Internet connection. Then you plug a regular phone into the TA, and you're ready to go.

Several VoIP companies sell combined routers (see Chapter 4) and VoIP terminal adapters through electronics stores. In that case, you set up your Internet connection with the router. Then you use your computer's Web browser to go to the VoIP company's Web site to activate the terminal-adapter part of the router, plug a phone into the phone jack on the router, and you're ready to go.

VoIP companies vary a lot, with local calling areas ranging from a single U.S. state to all of North America and Europe and large parts of Asia. Calls to other customers of the same VoIP company are always free, so you might want to use the same one your friends have. See our Web site at net.gurus. org/phone for some suggestions about VoIP companies.

If you have a cable modem, your cable company may also offer VoIP. If it does. the quality of service is better than what you get with independent VoIP providers, so it's worth a close look.

The nice thing about using a regular phone for VoIP is — it's a phone. When it rings, answer it. If you want to call someone, pick up the phone and dial. Most VoIP companies offer a full suite of phone features, such as voice mail, call forwarding, and caller ID, usually controlled from a Web page rather than from the phone itself.

Around the Virtual Town Pump

Typing or talking to a few people is fun and interesting, but for really good gossip, you need a group. Fortunately, the Internet offers limitless opportunities to find like-minded people and discuss anything you can imagine. Clubs, churches, and other groups use the Internet to hold meetings. Hobbyists and fans talk about an amazing variety of topics, from knitting to *American Idol* and everything in between. People with medical problems support each other and exchange tips. You get the idea — anything that people might want to talk about is now under intense discussion somewhere on the Net.

You can talk with groups of people on the Internet in lots of ways, including these:

- ✔ **E-mail mailing lists,** in which you exchange messages by e-mail.
- ✔ **Social networking sites,** such as MySpace and Facebook, described in Chapter 18.
- ✔ **Usenet newsgroups** (the original Internet discussion groups), which you read with a *newsreading* program. For a description of Usenet newsgroups and how to read them, see our Web site at `net.gurus.org/usenet`. Or, go to `groups.google.com` on the Web and search for topics that interest you.
- ✔ **Web-based message boards,** where messages appear on a Web page.

This section tells you how to participate in Internet-based discussions using e-mail mailing lists and Web message boards. These systems are *instant*, like instant messaging; you post a message, and hours or days later, you get a reply.

Mailing lists: Are you sure that this isn't junk mail?

An e-mail mailing list is quite different from a snail-mail mailing list. Yes, both distribute messages to the people on the list, but the messages on most e-mail mailing lists contain a discussion among the subscribers rather than junk mail and catalogs.

Here's how an e-mail mailing list works. The list has its own, special e-mail address, and anything someone sends to that address is sent to all the people on the list. Because these people in turn often respond to the messages, the result is a running conversation. For example, if the authors of this book hosted the *chocolate-lovers* discussion about the use and abuse of chocolate, and if the list-server program ran at `lists.gurus.org`, the list of the address would be `chocolate-lovers@lists.gurus.org`. (We run a bunch of lists, but not one about chocolate. Yet.)

Different lists have different styles. Some are relatively formal, hewing closely to the official topic of the list. Others tend to go flying off into outer space, topic-wise. You have to read them for a while to be able to tell which list works which way.

Mailing lists fall into three categories:

- ✔ **Discussion:** Every subscriber can post a message. These lists lead to freewheeling discussions and can include a certain number of off-topic messages.

- ✔ **Moderated:** A moderator reviews each message before it's distributed. The moderator can stop irrelevant, redundant, or clueless postings from wasting everyone's time.

- ✔ **Announcement-only:** Only the moderator posts messages. Announcement mailing lists are essentially online newsletters.

Who handles all this mail?

Something or somebody has to take on the job of keeping track of who's on the mailing list and distributing messages to all the subscribers. This job is *way* too boring for a human being to handle, so programs usually do the job. (A few lists are still run by human beings, and we pity them!) Most lists are run by *list servers* or *mailing-list managers*. Popular list manager programs include LISTSERV, Lyris, MailMan, Majordomo, and many others, as well as Web-based systems, such as Yahoo! Groups and Google Groups.

Talking to the human being in charge

Someone is in charge of every mailing list: the *list manager*. The list manager is in charge of helping people on and off the list, answering questions about the list, and hosting the discussion. If you have a problem with a list, write a *nice* message to the list manager. Remember that most list managers are volunteers who sometimes eat, sleep, and work regular jobs as well as maintain mailing lists. If it takes longer than you want, be patient. *Don't* send cranky follow-ups — they just cheese off the list manager.

The list manager's address is usually the same as the list address with the addition of *owner-* at the beginning or *-request* just before the @. For example, the manager of the `chocoloate-lovers@lists.gurus.org` list would be `chocoloate-lovers-request@lists.gurus.org`.

Urrp! Computers digest messages!

Some mailing lists are *digested.* No, they're not dripping with digital gastric juices — they're digested more in the sense of *Reader's Digest.* All the messages over a particular period (usually a day or two) are gathered into one big message with a table of contents added at the front. Many people find this method more convenient than receiving messages separately, because you can easily look at all messages on the topic at one time.

We prefer to receive our messages individually, and to tell our e-mail program to sort our incoming messages into separate folders, one for each mailing list we subscribe to. Thunderbird, Windows Live Mail, and many other e-mail programs can sort your messages.

Getting on and off lists

To find out how to subscribe to a list, or how to unsubscribe to the list, take a look at the instructions that (with luck) came with whatever information you received about the mailing list. With most lists, you can subscribe, unsubscribe, and change your subscription settings from the Web — you go to a Web page and fill out a form. Generally, you enter your e-mail address in a box on a Web page and click a Send or Subscribe button, and you're on the list. This strategy is often more convenient than sending a command by e-mail.

Before you subscribe, be sure that you see a way to get *off* the list (an option that some marketing-oriented outfits neglect to provide).

You should receive a chatty, machine-generated welcoming message telling you that you have joined the list, along with a description of some commands you can use to fiddle with your mailing-list membership. Usually, this message includes a request to confirm that you received this message and that it was really you who wanted to subscribe. Follow the instructions by clicking a link or replying to this message, or doing whatever else the instructions say to do. Confirmation helps lists ensure that they aren't mailing into the void, and keeps people from sticking you on lists without your knowledge. If you don't provide this confirmation, you don't get on the list.

Save the chatty, informative welcome message that tells you about all the commands you can use when you're dealing with the list. For one thing, it tells you how to get *off* the mailing list if it's not to your liking. We have in our mail program a folder named Mailing Lists, in which we store the welcome messages from all the mailing lists we join, so that we don't have to embarrass ourselves by asking for help with unsubscribing later.

Boing!

Computer accounts are created and deleted often enough and mail addresses change often enough that a large list always contains, at any given moment, some addresses that are no longer valid. If you send a message to the list, your message is forwarded to these invalid addresses — and a return message (reporting a bad address) is generated for each of them. Mailing-list managers (both human and computer) normally try to deflect the error messages over to the list owner, who can do something about them, rather than to you. As often as not, however, a persistently dumb mail system sends one of these failure messages directly to you. Just ignore it because you can't do anything about it.

Sometimes you may see an "I'm away on vacation" message or a "Click here if you're not a spammer" message in response to list messages you send. *Don't respond to those, either* — vacation and antispam programs shouldn't even be responding to list mail. Forward those messages to the list manager, though, so that she can suspend those recipients' subscriptions until they get their software under control.

To get off a list, you again visit the Web page for the list and follow the unsubscription instructions. *Don't* send a message to the list saying "Please unsubscribe me" because it just wastes the other subscribers' time.

Stupid mailing-list tricks

Most list servers know some other commands, including commands to hold your mail for a while, send you a daily message that includes all postings for the day, and see a subscriber list. For the exact commands, which vary depending on the list server software, refer to the instructions you received when you subscribed to the list. (You did save the welcome message, didn't you?)

Sending messages to mailing lists

Okay, you're signed up on a mailing list. Now what? First, wait a week or so to see what sort of messages arrive from the list — that way, you can get an idea of what you should or should not send to it. When you think that you have seen enough to avoid embarrassing yourself, try sending something in. That's easy: You mail a message to the list address, which is the same as the name of the list — `chocolate-lovers@lists.gurus.org` or `dandruff-1@bluesuede.org` or whatever. Keep in mind that because hundreds or thousands of people may be reading your pearls of wisdom, don't send anything until you have something to say, and try to spell things correctly. (You might think that this advice is obvious, but you would be sadly mistaken.) On popular lists, you may begin to get back responses within a few minutes of sending a message.

Some mailing lists have rules about who is allowed to send messages, so just because you're on the list doesn't automatically mean that any messages you send appear on the list. Some lists are *moderated:* Any message you send in is sent to a human *moderator* who decides what goes to the list and what doesn't. Although this process may sound sort of fascist, moderation can make a list about 50 times more interesting than it would be otherwise because a good moderator can filter out the boring and irrelevant messages and keep the list on track. Indeed, the people who complain the loudest about moderator censorship are usually the ones whose messages most urgently need to be filtered out.

Another rule that sometimes causes trouble is that many lists allow messages to be sent only from people whose addresses appear on the list, to prevent the list from being overrun with spam. If your mailing address changes, you have to resubscribe or else you can't post anything.

The fine points of replying to list messages

Often, you receive an interesting message from a list and want to respond to it. When you send your answer, does it go *just* to the person who sent the original message or to the *entire list?* It depends on how the list manager set up the list. About half the list managers set up their lists so that replies go automatically to just the person who sent the original message, on the theory that your response is likely to be of interest to only the original author. The other half set up the lists so that replies go to the entire list, on the theory that the list is a running public discussion. In messages coming from the list, the mailing-list software automatically sets the Reply-To header line to the address to which replies should be sent. (Which way to set it up is a topic that can provoke great and prolix passion, so don't ever suggest that they change it.)

Fortunately, you're in charge of that feature. When you start to create a reply, your mail program should show you the address to which it's replying. If you don't like the address it's using, change the address. Check the To and Cc fields to make sure that you're sending your message where you want. Don't run the risk of sending a message such as, "I agree with you — aren't the rest of these people idiots?" to the whole list if you intend it for only one person.

While you're fixing the recipient's address, you may also want to fix the Subject line. After a few rounds of replies to replies to replies, the topic of discussion often wanders away from the original topic. Change the subject to better describe what is really under discussion, as a favor to the other folks trying to follow the discussion.

How to avoid looking like a dimwit

After you subscribe to a list, don't send anything to it until you read it for a week. Trust us — the list has been getting along without your insights since it began, and it can get along without them for one more week.

You can determine which topics people really discuss and the tone of the list, for example. It also gives you a fair idea about which topics people are tired of. The classic newcomer gaffe is to subscribe to a list and immediately send a message asking a dumb question that isn't germane to the topic and that was beaten to death three days earlier.

The number-two newcomer gaffe is to send a message directly to the list asking to subscribe or unsubscribe. This type of message should go to the list manager or list server program, *not* to the list itself, where all the other subscribers can see that you screwed up.

One more thing not to do: If you don't like what another person is posting (for example, some newbie is posting blank messages or "unsubscribe me" messages or is ranting interminably about a topic), don't waste everyone's time by posting a response on the list. The only thing stupider than a stupid posting is a response complaining about it. Instead, e-mail the person *privately* and ask him to stop, or e-mail the list manager and ask that person to intervene.

Posting to message boards

Mailing lists are great if you want to receive messages by e-mail, but some people prefer to read messages on the Web. These folks are in luck: *Message boards* are Web-based discussion groups that post messages on a Web site. They're also called *discussion boards*, *forums*, or *communities*. Like mailing lists, some message boards are readable only by subscribers, some allow only subscribers to post, and some are *moderated* (that is, a moderator must approve messages before they appear on the message board). Other message boards are more like bulletin boards: Anyone can post at any time, and there's no continuity to the messages or feeling of community among the people who post.

Many Web sites include message boards. Some Web sites are dedicated to hosting message boards on lots of different topics. Some sites host message boards that can also send the messages to you by e-mail, so they work as message boards and mailing lists rolled into one.

Web-based discussion sites

Here are some of our favorites:

- ✔ **About.com, at** `www.about.com`: About.com hires semipro experts in a wide variety of fields to host sites about each field. For example, the knitting site at `knitting.about.com` is run by a world-class knitter who posts articles and patterns and hosts one or more message boards about knitting. Find the Forums or My Forums link to join in. Figure 16-4 shows a discussion of knitting techniques.

- ✔ **Google Groups, at** `groups.google.com`: Google Groups started as a way for people to participate in Usenet newsgroups over the Web. Then Google provided a way to set up new groups, too. You can search by topic for groups or messages of interest.

Figure 16-4: About.com hosts sites about hundreds (thousands?) of topics, each with a message board.

- ✔ **Yahoo! Groups, at** `groups.yahoo.com`: Yahoo! Groups includes message boards and file libraries, and you can read the messages either on the Web site or by e-mail — it's your choice when you join a group. Yahoo! Groups also features calendars for group events and real-time chats right on the Web site. To join, you must first sign up for a free Yahoo! ID, which also gets you a mailbox and free Web space — what a deal! You can also create your own Yahoo! group by clicking links — either a public group for all to join or a private group for your club or family.

Finding interesting online communities

Tens of thousands of communities — in the form of mailing lists, message boards, and hybrids of the two — reside on the Internet, but there's no central directory of them. This is partly because so many lists are intended only for specific groups of people, like members of the board of directors of the First Parish Church of Podunk or students in Economics 101 at Tech State.

You can find some communities by searching the Web (as we describe in Chapter 8) and including the word or phrase, mailing list, community, forum, or message board. Or, start at `www.about.com`, `groups.google.com`, or `groups.yahoo.com` and search for your topic.

Subscribing and participating

Most good message boards require you to register before you can subscribe, which means that you choose a username and password, and possibly provide your e-mail address, and respond to a message sent to that address. Registration makes it harder for spam-posting robots to take over the message board.

To subscribe to a community on one of these Web sites, just follow the instructions on the site. Some community Web sites let you read the messages posted to their lists without subscribing — you can click links to display the messages in your Web browser.

You can set up your own mailing lists or message boards, too. It's free because the sites display ads on their Web pages, and may even tack on ads to the postings on the list. If you have an unusual hobby, job, interest, or ailment, you may want to create a list to discuss it. Or, set up a list for a committee or family group to use for online discussions.

Look Who's Chatting

If mailing lists and message boards are too slow — if you want to chat with strangers right now — you might want to try online chat, which is similar to CB radio. Online chat differs from IM chat because it's public and you usually don't know the other people in the discussion.

You begin chatting by entering an area of the Internet called an electronic *chat room* (AOL calls them *channels*). After you join a room, you can read onscreen what people are saying and then add your own comments just by typing them and clicking Send. Although several people participating in the chat can type at the same time, each person's contribution is presented onscreen in the order received. Whatever people type appears in the general conversation window and is identified by their screen names. On some chat systems, such as AOL, each participant can select a personal type font and color for his comments.

If one of the people in a chat room seems like someone you want to know better, you can ask to establish a *private room* or *direct connection,* which is a private conversation between you and the other person and not much different from instant messaging. And, of course, you might get such an invitation from someone else. It's not uncommon for someone to be in a chat room and be holding several direct conversations at the same time, although it's considered rude (not to mention confusing!) to overdo this.

You might also be asked to join a private chat room with several other people. We're not really sure just what goes on in those rooms because we've never been invited.

Where is everyone chatting?

Which groups of people you can chat with depends on which chat system you connect to. Here are a few places you can find groups of people chatting online:

- ✔ **America Online:** If you have an America Online account, you can chat with other AOL users. Get *AOL For Dummies,* by John Kaufeld and Ted Leonsis (Wiley), for a full description of AOL chat rooms. Or, after you have an AIM account, start at `chat.aim.com` and click See All Chats to see which topics are active.

- ✔ **Skype and other VoIP systems:** If you use Skype (described in the section "Internet Phones and Voice Chat," earlier in this chapter), you can choose the Live tab to join a public voice chat or choose Chats⇨Start Public Chat to start your own.

- ✔ **Web sites.** Some Web sites include chat rooms, using a plug-in program that allows people to type at each other.

- ✔ **Yahoo! Messenger:** In Yahoo! Messenger, you can choose Messenger⇨ Yahoo Chat.

Chatting is pretty much the same from system to system, although the participants vary. This section gives a sense of the essence of chat no matter where you go to do it. We describe how to use Web-based chat rooms later in this chapter.

Each chat room has a name; with luck, the name is an indication of what the chatters there are talking about or what they have in common. Some channels have names such as *lobby,* and the people there are probably just being sociable.

Who am I?

No matter which chat facility you use, each participant has a *screen name,* or *nickname,* often chosen to be unique, colorful, or clever and used as a mask. Chatters sometimes change their screen names. This anonymity makes a chat room a place where you need to be careful. On the other hand, one attraction of chatting is meeting new and interesting people. Many warm and wonderful friendships have evolved from a chance meeting in a chat room.

When you join a group and begin chatting, you see the screen names of the people who are already there and a window in which the current conversation goes flying by. If the group is friendly, somebody may even send you a welcome message.

As in real life, in a room full of strangers you're likely to encounter people you don't like much. Because it's possible to be fairly anonymous on the Internet, some people act boorish, vulgar, or crude. If you're new to chat, sooner or later you'll visit some disgusting places, although you'll find out how to avoid them and find rooms that have useful, friendly, and supportive conversations. Be very careful about letting children chat unsupervised (see Chapter 3). Even in chat rooms that are designed for young people and provide some supervision, unwholesome goings-on can take place.

Type or talk?

The original chat rooms consisted entirely of people typing messages to each other. Newer chat systems include *voice chat* (which requires you to have a microphone and speakers on your computer) and even video (which requires a Webcam if you want other people to be able to see you).

Getting Used to Chat Culture

Your first time in a chat room can seem stupid or daunting or both. Here are some things you can do to survive your first encounters:

- ✔ Remember that when you enter a chat room, a conversation is probably already in progress. You don't know what went on before you arrived.

- ✔ Wait a minute or two to see a page full of exchanges so that you can understand some of the context before you start writing.

- ✔ Read messages for a while to figure out what's happening before sending a message to a chat group. (Reading without saying anything is known as *lurking.* When you finally venture to say something, you're *de-lurking.*) Lurking isn't necessarily a bad thing, but be aware that you might not always have the privacy you think you have.

✔ Some chat systems enable you to indicate people to ignore. Messages from these chatters no longer appear on your screen, although other members' replies to them do appear. This strategy is usually the best way to deal with obnoxious chatters. You may also be able to set your chat program not to display the many system messages, which announce when people arrive or leave or are ejected forcefully from the chat room.

✔ Scroll up to see older messages if you have to, but remember that on most systems, after you have scrolled up, no new messages appear until you scroll back down.

Chatting etiquette isn't much different from e-mail etiquette, and common sense is your best guide. Here are some additional chatting tips:

✔ The first rule of chatting is not to hurt anyone. A real person with real feelings is at the other end of the computer-chat connection. Don't insult people, and don't use foul language, and don't respond to people who do.

✔ The second rule is to be cautious. You really have no idea who the other people are. Remember, too, that people might be people hanging out in a chat room and quietly collecting information, and you might not notice them because they never say anything. (See the "Safety first" section in Chapter 2.)

✔ Keep your messages short and to the point.

✔ Create a profile with selected information about yourself. Most chat systems have provisions for creating profiles (personal information) that other members can access.

Don't give out your last name, phone number, or address. Extra caution is necessary for kids: A kid should never enter her age, hometown, school, last name, phone number, or address. Although you don't have to tell everything about yourself in your profile, what you do say should be truthful. The one exception is role-playing chat, where everyone is acting out a fantasy character.

✔ If you want to talk to someone in private, send a message saying hi, who you are, and what you want.

✔ If the tone of conversation in one chat room offends or bores you, try another. As in real life, you run into lots of people in chat rooms that you *don't* want to meet — and you don't have to stay there.

As in society at large, online chat involves some contact with strangers. Most encounters are with reasonable folks. For the rest, common sense dictates that you keep your wits about you — and your private information private. See Chapter 2 for some guidelines for staying safe while chatting with strangers.

Let's Chat

Whatever chat service you use, the idea is the same: You read other people's messages and chime in with your own. In this section, we describe Web-based chat because it's available to all Internet users without installing any extra programs.

Web-based chat sites have Java-based chat programs that your browser can download and run automatically. Some other Web chat sites require that you download a plug-in or an ActiveX control to add chat capability to your browser. (See Chapter 7 for information on how to use plug-ins.)

Finding some action

Some Web chat sites include

> ✔ ICQ Chat, at `www.icq.com/icqchat`
>
> ✔ AIM Chat, at `chat.aim.com`
>
> ✔ The new Google Wave at `wave.google.com`
>
> ✔ Userplane, at `www.userplane.com`, which supports text, voice, and video chat. Click the Directory box near the bottom of the page to find active chats.

Many other Web sites have chats on the specific topic of the site. Search for *chat at* `www.google.com` for a variety of chat venues.

Starting to chat

Most chat sites have directories or search boxes so that you can find a group talking about a topic of interest. We find that after you enter the chat room, 93 percent of chats are about nothing at all, or general flirting, so you may need to shop around. Also, you may make a number of tries before you find a chat room where people are actually chatting — sometimes, everyone appears to have wandered off.

Most Web-based chat pages have a large window that displays the ongoing conversation, a smaller window that displays the screen names of the participants, and a text area where you type messages. After you type your message, press Enter or click Send and the message appears in the message window for you and everyone else in the chat room.

In some chat rooms, you can click a name in the list of participants to see more information about that person, perhaps a name, location, or picture. Some chat rooms have links or buttons that enable you to turn on voice capability so that you can talk into your computer's microphone and hear other people from the speakers. And, some have video buttons or links that can enable your Webcam.

Chapter 17

Games and Worlds on the Web

*W*e're sure that you're reading about the Internet to become a more useful, productive member of society and bring positive change to the world. Or maybe not. You wouldn't be the only person on the planet who uses the Internet primarily to have fun. Enterprising game designers have found myriad ways to meet and exceed the time-wasting needs of the most demanding Internaut. Your options include traditional games, single-player games, multiplayer games, and Brave New Worlds you can create.

A Solitaire-y Pastime

When people say "online gaming," we often assume that they mean multi-player games, and for good reason: The Internet is fundamentally a communication technology, and the biggest advantage to online games is the enormous pool of other players available at any time.

If you're feeling antisocial, though, plenty of single-person games can be found, from classic solitaire to video games to games that are secretly teaching you something. Here are some places to look:

✔ **Games.com:** The site `www.games.com` (from AOL) has numerous solitaire games available to anyone willing to create a free account. (Read the sidebar "Who am us, anyway?" later in this chapter, to see how to create an account.)

✔ **AddictingGames:** One of countless Web sites dedicated to solitary gaming is `www.addictinggames.com`, shown in Figure 17-1. A good search engine can help you find others, like Miniclip (`www.miniclip.com`).

miniclip

Figure 17-1:
Getting
addicted
to online
games.

✔ **Game Show Network:** The GSN cable-television games network has a Web site where you can play along with the shows, at `www.gsn.com`. If you win, your name may even appear on TV!

✔ **Merchandising advertising**: Many corporations advertise their products in downloadable games. If you like Legos, try `play.lego.com`. The Web sites for some action movies offer related games.

✔ **MSN Games:** Puzzle, card, word, trivia, and other types of games are available at the Microsoft site `zone.msn.com`. Yahoo! Games at `games.yahoo.com` is the same idea.

✔ **Neopets:** You can play action, puzzle, and word games at `www.neopets.com` to earn virtual money (not the real stuff, unfortunately) to buy products for your virtual pets. Neopets allows for some degree of interaction between players, but most activities are solo.

✔ **VirtualNES:** If you loved your old Nintendo game console, you'll love `www.virtualnes.com`. It offers classic Nintendo Entertainment System games for free. (It's legal because the games are now out of copyright.)

Start playing in a Flash

Most games use interactive moving graphics, written in a system from Adobe Systems named *Flash*. To play these games, you download and install Flash Player, a plug-in for your browser that enables it to play Flash games. YouTube, the popular video-sharing site, uses Flash, too. (See Chapter 9 for more about Web-based video.) No matter what kind of games you play, you want Flash Player.

You can download Flash Player from `get.adobe.com/flashplayer`. If you try to play a Flash-based game and you don't have the player loaded yet, your browser will probably display a message and suggest installing it. Adobe updates Flash fairly frequently, generally to add whizzo features or fix security bugs, so if your browser suggests a Flash update, surf over to the Adobe Web site and install it.

Plays Well with Others

Anyone who spends much time playing games on the Internet will probably eventually want to play with other people. Most of us simply find more thrill in facing off with another human being than with an electronic box.

When looking for a game to play online, don't think that you need to sift through the overflowing shelves of the local video game store. An easy way to start is with games you already know.

A great many classic games have been adapted for online play, both proprietary ones, such as Scrabble and Monopoly, and ancient ones, such as chess and Go. Chances are good that you already know how to play at least one of them, so look for a free site on which to play. Here's what to do:

1. Choose a game — one you're comfortable with already. The field is wide open!

2. Consult with friends who play the game; they may recommend a Web site, or you may end up referring them to *your* choice.

3. If you have an AOL account (perhaps you use AIM), you'll find its game service (at `games.aol.com`) mostly free and easy to use. If not, try the MSN game site (`games.msn.com`).

4. If you use Facebook (described in Chapter 18), you can play online games solo or with other Facebookers. Type *games* into the search box, click Applications from the list of types of search results, and choose from the games. Our favorite is Bananagrams.

5. Try typing *online game* in your favorite search engine. You can find many free, independent sites, like OKbridge (at `www.okbridge.com`) or Miniclip (`www.miniclip.com`).

Who am us, anyway?

For many of the games described in this section, you need to create an *account*, which is simply an online identification that helps the site owners distinguish you from your neighbor. Creating an account generally involves these steps:

1. **Find the Create Account or Register link and click it.**

   It's on the home page of the Web site. If you see a Sign In link, click it because it probably leads to a page with a link to register.

2. **Enter your information, including a username and password.**

   Make up a username that you can remember and that reflects the kind of character you want to be in the game. Choose a password that isn't in the dictionary and isn't the same as any nongame passwords.

   Remember: Don't choose the same password you use for online banking or making purchases! See "What's the secret word,

Mr. Potter?" in Chapter 2 for advice on picking passwords. We keep our passwords in the KeePass program (downloadable from `www.keepass.info`).

3. **Check your e-mail for the activation code.**

   Generally, the Web site sends you an *activation code* that you must enter in order to activate your account. This system allows the Web site to confirm that your e-mail address is really yours.

4. **Play!**

What type of information do game Web sites ask for? Generally, they want your name and e-mail address. (If they ask for your birthdate, feel free to make one up. What business is it of theirs?) For games that cost money, you have to provide credit card information. Providing it is never entirely without risk but, as we discuss elsewhere in this book, not nearly as dangerous as you might think.

Looking to become a bridge master? At certain sites, like the American Contract Bridge League (at `www.acbl.org`), you can earn master points by playing online.

Games You Can Play at Any Computer

Some computer games don't involve online play — one of our kids loves strategy games that simulate battles from Rome to Gettysburg to WWII. These games traditionally come on CDs or DVDs because they include enormous amounts of high-quality graphics (along with sound and video). These CDs are copy-protected and can be installed on only one or two computers. If you lose the CD or you buy a new computer, you may lose your games and have to repurchase them.

Steam (at `steampowered.com`) is a way of buying games for your computer without waiting for the letter carrier to deliver it in a box. You can search for games and purchase them for (usually) slightly less than the boxed games from a store. Rather than send you a CD or DVD, Steam simply downloads the game to your computer. Downloading can take several hours, depending on the computer and your Internet connection. The advantage, in addition to saving postage and receiving them right away, is that your games aren't tied to your computer. If you're away from home, you can get on your Steam account from any computer, download your games to the computer, and play them. (Steam allows you to play from only one computer at a time.) This system means that you don't lose your games regardless of what happens to your computer. (Just don't lose your password!) In addition, the system keeps all your games currently downloading and installing updates automatically.

Here's the bad news: Steam is free, but the games are not. Steam runs only on PCs, not on Macs. And, if you want to play your games on a computer that's never connected to the Internet, you're out of luck.

MMORPGs Are More Fun than They Sound

MMORPGs (massively multiplayer online role-playing games) are one of the biggest online gaming industries, and something of a pop culture phenomenon. You may not have heard the term, but if you spend any time around gamers, you hear the names — _RuneScape, World of Warcraft, Guild Wars,_ and _EverQuest_ among them.

What's all the fuss about? Read on, and we'll show you.

The general idea

MMO, or _massively multiplayer online,_ just means that it's a big online game with lots of people playing together at one time. RPG stands for _role-playing game,_ which may require more explanation. In a role-playing game, you invent a character, a fictitious personality who represents you in a fictional world and whose actions you control. You play the role of a fictitious personality while exploring an imaginary world.

Computer RPGs generally ask you to take on the role of a warrior or an adventurer, and the main activities of your alter ego are fighting and treasure-hunting, although many MMORPGs also have possibilities for trading, crafting, nation-building, and more. These RPGs are as much about developing your character's abilities as his or her personality; as you fight, your character gains levels of skill, experience points, and better equipment, with which you can fight more dangerous monsters and earn yet more levels and equipment.

One of the earliest commercially successful RPGs, the pen-and-paper game *Dungeons & Dragons,* has a fantasy setting, a tradition that many modern RPGs uphold. If elves and dwarves leave you cold, there are MMORPGs for you, with themes ranging from crime fiction to comic books to the occult. For a long list, go to Wikipedia (en.wikipedia.org) and type *List of free MMOGs* or *List of MMORPGs* in the search box.

Some groups of players like to hang out in online chat rooms where they can discuss the action. The most popular chat space for online players seems to be Internet Relay Chat (IRC), which we describe at net.gurus.org/irc. See Chapter 16 for more about chatting with groups online.

Who's playing?

Many people think that MMORPGs are the exclusive playground of geeky, straight, white, male gamers. (Of course, we know that *you* don't hold that narrow-minded view!) Without getting into nature-versus-nurture debates, our experience suggests that there's some truth to this stereotype.

Whether it's a cause or an effect of their scarcity, minority gamers may sometimes feel less than welcome in the online world. You may find that other players, emboldened by anonymity and able to assume that other users are just like them, express offensive sentiments more freely than they might in person. Every game has antiharassment policies, but many games are used by so many players that enforcement is sometimes patchy.

Regardless, MMORPGs are *not* purely white men's spaces, nor are they used only by stereotypical gamers. Most MMORPGs depend more on quick thinking than on quick reflexes, and are thus accessible to those without much video game experience. *World of Warcraft* has more than 11 million players — we're sure you'll find like-minded people to hang out with.

If you feel like an outsider among gamers, you should know that alternative gaming communities exist in which you may feel more comfortable. Rather than be discouraged by the occasional bigoted remark, why not seek out a feminist mercenary guild, Chicano raiding team, or band of gay-friendly orcs? Believe us, they exist!

Of course, there are bad apples in any online barrel, and you may run into *trolls*, players who deliberately annoy other people just for the fun of it. (The activity is *trolling*.) Your best defense is to ignore them.

Choosing a server

After you choose an MMORPG to play, create an account, and provide your credit card information, you may need to choose a server. Large games may have tens of thousands of people playing simultaneously. To avoid overloading the system, players are divided over a number of servers. Each *server* is a separate computer system running a separate copy of the "world," to prevent it from getting too crowded. For the most part, all servers are equally usable, but here are some thoughts to consider:

✔ **Location:** Servers located near you physically are less likely to lag, which is important if you have a slow machine. The amount of time it takes your command to travel halfway around the world to a distant server may prove annoying.

✔ **RP:** Some designated "role-play" servers require users to speak with medieval affectations and eschew modern slang and game terms, forsooth.

✔ **PvP:** Some servers are all about player-versus-player combat, whereas others forbid it.

✔ **Population:** On a smaller server, your connection is slightly faster, but it may be harder to find players to trade or fight with.

✔ **Friends:** If you know someone who plays, ask which server she's on and join that one.

Roaming around RuneScape

RuneScape is a popular fantasy MMORPG aimed mainly at children and teenagers. Its chief claim to fame is its price tag: $0. *RuneScape* has a simplistic but serviceable combat engine and many nonviolent pastimes, such as mining, cooking, and other handicrafts.

The advantages of *RuneScape* include these:

✔ It's freely available online.

✔ It has manageable system requirements.

✔ It has useful guides and manuals, and may be less intimidating than more advanced RPGs. Its tutorial explains how to play the game and gets you started easily, and the information applies to other online games as well.

However, *RuneScape* has some disadvantages:

- ✔ If you prefer gaming with adults, the low *RuneScape* price attracts a younger population.

- ✔ Its graphics are less sophisticated than those in pricier games.

- ✔ It has less character customization than other RPGs. (All characters are human, for instance).

- ✔ It isn't *completely* free. Some skills and areas are available to only those who pay for membership, which starts at $5 per month.

Want to try it out? Find it at www.runescape.com. After you make your account, we recommend jumping right in. The beginning of the game is a handy tutorial. After you play around a bit, you may want to go back and read the online manual, which makes more sense in context.

RuneScape isn't the only free online RPG. Many others are on the Web, including the two-dimensional *AdventureQuest* (www.battleon.com), the chess-based *Tactics Arena Online* (www.tacticsarena.com), and the text adventure *Kingdom of Loathing* (www.kingdomofloathing.com).

Crafting war in World of Warcraft

The MMORPGs *World of Warcraft* (at www.worldofwarcraft.com), *EverQuest* (www.everquest.com), *EverQuest II* (www.everquest2.com), and *Final Fantasy XI* (playonline.com/ff11us) are examples of from mainstream game developers. These games have more content, more options, and snazzier graphics than do free online games. They're also significantly more expensive.

Your first step, if you choose to play one of these games, is to acquire the software. Unlike the games we describe earlier in this chapter, which you can play in your Web browser, these fancier games require special programs on your computer. For *World of Warcraft*, you'll probably make a pilgrimage to your local game shop to buy the game.

After you install it, you (as usual) set up an account, enter your credit card information, and decide how to pay for the game. Most of these games require a monthly fee, like magazine subscriptions do. Also like magazines, they give you a bulk discount, and you can cancel at any time.

Rather than make a long-term commitment early, get a free trial of the game and then decide how to pay after it ends. Here are some ways to acquire a free trial:

- ✔ **Referrals:** Many games let current members give their friends free trial accounts.

- ✔ **Out of the box:** Often, you get a free trial when buying the game. These games are released and rereleased frequently, so do some comparison shopping and make sure that the edition you buy gives you enough time to evaluate.

- ✔ **Demo disks:** We have gotten free software and trial periods from magazine promotions and the like.

- ✔ **Special offers:** As in any industry, good deals often exist for the persistent and discerning on the game Web sites.

You can read instructions for *World of Warcraft* at `worldofwarcraft.com/info` — click the Introduction or Getting Started links in the Game Guide listing. In the game, you can click the flashing exclamation point icon at the bottom of the screen for help, too.

After you start playing *World of Warcraft,* you can pick a race (elf, orc, gnome, or undead, for example) and a class (fighter, wizard, healer) for your character. The races belong to one of two factions — the Alliance or the Horde — who are locked in never-ending combat to control the world of Azeroth. Choosing wisely is important — if you dislike your character, you generally have to start again from the beginning. However, the rule books don't indicate what you'll enjoy, so we recommend trying a few different characters briefly before settling on one.

The basic activities of the game are killing monsters for levels and rare items, a process that can sometimes grow tedious. To liven it up and speed things along, consider working together with other players. Either arrange to play at the same time as your friends or ask around online to find others looking for a group. Some classes are more popular in groups than others, something you might consider when designing your character.

After you've played for a while, you may want to consider joining a *guild,* which is simply an association of like-minded players who cooperate to earn power, wealth, and prestige. The chief benefit is the ease with which you can recruit party members, but most games also offer mechanical incentives to join guilds. Of course, many people join more for the camaraderie and guild-marked clothing than for any material benefit.

One recent game that's quite different from those discussed here is *Guild Wars,* at `www.guildwars.com`; it has no monthly fees. Joining a guild should be your first priority because the focus of the game is guild-on-guild combat. The monster-hunting, treasure-finding part of the game has been abridged and streamlined to let you jump into player-versus-player (PvP) mode rather than player-versus-computer mode action that much faster.

It's a Whole New World

Second Life (at www.secondlife.com) is a game unlike any other, if it can even be accurately termed a game. It's a complex phenomenon that shares properties of MMORPGs and social networking sites, like Facebook (described in Chapter 18).

Second Life is essentially a simulated world — not our exact world, but rather another world with towns and people. It started with land, sea, and sky, and players have created towns, cities, building, parks, and businesses. (Go to maps.secondlife.com to see what's there.) In *Second Life,* you can run a store, buy and sell clothes, visit night clubs, or do practically anything else that some daring user has programmed. Although you create a character to represent you, as in an RPG, you don't fight monsters (unless that's what you truly want to do) and you don't accumulate levels. Rather, the game attempts to simulate the real world in its entirety — or at least an alternative reality populated by players who appear as 20-something hipsters and a smattering of dragons and talking raccoons.

Whom might you meet in *Second Life?* Almost anyone. The population skews slightly male and geekier than the average population, but it's certainly not used only by gamers and programmers. You find artists, stay-at-home moms, and presidential candidates as well (no joke!). A few corporations own islands in *Second Life* in which they hold virtual business meetings. You can even attend religious services (for example, from maps.secondlife.com, search for *unitarian* to find the First Unitarian Universalist Church of Second Life).

By the way, if you want a simulation of *this* world, go to www.twinity.com, which is creating online copies of real cities, starting with Berlin and Singapore.

A day in the Second Life

At the www.secondlife.com Web site, you can acquire the free *Second Life* software. You must be at least 18 to play; minors 13 and older should check out teen.secondlife.com. Either way, the first thing you want to do is create an account and download the software.

The basic version of *Second Life* is free, although if you provide your credit card information, you get some free Linden dollars, the currency of *Second Life.* We recommend that you do this. Providing your information now makes it easier for you to be tempted to spend money later, but you don't get far in *Second Life* without a few Linden dollars.

When you set up your account, you choose a name for your character. Your name matters. You're offered a selection of last names from which you must pick (although you can see a different selection by reloading the page), and your first-name-last-name combination must be unique. You cannot change your name after you have created the account. Most people opt for names with standard capitalization and no numbers, but your mileage may vary. Some people choose names based on their real names, and some go for creative names, puns, or homages to favorite fictional characters. (Thanks to Second Lifer Kenneth Sutton for this advice.)

You start off on Tutorial Island, shown in Figure 17-2. You learn how to create and dress your *avatar,* which is the *Second Life* version of you. The screen prompts walk you through changing the appearance of your avatar, walking, flying, picking up items, and looking around. At that point, you can head off to the mainland.

Figure 17-2:
Watching
Second Life
go by.

Absolutely the first thing you should do is change your clothes. Tutorial Island gives you three stylish outfits to choose from; don't wear them. Seize the chance for a little self-expression and design something that doesn't mark you as so obviously new. Fashion snobbery is alive and well on the Internet, but you generally get an A for effort. As long as your attire reflects you, and not corporate homogeneity, you'll be fine. If not, you can change outfits instantly. The Library folder in your Inventory has a variety of designer avatars from which you can mix and match to get started.

The easiest way is to right-click your character, choose Edit Appearance, and take off all your clothes. Then you can design new costume pieces one by one and click Save As Outfit to name them. Don't neglect the Create Skirt button, even if your character is male — with a few tweaks, it can be used to create coats, cloaks, and capes.

After you've done that, you can begin your *Second Life* journey. A few things you may be interested in doing are listed here:

- ✔ **Collect free stuff:** Search for *freebies* or ask around for places with free clothes, tools, or animations.

- ✔ **Join a group:** Search for groups through the search engine or look in the profiles of interesting people you meet.

- ✔ **Shop:** Everywhere you go are items for you to spend your money on.

- ✔ **Build:** Search for a "sandbox" area where you can use the builder to construct more elaborate objects. This process takes a while to get good at, but can be quite rewarding. You can use in-world scripting and particle tools for programming objects.

Who's Linden?

Linden dollars are the currency of *Second Life.* As in the real world, you don't get far without them. Fortunately, you don't need to buy food or transportation, but you can still empty your virtual pocketbook in plenty of ways. Here are some uses for Linden dollars:

- ✔ **Shopping:** If you don't want to create everything yourself, you want some Linden dollars to decorate and adorn your character (and home, if you have one). You can buy better clothes than standard issue or items for your home, such as furniture and trees.

- ✔ **Designing:** You must pay a small fee to upload objects and screen shots into *Second Life.* At this point, you can sell them, give them away, or trade them with other players.

- ✔ **Buying land:** You need a premium account to do this, but you can buy virtual property to use a house, club, clubhouse, store, or whatever strikes your fancy. If you don't want to pay for an account, you might want to rent from another resident.

We hope that you already have a few Linden dollars. If not, look into acquiring some. Here are a few ways to make money:

✔ **Sign-up bonus:** You get this money just for registering.

✔ **Direct purchase:** If you can afford it, you can simply exchange U.S. dollars for Linden bucks.

✔ **Stipend:** A more effective way to get money may be to shell out for a premium account. You pay a monthly fee but get a weekly stipend and the right to own land.

✔ **Sales:** Write scripts, design objects, write music, or take pictures and you can sell them to other players. You need some money to get started because it costs a small number of Linden dollars to upload your creations, but after that, it can be both fun and rewarding. You also retain real-world rights to your creations.

Is virtual stuff worth something in the real world?

After lots of people started playing in virtual worlds (gaming worlds and *Second Life*), they began creating things of value, even if these "things" exist only as ones and zeroes in a computer. (Hey, your checking account exists in your bank's computer in the same way.) An online character with lots of experience points, a beautifully designed costume (or body), or a well-placed chunk of real estate (virtual estate?) can be an object of envy to other gamers.

Naturally, an industry sprouted as soon as gamers figured this out. Experienced players realized that they could create a valuable character or item in the game and then sell it to a newbie for real money, and began doing so. An entire industry, *gold farming*, was born, and third world countries, with low-wage workers make up the bulk of it. Chinese workers can make good money playing *World of Warcraft* or other games in ten-hour shifts to gain points or experience level for gamers too lazy — er, too *busy* — to do it themselves. When one study was done in 2007, 1000g (an amount of virtual gold in *World of Warcraft*) on U.S. servers was worth about $260 in real dollars. Online game companies usually outlaw gold farming and close their accounts, but where there's demand, there will always be supply.

Part V
Putting Your Own Stuff on the Net

The 5th Wave   By Rich Tennant

"Ooo-wait! That's perfect for the clinic's home page. Just stretch it out a little further...little more..."

In this part . . .

The Internet is different from other computer networks because it's *flat* — every computer is, in principle, equal to every other. So, there's no excuse for being a virtual couch potato and just looking at other people's stuff — you can publish your own. We look at different ways you can make or contribute to Web sites, such as photo gallery sites, video sharing sites, blogs, and social networking sites such as Facebook and MySpace, including making your own Web site, either from scratch or (the easy way) by using a wiki or page creator site.

Chapter 18

Making a Splash Online

*B*ack at the dawn of the World Wide Web (in 1989), the plan was that people all over the world would communicate among themselves — a virtual rustic global village. That's not exactly how it turned out, with giant megamalls like Amazon.com making the Net a distinctly nonrustic experience. However, after you've used the Internet and browsed the Web for a while, you'll probably think of putting your own material on the Web. Hey, you've got interesting things to say, probably more interesting than a lot of Web sites you've surfed past!

Yes, it's time to stop just browsing the Web and start putting yourself out there in various ways. This chapter takes you through a bunch of ways you can post information on the Web, and explains how to use the ones that are the easiest to start with.

Ways to Go Public on the Web

You can post information on the Internet in lots of different ways. Some require more start-up effort than others. Here's an overview of the best methods for putting your own information online:

✔ **Join a social network:** Web sites such as Facebook, LinkedIn, and MySpace started as glorified personal ads, and have expanded to include photos, video, e-mail, blogs, polls — you name it. See the section "Presenting Your Online Self," later in this chapter.

✔ **Create photo galleries:** Many sites enable you to create an online gallery of photos or other pictures. Make your gallery public or share it with only friends and family. See the later section "Say 'Cheese!'"

✔ **Share videos:** If you have home videos, animated movies, or other digital video you created or edited using software on your PC or Mac, you can post it on a number of video sites. See the section "The Internet's Funniest Home Videos," later in this chapter.

✔ **Share documents, spreadsheets, and calendars:** Post word processing documents or spreadsheets that selected others can view or edit, and create calendars that others can see and change. See the section "Sharing Documents and Calendars," later in this chapter.

✔ **Sell stuff:** Sell goods or services in an online storefront or auction. See the section "Setting Up an Online Shop," at the end of this chapter.

✔ **Write a Web log (blog):** Create an online diary or journal with chronological entries. Chapter 19 describes how to read blogs and write your own blog.

✔ **Use Twitter to let your friends know what you're up to:** Twitter is a little, tiny blog where you post short messages *(tweets)* and read other people's messages. See Chapter 19.

✔ **Produce podcasts:** If you're a musician, storyteller, minister, or teacher or you just think you have something to say, you can post digital recordings on the Web. See Chapter 19.

✔ **Create a collaborative Web site:** A *wiki* enables you and your friends or co-workers to edit a set of Web pages together. See Chapter 20.

✔ **Build a handcrafted Web site:** You can use Google Sites, Homestead, Weebly, or a Web page editor to create a Web site with pages of your choosing. See Chapter 20 to find out how.

Presenting Your Online Self

Facebook, LinkedIn, and MySpace are *social networking* sites, which make it easy to make a Web page about yourself without having to know how to use HTML. Then you can use your Web page to communicate with friends, organize events, create committees, and meet new people.

Social networking sites have become hugely popular with all kinds of people. Facebook (www.facebook.com) was started for college students and expanded to teenagers in general, but the fastest-growing group of users these days is folks over 40. Now, every political candidate who's serious needs a Facebook presence. LinkedIn (www.linkedin.com) is designed for making business contacts. Many musical groups (especially rock bands) have also found MySpace (www.myspace.com) to be a good place to communicate with fans.

Since their creation, these sites have been a way for people to publish their thoughts and ideas on the Internet, for free. The sites have also opened a huge window for up-and-coming musicians, poets, and other performers, helping many people rise in their careers.

Figure 18-1 shows a typical Facebook page (okay, it's the page of one of the authors), also known as a *profile.* Your page can include photos, videos, a blog (described in the later section "What's in a Blog?"), and other elements to present the Real You (or, optionally, the Fake You).

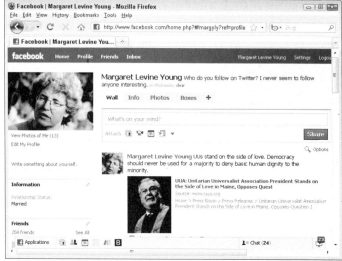

Figure 18-1: Social networking sites display information about you and make links to your friends.

You can find a bunch of social networking sites on Wikipedia (`en.wikipedia.org`); search for *list of social networking sites.* Facebook is the most popular, so we describe it in this section. How do you decide which social network to join? Ask your friends which networks they belong to.

Because social networking is trendy, it has a vast number of sites, most of which will never amount to anything. Some sites are popular in such specific niches as Spoke.com which is popular among salespeople, and Google's Orkut.com which is inexplicably popular among Brazilians, but if you've never heard of a site, likely nobody else has heard of it, either. Before joining a site, think of people you'd expect to find there, and search for them. If you don't find at least a few of them, the site isn't likely to interest you. Some sleazier wannabe sites scoop all the addresses out of members' address books and send invitations "from" them, so if you receive an invitation you weren't expecting, first write back to the alleged sender and see whether they intended to invite you.

Different sites have different age restrictions for users, along with rules that apply to all users regardless of age. Facebook, like most networking sites, requires users to be 13 or older.

Setting up your social site

To create your own page on a social networking site, the steps work like this:

1. **Go to the Web site where you want to create a site, such as** www. facebook.com.

2. **Find the Sign Up or Register button.** Follow the instructions to create an account, which is free. Some sites send a confirmation message to your e-mail, containing a link that you must click to prove that your address is what you say it is. On Facebook and MySpace, you specify a username that becomes part of the Web address of your site. (If your username is elvispresley on Facebook, your site is www.facebook. com/elvispresley).

3. **Set up your account.** Depending on the site, you're asked for different kinds of information. Facebook prompts you to join one or more networks based on geography (people in your town), people who went to your college, or people at your company.

4. **Edit your profile.** Click the Profile or Edit Profile button or link to enter the information you want to display on your pages. You may be asked for your gender, age, political leanings, religious views, hometown, phone number, mailing address, school name (current or past), sexual orientation, marital status, activities, favorite music — you name it. Enter only what you're comfortable sharing!

5. **Choose your security settings.** Look for settings that enable you to control who can see this information; we recommend that you not share your hometown (unless it's a big, big city), birthdate, or other identifying information. In Facebook, click Settings and then Privacy Settings to control who can see what. While you're at it, set your notifications; Facebook can e-mail you or send a text message when you receive various types of Facebook events.

6. **Take a look at your page.** In Facebook, click Profile. In MySpace, click Home. Make sure that you're comfortable with the entire world reading the information that's there — keeping in mind your boss, your minister, your kids, your parents, and that creep who compelled you to change your phone number to get away from him. (You get the idea.)

7. **Upload pictures, if you want.** You can upload photos from your PC, organize them into albums, add captions, and even click individual faces in your photos and identify them. (Very cool.) The Facebook system notifies any other Facebook users you identify in your photos so that they can take a look.

Finally, you have your own home page! At Facebook, you're at www. facebook.com followed by your username. At MySpace — same idea.

Keeping your page current

Some people check their profiles once a week to see whether new comments or messages are posted online. Others feel the need to update and redesign their accounts daily. (Perhaps these people check their voice mail every hour, too.) It's all up to you — that's why they call it MySpace.

Updating pictures is an easy way to keep your page current. New photos change the look of your profile and allow users to comment ("Where were you and what were you doing?!" "New shirt?").

MySpace and Facebook enable you to add other elements to your profile, like a Weblog (blog) of your news and musings or posting notes on your and your friends' "walls" (a section of your Facebook page).

Updating from Your iPhone

If you have an iPhone or iPod touch, download the free Facebook or MySpace Mobile app so that you can view and update your site from that cute little device. The app enables you to post profile updates, read messages, and look at your friends' pages, as shown in Figure 18-2. When you take a picture or video, you can send it directly to Facebook or MySpace for posting.

Figure 18-2:
Use a smartphone "app" to update your profile from anywhere.

Making connections

The whole point of social networking sites is, believe it or not, social networking. Your site isn't complete until it includes links to lots of friends — preferably, people you actually know. (Why add a stranger as your friend if the person is a stranger?)

On Facebook, click Friends and then click the Find Friends tab. If you store your friends' e-mail addresses in your Yahoo! Mail, Google Gmail, Windows Live Hotmail, or AOL, Facebook offers to search your address book for the addresses of people who have Facebook accounts. A scary feature (but we tried it anyway) was uploading the address book from our e-mail program so that Facebook could identify people with Facebook accounts that we might want to invite to be our Facebook friends. Or, you can search for friends, relatives, or classmates. Click Friends and type names in the Search Friends box.

After you have friends, you can send them messages, look at their pages, view their photos, look at their friends, and (depending on people's privacy settings) look at their friends' pages. You see their *walls*, which you can write on (leave a note) — it's a kind of personalized digital graffiti.

LinkedIn works a little differently because its emphasis is on making business connections. After you've linked up to your business contacts, you can write recommendations of other people, pose questions, and answer questions. The idea is to garner recommendations and write useful answers so that people looking for employees or contractors see your profile and decide to contact you through a mutual connection.

Say "Cheese!"

We love sharing our family photos with other people, and the Web makes it easy. Also, sharing over the Web saves you the cost of making extra prints of your snapshots, and it's quick. Several Web sites enable you to upload your digital pictures to the sites and share the pictures with your friends and family. These free photo-sharing sites make their money by selling prints — after your family sees that gorgeous shot of little Mary finger-painting with pudding, they'll *have* to have a copy for the fridge!

Of course, the most popular way to share pictures is on Facebook!

You can try one of these photo-sharing sites:

✔ **Flickr** (part of Yahoo!), at `flickr.com`: This is probably the biggest photo-sharing site. Upload pictures from your computer, e-mail them, or send them from your phone — videos, too. Flickr gives you the choice of making photos public to all Flickr users, accessible only to specific groups of people, or completely private.

✔ **Picasa** (from Google), at `picasa.google.com`: Picasa combines a free photo-organizing program with a web-based picture-sharing site, at `picasaweb.google.com`.

✔ **Photobucket** (owned by Fox), at `photobucket.com`: This site hosts both pictures and video.

✔ **Windows Live Photos,** at `profile.live.com` or `photos.live.com`: When you log in with your Windows Live ID, you get a profile that includes calendars, instant messaging, and (most germane to file-sharing) a Photos section where you can create albums and upload pictures. You can also see photos that your friends have tagged as containing you. Click Photos and then Create a Photo Album, type a name for the album, and then choose the photos to update into your new album.

✔ **HP Snapfish,** at `www.snapfish.com`, lets you set up online photo albums using either photos you upload or rolls of film you mail in to the site. You can share the albums and order prints.

Picture formats

Pictures come in dozens of formats. Fortunately, only three picture formats are in common use on the Web: GIF, JPEG, and PNG. Many lengthy — er, *free* and *frank* discussions have occurred on the Internet concerning the relative merits of these formats. John, who is an Official Graphics Format Expert, by virtue of having persuaded two otherwise reputable publishers to publish his books on the topic, suggests that photographs work better in JPEG format, whereas clip art, icons, and cartoons are better in PNG or GIF. If you're in doubt, JPEG files are smaller, and download faster. PNG is a superior, new replacement for GIF, and its only disadvantage is that people with very old browsers (Netscape 3.0 and older, for example) can't easily view PNG files.

If you have a picture in any other format, such as BMP or PCX, you must convert it to GIF, JPEG, or PNG before you can use it on the Web. Windows comes with Paint, which you can run by choosing Start➪All Programs➪Accessories➪Paint. Or, check out Tucows at `tucows.com/downloads/Windows` or try Download.com at `www.download.com` for graphics programs that can convert file formats. For the Mac, consider GraphicConverter at `www.lemkesoft.de` and click the American flag for the English version of the site.

After you create an account at one of these sites, you can upload photos into online photo albums by filling out forms on the Web site. Then you can share your albums with your friends. If you want, you can make your photos on these sites invisible to the general public — only to the people with whom you share the album.

You (and your friends) can also order prints of your uploaded photos — that's how these sites make their money. The prices for prints are reasonable, and we find these systems convenient. You can print your photos as calendars, cards, books, and even postage stamps.

Another way to share photos is to include them on a blog, as described in Chapter 19. Blogs are useful if you want to use your photos to illustrate a narrative, like the story of your trip to Spain.

Organizing your photos, too

Several programs help you organize the pictures on your computer as well as uploading and sharing them online. Picasa is the Google photo management program, which you can download from www.picasa.com or picasa.google.com. The program finds the photos on your computer (identifying them by their filename extensions) and helps you organize, caption, and edit them. They then enable you to upload the photos or albums to their Web site for sharing with your friends and family. Figure 18-3 shows the Picasa photo-sharing Web site.

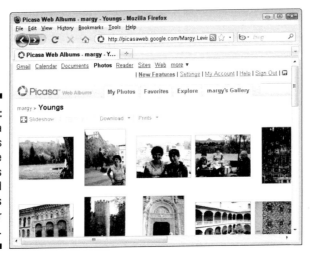

Figure 18-3:
Picasa helps organize your photos and upload them to its Web site for sharing.

Windows Live Gallery comes as part of a bundle of programs that you can download for free from download.live.com, as described in the sidebar "Windows Live Essentials" in Chapter 13. Like Picasa, this program organizes and uploads your photos.

The Internet's Funniest Home Videos

It would be hard to live in the 21st century and not have heard of YouTube (at youtube.com), the popular video-sharing Web site owned by Google. YouTube and similar sites, like Dailymotion (dailymotion.com/us), Flickr (flickr.com), Google Video (video.google.com), Photobucket (photobucket.com), Veoh (www.veoh.com), and Yahoo! Video (video.yahoo.com), store huge libraries of videos that you can search and watch. To watch videos on YouTube and other video-sharing sites, see the section "Watching Movies on the Net" in Chapter 9.

You can post videos on these sites, too, as long as your video isn't longer than about ten minutes. (Different sites may have different limits.) Use your video camera, digital camera, or phone to shoot a short movie and transfer it to your PC. Then you can upload your video. On YouTube, you sign up for a free account first and then click the Upload Videos link on any YouTube page.

If you have a cellphone that takes video, you can upload videos from your cellphone and post them to social networking sites like Facebook. The built-in iPhone Camera program enables you to shoot video, and then gives you the option of e-mailing or uploading it to YouTube.

Sharing Documents and Calendars

Have you ever wished that you could share a spreadsheet or word processing document with other people, and maybe even let them let them make changes? For example, you're the commissioner of a fantasy football league and you want to share a spreadsheet of players and their statistics with the other players. Yeah, you could print the spreadsheet and pass it around, but what if you make updates? Instead, you can upload the spreadsheet to a document-sharing site and share it with the other players.

Or, a document or spreadsheet might be just for you, but you need to be able to edit from more than one computer. Our kids use a document-sharing site to work on their school papers both at home and at school — it's much easier than copying their files to a thumb drive or disk, which they'd probably forget on the kitchen counter, right next to their lunch.

Several document-sharing sites allow you to use the Web as your word processing, spreadsheet, or presentation program, storing your files online. You can see, edit, and print your documents, spreadsheets, and presentations from any computer that's on the Internet. In fact, these sites are so good that some people use them for all their documents and spreadsheets, even if they have word processing and spreadsheet programs on their computers.

Making a Google Doc

The most popular document-sharing site is Google Docs, at `docs.google.com`. Google Docs doesn't support every advanced feature of Microsoft Word and Excel, but it handles all the basics. Figure 18-4 shows a Google spreadsheet. The toolbar just above the spreadsheet provides formatting options, like a "real" spreadsheet, and the menu bar (File, Edit, View, and so on) provides other spreadsheet features. You can print your spreadsheet, presentation, or document or export it in a standard format.

Figure 18-4:
A group of people can view and edit a Google Docs spreadsheet.

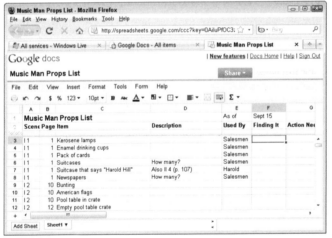

To get started with Google Docs, follow these steps:

1. **Sign in at** `docs.google.com` **with your Google account username and password.**

   Or, if you're already signed in at another Google site, click Documents on the list of Google services at the top of the screen. Either way, you see the Google Docs screen, with a list of the documents and spreadsheets that you can view or edit.

2. **To upload a word processing document, presentation, or spreadsheet from your computer, click Upload, click Browse, and select the file to import. Then click Upload File.**

   Google Docs uploads the file and creates a new document, presentation, or spreadsheet that you can edit and share.

3. **To create a new document, presentation, or spreadsheet from scratch (rather than uploading it), choose New⇨Document, New⇨Presentation, or New⇨Spreadsheet.**

   Hey, the New menu has a bunch of other options, too (maybe more since we wrote this chapter), like Presentation, which enables you to create a PowerPoint-style set of slides.

   Google creates a new element of the type you chose and displays it on the screen, with the appropriate menu bar and icons for editing.

4. **If you created the file from scratch, give it a name. Choose File⇨Rename from the menu bar in Google Docs (not the menu bar at the top of your browser window) and type a name.**

5. **Type in the document, presentation, or spreadsheet as usual.**

   If you made a spreadsheet, click in a cell and then type in it. To edit a cell, double-click it or click it and press F2.

6. **When Google Docs asks whether to start autosaving your information, click Start Autosaving.**

   Google saves your data in the *cloud*, that is, the innumerable Web servers that Google maintains and that we never have to see or worry about. It saves your changes every few minutes, so you're unlikely to lose your work.

Sharing the wealth

After you have a document or spreadsheet (or presentation) in Google Docs, you can share it with other people. Click the Share button and choose Invite People. Cut and paste or type the addresses of people you want to share the information with. Click To Edit if you want to allow them to make changes to your document or spreadsheet, or To View if they can look but not touch. Enter the subject and text of the e-mail message that Google Docs will send to invite them to look at your document or spreadsheet, and click Send.

Your invitees receive a message explaining how to access the information you're sharing.

You can also give people a Web address they can use to view the document or spreadsheet (no editing). Click Share and choose Get the Link to Share to see a rather long URL that you can e-mail or IM to people so that they can take a look.

Making and sharing an online calendar

Another kind of information you can share is an online calendar. Maybe your club, church, theater, or whatever holds public events. Or, maybe they have a schedule of meetings to share with a small group of people. Either way, you can make an online calendar, enter events or meetings on it, and make it available for viewing or editing.

Google Calendars, at `calendar.google.com`, enables you to make one or more calendars, share them with other people, and make them public. You can display more than one calendar, overlaid in different colors, so that you can see your own events alongside your friends or co-workers. Microsoft has a similar service at `calendar.live.com`.

Margy's family has a Google calendar for our family events. On the computer in her kitchen, family members refer to the online calendar rather than to the traditional coffee-stained paper wall calendar. We sync our Google calendar with the calendars on our smartphones or other devices, such as the iPhone or iPod touch. Okay, we *are* geeks, but it sure is convenient to have a shared family calendar with us all the time!

Beyond Google Docs

Google Docs isn't the only online document-sharing site. Zoho (`www.zoho.com`) offers free accounts (you can even log in using your Google account name) that you can use to create a share several types of files. Zoho Writer has more formatting options than Google Docs. Zoho Sheet provides online spreadsheets. Zoho Show makes slide show presentations. Holy cow — it's a complete Microsoft Office-like set of programs, all for free!

Not surprisingly, Microsoft has decided to play this game, too. If you go to Microsoft Office Live, at `www.officelive.com`, you can create (surprise!) documents, presentations, and spreadsheets by uploading them or making them from scratch. To get started, sign in with your Windows Live account (or make one for free).

Setting Up an Online Shop

Selling stuff on the Internet used to take hundreds of thousands of dollars worth of software and programming talent. A number of sites now let you create Web stores for very modest fees. Here are a few:

✔ **Amazon.com Marketplace**, at `sellercentral.amazon.com`, is easy to set up. Sign in with an Amazon.com account (the same account you use if you buy books or other items on the site), click Your Account, and click Your Seller Account to find out how to set up a seller account. Or, search Amazon.com for the item you want to sell and click the Sell Yours Here button. The site even processes credit card sales for you, eliminating what was once a horrible pain in the neck.

✔ **eBay.com Stores**, at `pages.ebay.com/sellercentral`, enables you to sell items in auctions (for which eBay is famous) or at fixed prices (using the Buy It Now option). Your store can have its own name and logo, and items in your store show up when people search eBay for merchandise.

✔ **Yahoo!**, at `smallbusiness.yahoo.com`, lets you create a storefront for a monthly fee.

To set up a store, you sign up for a free account at the Web site and then click the link to create the store. You provide information about the items you sell, including descriptions, prices, and shipping costs.

If you don't want to set up a whole store, you can still sell individual items either on consignment at sites like `www.half.com` or at auction at sites like `www.ebay.com`. eBay owns Half.com, so when you set up an account to buy or sell items on one, you're ready to buy or sell on the other, too.

To sell an item on Half.com (or any other consignment site), first find the item you want to sell, as shown in Figure 18-5. Half specializes in books, movies, and music, and it has almost everything in print in its database. When you find your item, click the Sell My Copy link, specify the condition of the item, add a description, and state your asking price. When you click the List Item link, your listing goes into the Half.com database and appears on the site within an hour. When you sell your item — which could be minutes, hours, or months later — Half.com keeps a commission.

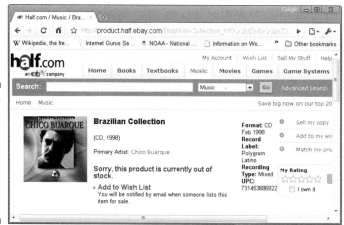

Figure 18-5:
If you have a rare Brazilian CD to sell, click Sell My Copy on Half.com.

Selling an item on eBay is similar for books, CDs, and DVDs, but for other items it can be a little more complicated. You write a description for the item and take or scan a digital picture of it. Start at www.ebay.com, click the Sell tab or link, and follow the directions. Auctions can last as long as seven days, or you can set up a fixed-price offer with no end date. eBay charges you a listing fee, although if your item doesn't sell, you can usually relist it (try again, perhaps with a lower starting price) for free. Click Help at the bottom of any eBay page, and then Selling Basics, for instructions and hints for selling.

Chapter 19

Blogs and Twitter

. . . .

In This Chapter

▶ Reading other people's online diaries (also known as blogs)

▶ Making your own blog

▶ Tweeting what's happening right now on Twitter

. . . .

Diaries are as old as writing. (We made up that statement, but it may well be true.) However, diaries that every single person on the entire Internet can read are a more recent invention. Not many people have always dreamed of publishing their diaries, but lots of people want to write regular columns where they can express their opinion, tell stories, or post pictures. Blogs have made that expression possible, easy, and free.

If you're not an enthusiastic and voluminous writer and you want to post tiny articles or journal entries, Twitter was invented for you. This chapter explains how blogs work, including microblogs (the technical term for what Twitter is).

What's in a Blog?

A *Weblog*, usually abbreviated as *blog*, is a public online diary where someone posts more or less regular updates. A blog uses software that lets you easily post entries by using your Web browser — no additional software is needed. You can even post updates from your mobile phone.

Most blogs are updated frequently by one author and contain short, dated entries, as in a diary, with the newest ones at the top. Other blogs are more complex, with multiple topics or pictures as well as or instead of words, but they retain the idea of relatively short entries, updated relatively often. Figure 19-1 shows the political blog of a friend of ours, Doug Muder (weeklysift.blogspot.com).

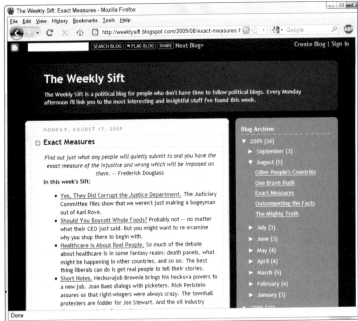

Figure 19-1:
The value
of a blog
depends on
whether its
author has
anything
interesting
to say.

The best blogs offer cutting-edge journalism and commentary and brilliant, witty, sparkling writing, whereas the worst disprove the old cliché that a million monkeys at a million typewriters would eventually produce the works of Shakespeare. If you search Google.com for the word *blog* or *weblog* and some topic words that are of interest to you, you'll invariably find someone blogging away at it. But keep reading to find out better ways to discover and organize the blogs you read.

As blogs have become more popular, many Web sites have added blogs to post news, gossip, or behind-the-scenes stories. Every *New York Times* columnist (at www.nytimes.com) has a blog — go to nytimes.com/blogs to see a list. Some sites show the latest blog posting or two in a prominent spot, and you can click a link to see older posts.

How to read a blog

Reading a blog is easy because blogs are just Web pages. Point your browser at the home page of the one you're interested in and read it. (Bet you thought it would be more complicated than that.) If you want to see more information about a particular story, click the link in the story.

Reading one blog is like eating only one potato chip, which never happens. When you find one blog, it usually has links to other blogs. If you search for one blog on a particular topic, you find a dozen blogs on that subject, and before you know it, you're mired deep in the swamps of Blogistan, with far too many interesting blogs to keep track of.

Because blogs change frequently (at least they're supposed to), you might want to bookmark your favorite ones in your Web browser so that you can find them again. As you find more blogs, you soon find your bookmark folder and your brain exploding from trying to keep track of them.

Luckily, you can subscribe to blogs so that you don't have to remember to return to each blog Web site to read the latest postings. When you subscribe to a blog, the new entries arrive on your computer automatically, so you don't have to check the blog Web site.

An *RSS feed* is the blogging feature that enables you to subscribe to the blog and receive new postings automagically. (*RSS* stands for Really Simple Syndication.) An RSS feed is a special Web address (URL) that usually ends with `.rss`. When you're reading a blog in your Web browser, look for a Subscribe or RSS link, which should display information about the site's RSS feed. Some blogs use a URL at `feedburner.google.com` for their feeds.

The system you use to subscribe is an *aggregator*, although almost no one uses the term. One type of aggregator is Web based, a Web site that tracks and shows you all your favorite blogs. The other is desktop based, a program that lets your computer track and show your favorite blogs.

Your favorite blogs

The following sections describe three of our favorite aggregator Web sites, all free.

Bloglines

```
www.bloglines.com
```

Bloglines, shown in Figure 19-2, is the premier site for people who want to follow a whole lot of blogs. To get started at Bloglines, you set up a free account and then tell it to subscribe to the blogs you're interested in. If you know the RSS feed's URL, you can enter it directly, but it's usually easier to use the built-in search engine. Type a few words describing blogs you might like and pick the likely-looking ones. Many blogs also have a Bloglines button you can click to open the Bloglines site and add that blog to your account.

For each blog, Bloglines tracks the items in the blog and remembers which ones you've looked at, reporting the number unread in parentheses after the name of each blog. That makes it easy to cruise by and catch up on what's new. You can mark stories of interest to add to your private clipping folder, and you can also publish a blog of clippings and, optionally, add notes to each clipping. (Your clipping blog is a real blog with its own RSS feed, so your friends can read it and save entries, and their friends can read their clipping blogs, offering nearly theological blogs within blogs within blogs.)

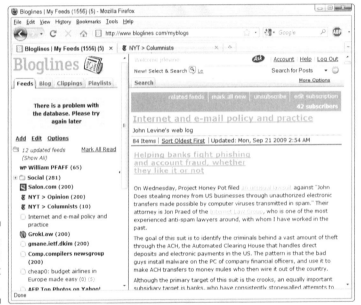

Figure 19-2:
All blogs, all the time, at Bloglines.

Google Reader and iGoogle

```
www.google.com/reader
google.com/ig
```

After you log in to your free Google account, you can start subscribing to blogs. (This Google account works with all Google services; if you don't already have an account, click a link to create one.) Google Reader offers bundles of popular feeds to get you started. To add a blog from Blogger (Blogspot), Facebook, Flickr, LiveJournal, MySpace, or several other popular blog sites, you can select the site and type the name of the blog. You can either click the Add Subscription link at any time to search for a blog by name or topic (this is Google, after all) or paste in an RSS feed.

Or, you can add blogs to your Google home page, a.k.a. your iGoogle page. When you log in to `google.com/ig` using your Google username and password, you see your iGoogle page, which you can configure to display the weather, calendars, news, and (of course) your favorite blogs.

My Yahoo!

`my.yahoo.com`

My Yahoo! lets you mix and match the site's own material with RSS feeds, in a two- or three-column format that lets you pack an amazing amount of information into one Web page. Any resemblance to iGoogle shows that Google knows good ideas when it sees them.

Because Bloglines, iGoogle, and My Yahoo! are quite popular, many blogs offer a one-click way to add the blog to your subscriptions.

Writing Your Own Blog

Now that you've read other people's blogs, how about starting your own? People read blogs for their brilliant, witty, sparkling content. Sparkling is hard, and sparkling regularly is exhausting. If you start your own blog, try blogging for a while on your own before telling all your friends about it. Otherwise: "It was okay at the beginning, but now, big yawn."

Many blogging sites accept text, phones, and even video as part of your blog. You don't have to decide in advance what kind of material you'll include.

Can I make big buck$ with my blog?

Probably not. The alleged path to blog riches is that you start a blog, fill it with fabulous writing, and add some ads down the side and then millions of people flock to your blog and click the ads, and your share of the advertising income buys a tropical island where you retire.

A few famous blogs have succeeded with this plan, such as Boing Boing (`www.boingboing.net`, for eclectic technogossip) and Wonkette (`www.wonkette.com`, for Washington, D.C. political gossip), but you can probably count them on your fingers, and running each one is a full-time job. We've experimented with ads on some of our bloggish Web sites, such as John's airline information site at `airinfo.travel` or his blog about Internet and e-mail policy, at `weblog.johnlevine.com`, and we've never seen more than a few dollars a day, which means that our tropical island will be limited to about four square inches.

You can put up a blog with ads for free at Blogger (`www.blogger.com`), so you have nothing to lose but your time and perhaps your self-esteem. Don't quit your day job quite yet.

Finding where to put your blog

Many big blog sites let you blog away without having to install anything. These sites offer a basic usable blog for free. Some also have extra-cost add-ons that they hope you'll use. For reasons that will shortly become apparent if you read this entire section, we suggest that most of our users try Blogger.

Here are some popular blog-hosting sites:

Blogger

www.blogger.com

Also known as Blogspot, Blogger is now part of the Google empire, although Google hasn't Google-ized it, at least not yet. After you create an account, you can add and edit blog entries through the Web site, customize it in any of a zillion ways, and publish your blog. Blog entries can include photos and videos. You can even post text and pictures from your mobile phone.

Blogger is remarkably uninterested in asking for your money. As far as we can figure out, its reason for existence is mostly to be a place for people to display Google ads. That's fine — it's a nice site, and the ads are entirely optional.

LiveJournal

www.livejournal.com

The cliché LiveJournal user is a college student who needs to provide too much information to his 100,000 closest friends on topics ranging from taste in music to short-term party plans to personal political philosophy. If this sounds like you, LiveJournal is the place. Blog entries can include photos, video, and other cool stuff.

WordPress

www.wordpress.com

WordPress can provide you with a customizable blog for free. Because its software is widely used, lots of plug-ins allow you to mix photos from Flickr, posts from Twitter, and other kinds of information directly into your blog. You can also create nonjournal pages, such as an About Me page.

Xanga

www.xanga.com

Top five reasons not to start your own blog

Blog entries are usually short, so in that spirit, we offer you a short list:

5. You work on your blog when you should be working on your day job, annoying your co-workers and boss, and you spend hours reading *other* blogs, looking for topics to comment on or borrow.

4. Every conversation or experience becomes a potential blog entry rather than part of your life (also known as novelist's syndrome).

3. You try to have strange conversations and experiences in order to have something to blog (bad novelist's syndrome).

2. Everything, no matter how trivial, takes on a deep bloggable meaning. ("Did you ever notice all the different ways that rain streaks the dirt on the side of a city bus?")

1. You realize that you have nothing to say.

We practice what we preach here. None of us has a personal blog, just work-related ones.

Xanga is a lot like LiveJournal except that the average user seems to be about five years younger. Unlike the other two sites, Xanga shows its ads on your blog unless you buy a premium account. Xanga also includes some social networking features, like Facebook and MySpace.

You can also add a blog to your Facebook, MySpace, or other social networking site. See the section in Chapter 18 about setting up your social site.

When you create a blog at one of these sites, you choose a name for the blog and this name plus the site name becomes the Web address of your blog. For example, if you name your blog Weekly Sift at blogspot.com, the address of the blog is `weeklysift.blogspot.com`.

Going postal

When you're ready to post an article, diary entry, story, or rant to your blog, you have a number of options:

- ✔ **Use your Web browser.** Go to the blog's Web site in your Web browser and click the Create Post or New Post link. Type your article, or cut and paste it from your word processor. Most blog sites allow you to preview your posting before publishing for the world to see.

- ✔ **Use a blogging program.** The Windows Live package includes Windows Live Writer, which can manage blogs on most of the popular blogging services as well as on Microsoft's own `spaces.live.com`.

✔ **Mail it in.** At some blog sites in this list, you can e-mail articles to a special address. In Blogger, you click Settings and then Email to set up the address.

✔ **Text it in**. Some blog sites — notably, Twitter (see the later section "Twittering about Your Life") @md let you send them text messages that are then posted to your blog. You can either set up the blog from your phone or register your phone to post messages on a blog you already created. Go to `go.blogger.com` if you use Blogger. A number of third-party iPhone apps are available for posting to all the major blogging sites.

For more ways to blog, see *Blogging For Dummies,* by Susannah Gardner and Shane Birley.

Illustrating your blog

Text is so 20th century. (Actually, it's more 15th century, but who's counting?) If you find text constraining, just about every blog site, including the ones we describe in the preceding section, lets you include pictures as part of your blog, often uploaded directly from your mobile phone.

For example, when you're creating a new post on Blogger (also known as Blogspot), you can add a picture or video to your post. You upload it and there it is, in your blog!

Blogging in song

If you're a storyteller or musician, or you just have a lot to say, you can post your digital recording on the Web as a *podcast*, which is an audio blog. You can upload any audio file you created yourself, containing music, speech, or any sounds you like, and other people can subscribe to it, just like on a blog. Chapter 9 describes how to find and subscribe to podcasts.

Several Web sites will host your podcast for free or for a small monthly fee. Here are two:

✔ **Liberated Syndication,** at `www.libsyn.com`, offers accounts starting at $5 per month.

✔ **PodBean,** at `www.podbean.com`, is free for the first 100MB of audio files. To store more files, you need to pay a modest monthly fee.

Gack — it's a trackback

Bloggers frequently comment on each other. Sometimes the comments are nice, sometimes they're not so nice, but they're certainly, uh, involved. Most blogs let visitors leave comments, but the serious discussions are often between two or more blogs, with each one containing comments on the other blog. Anyone reading the blog with comments can see the reference to the original blog, but there's no way for someone reading the original to know where to look for comments. That's where *trackbacks* come in.

Let's say that one blogger — call him John (not his real name) — posts a provocative entry in his blog. Then a second blogger, Margy (not her real name, either) posts "For an utterly priceless example of disenchronia, check out this entry in John's blog" with a link to John's blog. If John's blog software is set up to handle trackbacks, Margy's blog system can tell John's blog about the new link so that John's blog adds a trackback note with a link to the comment, thereby making the connection two-way.

The original vision of hypertext, of which the Web is a quick-and-dirty, hacked-up version, made all links two-way. Trackbacks bring the real-life Web closer to what it was originally supposed to be.

After you have a podcast, be sure to submit it to the iTunes Store so that people who use iTunes can easily subscribe: Run the free iTunes program (which is useful even if you don't own an i-Anything), click iTunes Store, click Podcasts, and click Submit a Podcast. (See Chapter 9 to find out how to use iTunes.)

Twittering about Your Life

Blogs can let the world know the details of your life as it happens. But what about the times you're away from your computer? How can you tell your friends right away that you found an outstanding purchase at the mall or that you're stuck in traffic? And, how can you receive these vital messages from your friends when you're on the road? Twitter (at www.twitter.com) is the answer. It's a *microblogging* service that lets you send in updates as often as you want, no matter where you are. This level of detail can, of course be a mixed blessing — a friend of ours likens Twitter to a continuously updated Christmas letter.

When you create a free Twitter account, you create a blog that allows only very short entries, no more than 140 characters each, known as *tweets*. You can send as many tweets as you want, and some people send in many indeed. The simplest way is to log in to Twitter and type a line in the box at the top of the page, but you can also tweet from any of a vast number of Twitter-compatible programs, plug-ins on Web sites such as Facebook, as well as from your mobile phone. (See the nearby sidebar "Tweeting from your phone.")

Tweeting from your phone

You can post to Twitter by text-messaging from your mobile phone. First, you link your phone number to your Twitter account; click the Settings button at the top of the page, click the Devices tab, and follow the instructions, which include sending a text message to prove that the number is yours. After that, whenever you send a text to the special phone number 40404 in the United States or 21212 in Canada, Twitter posts the message on your Twitter page. If you turn on Device Updates on that page, the service also sends you a text for each direct message and each tweet in the feeds you follow.

The Twitter service is free, but you pay the usual charge for sending and receiving messages. If you receive as few as five messages a day, that's 150 messages a month, so be sure that your phone plan includes enough messages that you don't end up paying by the tweet.

iPhone users can download and install apps to display and send tweets, too. The figure here shows the free TweetDeck app displaying the results of a search. As you can see in the figure, iPhone apps can display information from Twitter, like what people are saying about "Mad Men."

Each user's tweets are visible on a Web page such as `twitter.com/barackobama`. Because it would be tedious to have to check every page of every person you're interested in, you can *follow* other Twitter users by clicking the Follow button under their names on their Twitter pages. Then on your Twitter home page, you see, in one chaotic list, all the tweets from everyone you're following, as shown in Figure 19-3. Twitter indexes all tweets, and you can search for words and phrases to find recent tweets of interest.

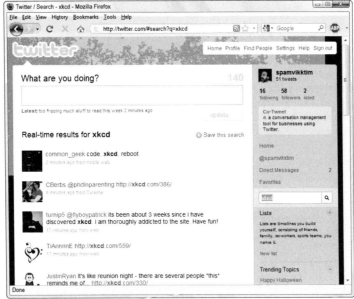

Figure 19-3:
Twitter has
extremely
short
articles —
and you can
search the
world of
tweets by
topic.

Private tweeting

Normally, your Twitter account is public, which means that anyone can follow your tweets. If you're one of the rare people who would rather not have every random person in the world watching what you say, you can go to the Settings page and select the Protect My Tweets check box to limit your tweets to people you approve.

If your organization wants to create its own private Twitter, you can use Yammer, at yammer.com

Using @replies and direct messages

Sometimes, you may want to reply to another user's message. If you start a message with an @ sign and the name of a user, that message is a reply to that user. Or, you can insert *@user* in the middle of a tweet, as a mention. In either case, the user you reply to or mention will see your message when she clicks the *@user* button on the Twitter home page. You can also send a *direct message* by typing the letter D, a space, the username, and the message. This message isn't visible to anyone else — only to the person you sent it to.

Specifying a topic by using hash marks

If you particularly like someone's tweet, on your Twitter home page you can mark it as a favorite by clicking the star that appears when you put your mouse cursor to the right of the tweet. Put #*tag* in a tweet to specify that it's related to other tweets with the same topic tag to help people find it.

Twitter has a culture all of its own, but it's easier just to watch the tweets go by and see the style rather than try to explain it.

A surprising number of people and organizations use Twitter to send out announcements and updates. They range from pop stars (with Twitter account mileycyrus) to politicians (Schwarzenegger) to fictional super-reporter Roland Hedley (Roland_Hedley). Enter a person's name or Twitter account name in the search box to see the most recent tweets.

Including a Web address in your tweet

Web addresses can be long, and tweets have to be short. What to do? A number of URL-shortening Web sites can provide a shorter Web address that redirects to the real Web address. The most popular URL-shortener is bit.ly. Here's how to use it:

1. **Go to `bit.ly` in your Web browser.**

   (It has no `.com` on the end.)

2. **In the text box on the bit.ly page, type or paste the Web address you want to include in a tweet, and then click the Shorten button.**

   Bit.ly displays a short Web address (starting with `http://bit.ly`) that redirects to the address you provided.

3. **Click the Copy button to copy the shorter address to your clipboard.**

4. **Paste (or type) the address into your tweet.**

   Or, use it anywhere else you want a shorter Web address, such as in an e-mail message.

Making Twitter lists

A recent addition to Twitter is *lists*, where you can create a list of Twitter users that have something in common. For example, you can make a list of your friends, players on your favorite team, or people who post about a topic you find interesting. Your list can be public (so anyone can see it), or private (just for you). The list appears on your Twitter page so you can click it to see tweets from all the people on that list. If you follow a lot of people, lists allow you to separate the tweets into topics, so you aren't stuck seeing them all mixed together.

If you make a list public, people can see your list at www.twitter.com/ *yourname*/*listname*, where *yourname* is your Twitter username and *listname* is the name of the list.

Even more ways to tweet

Twitter is so popular that many programs are available to make it easier to send tweets, follow people, and find tweets on specific topics. For example, TweetDeck (at www.tweetdeck.com) runs on Windows, Macs, and iPhones and displays tweets from people you follow, tweets that mention specific topics, and newsfeeds from Facebook and MySpace in one window. To find other Twitter-related programs search the Web for *Twitter applications*.

Chapter 20

Making Your Own Web Site

*I*n Chapter 18, we list a bunch of ways that you can put information on the Web, like posting pictures on a photo-sharing site, participating in a social networking site, or writing journal entries or articles on a blogging site. Those ways are terrific, just terrific — we love them all — but they may not be enough for you. What if you want more? What if you need a Web site with a bunch of pages, with titles you choose, about topics you choose, and maybe even with your own domain name? Okay, you're ready for the next step.

There are (as usual), several ways to create a site over which you have more control than the types of sites described in Chapters 18 and 19. This chapter describes how you can use a *wiki* to make a site with as many pages as you like and how to use a *page creator site,* such as Weebly or Google Sites. Finally, we tell you how to register a domain name. (However, we have to warn you that all the short and pronounceable domain names are already taken.)

Working Together on a Wiki

Wikis were designed to enable groups of people to work together to make and maintain Web sites, but wikis are helpful for setting up single-creator sites, too. A wiki (named for the interterminal bus at Honolulu International Airport, which is in turn named for the Hawaiian word *wiki-wiki,* which literally means "in a hurry" — no, really) can have an unlimited number of authors, all of whom can add and change pages within the wiki Web site.

Unlike a blog, it doesn't have to be a sequence of journal entries. Instead, you can organize your text any way you like, including making as many new, interlinked pages as you like.

If this process sounds potentially chaotic when you have more than one author, it is, but most wikis have ground rules that keep the group moving in more or less the same direction. A wiki can work well if it has a single author or if it has a group of people who trust each other to edit each other's writing. For example, a group of co-workers can make a wiki that contains information about a project they're working on. A church or club can make a wiki with committee meeting minutes, mission statements, plans, and schedules.

The biggest wiki of them all is *Wikipedia,* shown in Figure 20-1, at `www.wikipedia.org`, a collaborative encyclopedia which, with more than 3 million entries (in English, plus millions in other languages), is well on its way to including all human knowledge. Most pages have an Edit link so that you can add what you know. Some pages have a sidebar with complaints about the article from the Wikipedia editors, begging you to help improve it.

Figure 20-1:
The Wikipedia has articles on almost everything — and you can add missing articles.

Weaving your own wiki

You can create your own wiki in one of two ways:

✔ **Set up a Web site and install wiki software.** The wiki program that Wikipedia uses is MediaWiki (at `www.mediawiki.org`). This method assumes that you know how to install a program on a Web server, so it probably isn't your best option.

> ✔ Use a *wiki farm*, **which is a Web server that already runs wiki software.** Wikipedia has a list of wiki farms — look up *wiki farm*. We've had good luck with Wikispaces at `www.wikispaces.com`. Another site is Wetpaint, at `www.wetpaint.com`, which includes social networking features.

When you sign up for a wiki at a wiki farm, you may need to pay a monthly or yearly fee, or you may have the option to run the wiki for free in return for displaying ads. After you create your account and name your wiki, you can invite your collaborators to use it, usually by typing or pasting their e-mail addresses into a form so that the system can send them invitations. Every user has a username and password so that only they can make changes to the wiki content.

Wiki farms usually let you name your wiki, and the Web address of the wiki combines your name and their name. For example, Figure 20-2 shows a church that uses a wiki for its Web site. The leaders of the congregation have permission to edit the pages, and others can just look at them. The site is hosted at Wikispaces, so its Web address is `cvuus.wikispaces.com` because the initials of the congregation's name are CVUUS.

Figure 20-2:
You can use a wiki to make a Web site about anything, as long as you aren't picky about the page layout.

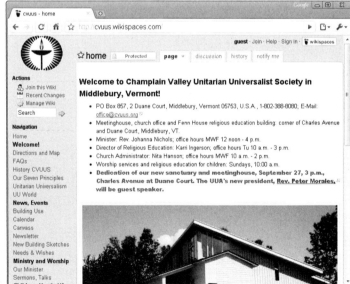

Wiki pros and cons

There's a lot to like about wikis, but they aren't perfect. Some advantages are described in this list:

- ✔ Wikis are free, if you don't mind ads. Some wiki farms give adfree accounts to schools and other nonprofits. Some allow you to pay an annual fee to eliminate the ads.

- ✔ Wikis are quick to set up — you can usually get started in minutes.

- ✔ You don't have to have special software (like a Web site editor) to edit wiki pages. Instead, you click the Edit link on a page and make changes directly in your browser. You may have to learn a simple set of punctuation *(wiki markup)* to create headings and apply bold and italics. Or, your wiki software may provide a WYSIWYG (*w*hat *y*ou *s*ee *i*s *w*hat *y*ou *g*et) visual editor.

- ✔ Wiki markup is simpler to learn than HTML, the markup language that all Web pages use, as described in the nearby sidebar "Why you don't care (much) about HTML."

- ✔ You can upload pictures and make them appear on wiki pages.

- ✔ At some wiki farms, you can register your own domain name and use it as your wiki's address. (See the section "Be the Master of Your Domain," later in this chapter.)

- ✔ A group of people can collaborate on a wiki, each person making changes to the pages and creating new ones.

So what's wrong with wikis? Here are some drawbacks:

- ✔ On most wikis, you can't control who can edit which page. Someone who has permission to edit pages can edit any page. (Better wiki software may be on its way, though.)

- ✔ You have limited control over the format of your wiki pages. Links are usually listed down the side with a title at the top and a single column of text and pictures. Making more columns is hard.

- ✔ Most wikis require that all pages in your site have the same layout — the same look. You can't control where your navigation links appear or the background color of your pages. Some wikis display Main Page as the title of your home page, which is particularly ugly.

A wiki is an excellent way to get started with a Web site. Wikis are cool, but you don't have much control of how your pages look. Wikis emphasize collaboration over graphic design. If you become frustrated by the limited formatting options, you'll know that you're ready to move to a more customizable program. In the meantime, refer to *Wikis For Dummies,* by Dan Woods and Peter Thoeny.

Why you don't care (much) about HTML

Just so you know what *HTML* is, in case someone asks, it stands for *HyperText Markup Language,* the language used for formatting Web pages. Web pages are made up of text and pictures that are stuck together and formatted with HTML codes. Fortunately, you have waited until now to start creating a Web page: Clever page-creator Web sites and programs are available that let you create your pages and then write the HTML codes for you automatically so that you don't have to write the codes yourself.

If you want to write a lot of Web pages, you should eventually master some HTML. Although complex, interactive pages require a fair amount of programming, the basics aren't all that complicated. The HTML for **complicated** is `<b>complicated</b>` (that's `<b>` for bold type). In case you decide that you want to be in the Web-page creation business, entire books have been written about how to do it. Stick to recent titles because extensions to HTML are evolving at a furious pace, and the books go out of date in less than a year. We recommend *HTML, XHTML & CSS For Dummies,* 6th Edition, written by Ed Tittel and Jeff Noble (Wiley) for the basics, and *Web Design in a Nutshell,* 3rd Edition, written by Jennifer Niederst (O'Reilly Media) for more advanced information.

Page Creator Sites to the Rescue

If you're ready to take more control over the look of your Web site, consider using one of a number of *page creator sites* that have sprung up. These sites enable you to you design what you want your site to look like, create a home page for the site, and create as many other pages as you want. Different pages can have different layouts.

Page creator sites offer a variety of features, so look carefully before choosing one:

- ✔ The site may be free or may incur a monthly charge. Free sites often display ads over which you have little control.

- ✔ Some page creator sites allow more customization of the design than others. Some let you see the HTML (Web page code) that makes up your pages and tweak it so that your pages look just right. Others don't allow this.

✔ Your site can be a subdomain of the page creator site (that is, your Web address is their address with www replaced by a name you choose).

✔ Page creator sites offer lots of standard designs. See whether any sites have a design you like.

✔ Some sites let you include message boards, guest books, blogs, calendars, photo galleries, and video on your site. Some help you sell items on your site, with connections to PayPal for checkout.

✔ The amount of information you can store on your Web site varies, along with the maximum number of pages.

Here are some page creator sites we know about:

✔ **Google Sites** (at `sites.google.com`) is a free page creator site run by (who else?) Google. The layout isn't completely customizable.

✔ **Homestead** (at `www.homestead.com`) is for small businesses and lets you start from more than 2,000 business templates.

✔ **Moogo** (at `www.moogo.com`) shows ads on your site.

✔ **Moonfruit** (at `www.moonfruit.com`) is a British page creation site that helps you connect to Facebook and Twitter.

✔ **uCoz** (at `www.ucoz.com`) hosts Web sites for free, and lets you include photos, videos, photo albums, polls, guest books, and forms that e-mail you the information that people fill in. It's one of the most popular sites in Russia.

✔ **Viviti** (at `www.viviti.com`) is free for one small, personal Web site, and a modest fee for larger or commercial sites. You can include Twitter messages, Google maps, and other fancy components on your pages.

✔ **Weebly** (at `www.weebly.com`) has a nice drag-and-drop system for setting up your site — and no ads.

✔ **Webs** (at `www.webs.com`) has lots of design templates and can host photos, videos, blogs, and message forums.

✔ **Wix** (at `www.wix.com`) hosts Flash-based sites — animated, graphics-based sites that can have fancier formatting than most of the other sites. If you're more of a word person, look elsewhere.

✔ **Yola** (at `www.yola.com`) used to be SynthaSite. It's another well-regarded page creator site.

All these sites make it incredibly easy to make your own Web site — for free. (Of course, you have to decide what to say — see the sidebar "What do you say?")

What do you say?

Creating a Web page is easy. Choosing what to put on your page, however, is harder. What is the page for? What kind of person do you want to see it? Is it for you and your family and friends and potential friends across the world, or are you advertising your business online?

Consider which information you want the entire world to know, because a Web site is potentially visible to absolutely anyone, including that guy who has hated you ever since fifth grade. If your page is a personal page, don't include your home address or phone number unless you want random people who see the page potentially calling you up. If it's a business page, include your address, phone number, and any other information that potential customers might want.

If you put your e-mail address on your Web site, you can expect lots more spam because spammers *scrape* Web sites: Their programs visit Web sites looking for text with at-signs (@) in it. You can deter these programs somewhat by inserting a space on either side of the @ (as in `internet12 @ gurus.org`) or replacing it with the word *at* (like `internet12 at gurus.org`), although these programs may get wise to this trick.

Setting up your site

To give you an idea of how easily you can use these page creator sites, try Weebly, a free site with lots of nice features. You can set up one Web page or a set of pages, including text, pictures, and links to other pages. Your Web site is then at *username*`.weebly.com`, where *username* is a name you choose. If you want to pay for a domain name (described later in this chapter), you can register a name that doesn't include `weebly.com` in it.

At any page creator site, you create an account (usually for free) with a username. Because this username becomes part of your Web address, choose it with care. In our example, we make a Web site for the Maiden Vermont Women's Barbershop Chorus of Middlebury Vermont, so the username `maidenvermont` or `maidenvt` is a good pick. Weebly lets you choose for your Web site a name that's different from your username, but not all page creator sites allow it.

In your Web browser, start at `www.weebly.com` (or the Web site of the page creation site of your choice) and sign up to create an account. Be sure to read the terms of service to ensure that you know your rights and responsibilities; for example, make sure that you (and not they) own anything you post.

After you sign in, you begin to create the site. Weebly asks for a title for the Web site and then shows you an empty home page with a basic design, as shown in Figure 20-3. Your next steps are to add text and pictures and to refine the design.

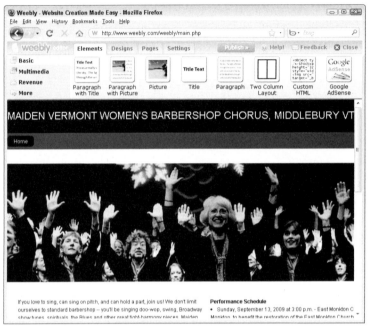

Figure 20-3:
Create a
Web site at
Weebly by
using only
your Web
browser.

Editing a page

Each page creator site has its own, nifty way of helping you make your pages. Weebly has this set of tabs along the top (as of the fall of 2009):

- ✔ **Elements:** Add pictures, text, columns, and other items to the page.

- ✔ **Designs:** Choose the overall color scheme and page layout.

- ✔ **Pages:** Add more pages or blogs.

- ✔ **Settings:** Edit the Web site's title, password, and other options that affect the entire site.

First, decide on a format for your entire site. In Weebly, you click the Designs tab and choose a likely-looking color scheme and page layout. Don't worry about the text and pictures in the samples that appear — you change those elements later. Choose an overall look that you like.

To edit the page, you use the Elements tab, which shows a series of items you can put on your page, such as paragraphs of text and pictures. If you click Multimedia at the left end of the tab, you see more options, including a photo gallery, videos, and Google Maps. Find an item you want to add to your page, drag it where you want it, and then add whatever information is missing. For text, cut and paste or type the text you want to appear. For pictures, upload photos or clip art from your computer. (See the section "Producing Pictures for Your Site," later in this chapter, for how to find or make graphics.)

Spruce up your home page in these ways:

- ✔ **Add text.** Weebly includes a few paragraph-formatting options among its elements — drag one to your page. When you click in the new text area, you see a toolbar with buttons for boldface, italics, bullets, font color, typeface, type size, and text alignment, just like in a word processor.

- ✔ **Add pictures.** For icons, clip art, or photos, drag the Picture element to the place on your page where you want a picture to appear. Then upload the file that contains your picture. If you put the image in the wrong place, you can drag it around the page with your mouse.

- ✔ **Add links to other pages.** You can convert any text or picture into a link. Select the text or image with your mouse and click the Link button on the editing toolbar. Choose whether you're linking to a page on your own site or to a Web page that's not in your site or to an e-mail address (so that when a visitor clicks the link, her e-mail program opens with a new message addressed to that address). You can also upload documents (like Word documents or PDF files) and link to them.

- ✔ **Add other cool stuff.** Most page creator sites provide a bunch of other items you can add to your pages, such as a calendar, a weather report, a Google map, a blog, an MP3 music player, and videos. For example, you can include a map to your church's or club's meeting location.

- ✔ **Edit the HTML.** As you make changes to your page, the page creator writes the HTML to display the page. If you're a glutton for punishment, or if you want to tweak the look of your page, many sites enable you to see and edit the HTML — in Weebly, click the Custom HTML link.

Publishing your first Web page!

When you like the look of your page, click the Publish button to save your changes. The system may ask you to confirm the address you're going to use for your site. Now you can look at your new site in your browser! To see your site, type *sitename*.**weebly.com** (replace *sitename* with the name you specified) into your browser's address box.

Naturally, you won't get it right the first time. (We never do.) You can go back to Weebly.com, make changes, and publish again until you like the way the site looks.

One page is not enough

One Web page is rarely enough. How about an About Us page or a Links page with the names and links to related Web sites?

To add more pages in Weebly, click the Pages tab (shown in Figure 20-4) and then click the New Page link. Give the page a name and decide whether a link to it should appear on your site's navigation bar (the main series of links, which may appear along the top of the page or down one side, depending on your page layout).

Figure 20-4:
Adding
pages in
Weebly.

Be sure to create links among your pages so that your visitors have a way to see them (without requiring them to guess the page names and type them as part of the Web address).

Producing Pictures for Your Site

Most Web pages contain graphics of some sort. Each picture that appears on a Web page is stored in a separate file. To add an image to a Web page, you add an HTML *tag* (command) — or your page creator site's equivalent — to indicate where it should appear, along with a caption for the visually impaired, and positioning information (whether you want the pictures to the left, center, or right and whether text should flow around it).

Where do pictures come from? You can draw them by using a paint program, scan in photographs, or use that fancy digital camera you got for Christmas (or your cellphone). Then use Paint or a better graphics editor to crop your pictures, fix the red-eye effect, and generally spiff up your pictures. Save your files as GIF or JPEG files, and resize them to be fewer than 500 pixels wide and smaller than 200KB in file size.

If you need graphics that you can't produce yourself, you can find lots of sources of graphical material:

✔ Plenty of freeware, shareware, and commercial clip art are available on the Net. Try the Clip Art page at our favorite Web directory, the Open Directory Project list, at www.dmoz.org/Computers/Graphics/ Clip_Art.

✔ If you see an image you want to use on a Web page, write to the page's owner and ask for permission to use it. More likely than not, the owner will let you use the image.

✔ You can subscribe to a clip art site. We use clipart.com, which has subscriptions starting at $15.

Clip art, like any art, is protected by copyright laws. Whether it has already been used on a Web page or whether a copyright notice appears on or near the image doesn't matter. It's all copyrighted. If you use someone else's copyrighted art, you must get permission to do so. Whether your use is educational, personal, or noncommercial is irrelevant. If you fail to secure permission, you run the risk of anything from receiving a crabby phone call from the owner's lawyer to winding up on the losing end of a lawsuit. Most people are quite reasonable whenever you ask for permission to use their work. If an image you want to use doesn't already come with permission to use it, check with the owner before you decide to add it to your own Web page.

Linking to Other Pages and Sites

The *hyper* in hypertext is the thing that makes the Web so cool. A *hyperlink* (or just *link*) is the thing on the page that lets you go from page to page by just clicking the link. A Web page is hardly a page if it doesn't link somewhere else.

The immense richness of the Web comes from the links that Web page authors place on their pages. Contribute to this richness by including links to places you know of that the people who visit your page may also be interested in. Try to avoid including links to places that everyone already knows about and has in their bookmarks. For example, everyone knows where to find Google and Yahoo!, so leave them off. If your home page mentions your interest in one of your hobbies, however, such as canoeing or volleyball or birding or your alma mater, include some links to related sites you know of that are interesting.

Creating a Web Site with Your Bare Hands

If you're an old-fashioned person, or just someone who likes to get your hands dirty (bits and bytes can be particularly hard to wash off), you can use the time-honored tools or our Web-site-making forebears — Web editors and file transfer programs. Making a Web site from scratch gives you full control over the layout of the site and enables you to add database-driven or other advanced features. Here's a quick overview of how the process works:

1. **Sign up for Web server space.**

   Lots of Web hosting companies are out there, ready to charge from $5 to $20 per month to store your Web pages on their *Web servers* — computers where Web pages live. We've used pair.com, dreamhost. com, ipowerweb.com, and myhosting.com but lots of other good ones are out there. Your Internet service provider (ISP) may include Web hosting in your Internet service, so you may already have Web server space. Your ISP or Web hosting company gives you a server name, username, and password so that you can upload your pages to its site.

2. **(Optional) Buy a domain name.**

   You don't have to have a domain name (that is, something-or-other. com or .net or .org or .us) to have a Web site, but it's classier. Your ISP or Web hosting company can help you find out whether the domain name you want is already taken (all the good names are long gone) and can help you buy it. Domain names cost from $7 to $20 per year, although many Web hosts will throw in a domain name if you sign up for a year or longer. See the section "Be the Master of Your Domain," later in this chapter.

3. **Write some Web pages.**

   Start with one page. You can use any text editor or word processor, but spiffy Web-page authoring programs designed for this purpose are available — and some are free — so you may as well use one. Dreamweaver is the most widely used Web editor, but it costs several hundred dollars. KompoZer (the successor to the free Nvu, which was the successor to the Web editor that was a part of the precursor to Firefox) is an open source Web editor that includes a file transfer (FTP) program; you can download it from `www.kompozer.net`.

Save the pages in files on your computer's hard drive, using the filename extension `.htm` or `.html`. You can see how the pages look by opening them in your browser and choosing the File⇨Open File command (or press Ctrl+O and browse to the file).

4. **Upload your Web pages to your Web server.**

   The rest of your world can't see Web pages that are stored on your disk. You have to copy them to your ISP's or Web hosting company's Web server. You can use an FTP program such as FileZilla (from `filezilla-project.org`). Or, your Web editor may have a built-in FTP program (KompoZer and Dreamweaver do). Or, if you're a real he-man — uh, he-person — you can use the command line FTP program included with Windows.

See *Building a Web Site For Dummies,* 3rd Edition, by David A. Crowder (Wiley) for a more detailed explanation of how to create a Web site, add pictures, make links among your pages and from your pages to other sites, and publicize your site.

Content management systems (CMSs) rule!

As Web sites grow large, they become difficult to maintain. For a Web site to look professional, or at least not actively embarrassing, all its pages should be formatted in the same way and should include a consistent set of sitewide navigation links so that visitors can find their way around. Making pages by hand becomes increasingly cumbersome as all these features are added. Naturally, some clever person realized that what we needed to help manage large Web sites is a computer program!

A *content management system* (or *CMS*) is a program that creates Web pages for you. You configure the CMS with all the formatting your pages will use, including links, menus, colors, graphics — you name it. The CMS stores this information in a database. Then you create Web pages for your site, usually by cutting and pasting text into CMS-generated Web forms — the CMS stores all content from your pages in its database, too. As you complete each page and click Publish (or an equivalent link), the CMS creates the Web page and stores it on your Web server for the public to see.

Many CMS programs are available, but you need to have your own Web server space and know how to install programs in order to use one. Search for *list of content management systems* at `www.wikipedia.com` to see a page that includes tables of CMS software with features and pricing. All CMSs have quirks and peculiarities that can take a while to figure out, so if you have a friend who's already familiar with a CMS, use the same one and share the wisdom.

Be the Master of Your Domain

A home page address like this one:

```
www.people.stratford-upon-avon-internet.com/~shakespeare/
              PrinceOfDenmark/index.html
```

just doesn't attract as many visitors as

```
www.hamlet.org
```

Getting your own domain name is a lot easier and cheaper than you might think. Follow these three steps:

1. **Choose a name.**

   Pick one that's easy to remember and to spell. Pick out a couple of alternative names in case the one you want is taken. Don't use a variation of a popular trademark like Coke or Sony (or *For Dummies*) unless you like dealing with lawyers. Also be sure that the name isn't already taken; whoever you pick to register your domain will have a lookup service to see what's available.

2. **Ask your ISP or Web hosting company to host your name.**

   Hosting your name means that your ISP or Web hosting company (wherever you store your Web pages — perhaps a wiki farm or page creator site) breathes some incantations that tell the Internet where to go when someone types your Web address. Many ISPs charge a fee for this service, but a few do it for free. Your ISP may be able to handle the next step, registration, for you too.

3. **Register your name if your ISP doesn't.**

   Hundreds of registrars compete for business in the popular .com, .net, .org, .biz, .us, and .info categories. The going rate is between $7 and $20 per year unless your Web host offers a package that includes it.

   If your ISP wants to charge you big bucks (more than $10 a month) to register your name and host your pages, consider using a Web hosting service. Pair Networks at pair.com and MyHosting at myhosting.com are both reputable, reliable, and cheap.

Shout It Out: Getting Your Web Site Found

After your pages are online, you may want to get people to come and visit. Before you create any online publicity, make sure that your pages have two types of information that search engines and Web directories look for:

- ✔ **Page description:** You can store a one-sentence description of your page in the *metatags* (hidden codes) at the beginning of each Web page. Yahoo!, Google, Bing, and other sites display this text when your page appears in their listings, and they use the text to determine how to categorize the page.

- ✔ **Keywords:** You can provide a list of key words and phrases that people might search for if they want to find your page. Display the HTML codes that make up your page, and skim down until you find `</head>`. Just above that, add a tag like this one:

```
<meta content="chickens, hens, eggs, poultry, domestic poultry"
        name="keywords">
```

Replace the list of chicken-related terms with your own. These words don't appear on the page; they are part of the *metainformation* stored about your page. Keep your list reasonably short or else search engines will ignore it.

After your page description and keywords are in place, upload your pages again.

To publicize your site, visit your favorite Web directories and search engines, such as Google (`google.com`), Yahoo! (`yahoo.com`), and Bing (`bing.com`), and submit your URL (the address of your page) to add to their databases. All these sites have on their home pages an option for adding a new page — the option is usually labeled Suggest URL or Suggest a Site or Add Your Site. (Sometimes it's a teeny link near the bottom of the page.) Automated indexes, such as Google, add pages promptly, but manually maintained directories, such as the Open Directory Project, may not accept them.

Don't pay to have your site included: Every respectable search engine and directory has an option for adding your noncommercial site for free, although it make take a while for your site to show up.

Getting lots of traffic to your site takes time. If your site offers something different that's of real interest to other folks, it can build a following of its own. Even we *For Dummies* authors have gotten into the action: A few of our homegrown sites are Margy's Great Tapes for Kids site (at `www.greattapes.com`), John's Airline Information On-Line on the Internet site (at `airinfo.travel`), and Arnold Reinhold's Math in the Movies page (at `www.mathinthemovies.com`). Just imagine what you can come up with!

Part VI
The Part of Tens

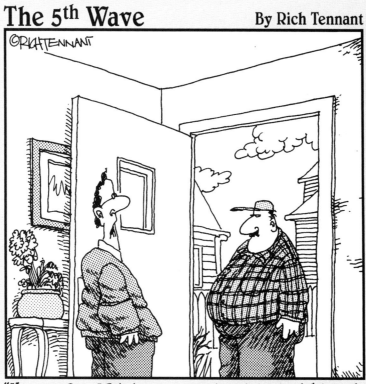

The 5th Wave   By Rich Tennant

©RICHTENNANT

"Honey! Our Web browser got out last night and dumped the trash all over Mr. Belcher's home page."

In this part . . .

We have lots of interesting odds and ends we want to tell you about, so (to provide the illusion of organization) we grouped them into lists. By the strangest coincidence, each list consists of exactly *ten* facts. (*Note to the literal-minded:* You may have to cut off or glue on some fingers to make your version of ten match up with ours. Perhaps it would be easier just to take our word for it.) Note that the glossary appears after this part of the book.

Chapter 21

Ten Problems and Ten Solutions

In This Chapter

▶ My computer is messed up with something it caught on the Internet

▶ I have a program that won't run without displaying ads

▶ I can't e-mail family pictures to my relatives

▶ I need to protect myself from ID theft

▶ I can't remember all those passwords

▶ My e-mail messages come back as undeliverable

▶ I want to keep my privacy online

▶ Other family members are hogging the computer

▶ I need to know what to do about "404 not found" messages

▶ I don't know whether to put my e-mail address on my Web site

*G*osh, using the Internet is exciting. But sometimes things get so fouled up that you want to push your computer out the window and go back to the communication methods our ancestors used, like newspapers, telephones, and smoke signals.

Don't give up just yet. This chapter offers up some common problems that many Internet users encounter, as well as some solutions to those problems.

My PC Takes Forever to Boot and Pop-Up Ads Have Taken Over the Screen

Slow start-up, sluggish operation, and annoying pop-ups all suggest that your computer is infested with *malware,* sneaky programs that do bad things to your computer, including spyware (which arrives by way of your Web browser), viruses (which arrive by e-mail) and worms (which arrive all by themselves). A full-scale war is being waged in cyberspace for control of the world's PCs, and your computer is likely a casualty. Chapter 2 describes both types of malware, Chapter 4 suggests strongly that you install virus-checker and antispyware programs, and Chapter 14 describes how to configure your virus checker. Make sure that you have downloaded the latest improvements to your Windows operating system, and ensure that your virus checker and spyware removers are up to date. And, if you still use Internet Explorer to browse the Web, consider trying a different browser, such as Firefox.

We like these antispyware programs, all three of which we use:

- ✔ Ad-aware, from Lavasoft, at www.lavasoftusa.com (shareware)
- ✔ Microsoft Windows Defender, at www.microsoft.com/athome/ security/spyware/software (free, already included in Windows 7 and Vista)
- ✔ Spybot Search & Destroy, from www.safer-networking.org (shareware)

For all three programs, download, install, and run them, and be sure to download updates regularly.

The nuclear option

If you have installed and run antivirus and antispyware programs and you still have problems, it may be too late for Band-Aid remedies. Your computer may be so thoroughly infested that you have no choice but to blow everything away and start over.

Before you reinstall Windows, you *must* get a firewall to protect your computer. Most distributed versions of Windows are so insecure that you simply cannot install the program and all its security updates before you're reinfected with viruses and worms. (Installing and updating Windows and your application programs take a couple of hours. Infection takes perhaps ten seconds.) The routers we mention in Chapter 5 that let you connect several computers to your Internet connection include adequate firewalls that are quite cheap. Even if you have only one computer, the $30 you spend for a router is well worth it.

Before you can reinstall Windows, be sure to make a copy of all your files. If you haven't been backing up regularly, make two copies, just to be safe. Back up at least one copy to more reliable CD-Rs or DVD-Rs rather than to rewritable media. Make sure that you have the installation CD or DVDs and all the registration codes, license codes, and key codes for all applications you use.

Before reinstalling Windows, you may want to get a copy of *Windows For Dummies* (written by Andy Rathbone and published by Wiley) or *Windows XP Home Edition: The Complete Reference,* or *Windows Vista: The Complete Reference.* (The latter two books were written by John and Margy and — published by Osborne/McGraw-Hill.) These books contain more details about how to reinstall Windows than we have room for here. You need the original CDs that came with your computer or a new copy of Windows XP or later. Put the Windows CD or DVD in your CD or DVD drive and reboot. Follow the instructions to where it asks whether you want to rewrite or destroy all information on your hard drive. To find it, you may need to select advanced options. Take a deep breath and answer Yes and then Yes again to all warnings indicating that all your files will be erased. They will — that's why we have you back them up — but they'll erase the worms, too.

When the reinstallation of Windows is complete, follow the onscreen instruction to reenter your Internet settings. Then go immediately to `windowsup date.microsoft.com` (which works only with Internet Explorer — sigh) and download all suggested updates to Windows, which takes quite a while. Load your antivirus and antispyware software and get their latest updates. Then reinstall all your applications. Yes, this process is a real pain.

Next, place your data backup CD in the CD drive and have your antivirus program scan it. We recommend that you do not reinstall all your data files at first; just the ones you need to use. If you made two copies as we told you to, keep them in two different places — preferably, in two different buildings.

Finally, create separate, password-protected accounts for everyone who will use the computer, and make them all Limited rather than Administrator accounts unless they have a good reason to be installing their own programs. Have a talk with everyone about the risks of free downloads and online game sites. Suggest that, in case you have to repeat this process, their use of your computer will be terminated. This isn't the kind of problem you want to keep dealing with, as you have no doubt concluded if you just had to rebuild your system.

The thermonuclear option

Because you can buy a reasonable computer for less than $400 these days and you can use the same printer and screen (if your computer isn't a laptop) you have now, sometimes if you've had your old computer for a while, it's easier to buy a new computer and start over. The nice people at the computer store should be able to help you extract your files from your old, messed-up computer, perhaps for a modest extra charge, and install them on a new one. Even if the new computer is all configured and updated at the store, which it should be, you still should get a router to deter future hostile invasions.

The switcheroo

Plan B is to consider getting an Apple Macintosh computer, even if only for your e-mail and Web surfing. As of this writing, no serious online threats exist for Apple's Mac OS X. This situation could change, but at least Apple has a head start over the hackers, rather than the other way around for Microsoft. You should still keep your Mac's operating system up to date and rebuild your PC if you still plan to use it. If you need certain programs for work, look for Mac equivalents or check out Boot Camp (`www.apple.com/macosx/compatibility`), which lets you run your Windows system and programs on your Mac.

This Nice, Free Program Doesn't Run If I Turn Off the Ads

Lots of free programs are supported by advertising. That's the deal. You may be able to find equivalent programs that don't show ads, or you can pay to register the program and make the ads go away. Even if you're willing to trade ad-watching for free software, we do *not* recommend that you use any program that shows Web-based ads — *adware* — while other programs are running. (Ads displayed in the program itself rather than in your browser, such as the Eudora mail program and Opera Web browser, are fine.) Adware companies swear up and down that it's not spyware and that they don't compile personal dossiers of all the Web sites you visit to decide which ads to send to your computer, but we don't trust them.

I Can't Send Large E-Mail Attachments

Some Internet service providers and some system administrators limit the size of files you can send or receive by using their mail servers. In the case of problems at work, the solution may be as simple as talking to the person in charge of your Internet access and asking for the limit to be changed. Your ISP might not be so accommodating.

We have other ways to move giant files from point A to point B.

One is to open an account on a webmail provider that handles large attachments. Google Gmail allows attachments of as much as 25MB, Yahoo Mail allows 10MB for the free version and 20MB for the paid Plus version, and Windows Live Hotmail allows 10MB. The process of attaching a file to a message increases its size by about 20 percent, so the maximum file size is smaller than the maximum attachment size.

For local file transfers, *sneakernet* (transferring files by walking them from one computer to another) has made a comeback in the form of USB flash drives. Flash drives work with recent versions of all major operating systems. They operate like removable disk drives but are about the size of your thumb (or smaller, especially if you have big thumbs) and have a shiny, rectangular plug at one end. Some geeks carry one on a lanyard around their necks or on their keychains. To use one, just plug it into a USB port on your computer. For very large files (many gigabytes), you can use an iPod as a portable USB hard drive. After you copy whatever files you want, you need to tell your operating system that you're done with the drive before you unplug it. Windows uses a tiny icon in the system tray that does this. On Macs, drag the disk's icon to the trash.

If your computer has a CD or DVD writer, you can also burn your files on a CD or DVD to give to your friend. It's not as cute and compact as a USB drive, but it's more durable. Your camera's memory card can also hold files.

I'm Worried about ID Theft

The U.S. Federal Trade Commission (www.ftc.gov/idtheft) offers this advice to prevent identity theft: First, look out for *phishing,* e-mail that claims to come from a bank or another online account, such as eBay, and claims that your account has a problem that you can clean up by clicking a link in the message. These messages are never real, but they're very dangerous. If your bank thinks that a security problem exists, it doesn't tell you by e-mail. If you're not sure, contact the company by phone or type its Web address (for example, www.yourbank.com) into your browser by hand and look for the customer service section. See Chapter 2 for more about phishing.

The Internet isn't the only source of information about you. Keep bills and other documents that bear your account and Social Security numbers in a safe place, and tear up or shred old bank statements and credit card bills. Get a shredder that cross-cuts the paper into short strips rather than the cheaper shredders that make strips the length of the page; patient thieves can paste those together. Those offers for preapproved credit cards are also dangerous if they fall into the wrong hands. Shred them or stop them altogether by calling 1-888-5OPTOUT or visiting www.optoutprescreen.com. If your driver's license still has your Social Security number on it, get a new license issued.

Get in the habit of looking over your bank and credit card statements when they arrive (or even earlier, online). Don't worry about the bank's arithmetic, but look for charges that you don't remember incurring. If you find any, contact your bank or credit card company immediately. After you verify any fraudulent charges, tell the bank that you want new accounts with new credit card numbers. You may need to file a police report, although in our experience, if you have fraudulent charges, the bank will issue new cards without hassle.

I Can't Remember All My Web Site Passwords

The standard advice is to construct passwords from a mixture of letters, numbers, and special symbols; to have a different password for each account; to never write down passwords; and to change them every few months. Most Internet users who have dozens of accounts ignore this advice because only a truly unusual person can remember dozens of different random passwords and which account goes with each on.

We suggest a compromise. Make up one good password to use on all your low-risk accounts — accounts in which letting someone else gain access has little consequence, such as online newspaper subscriptions. Use different passwords for the accounts that really matter, such as online banking. If you feel that it's necessary, writing down those passwords and keeping them in a safe place is better than picking a password that's easy for someone to guess. Don't list your passwords in your desktop Rolodex or on a sticky note stuck to your computer's monitor. *Never, ever* choose a password that is a regular English word (a word that appears in a dictionary) or a common name.

Another option is to store your passwords in a password-protected file. The free, open source KeePass program (available for download from `www.keepass.info`) enables you to create an entry for each Web site or other password you need to remember. You can enter a username, a password, a Web address (URL), and notes about the account, and you can organize accounts into categories (for example, Home Banking, Email and Chat, and Shopping). KeePass can also suggest very strong passwords for you (made of random strings of characters) and can copy a username and password into your computer's Clipboard for pasting into your browser. Of course, you need to remember the password to your KeePass file — don't write it anywhere!

Some decent programs are available for safely storing passwords on smartphones and the iPod touch, too. We like the free, open-source *Keyring* for Palm smartphones, available at `gnukeyring.sourceforge.net`. Be sure to pick an extremely strong master password and have a backup plan for when your phone falls into the bathtub and dies. (Ink on paper has stood the test of time.)

I Get Messages Telling Me That E-Mail I Never Sent Is Undeliverable

You can't do much about this problem after it has happened. Most spammers use computers that have been taken over by worms or viruses to send spam, using faked return addresses taken from the list of spam addresses. Make sure that your computer isn't the source of this type of unwanted message by keeping its operating system and antivirus software up to date, using a router as your firewall (see Chapter 5), and turning off the computer (or at least its connection to the Internet) when it's not in use.

People Seem to Know a Lot about Me

The rate at which we're all losing our privacy scares us, too. Here are a few tips.

Get rid of spyware that may be lurking on your machine

Spyware does just what it sounds like — it spies on you and your activities. You think your Internet activities are private, but unless you keep your PC spyware free, they're not. Browse one mortgage lender site and you'll hear from the universe of mortgage lenders. Buy from one pharmacy and you'll receive solicitations from other companies for drugs you didn't even know existed. Your inbox is full of names that closely resemble — but aren't quite — people you actually know. If all this sounds familiar, chances are good that software is recording your every keystroke. Get rid of it! (The software, not the keyboard.) When we use Internet Explorer (some folks still have Web sites that work only with Internet Explorer), we often have to clean our machines because worms and viruses often sneak through security holes in it. Because it's so widely used, it's targeted by hackers all over the world, which is why we use Firefox or Google Chrome instead (see Chapter 6).

Don't be dumb

Don't put information on your Web page that you don't want everyone in the world to know. In particular, don't include your home address and phone number unless you want calls and visits. We know at least one person who received an unexpected phone call from someone she met on the Net and wasn't too pleased about it. Why would Net users need this information, anyway? They can send you e-mail!

Don't order stuff while using a public PC

Normally, ordering stuff over the Web or by e-mail is safe — at least as safe as handing your credit card to a waiter! However, some shopping sites store information about you (including a link to your mailing address and payment info) on your computer in a file known as a *cookie.* This system works perfectly when you're ordering from your own computer — you don't have to retype all that info when you visit the site the next time you order. But when you order stuff at the library or at a cybercafé, this personal information may be stored on that computer. The next person who uses that computer and goes to that site then has all your personal data available and may be able to use it to place an order. Better not chance it.

I Can't Get My Kids, Spouse, or Significant Other Off the Computer

Games and instant messaging are highly addictive and seem to be becoming more so. Microsoft's Steve Ballmer brags about the addictive nature of the games his company sells and smiles as he says he wouldn't let *his* kid play them. That ought to give you a hint.

Set clear limits on computer usage and stick to them. Have a talk with your spouse or significant other about which kinds of online chatting are okay and which aren't. Also think about how much time *you* spend in front of a computer screen. Use some of your Internet time to make a list of outside activities you enjoy and stick it next to your computer screen. Promise yourself you'll do at least one fun off-computer activity every day. Internet addiction is serious — you may need professional help to quit the habit.

On the other hand, if it's your spouse, sometimes it makes more sense to squander $400 on a second computer (see Chapter 5 for hints on connecting them both to the Net using a single account) than to squander your marriage.

When I Click a Link, My Browser Says "404 Page Not Found"

Web pages move about or disappear on the Internet. If you type a URL from a printed source, make sure that you type it exactly as it was printed, including capitalization. If you read a URL that's part of a sentence, watch out for the comma, period, or hyphen at the end. That comma, period, or hyphen may or may not be part of the URL — or it may be punctuation for the sentence.

If you clicked a hypertext link or you're sure that you typed the URL correctly and you still see this error message, the data on the site may have been reorganized. Try "walking up" the URL by deleting the portion back to the last slash character and trying again; then delete the portion back to the next-to-last slash character; and so on.

If you see a File Not Found message when you try entering this line, for example:

```
epicurious.com/cooking/menus/cooknow/omelettes.html
```

try entering these lines, in order:

```
epicurious.com/cooking/menus/cooknow
epicurious.com/cooking/menus
epicurious.com/cooking
```

At one of these levels, you may find a hint about where the file you seek can be found. Alternatively, go to your favorite search engine and search for it.

A page long gone may still be found on the Wayback Machine at `www.archive.org`, a free site that has attempted the daunting task of periodically saving snapshots of the whole World Wide Web.

I Want to Include My E-Mail Address on My Web Page

Including your e-mail address in a Web page is a sure way to attract spam. Spammers have programs that crawl the Web looking for e-mail addresses to spam. You can thwart them by *describing* your e-mail address rather than just typing it out — "It's `al` at `blahblah.com`" — or use obscure HTML coding on the Web page. At the least, we suggest that you set up a separate e-mail address for your Web site at a free webmail site, such as `www.gmail.com`, `www.hotmail.com`, or `mail.yahoo.com`. If the flood of unwanted mail becomes too great, you can abandon that account and set up a new one.

One useful trick is to ask Web site visitors to include a special word in the subject line of their messages. For example, if your Web page is about belt buckle collecting, you can ask correspondents to include *buckles* in the subject line. You can send the rest of the messages to the trash.

Chapter 22

Ten Fun or Worthwhile Things You Can Do Online

*Y*ou can use the Internet in hundreds of ways for work and profit. In this chapter, we focus on some of the fun you can have out there. If you'd like to spend your time online doing something more worthwhile — we're sure you do! — the Internet also offers ways to make the world a better place, by working directly on projects or making it possible for other people to do so. When you find other ways to improve the world or other new and fun things to do on the Net, let us know by sending us an e-mail at internet12@ gurus.org.

Share Pictures and Videos with Your Friends and Family

E-mail attachments (see Chapter 15) are an excellent way to ship snapshots anywhere in the world for free. You don't even need a digital camera; your phone can probably take sttgills and maybe even video.

If you have more than one or two pictures or videos and you want to share them with more than one or two people, making an online photo album is a more convenient way to go. Make an account at Flickr (at www.flickr.com) or Photobucket (at www.photobucket.com), upload your photo and video files, and tell the site who else can see it. You can point your friends to your album by giving them the URL, and they can view the pictures online. Some of the sites listed in the section "Say Cheese!" in Chapter 18 can also sell your friends prints of the ones they especially like.

Entertain Yourself with TV and Radio

There are more and more ways to entertain yourself online than these days than ever before, and the day when you don't need a TV or a stereo is at hand. Here are just a few of the things you can find to kill some time.

Watch movies, TV, and ads

The Internet has created a new way for makers of short and experimental movies to find an audience. Many sites feature miniflicks that you can watch for free. The most popular is Google's YouTube at youtube.com, whose users upload vast amounts of video, from the profound to the inane. Try looking for *airplane landings*. You can upload your own videos, too, as long as you made them yourself, they're no more than ten minutes long, and they follow other YouTube guidelines.

Hulu, at www.hulu.com, puts television on the Web, so you can watch early episodes of shows that you tuned in partway through. It's supported by ABC, Fox, NBC, and others, so you get the real shows, not chopped-up captures of shows, although shows are prefaced with advertisements because something or someone has to pay the bills. Blip.tv (at blip.tv — no *.com* at the end) hosts shows you may never have heard of because they're made by independent creators.

The entire original 1960s *Star Trek* series is available on YouTube, complete and without ads. Visit www.youtube.com and search for *Star Trek*.

If for some reason you don't see as many ads on TV as you want, visit www.advertisementave.com, where you can catch up on all the ads you've missed. The excellent AdCritic (creativity-online.com/adcritic) also features the best current ads and classics. Either way, now you can catch those great Super Bowl ads without having to watch the tedious football.

These film sites mainly use Flash, which plays videos directly in your Web browser. See Chapter 9 to find out how to watch videos on the Web.

Listen to current and classic radio programs

Have you ever turned on your radio, found yourself in the middle of a fascinating story, and wished you could have heard the beginning? National Public Radio in the United States keeps many of its past programs available online. If you want to hear the whole program, visit `www.npr.org`. You can also use the site's search feature to browse for stories you missed completely. Some radio shows also have their own Web sites, like Car Talk (shown in Figure 22-1).

Figure 22-1: The Car Talk podcast offers advice about cars any time you need it.

Many NPR affiliates and other radio stations have live streaming audio of their programs, so you can listen live to stations all over the country — go to Google and search for the station call letters or the program name. (John recommends his local station at `wrvo.fm`, especially the old shows from the 1930s through 1950s, which they play in the evening.) Many other radio stations now let you listen to their live programs over the Internet, which is particularly handy in large office buildings with poor radio reception. You can listen to stations from around the world and get a taste of world music firsthand or hear the news from different perspectives.

If you have an iPod or another MP3 player, you can download audio files and listen to many radio shows at any time. See Chapter 9 to find out how to subscribe to podcasts.

Find Out What Your Stuff Is Worth

You already know about eBay, the online auction site where you can buy and sell almost anything. (If not, flip back to Chapter 10 to read about it.) But you may not know that you can use it to find out the value of almost anything — at least, anything that has sold on eBay in the last 90 days — by searching completed eBay auctions.

You need an eBay account to search completed auctions, so start at www. ebay.com and register for a free account if you don't already have one. Then click the Advanced Search link (we can't tell you exactly where it is, since Web site designs change so often, but it's probably next to the search box or the Search button). Type key words about your priceless treasure into the search box and select the Completed Listings check box. When you click the Search button, you see all the auctions with those keywords, and what the final selling price was. If any of the merchandise is similar to your fabulous object, you can see what people are actually paying for it.

(Warning to all you Beanie baby speculators: You may be depressed to find out what vintage, rare, one-of-a-kind, limited-edition, collectible Beanie Babies are selling for.)

Have Some Fun and Play Games

There are too many sites with games and puzzles to list here, so we had to go with a select number of the fun places to visit online.

Play checkers or bridge

. . . Or chess, poker, hearts, backgammon, cribbage, go, or any other board game or card game. The classic games hold up well against the ever-more-bloody electronic games. Now you don't need to round up live friends to play with — you can find willing partners at any time, day or night, at sites such as games.yahoo.com or games.aol.com. If you used to play Diplomacy, our favorite board game, back in the 1970s, try www.playdiplomacy.com.

True bridge aficionados like to think of bridge not as a card game but, rather, as a way of life. You can round up a bridge foursome at www.bridgebase.com (for free) and www.okbridge.com ($99 per year after a free trial period). Many free and fee sites are listed at www.greatbridgelinks.com.

See Chapter 17 for more elaborate games for one, two, four, or thousands.

Build your own world

Virtual worlds are electronic places you can visit on the Web — kind of like 3D chat rooms. Rather than create a screen name, you create a personal action figure, or *avatar,* that walks, talks, and emotes (but doesn't make a mess on your floor). When you're in one of these worlds, your avatar interacts with the avatars of other people who are logged on in surroundings that range from quite realistic to truly fantastic. In some virtual worlds, you can even build your own places: a room, a house, a park, a city — whatever you can imagine. Other worlds let you make money, gain status, and battle complete strangers. People who enjoy role-playing games can disappear into online games for hours, days, or months at a time.

Most virtual worlds require you to download a plug-in or special software. Some are free, whereas others require a monthly or an annual subscription. See Chapter 17 for some virtual worlds to consider. For example, *Second Life,* at secondlife.com, lets you create your own part of a shared online world, including spending real-world money.

Web-based online worlds are an outgrowth of MUDs (which stands for Multi-User Dimensions or Multi-User Dungeons or various other names, depending on whom you ask), which were text-based virtual online worlds long before there was a Web.

Build Your Own Jumbo Jet

Even staid corporate sites have the occasional goodies tucked away. Airbus builds airplanes, including the very, very, very large A380 superjumbo. Normally, an A380 lists for $300 million, but if that's a little out of your price range, Airbus Goodies has some paper versions you can print, cut out, fold, and fly, at www.airbus.com/en/myairbus/goodies.

Visit Art Museums around the World

Art museums are great places to spend a rainy afternoon. Now you can visit museums and galleries all over the world by using your browser. Not all museum Web sites have online artwork, but many do. Our favorites include the Louvre in Paris (www.louvre.fr, click English in the upper right corner if you don't read French), Boston's Museum of Fine Arts (www.mfa.org), the Metropolitan Museum of Art in New York (www.metmuseum.org), the Rijksmuseum in Amsterdam (www.rijksmuseum.nl), and the State Hermitage Museum in Russia (www.hermitagemuseum.org). Check out the spectacular color photographs from Tsarist Russia by Sergei Prokudin-Gorskii, digitally reconstructed by the Library of Congress, at www.loc.gov/exhibits/empire, and the amazing American Memory collection of historical photos at memory.loc.gov (shown in Figure 22-2).

Figure 22-2: The American Memory collection at the Library of Congress.

Take a Trip around the Planet and the Stars

The Internet offers many wonderful simulations of activities such as flight and space travel. So if you've ever wanted to be a pilot or an astronaut but lacked the time or the money to commit, here's a few places to take a look at.

Tour the earth

The modestly named Google Earth at `earth.google.com` is a download-able program that lets you fly around the earth and zoom in and out. After you get fairly close to the ground, you find links to pictures contributed by users (including some impressively remote places — try looking for South Georgia), Wikipedia links, and enough to keep you busy for hours, days, or even months, if you're not careful.

Or, check out Google Maps Street View: Start at `maps.google.com`, go to an urban area (try **1 5th Ave, NY NY 10011**), and click Street View. You can make a 360-degree pan of that spot to see what it looked like the last time a Google employee was there with a camera.

Lots of other interesting maps are on the Web. Watch the "walmartization" of the United States at `projects.flowingdata.com/walmart`. A wonderful analysis of the red-state-versus-blue-state political landscape is at `www.personal.umich.edu/~mejn/election/2008`.

Tour the solar system

The last half of the 20th century will go down in history as the time when humans began to explore outer space. Probes visited several comets and asteroids and every planet except Pluto. The probes sent back amazing pictures: storms on Jupiter, oceans on Europa, mudslides on Mars, and the Earth at night.

Which generation will get to play tourist in the solar system remains to be seen; here are some great space sites:

✔ You can follow the adventures of the Mars rovers at `marsrovers.jpl.nasa.gov`, and virtual tours are available now at sites such as `sse.jpl.nasa.gov`.

✔ Be sure to bookmark the astronomy picture of the day at `apod.nasa.gov/apod`.

✔ Above all, don't miss the incredible NASA montage of human civilization at `antwrp.gsfc.nasa.gov/apod/image/0011/earthlights_dmsp_big.jpg`.

Do Some Cool Things with Books Online

No longer must you carry around that hardback bunch of paper with words printed in ink. No. Today you can find references online, help turn print books into digital ones, and even go check out some comics.

Edit an encyclopedia

Wikipedia (en.wikipedia.org) is not only a free encyclopedia, it also lets you edit its articles. If you feel knowledgeable about a topic, look it up in Wikipedia. If you find mistakes or have more to say, just set up a free account, then click the Edit tab. If no article exists, Wikipedia offers to let you create one. Read en.wikipedia.org/wiki/Help:Contents/Editing_Wikipedia for more information on how to edit existing articles and write new ones, following the rules of Neutral Point of View. See the section "Working Together on a Wiki" in Chapter 20 for more about how groups can edit a Web site communally using a wiki.

Digitize old books

Many Web sites require that you decode some blurry text known as a CAPTCHA (which allegedly stands for **C**ompletely **A**utomated **P**ublic **T**uring test to tell **C**omputers and **H**umans **A**part) before it will let you set up an account or post a message. The reCAPTCHA project at Carnegie-Mellon University uses CAPTCHAs to help digitize old books and newspapers. The scanning process first makes a photographic image of each page, then tries to identify the words in the text. It can recognize most of the words but some are just too blurry or obscure for automatic identification. That's where you come in. Each reCAPTCHA challenge shows you two words (see Figure 22-3); one that's already been decoded and one that hasn't. When you type in the two words, it checks the one it knows, and if you get that one right, it assumes you probably got the other one right, too. Just to make sure, it'll show each unknown word to several different people, and if they all agree, it's been decoded. ReCAPTCHA is used by thousands of Web sites all over the world, showing about 30 million CAPTCHAs a day. Not all of them are solved, of course, but that's still a lot of words decoded.

You're helping the reCAPTCHA project every time you solve a two-word reCAPTCHA challenge. For more information, see their Web site at www.recaptcha.net.

Figure 22-3:
Convert those print books into digital books with CAPTCHA.

Read the comics

Why get newsprint ink on your hands just to read your favorite comic strip? Ours are

- ✔ *Dilbert,* at `dilbert.com` (okay, you knew we were geeks!)
- ✔ *Doonesbury,* at `doonesbury.com`
- ✔ *Foxtrot,* at `foxtrot.com`

Comics.com has lots of other comic strips, including vintage *Peanuts* strips.

Search for Extraterrestrial Life or Cure Cancer

SETI@home (`setiweb.ssl.berkeley.edu`) is a scientific experiment that uses Internet-connected home and office computers to search for extraterrestrial *i*ntelligence (SETI). The idea is to have thousands of otherwise idle PCs and Macs perform the massive calculations needed to extract the radio signals of other civilizations from intergalactic noise. You can participate by running a free program that downloads and analyzes data collected at the Arecibo radio telescope in Puerto Rico.

If eavesdropping on space aliens seems a bit far out, you may enjoy lending your computer's idle time to solving problems in cryptography and mathematics. Distributed.net (`www.distributed.net`) manages several projects. (Feel free to join the Internet Gurus team there.) When you sign up to help a project at Distributed.net, you agree to run its program on your computer when the computer isn't otherwise occupied, and your donation of computer time helps achieve the goal of the project.

If math and cryptography don't ring your chimes, consider joining the Folding at Home project at `folding.stanford.edu`. This project studies how proteins get their three-dimensional shapes, an important question in medical research. By signing up to run its program, you're helping with basic research that may help find a cure for "Alzheimer's, Mad Cow (BSE), CJD, ALS, Huntington's, Parkinson's disease, and many cancers and cancer-related syndromes."

Do Something Nice and Help Save the World

Microfinance pioneer Muhammad Yunus won a Nobel Peace Prize for starting the Grameen Bank, which makes tiny loans to people in Bangladesh and other developing countries to start small rural businesses. Kiva (`www.kiva.org`) lets you become your own microfinance lender to groups of people in Latin America, Africa, and Asia for projects like starting a sewing business, delivery service, or fish market. Loans start at $25.

Heifer International (`www.heifer.org`) provides livestock and other resources to poor farmers for both food security and income. A heifer (that's a young cow for you city folk) costs $500, a share of a goat or pig starts at $10.

Do you surf the Web for hours each day? Maybe your life needs more meaning. Adopting a child is more of a commitment than upgrading to the latest Microsoft operating system, but at least kids grow up eventually and you don't have to reinstall them to get rid of viruses. Here are two excellent Web sites that list special children in need of homes: `www.rainbowkids.com` and `www.capbook.org`. It can't hurt to look.

Glossary

404 Not Found: An error message that your Web browser frequently displays when it can't find the page you requested; caused by mistyping a URL (your fault) or clicking a broken link (not your fault).

ActiveX: A Microsoft scheme for downloading little programs, sometimes known as objects. Internet Explorer supports ActiveX. Unfortunately, these little programs may contain spyware.

address: A destination for either an e-mail message or a Web page. An e-mail address almost always contains an @ symbol, and a Web page address is more properly termed *URL*.

AIM (AOL Instant Messenger): A free instant messaging program that you can use whether or not you have an AOL account.

AOL (America Online): A value-added, online service that provides many services in addition to Internet access, including access to popular chat groups. Go to `www.aol.com` for more information. AOL also offers free webmail at `mail.aim.com`.

app: A small application, such as a program for an iPhone.

applet: A small computer program written in the Java programming language, often downloaded and run using a Web browser. An applet runs in a special "sandbox" that makes it difficult for it to do damage to your computer.

archive: A single file containing a group of files that have been compressed and glommed together for efficient storage. You have to use a program such as Windows Compressed Folders, WinZip, tar, or StuffIt to pull out the original files.

attachment: A computer file electronically stapled to an e-mail message and sent along with it.

BCC (blind carbon copy): A way to send a copy of your e-mail to someone without other recipients knowing about it. *See also* CC.

binary file: A type of file that contains information other than text. A binary file might contain an archive, a picture, sounds, a spreadsheet, or a word processing document that includes formatting codes in addition to text characters.

Bing: The latest Microsoft Web search site, at `www.bing.com`.

bit: The smallest unit of measurement for computer data. Bits can be *on* or *off* (symbolized by 1 or 0, respectively) and are used in various combinations to represent different types of information.

bitmap: Little dots put together in a grid to make a picture.

BitTorrent: A method for transmitting large files over the Internet that spreads the load among many cooperating computers.

biz: The last part of an Internet domain name (such as `example.biz`) to indicate that the host computer is run by a commercial organization that couldn't get the `.com` address it really wanted.

blog: Short for W*eb log,* which is a personal diary on the Internet. Any fool can publish a blog, and many fools do.

bookmark: The address of a Web page to which you may want to return, stored in your browser. Firefox and Google Chrome let you maintain a list of bookmarks to make it easy to return to your favorite Web pages. Also known as a *favorite.*

bounce: To return e-mail as undeliverable. If you e-mail a message to a bad address, it sometimes bounces back to your mailbox.

broadband: A fast, permanent connection to the Internet, such as one provided by DSL, cable modem, or satellite. *See also* DSL.

browser: A program that lets you read information on the Web. Some all-singing, all-dancing browsers can send and receive e-mail and do other things, too.

byte: A group of eight bits, enough to represent a character. Computer memory and disk space are usually measured in bytes.

cable modem: A box that connects your computer to your cable TV company's wiring; needed for a cable Internet account.

CC (carbon copy): A type of address in which addressees receive a copy of your e-mail and other recipients are informed of it if they bother to read the message header. *See also* BCC.

certificate: Cryptographic data that identifies one computer or person to another.

chat: To talk (or type) live to other network users from any part, or all parts, of the world. To chat on the Internet, you use an instant message program (such as AIM, Yahoo! Messenger, or Windows Live Messenger) or an Internet Relay Chat (IRC) program such as mIRC, or you chat by way of a Web site like Facebook.

Chrome: The Google Web browser, available for free at `chrome.google.com`.

client: A computer that uses the services of another computer or a server (such as e-mail, FTP, or the Web). If you dial in to another system, your computer becomes a client of the system you dial in to (unless you're using X Windows — don't ask). *See also* server.

com: The last part of an Internet domain name (in `www.google.com`, for example), originally intended to indicate that the host computer is run by a commercial organization.

cookie: A small text file stored on your computer by a Web site you have visited; used to remind that site about you the next time you visit it.

cyber-: A prefix meaning the use of the computers and networks that comprise the Internet, as in *cyberspace, cybersex,* or *cybercop.* Used by itself, it's short for *cybersex,* referring to licentious online conversations.

default: Information that a program uses unless you specify otherwise.

DHCP (Dynamic Host Configuration Protocol): A system that assigns IP addresses for a local-area network (LAN) or a broadband system that doesn't require individual logins. *See also* PPPoE.

dialup connection, dialup networking: The built-in Internet communication program in Windows that connects over ordinary telephone lines.

digest: A compilation of the messages that have been posted to a mailing list recently.

domain: Part of the official name of a computer on the Internet — for example, `gurus.org`. Also the Microsoft name for groups of computers on a LAN controlled by a Windows server.

domain name server (DNS): A computer on the Internet that translates between Internet domain names, such as `xuxa.iecc.com`, and numeric IP addresses, such as `208.31.42.42`. Sometimes just *name server.*

download: To copy a file from a remote computer "down" to your computer.

DRM (Digital Rights Management): A type of technology that attempts to restrict what you can do with material you find on the Internet.

DSL (Digital Subscriber Line): A type of technology that lets you transmit data over phone lines at high speed, as much as 7 million bps. It's a nice feature if you can get it — ask your phone company.

DSL modem: A box that connects your computer to a DSL line.

dummies: People who don't know everything but are smart enough to seek help. Used ironically.

eBay: The original and most successful Web-based auction site, at `www.ebay.com`.

edu: The last part of an Internet domain name (`middlebury.edu`, for example) for an educational institution, usually a college or university.

e-commerce: Electronic commerce; mainly buying and selling goods and services over the Internet.

e-mail, email: Electronic messages sent over the Internet.

emoticon: A combination of punctuation or punctuation and letters intended to communicate emotion on the part of the writer, especially in e-mail, chat, or instant messages. Emoticons include smileys (see later in this glossary) and combinations like <g> for "grin." Don't overdo it.

Facebook: A social networking Web site, at `www.facebook.com`.

FAQ (Frequently Asked Questions): An article that answers questions that come up often. Many mailing lists and Usenet newsgroups have FAQs that are posted regularly. FAQs are frequently found at `www.faqs.org`.

favorites: A list of files or Web pages you plan to use frequently. Internet Explorer lets you maintain a list of your favorite items to make it easy to see them again. Same idea as *bookmarks.*

Firefox: A popular, free browser from the Mozilla Foundation that competes with Internet Explorer and has fewer safety issues.

firewall: A type of security software, often running in a router or a user's computer, that connects a local network to the Internet and, for security reasons, lets only certain kinds of messages in and out.

flame: To post angry, inflammatory, or insulting messages. Don't do it! Too much flaming between two or more individuals is a *flame war.*

Flash: A free program for viewing interactive multimedia on the Web. For more information about Flash and for a copy of the program's plug-in for your browser, go to `get.adobe.com/flashplayer`.

FTP (File Transfer Protocol): A method of transferring files from one computer to the other over the Net.

GIF (Graphics Interchange Format): A patented type of graphics file originally defined by CompuServe and now found all over the Net. Files in this format end in `.gif` and are *GIF files,* or just *GIFs.* Pronounced "jif" unless you prefer to say "gif."

giga-: A prefix meaning 1 billion (1,000,000,000).

Gmail: The free Google webmail service, at `gmail.com`.

Google: A search engine used for finding things on the Web, with extra smarts to look for the most useful pages. It's on the Web at `www.google.com`. Also, a megacorporation that offers a wide variety of free Web-based products and services.

gov: The last part of an Internet domain name (in `cu.nih.gov`, for example) run by a government body in the United States. Originally just the federal government, but now also open to state and local governments.

header: The beginning of an e-mail message, containing To and From addresses, subject, date, and other gobbledygook important to the programs that handle your mail.

home page: The entry page, or main page, of a Web site. If you have a home page, it's the main page about you. A home page usually contains links to other Web pages.

hostname: The name of a computer (or *host*) on the Internet (`net.gurus.org`, for example).

hotspot: A public area with Wi-Fi Internet access.

HTML (HyperText Markup Language): The language used to write pages for the Web. This language lets the text include codes that define fonts, layout, embedded graphics, and hypertext links. Web pages are stored in files that usually have the extension `.htm` or `.html`. Don't worry: You don't have to know anything about HTML to use the Web.

HTML mail: E-mail messages formatted with HTML codes. Most e-mail programs can display them.

HTTP (HyperText Transfer Protocol): The way in which Web pages are transferred over the Net. URLs for Web pages start with `http://`, although you almost never have to type it.

HTTPS: A variant of HTTP that encrypts data for security.

hypertext: A system of writing and displaying text that enables the text to contain *links* to related documents. Hypermedia extends the concept to images and audio. The Web uses both hypertext and hypermedia.

IM (instant message): A message sent from one person to another that appears immediately on the recipient's computer, allowing a text conversation. AOL's AIM, Yahoo! Messenger, and MSN Messenger are popular IM systems.

IMAP (Internet Message Access Protocol): A method used for storing and delivering Internet e-mail that lets you see the same view of your mailbox no matter what computer you check it from.

info: The last part of an Internet domain name, such as `mta.info`, to indicate (supposedly) useful information. Sometimes it even is.

Internet: All the computers that are connected into an amazingly huge global network so that they can talk to each other. When you connect your puny little computer to your Internet service provider, your computer becomes part of that network.

Internet Explorer: A Web browser vigorously promoted by Microsoft for Windows. *See also* Chrome, Firefox, *and* Safari.

Internet Relay Chat (IRC): A system that enables Internet folks to talk to each other in real time (rather than after a delay, as with e-mail messages). The granddaddy of instant message systems.

intranet: A private version of the Internet that lets people within an organization exchange data by using popular Internet tools, such as browsers.

IP, (Internet Protocol): The scheme used to route packets of data through the Net, often used with TCP as TCP/IP. A newer version, IPv6, allows many more addresses. *See also* TCP.

IP address: A four-part number, such as `208.31.42.252`, that identifies a host on the Internet.

iPhone: A smartphone that includes a Web browser, an e-mail program, and a YouTube viewer and allows you to download and install other Internet "apps" (application programs).

iPod: The Apple line of personal music players.

ISP (Internet service provider): The folks who bring the Internet to you — by way of dialup, DSL, or cable modem, including folks like AOL, Comcast, and MSN.

iTunes: The Apple music software and online music store. Also used to connect your computer to your iPod or iPhone.

Java: A computer language invented by Sun Microsystems. Because Java programs can run on many different kinds of computers, and most Web browsers can run chunks of Java code called *applets,* Java makes it easier to deliver application programs over the Internet. JavaScript is an unrelated language that also is widely used on Web pages.

JPEG: A type of still-image file found all over the Net. Files in this format end in .jpg or .jpeg and are *JPEG* (pronounced "jay-peg") files. Stands for Joint Photographic Experts Group.

K, KB, Kbyte: Kilobyte, or 1,024 bytes. Usually used as a measure of a computer's memory or hard drive storage, or as a measure of file size.

kilo-: Prefix used by marketers to mean one thousand (1,000) and by engineers to mean 1,024.

LAN, or local-area network: Computers in one building or campus connected by cables so that they can share files, printers, or an Internet connection.

link: A hypertext connection that can take you to another document or another part of the same document. On the Web, links appear as highlighted text or pictures. To follow a link, you click the highlighted material.

LinkedIn: A social networking Web site (at www.linkedin.com) used primarily by businesspeople.

Linux: A version of UNIX; an operating system that runs on a wide variety of computers, including PCs. Many Internet servers run UNIX or Linux.

list server: An e-mail mailing list management program; a program that maintains a subscriber list and distributes list postings to those subscribers. Common list servers include LISTSERV, Lyris, Mailman, and Majordomo. The names of mailing lists maintained by LISTSERV often end with -L.

lurk: To read a mailing list or chat group without posting any messages. Someone who lurks is a *lurker.* Lurking is okay and is much better than flaming.

mailbomb: To send someone vast amounts of unwanted e-mail.

mailbox: A file on your incoming (POP or IMAP) mail server where your e-mail messages are stored until you download them to your e-mail program. Some e-mail programs also refer to the files in which you store messages *mailboxes.*

mailing list: A special type of e-mail address that remails all incoming mail to a list of subscribers to the mailing list. Each mailing list has a specific topic, so you subscribe to the ones that interest you. Often managed by using LISTSERV, Lyris, Majordomo, Mailman, or another list server program.

mega-: A prefix meaning one million.

mil: The last part of an Internet domain name, such as `www.army.mil`, run by some part of the U.S. military.

MIME (Multipurpose Internet Mail Extension): The scheme used to send pictures, word processing files, and other nontext information through e-mail.

mirror: An FTP or Web server that provides copies of the same files as another server. Mirrors spread out the load for more popular FTP and Web sites.

MMORPG: A massively multiplayer online role-playing game.

mobi: The last part of an Internet domain name, such as `amtrak.mobi` or `giggle.mobi`, used for Web sites intended to be used on mobile phones.

modem: A gizmo that lets your computer talk on the phone or on cable TV. Short for *modulator/dem*odulator.

moderator: The person who looks at the messages posted to a mailing list, newsgroup, or chat forum. The moderator can nix messages that are stupid, redundant, off the topic, or offensive.

Mozilla: The foundation (at `www.mozilla.com`) that supports and enhances open source software originally from Netscape. The foundation distributes the Firefox browser and the Thunderbird mail program.

MP3: A music file format available on the Net.

MPEG: A type of video file found on the Net. Files in this format end in `.mpg` or `.mpeg`; stands for Moving Picture Experts Group.

MSN: Microsoft Network, the Microsoft Internet provider.

MySpace: A social networking Web site (at `www.myspace.com`) used primarily by teenagers and music groups.

Napster: An online music source that charges a flat monthly fee for all you can listen to.

net: A network, or (when capitalized) the Internet itself. When these letters appear as the last part of an address (in `www.abuse.net`, for example), it nominally means a networking organization.

.NET: The Microsoft platform for Web services, which allows applications to communicate and share data over the Internet. No relation to `.net` addresses.

network: A group of computers that are connected. Those in the same or nearby buildings are in a *local-area* network; those who are farther away are in a *wide-area* network; and, when you interconnect networks all over the world, you get the Internet!

newsgroup: A topic area in the Usenet news system. (See the Web page `net.gurus.org/usenet` for a description of Usenet newsgroups.)

org: The last part of an Internet domain name (in `www.uua.org`, for example), probably run by a noncommercial organization.

Outlook: An e-mail program (among other things) that is part of Microsoft Office. Powerful, flexible, and notoriously susceptible to worms and viruses.

page: *See* Web page.

password: A secret code that's used to keep things private. Be sure to pick one that's hard to guess — preferably, two randomly chosen words separated by a number or special character.

PayPal: A Web-based service (at `www.paypal.com`) through which you can make and receive payments by e-mail or from links on Web sites. Owned by eBay.

PDF (Portable Document Format) file: A method for distributing formatted documents over the Net. Windows and Linux users need the special reader program Acrobat. Get it at `www.adobe.com/products/acrobat`.

phishing: Using e-mail or IM to trick people into revealing personal information, such as credit card numbers.

ping: To send a short message to which another computer automatically responds. If you can't ping the other computer, you probably can't talk to it any other way, either.

plug-in: A computer program you add to your browser to help it handle a special type of file.

podcasting: A system for distributing audio files with timely content that is meant to be heard on personal music players, such as the Apple iPod.

POP (Post Office Protocol): A system by which a mail server on the Net lets you pick up your mail and download it to your PC or Mac. A POP server is the computer from which you pick up your mail. The most recent version is POP3.

POP server: A server that stores your incoming e-mail messages until you download them to your e-mail program.

pop-up: A new, usually annoying, window that appears in response to an action you took. Pop-ups are often used for advertising.

port number: An identifying number assigned to each program that is chatting on the Net. You hardly ever have to know these numbers — the Internet programs work this stuff out among themselves.

portal: A Web site designed to be a starting point for people using the Web. A popular one is my.yahoo.com.

PPP (Point-to-Point Protocol): The most common way a computer communicates with the Internet over a dialup phone line.

PPPoE (PPP over Ethernet): The way you log in to a broadband account that requires an account and a password. *See also* DHCP.

protocol: The agreed-on rules that computers rely on to talk among themselves. A protocol is set of signals that mean "go ahead," "got it," "didn't get it, please resend," or "all done," for example.

proxy server: A program that translates between a LAN and the Internet.

QuickTime: A video and multimedia file format invented by Apple Computer and widely used on the Net. You can download it from www.apple.com/quicktime.

RealPlayer: The program that plays RealAudio streams, available from www.real.com. Helix is the open source version.

router: A device that connects two or more networks. Can be a separate piece of equipment or software running on a PC.

RSS (Really Simple Syndication): A Web technology that lets you track multiple information sources, with automatic checking for new content.

Safari: The Web browser that comes with Mac OS X, also available for Windows.

search engine: A program used to search for information on the Web. Google is a fairly popular one.

secure server: A Web server that uses encryption to prevent others from reading messages to or from your browser. Web-based shopping sites often use secure servers so that others cannot intercept your ordering information.

server: A computer that provides a service — such as e-mail, Web data, Usenet, or FTP — to other computers (known as *clients*) on a network. In online gaming, each server is its own world, and players on one server don't interact with players on other servers.

shareware: A type of computer program that is easily available for you to try with the understanding that you will pay for the program if you continue using it. A great deal of good stuff is available, and people's voluntary compliance makes it viable.

skin: The arrangement of buttons, menus, and other items displayed by a program. Some programs (such as Opera and Firefox) let you choose from several skins.

Skype: A software product for making free or low-cost long-distance and international telephone calls over the Internet, downloadable from www. skype.com.

smartphone: A cellphone capable of Internet functions, such as e-mail and Web browsing.

smiley: A combination of special characters that portray emotions, such as :-) or :-(. Although hundreds have been invented, only a few are widely used, and all are silly. A smiley is a type of emoticon.

SMS (Short Messaging System): A system to send short text messages to and from mobile phones.

SMTP (Simple Mail Transfer Protocol): The optimistically named method by which Internet mail is delivered from one computer to another.

SMTP server: A server that accepts e-mail messages for delivery to local users or the rest of the Internet.

social networking site: A Web site where people can create online profiles, photo albums, and blogs, and can link to their friends' pages. See Chapter 18.

spam: Messages sent to large numbers of people who didn't ask for them. It's antisocial, ineffective, and often illegal. To fight spam, see www.cauce.org.

spyware: Software that sends information about you and how you use your computer to other people without your permission.

SSL (Secure Socket Layer): A Web-based technology that lets one computer verify another's identity and allow secure connections; used by secure Web servers. A newer version is known as *TLS*.

stationery: Formatted e-mail that you can use when composing messages to send to recipients by using graphical e-mail programs. (Not everyone's e-mail program can display formatted e-mail.)

streaming audio or video: A system for sending sound or video files over the Net that begins playing the file before it finishes downloading, letting you listen or watch with minimal delay. RealAudio (www.real.com) is the most popular streaming format.

surf: To wander around the World Wide Web and look for interesting stuff.

TCP (Transmission Control Protocol): The system that two computers use to synchronize data. Usually used with IP as TCP/IP to manage connections over the Net. *See also* IP.

telnet: A program that lets you log in to some other computers on the Net. Many prefer the more secure program ssh. See net.gurus.org/telnet.

tera-: A prefix meaning trillion (1,000,000,000,000).

text file: A file that contains only textual characters, with no special formatting, graphical information, sound clips, video, or what-have-you.

thread: A message posted to a mailing list or newsgroup, together with all the follow-up messages, the follow-ups to follow-ups, and so on.

Thunderbird: A popular e-mail client from the Mozilla Foundation. See Chapter 13.

top-level domain (TLD): The last part of an Internet domain or hostname. If the TLD is two letters long, it's the *country code* in which the organization that owns the domain is (usually) located. If the TLD is three letters or longer, it's a code indicating the type of organization that runs the domain.

troll: An online game player or mailing list member who lives to annoy other people pointlessly. Don't feed the trolls.

tweet: A short message (as many as 140 characters) posted on Twitter by way of the Web site, a smartphone app, or a text message.

Twitter: A microblogging site (at twitter.com) where you can post short text messages (tweets) to be read by your followers. See Chapter 19.

UNIX: A geeky operating system originally developed at Bell Labs. Used on many servers on the Net. Linux is now the most popular version.

upload: To copy your stuff to somebody else's computer.

URL (Uniform Resource Locator): A standardized way of naming network resources, used for linking pages on the World Wide Web.

Usenet: A system of thousands of newsgroups. You read the messages by using a newsreader. (See the Web page `net.gurus.org/usenet` for a description of Usenet newsgroups.)

viewer: A program to show you files that contain stuff other than text.

virus: A self-replicating program that piggybacks on e-mail messages or other programs, frequently with destructive side effects. *See also* worm.

virus checker: A program that intercepts and destroys viruses as they arrive on your computer.

vishing: Voice phishing; phone calls made usually by way of VoIP to try to trick you into revealing personal or financial information.

VoIP (Voice over Internet Protocol): A method for sending telephone calls over the Net. Go to `net.gurus.org/phone` for more information.

watermark: A message hidden in a music, an image, or a video file designed to detect copyright violations. *See also* DRM.

WAV: A popular Windows format for sound files (`.wav` files) found on the Net.

Web Folder: A Windows feature that enables you to use Windows Explorer to see, download from, and upload to an FTP or Web server.

Web page: A document available on the World Wide Web.

Web page editor: A program for editing files in HTML for use as Web pages.

Web server: A program that stores Web pages and responds to requests from Web browsers.

Web site: A collection of Web pages stored on a Web server. The Web pages belong to a particular person or organization.

Webcam: A digital video camera that attaches to your computer and transmits video over the Internet. The video can appear on a Web page or as part of a chat or conference.

Weblog: *See* blog.

Webmail: A Web-based e-mail service, such as `gmail.com`, `mail.yahoo.com`, or `mail.live.com`.

WEP (Wired Equivalent Privacy): A broken security system for Wi-Fi. Use WPA instead.

Wi-Fi: The most popular kind of wireless network. Also known as 802.11b/g, after the number of the standard that defines it.

wiki: Short for *wikiwiki,* which is Hawaiian for *fast.* A technology that lets you rapidly create and edit Web pages by using your Web browser.

Wikipedia: The open source, Web-based encyclopedia at `wikipedia.org`.

WiMax: A wireless broadband access technology that hopes to provide an alternative to cable and DSL.

wireless network: A network that uses radio waves rather than cables.

World Wide Web: A hypermedia system that lets you browse through lots of interesting information. The Web has become the central repository of humanity's information in the 21st century.

worm: A malicious program that spreads directly from computer to computer.

WPA (Wi-Fi Protected Access): A security system for Wi-Fi that's harder to break than WEP.

XML (eXtensible Markup Language): A markup language and set of related technologies that can be used to make information on the Internet sharable by different types of programs, not just by Web browsers.

Yahoo!: A Web site (at `www.yahoo.com`) that provides a subject-oriented guide to the World Wide Web and many other kinds of information.

YouTube: A video-sharing Web site (at `www.youtube.com`) owned by Google.

Zip file: A file with the extension `.zip` that has been compressed with ZipMagic or WinZip or another compatible program. Windows calls it *Compressed Folder.*

Index

• B •

• K •

• N •

Internet

Blogging For Dummies,
2nd Edition
978-0-470-23017-6

eBay For Dummies,
6th Edition
978-0-470-49741-8

Facebook For Dummies
978-0-470-26273-3

Google Blogger
For Dummies
978-0-470-40742-4

Web Marketing
For Dummies,
2nd Edition
978-0-470-37181-7

WordPress For Dummies,
2nd Edition
978-0-470-40296-2

Language & Foreign Language

French For Dummies
978-0-7645-5193-2

Italian Phrases
For Dummies
978-0-7645-7203-6

Spanish For Dummies
978-0-7645-5194-9

Spanish For Dummies,
Audio Set
978-0-470-09585-0

Macintosh

Mac OS X Snow Leopard
For Dummies
978-0-470-43543-4

Math & Science

Algebra I For Dummies
978-0-7645-5325-7

Biology For Dummies
978-0-7645-5326-4

Calculus For Dummies
978-0-7645-2498-1

Chemistry For Dummies
978-0-7645-5430-8

Microsoft Office

Excel 2007 For Dummies
978-0-470-03737-9

Office 2007 All-in-One
Desk Reference
For Dummies
978-0-471-78279-7

Music

Guitar For Dummies,
2nd Edition
978-0-7645-9904-0

iPod & iTunes
For Dummies,
6th Edition
978-0-470-39062-7

Piano Exercises
For Dummies
978-0-470-38765-8

Parenting & Education

Parenting For Dummies,
2nd Edition
978-0-7645-5418-6

Type 1 Diabetes
For Dummies
978-0-470-17811-9

Pets

Cats For Dummies,
2nd Edition
978-0-7645-5275-5

Dog Training For Dummies,
2nd Edition
978-0-7645-8418-3

Puppies For Dummies,
2nd Edition
978-0-470-03717-1

Religion & Inspiration

The Bible For Dummies
978-0-7645-5296-0

Catholicism For Dummies
978-0-7645-5391-2

Women in the Bible
For Dummies
978-0-7645-8475-6

Self-Help & Relationship

Anger Management
For Dummies
978-0-470-03715-7

Overcoming Anxiety
For Dummies
978-0-7645-5447-6

Sports

Baseball For Dummies,
3rd Edition
978-0-7645-7537-2

Basketball For Dummies,
2nd Edition
978-0-7645-5248-9

Golf For Dummies,
3rd Edition
978-0-471-76871-5

Web Development

Web Design All-in-One
For Dummies
978-0-470-41796-6

Windows Vista

Windows Vista
For Dummies
978-0-471-75421-3